THE LIVING LIGHT DIALOGUE

Volume 20

Reproduction of the cover image of the
1972 edition of *The Living Light*

[See the appendix for a discussion of the image's symbolism.]

THE LIVING LIGHT DIALOGUE

Volume 20

Through the mediumship of
Richard P. Goodwin

Living Light Books

The Living Light Dialogue Volume 20
Copyright © 2024 Serenity Association
Through the mediumship of Richard P. Goodwin.

All rights reserved. No portion of this book may be reproduced—electronically, mechanically, or via internet transmission—without advance, express written permission of the publisher except in the case of brief quotations embodied in critical articles and reviews. No derivative work—games, supplemental material, video—may be created without advance, express written permission of the publisher. For information address Living Light Books, P.O. Box 4187, San Rafael, CA 94913-4187.

Cover design copyright © 2024 by Serenity Association
Cover photograph by Serenity Association, 2024; copyright © 2024 by Serenity Association.

www.livinglight.org

Library of Congress Control Number 2007929762
ISBN: 978-1-947199-49-1

FIRST EDITION

This volume of teachings is dedicated to the spirit friends who brought to Earth the Living Light Philosophy. With eternal gratitude, we pray that we may demonstrate these principles and continue to bring to publication these teachings.

CONTENTS

Acknowledgment ix
Preface. xi
Introduction. xv
Class March 8, 1983. 3
Class March 10, 1983 5
Class March 11, 1983 15
Class March 13, 1983 31
Class March 15, 1983 39
Class March 16, 1983 43
Class March 18, 1983 45
Class March 22, 1983 57
Class March 26, 1983 65
Class March 29, 1983 81
Class April 1, 1983 83
Class April 3, 1983 91
Class April 5, 1983 93
Class April 10, 1983. 105
Class April 11, 1983. 115
Class April 12, 1983. 117
Class April 17, 1983. 119
Class April 19, 1983. 123
Class April 22, 1983. 145
Class April 28, 1983. 147
Class April 29, 1983. 149
Class May 15, 1983 151
Class May 18, 1983 197
Class May 24, 1983 201
Class August 16, 1983. 203
Class May 20, 1984 205

Class September 27, 1984. 269
Class September 28, 1984. 289
Class September 30, 1984. 311
Class August 17, 1986. 341
Membership Meeting April 8, 1972 359
Membership Meeting May 12, 1974 383
Membership Meeting May 11, 1975 397
Membership Meeting May 9, 1976 423
Membership Meeting May 13, 1979 445
Membership Meeting May 11, 1980 461
Membership Meeting May 10, 1981 469
Membership Meeting May 5, 1983 483
Membership Meeting May 13, 1984 491
Membership Meeting September 21, 1988. 513
Membership Meeting November 28, 1988 533
Appendix 541
Notes 555

ACKNOWLEDGMENT

Grateful acknowledgment is made to the many friends and associates for invaluable aid in compiling this book, for their helpful suggestions, for their loyal interest and encouragement.

Special acknowledgment is due to those who painstakingly and selflessly transcribed and proofread the text.

PREFACE

It was through the mediumship of the Serenity Association founder, Mr. Richard P. Goodwin, that a philosophy known as the Living Light was given in more than 700 classes over a twenty-five-year period.

To be specific, the philosophy was imparted through Mr. Goodwin by a magistrate who had lived on Earth some 8,000 years ago. The former magistrate is known to Living Light students as "the Wise One," and he narrated the journey of his soul on the other side of life, the experiences—especially the difficulties—he encountered in having to face himself, as well as the teachings he earned to help himself through the realms in which he traveled. It was his decision to share the teachings with souls on both sides of "the curtain."

Prior to the advent of the Wise One, Mr. Goodwin had prayed for a teacher from the realms of light. Mr. Goodwin, since age fourteen, had been the instrument through which spirit was able to communicate with those seeking help. But he saw that his mediumship brought only temporary solace, because the people he was trying to help soon became fascinated with the phenomena and ignored the help that spirit was imparting. He prayed for someone who would bring forth teachings that would benefit any soul seeking a path to a greater awareness of himself and of God.

His prayers were answered in 1964 when the Wise One came through for the first time. Mr. Goodwin, at first apprehensive about what this new teacher would impart, was taken into deep trance and not able to control what was being revealed through him. Upon hearing the recorded classes afterward, however, he became convinced of the goodness of the teacher and of the value of the simple, beautiful teachings. This, then, was the beginning of the Living Light Philosophy given to Earth through the mediumship of Richard P. Goodwin.

In carrying out the request of the Wise One and Mr. Goodwin, students of the Serenity Association transcribed from audiotape the classes that had been brought through. Because most are in the form of teacher-student interaction, the classes became known as *The Living Light Dialogue*; and the students were instructed to publish the classes as a multi-volume set of the Living Light Philosophy. *Volume 1* was published in the autumn of 2007.

The present volume contains thirty individual classes and eleven membership meetings. All the classes in this volume were given at the Serenity temple and were given only to students of the philosophy, and some were only given to a very small group of advanced students. Most of the classes have not been available in any form since the day they were given.

Many of these classes were recorded on a microcassette recorder, and in many of the recordings, the recorder was frequently stopped and started, often on the guidance of the spirit. That is, a sentence or two would be recorded, and then the recorder was stopped. The discussion would continue without being recorded, and, moments or minutes later, a few more sentences were recorded. The instances when the recorder was stopped are indicated by a line of five asterisks. Some classes that originally recorded more extensive interactions between the students and the teacher and were edited, at a later date, to remove some of the more personal topics. And in a few classes, the entire discussion was recorded and survives unedited. Due to the editing that occurred, the order of the teachings, as presented in this publication, may not be the order in which the which they were originally given. In several classes, the personal notes of students who were present in the class were consulted to resolve issues and to complete partial recordings.

Although considerable effort has been made to accurately date these classes, there is the possibility that they may not have been assigned to the correct date. A microcassette tape may have been labelled with one date, but the actual recording may have a different or even multiple dates. In addition, there is no guarantee that all the teachings on a dated tape were actually given on that date: a recording could have been added days or even weeks later, and the tape just happened to be the one that the recording technician picked when he was instructed to begin recording.

The classes are presented in chronological order and range in date from March 10, 1983, to November 28, 1988.

Although additional written teachings may be published, this is the last volume of recorded classes of the Living Light Philosophy, and the students of Serenity wish to take this opportunity to express our deep gratitude to the Wise One, the Spirit Council and their many angel helpers, and to Mr. Goodwin. It has been both our privilege and our sacred duty to publish this philosophy. Even though it has taken many years and required much effort to transcribe, proofread, and publish these beautiful teachings, that effort is a small token of the debt of kindness that we owe to all the angels who worked to bring these teachings to this world. To all the angels, to all the people who in any way helped in this divine endeavor, we say thank you.

The foundation of the classes—the foundation of the Living Light Philosophy itself—is the Law of Personal Responsibility which states, in part, that we are responsible for all our experiences, and that our experiences are the return of the laws that we have established with our thoughts, acts, and deeds. Through greater awareness of our thoughts and by exercising our divine right of choice, we may choose to establish laws of greater harmony and goodness.

The Living Light Dialogue teaches that we have come to Earth to learn the lessons that are necessary to free us from the dictates and limits of our own thoughts and judgments, which are the mental patterns that we follow through our own lack of awareness and are so very potent, forceful, and limiting. These teachings guide us in making the necessary changes in our thinking in order to free ourselves from those patterns and to express our soul consciousness.

The choice of guiding the direction of our life, as stated by the Wise One when he speaks of being with a person, place, or thing, is, in essence, of being in this world and not a part of this world. He further explains that no matter what experiences we encounter, no matter what we do or do not do, we—our spirit—may view the experience in objectivity from a soul level of consciousness where peace reigns supreme.

The teachings of this volume help us to restore harmony or balance in our life by flooding the consciousness with spiritual affirmations and prayers, a few of which can be found in the appendix. When reason is restored, by balancing our sense functions with our soul faculties, we will consciously experience peace. Without annihilating our ego or our sense functions, we will find a pathway of expression for our soul. Where there was once disturbance, now there is acceptance. Where there was disease, now there is poise. And where there was hopelessness and despair, now there is reason, divine neutrality; and peace shows the way.

If you make the effort to apply these laws, such as, "If man is a law unto himself, what are you doing with the law that you are?", and demonstrate the wisdom of patience, the truth of this philosophy will be your living demonstration.

As the teacher states in CC 130, "My journey of many centuries and much experience has brought me here to Earth to share with you these simple teachings that have come as the effect of a long, long, long journey. Let not *your* journey be so long in the realms of illusion. For it is not necessary for you. For in your evolution, you have earned an awakening. But it is up to you to do something that is constructive and worthwhile."

INTRODUCTION

[This introduction was written by Mr. Goodwin and originally appeared in The Living Light, *which were the first teachings of the Living Light Philosophy published in book form. The entire text of* The Living Light *was republished in* The Living Light Dialogue, Volume 1.*]*

"Think, children. Think more often and think more deeply."

The teachings in this book were given as a progressive series of lessons to a group of four students who were sitting for spiritual unfoldment with me beginning in January of 1964. The communications were regular until October of that year, when nearly a seven-year silence ensued, and resumed in 1971 to the present. They were received in three ways by me as a channel. The main text was taped from a direct control of my voice in deep trance at special sittings of our group, during which I had no experience of the voice or what was being transmitted. A few scattered verses were given independently when I was privileged to see and hear our teacher clairvoyantly. I have also been a channel for this communicant when speaking from the podium at church and in answering difficult questions at our public seminars.

Nearly all we know about our teacher is contained in the lectures. He reports that he had tried for sixteen years to break through an interference barrier that the channel had to deep trance. When our conditions were in resonance with his patient wisdom, he came through ready to teach his understanding. I have seen him as an old man dressed in white with long flowing white hair. He has blue eyes, slightly smiling and deeply compassionate. I have always called him the Old Man. The students liked to call him the Wise One. He is surely one of those often called a Teacher of Light. I do not know his country, although he indicated at one time that he was from 6000 B.C., and a form of a judge in his time.

The text is often difficult, but it is complete, having been transcribed word for word from the original tapes recording the trance voice. It is presented with a minimum of punctuation to be freer for the individual interpretation of each reader. The lessons given before the long silence are phrased with many allegories often paradoxical. There are repetitions and renewals of theme, but it is explained that if an understanding is not perceived, compassion dictates that it be said again. Some of the topics have but a simple mention with little development but all are revealed, we are told, according to merit.

The Old Man is a fine teacher. He has in a hundred ways intertwined his allegory, progressive explanations, unfolding exercises, and timely references to reach a multitude of levels of individual understanding. A notable change is his more direct style of presentation beginning in 1971.

There is an endearing intimacy of person that can be felt through his lectures, a meaningful and loving encounter with a wise friend. Like an old man, he makes a mistake and conscientiously corrects himself a few paragraphs later. He listens often and carefully to our earnest discussions of his words. He consults with a group of experts on evolution and cites their learning in his lesson. His use of the direct address "children" or "my children" is not patronizing but infinitely loving and supportive.

A word must be said about the teachings. The Old Man makes clear that his lessons are not dogma, a creed or a narrow way, but simply his own understanding offered to us as a form of instruction to aid us in our own individual progression. When he speaks of Laws, he does not refer to man-made rules or moral traditions but to the cosmic and atomic way-things-are, the natural world of what-is, the universal laws of life, part of the original creative design and through which creation is fulfilled. These laws are beyond the possibility of being changed, suspended, transcended, or destroyed but they are ever a tool of mankind, not his master. First, through our awareness of the universal laws and then slowly through our developed understanding, the powers of creation are accessible to us. Not power over men's minds or circumstances, but power over whatever is selfish and imperfect in ourselves is the way up the eternal ladder of progression. When the Old Man cautions us concerning the Law of Responsibility or gives us a thinking exercise to explore the Law of Identity in a dynamic manner, he prepares us to take another step. And all move in accordance with the Law of What Can Be Borne.

Our teacher shows us how the two worlds are drawn together. In his realm, he describes, there is a great diversity of thought, many schools of understanding; but the Light is always known by the Light. Because of the interdependence of the two realms, listening to our discussions helped to clarify his teaching to others on his side of the curtain. His love and gratitude he humbly equates with ours.

The lessons to be perceived are not new, they are very old, but they are new to certain levels of our being. I would personally advise the reader, after reading this volume of discourses in full, to make a daily habit (or when there is a feeling or need) to sit quietly with the book. Open it at random and be guided to the Light by the passage that is there for the day. This technique is still used by the original students who were given the lessons and by many students after them who have studied in unfolding classes with me through these teachings.

Go beyond the words into feeling, into the immediate meanings for you. Touch into the inspiration that flows into the form of this book. It is from the Divine.

RICHARD P. GOODWIN
San Geronimo, California
June, 1972

Individual Classes

Class March 8, 1983

[This class, as well as several classes given after this date, was recorded at the Serenity temple on a microcassette recorder. During many of the microcassette classes, the recorder was often paused. A few sentences might be recorded and then the recorder was stopped. The class may or may not continue while the recorder was paused. When the recorder was stopped, an audible sound was recorded on the tape. Typically, the teacher would silently signal the vice president to start and stop the recorder; so, usually there are no spoken words to indicate a break in recording. As a result, many of the microcassette classes do not read like the previously published classes. As an aid to understand the microcassette classes, the instances when the recorder is stopped are indicated by five asterisks. The pause between teachings could last a few moments or several hours. So, sometimes adjacent teachings are closely related, but often they are not.

In addition, some recordings, but not all, were edited to remove some of the more personal topics that were discussed. In a few classes, the transcribed teachings had to be reassembled from multiple tapes. While great effort was made to present the teachings in the order they were given, there is the possibility that some teachings are out of order because the proper order of the teachings could not be established from the surviving, edited tapes. The personal, hand-written notes taken by individual students during those classes were consulted to aid in establishing the order of the teachings.

Although some of the microcassette classes may seem incomplete, they are complete transcriptions of the surviving recordings. Also, be aware that some of the teachings were given only to a very small group of advanced students, while others were given to a larger group of students.]

Pinheads are pointed hearts that have limited, by dictate of their own ego, the power and goodness of God to the point of their dictate, through which they release the river of life. And God help all who are in its way.

*****

It's known as the force of mental substance. And plenty of force is behind you know what.

*****

May you awaken and accept your joy from God that you be not the victim of you know what.

*****

From urinate to eliminate, we shall be free. Eliminate - coming soon.

*****

The love of the soul becomes the control of the mind, for the mind offers self, the glory of need.

MARCH 8, 1983

Class March 10, 1983

[The following teachings were given to a small group of advanced students.]

Ready? *[The teacher may be inquiring about the microcassette tape recorder.]*

Yes, it's ready.

Yes. Formless, free Spirit has no awareness without a vehicle of design, for awareness exists only in the design. You hear?

Yes.

For example, if you take the element air—and it has no form through which it may flow—hmm?—

Yes.

—then there is no awareness that it is air.

Yes.

You see? The element air becomes aware of itself when, in its movement, there is what you might call a resistance to it.

Yes.

Hmm? Now the purpose of design is for that principle of an awareness, a self-awareness—you understand?—

Yes. Yes.

—an awareness of itself, to register. And that registration, that impingement is dependent upon design.

Yes.

Now, as the element air moves through design, there is an impingement or what you call a resistance.

Yes.

Well, at that point of contact you have awareness. Hmm?

Yes.

Now, this is now awareness, but it is not self.

Yes.

You hear?

Yes.

The next step in this so-called resistance or awareness is the actual form that garners up and is attracted unto the design.

Yes.

Hmm?

Uh-huh.

And as the elements of the design—

Yes.

—pull unto themself the substance, then you have self-awareness.

Oh, yes.

And that's where the problem is.

Uh-huh.

Because, you see, the denser the form—

Yes.

—means the more the resistance.

Yes.

And the more the resistance is now called belief—

Yes.

—in your world.

Uh-huh.

You hear? And so depending, of course, on the degree of belief is the resistance and the self-awareness.

Yes.

Now, from that man descends, the formless, free Spirit—

Yes.

—deeper into the resistance to the flow, to the freedom that man is.

Yes.

The more the resist—the more the belief, the more the resistance, because belief is the magnet that pulls the substance and increases the density of the form.

Yes.

Now, my good friend, you are the one who received some time ago—

Uh-huh.

—the intensity, intensity of density is measured by acceptance.

Yes.

Now, for example, a person believes that such and such is that way.

Yes.

Now, that is a very dense form.

Yes.

Their belief is very great. You introduce within the consciousness—

Uh-huh.

—the possibility that there is more than that way.

Yes.

There are other avenues; there are other and broader aspects.

Yes.

You understand?

Uh-huh.

What happens to that form of belief, which is now very, very solidified—

Yes.

—it begins to quiver and then to quake, like an earthquake.

Yes.

And you experience what you call an emotional trauma.

Yes.

That's the process of freedom. You've had a few traumas lately.

Yes.

A couple of earthquakes.

Uh-huh.

Do you understand?

Yes.

Well, this is what's taking place. And the purpose of design, you see—

Uh-huh.

You are not the design.

Yes.

You are not the thought.

Yes.

Hmm? So, if a person, you see, believes they are the thought, then what they are revealing unto themselves—you hear?—

Yes.

—is the bondage of self-awareness, solidified in the substance of belief—

Yes.

—you hear?—and rigidly turned into a pillar of salt by the power of God through what is known as the direction of the will of God, will power—

Uh-huh.

—Hmm?—

Yes.

—unto the self. You see?

Yes.

Now, I do hope I've presented that in terms that are understandable.

I think I understand it.

I feel that you do.

Uh-huh.

Now, this is taking place with all design, all thought, all form.

Yes.

That's what it is.

Uh-huh.

Now, if you understand what it is, you hear?—

Yes.

—and you understand the purpose of why it is—
Uh-huh.
—what it is—
Uh-huh.
—then you're on the first step of authority—
Uh-huh.
—and control over it. You use it for the good, you see.
Uh-huh.
You see, if you truly believe—remember, that's a bondage.
Yes.
But [it] can serve a good purpose if you are on the plane of objectivity.
Yes.
Then you say, "Yes, now that is belief. That is not me."
Uh-huh.
"I look at this. I use it intelligently for great good."
Yes.
Hmm? "First, unto myself."
Uh-huh.
For it cannot be good to another unless it is good to oneself.
Yes.
Hmm?
Yes.
Now remember that. The law is demonstrable.
All right.
We grant unto others what we have first granted unto our self for that is the demonstrable law.
Yes.
So when you want to do something good, remember, it is either good for you or it is not good in what you do.
Yes.
Hmm?
Yes.

Now, if you remember that, my good friend, you're well on the path. And your freedom is moment by moment. And those moments keep increasing.

Uh-huh.

They last longer.

Yes.

Well, you see, understand and apply the purpose of design.

Yes.

It is a tool.

Uh-huh.

You are not the tool. You never were the tool. Don't be a fool and think you're the tool.

Yes.

Will you remember that?

I will. Yes.

Don't be a fool and think you are the tool.

Yes.

Because from thinking you're the tool, you'll enter the bondage of believing—

Yes.

—you're the tool. And you know what a sad day that is.

Yes. Really.

Well . . . it's total bondage. *[It is difficult to transcribe a word.]*

Uh-huh.

That's what it offers—

Yes.

—to everyone, my child, not just to you. And so faith is the path. Faith is indispensable to any freedom.

Yes.

Faith in the Power that is. All these things, they come and go, for beliefs do change in time.

Uh-huh.

Yes. They—the concrete gets broken up with what you call your little jackhammers.
Yes.
Hmm?
Uh-huh.
See? You don't want that.
No.
You don't need that. You're an intelligent being. You have earned a spiritual awakening that is within your consciousness and each day rises more.
Yes.
In spite of your mind, which is the vehicle that believes.
Uh-huh.
Hmm?
Uh-huh.
And what does the mind believe? You want to know what the mind believes?
Yes.
The mind believes what it can control or has the slightest thought or the possibility and potential of controlling.
Yes.
And then, you see, they call that love, some people.
Oh, yeah.
Hmm?
Uh-huh.
Their belief that here, "This, I can control."
Uh-huh.
"That has potential for *me*!"
Uh-huh.
That's what they call love, child.
Yes.
Hmm!
Yes, yes, that's—

Then let us save ourselves from that, that love.
Yes.
There's one Power, one Light, and one Love. Hmm?
Yes.
And when it enters down into form, well, look out, unless the person that it is flowing through is demonstrating total consideration of their divine rights and, therefore, are qualified to grant it unto you.
Yes.
Otherwise, beware.
Uh-huh.
Bladder beware! *[The teacher laughs.]*
Yes.
Let's not have any more blue bladder Mondays—
No.
Or Thursdays.
No.
Hmm?
No.
No more. No more. In fact, I might drop that little tidbit to someone I see clearly here before me. That thing.
Uh-huh.
Perhaps I'll drop that: Let us free our self from blue bladder Mondays. *[The teacher and Student R laugh.]*
Yes.
You understand.
I do.
I just—Yes. I wouldn't want you shocked.
No. I'm not.
Well, I'll have to—be it in Divine order. We'll see—
Yes.
—what that can—I, I believe—and, you know—
Uh-huh.
—I'm down here in your world of belief.

Yes.

But I know it'll help some souls.

Good.

Hmm? A lot of people have blue bladder Mondays and Mon-nights.

Yes.

Maybe I should say Monday day and nights! *[The teacher laughs loudly.]*

Yes.

I don't want to leave out the night, child.

Right.

To have it misinterpreted, you know, and twisted around.

That's when the bladder gets the bluest. Reddy, stay down. Reddy, down.

Yes, yes, my good soul. Here, student.

Stay down.

Yes, I love you very much, you know. *[It seems the teacher is addressing Reddy, who is a dog.]*

You sit right here.

Yes, here, here. Old friend, friend. Yes. He's such a loyal student, you know.

He really is.

Oh, he's been very loyal. Always. Saved you more than once, child.

Yes.

His little soul. He loves you so much. You noted that.

Uh-huh.

He's scared you with his love because it's genuine.

Yes.

Hmm?

Yes. Didn't really know what to do with it.

There. See? Now where were we? On blue bladder Monday days and nights.

Yes.

Yes. And remember—no, I'll think I'll incorporate that. That's very wise. Now let us have no more blue bladder Mondays, for they're the bluest on Monday nights.

Yes.

Oh, I have to figure out something.

Yeah. I'm sure you'll come up with something very good. [The teacher laughs loudly.]

Ah! Let's remember, children, bladders are the bluest at night. So, let's have no more blue bladder Mondays. Doesn't that sound more diplomatic?

Yes. That sounds good. Yes.

[The teacher laughs again.] Well, be it in Divine order I won't forget. Any questions . . . *[The teacher laughs again and it is difficult to transcribe a few of his words.]* Peace, child. Peace. Tries to get in sometimes, you know.

Uh-huh.

Any questions you have on bladders are the bluest at night; let's not have any more of these blue bladder Mondays?

Right.

[The teacher laughs again.] I do enjoy that.

Yes.

Yes. Any questions, friend?

No, not now. Thank you.

Then, why don't you ask my channel—shut it off.

MARCH 10, 1983

Class March 11, 1983

[The following teachings may have been given to a larger group of students.]

A fallen be is a soaring me.

*****

And if you wonder what's soaring, just take a look at what it leaves.

*****

So beware of things that fly high.

*****

A wise man chooses a pen for he knows what he's doing.

*****

Fools choose pencils and do a lot of erasing.

*****

Their own mistakes.

*****

Crowns, like crosses, nail on tightly.

*****

Nails, like clutches, have to be hammered in.

*****

And the better the hammer, the greater the hold.

*****

A good carpenter makes one hit. A fool makes many.

*****

Has-beens, as you know, are holey bastards. Holey in the sense of *h-o-l-e*.

*****

Pen pals have no concern for they're not so foolish to use pencils that need erasers.

*****

[The following teachings may have been given to a very small group of advanced students.]

We'll chat here about love.

Uh-huh.

I said to my channel many years ago: Something's very popular in your world years ago: "Love is a simple thing, just like a silver ring." Hmm? And on and on. But we can stop at that point about love is a simple thing.

Now I want to speak first about love that is. Not what people say it is, but what it *is*.

Yes.

Love is a simple thing. For it's truth. It is simple. It's not hidden. It's not concealed. That's—it's like truth. That's what love is.

Uh-huh.

It's like a silver ring. The ring of the divine return. There's no motive. What is there—motive has to have a beginning and motive has to have an ending.

Uh-huh.

There's no beginning or ending to the divine circle of return, which is life itself.

Uh-huh.

And what is it? It's a silver ring. It's a simple thing, a silver ring. It's the silver of character.

Uh-huh.

It reveals itself in all of life's experiences. It's character. Unchanging. Unyielding. Freed from motivation. It just is.

Uh-huh.

And so, no matter what one does or what one does not do, that does not change love. One does not tell a person that they "love" them.

Uh-huh.

One demonstrates that in the Law of Divine Return.

Uh-huh.

One respects the rights of difference. One is true to one's own love, the love of truth, for that's what love is.

Uh-huh.

If love is not truth, child, then it's not love. It's something that the mental substance uses to—as you so were inspired, it is the ring in the nostrils. *[The teacher quietly laughs.]*

Uh-huh.

And only fools place rings in their nostrils for someone to latch a chain upon. You understand? So the love of mental substance is the ring in the nostril of the nose. And you know what that represents. And so one is a bit cautious in the awareness of the bladder.

Uh-huh.

So they're not bound by the nose.

Yes.

Instead of the toes.

Uh-huh.

If you must be bound, let it be the toe. It's terrible to be bound by the other part of your anatomy, you know.

Yes.

[The teacher laughs.] And so that's my feelings about love.

Uh-huh.

Love that is, and love of your peanut world.

Uh-huh.

And we'll take a little pause now.

*****

Gravity is not partial to the apple.

*****

A pointed heart is a soul in bondage, known to man as overidentification with self.

*****

So-called lost souls are wanderers, destined, someday, to return home.

*****

On the—you may record this on the infa action. *[The teacher says "infa", not "infra." Although he may be referring to "infra," when he says "infa" his words were transcribed as he pronounced them. On some occasions, the teacher does say "infra," and it is transcribed as such.]*
OK.
Yes. Now we were speaking on the development of what you call a photograph.
Yes.
And we were speaking on the indispensability in the process—
Yes.
—of what you call infa red.
Yes.
Is that not correct?
Yes.
We were also speaking on the necessity of the absence of light at a critical part of the developing process.
Yes.
Is that not true?

It is.

And that's where we were speaking on the necessity of infrared. Is that not true?

Yes.

Now, first let's go to basic principle. You understand from our teachings that red is the color of action.

Yes.

You also understand that "infa" is an abbreviated term of infinity.

Yes.

Therefore, the—we are now speaking of infinite action.

Yes.

Not finite, but infinite.

Yes.

So, in the development of anything, there is the ingredient—if we can put it in that [those] terms—of infinite action.

Yes.

Now we must ask our self the question, "What is infinite action? What is action of infinity to you? To your finite mind?" which we must work with.

Uh-huh.

[After a short pause, the teacher continues.] That's the question. What is the action of infinity?

It would be action beyond one dimension.

Correct. Correct. Action beyond the limits of one dimension. Correct?

Yes.

Now, is infinite action beyond the limits of two dimensions?

Yes, being infinite, it would count—or would encompass all dimensions.

Therefore, we are speaking of action beyond all limits. Is that not correct?

Yes.

And we term that in the process of development of what you call a photograph or picture—would you call a picture an illusion of that which is?

Uh-huh.

Ah! Now, we are now speaking of action, infinite, infinite action beyond the veil of illusion.

Yes.

Is that not correct?

Yes.

All right. We find that in order to experience the illusion of what you term, now, a photograph—

Uh-huh.

—in the developing—development of a photograph, which is an illusion—

Uh-huh.

—that we have the indispensable ingredient of infinite action in the process of the developing.

Yes.

Correct?

Yes.

So we find infrared a necessity to development of illusion.

Yes.

That illusion may know illusion through the action of infinity. Follow me, child?

Yes.

Ah, yes, indeed. So, one now in this process of development, such as you, my channel, all people are going through—

Uh-huh.

Hmm? We find what we term, as I listened attentively during your little break—

Yes.

—what you term as nublious.

Yes.

Now, *[The teacher laughs.]* you're getting to home base, believe it, whether you know it or not.

Uh-huh.

Through sharing, not comparing, you're going to get there.

Yes.

You will go beyond comparing, you know.

Oh, yes.

During your sharing.

Uh-huh.

You understand?

Yes.

It's a process. Hmm?

Uh-huh.

All right. Now, we now find that we have this, what we term and experience as nublious.

Yes.

Well, now the question must rise within your consciousness, "What is nublious?"

Uh-huh.

What is it? What is it to you? What is it to your finite mind? What is it to your developing process?

My awareness, conscious awareness—

Yes?

—deals with one dimension: the dimension of form or of creation. That to my mind or that to me that is nebulous or nublious would be—

I wouldn't want to make a mistake. Is it nebulous or nublious?

I'll use your word nublious.

[The teacher laughs.] Perhaps in your peanut world we should use nebulous. *[The teacher laughs again.]* It is *n-e-b*, isn't it?

Yes.

Yes. We'll leave out the *u*. *[The teacher laughs again.]* Not, not our *b*s, but leave out the *u*s.

All right.

Yes. All right.

Thank you. But then—

Did you say "nebulous"?

Well, I'll call it whatever you want.

Yes, nebulous is fine.

Nebulous.

Yes, you are now nebulous. *[The teacher laughs again.]*

All right. So, whatever is nebulous would be of other dimensions, ah, not, not the one that I'm consciously aware of, but those beyond my conscious awareness.

Ahh. And so we move in the developing process to—what? "I'm not familiar with this." Well, what is it? "Is it anything? Yes, I do sense something. I do feel something, but I don't see anything." Hmm?

Correct.

"I can't touch anything!"

That's right.

Correct?

Uh-huh.

The photograph is not yet complete. Hmm?

Right.

For, you see, you are experiencing the infrared.

Yes.

And, you see, the illusion is not yet solidified.

Yes.

Uh-huh. You did want to know about the action of infinity, called infrared, in the developing—development of illusion, didn't you, child?

I certainly did.

This is what we are discussing.

Yes, we are.

Hmm?
Yes.
You see? So, the experience—say that you're in a little—what [do] they call those things where shops are?—camera room.
Yes.
Ah! And you are in the process with the infrared.
Uh-huh.
Nebulous.
Uh-huh.
Hmm? Not yet appearing.
Yes.
Correct?
Uh-huh.
And you're waiting for it to happen.
Yes.
And it seems to take an infinity, doesn't it?
Uh-huh.
For you are identified in the moment of the infrared.
Uh-huh.
The action of infinity.
Yes.
Hmm? And through patience, is it not true?
Yes.
And the proper, uhm, chemicals—
Uh-huh.
—combined, properly—
Uh-huh.
—does not the illusion become solidified? You say, "Ah, yes, there it is."
Yes.
Paper? Hmm?
Uh-huh.
It has an imprint upon it.
Yes.

Correct?
Yes.
For you have used the proper chemicals.
Uh-huh.
Hmm? And now you say, "Oh, that does look like me."
Yes.
Why, yes! "Well, I didn't know I was so good looking!" *[The teacher and Student R laugh.]* "But it does . . ." *[The teacher laughs again.]* "But it does resemble me tremendously."
Uh-huh.
"Same height and color of the hair and etc. Could have had a little more light there."
Yes.
"Oh, no, that one is too much light."
Uh-huh.
"Next time, I'll have to take corrective measures." Now, you're beginning to understand a little bit about illusion.
Yes.
That which you think you are. Not, you see, not what you are, but what you think you are.
Yes.
That's the illusion.
Uh-huh.
The forms.
Yes.
You see? You see, and you are the little camera—
Uh-huh.
—that's taking the picture. Listen carefully.
Yes.
You're the lens.
Yes.
And you're doing the whole process within your consciousness. You're adjusting your camera. You're taking the

picture. And after you take the picture, my child, the actual chemicals of your being—you hear?—

Yes.

—are going through all that you go through in your camera processes of development.

Uh-huh.

You hear?

Yes.

Through the process of infinite action, you hear?

Ah, yes.

And they're going buzz. *[The teacher makes a sound that is difficult to describe, but suggests production or manufacturing.]*

Uh-huh.

And bam! *[The teacher makes another sound that is difficult to transcribe, but suggests the completion of the production process.]* Well, there it is!

There's the image.

In your consciousness and everyone else's.

Yes.

That's infrared.

Uh-huh.

That's the action of infinity. *[The teacher whispers and continues to whisper for some time.]*

Uh-huh.

You have charge over all creation because you are the one that controls the camera of your mind.

Uh-huh.

You understand?

Yes.

That deals with this.

Uh-huh.

Now you have control over the radio.

Yes.

You hear? And that deals with this—

Uh-huh.

—the receiver. And you also have control over the transmitter, you hear?

Uh-huh.

That deals with this.

Yes.

You hear? There, my child, move in greater understanding of the three vehicles. Just start working with the three that you have as a tool.

Yes. The body, mind, and soul.

Indeed, indeed. And look, you have the camera.

Uh-huh.

You have the radio.

Uh-huh.

You call it a radio.

Uh-huh.

And you have the transmitter.

Uh-huh.

Now that's what you should be studying and working with, through infrared!

Yes.

For what you call infrared, the action of infinity—

Uh-huh.

—placed to the radio or the transmitter—

Uh-huh.

—is given different terms in your world. Same principle.

Yes.

Hmm?

Uh-huh.

Now you have some background, you hear?

Yes.

And you have, definitely, an inclination towards a deeper understanding.

Uh-huh.

And it does exist within your consciousness. It's simply a matter of application.

Uh-huh.

Hmm?

Uh-huh.

They use those things against the Light, you hear?

Yes.

For they have awareness, for they have come from the Light.

Uh-huh.

And have chosen, through overidentification, what I gave to you earlier—

Yes.

—for your little machine, there. *[The teacher may be referring to the tape recorder.]*

Yes.

Hmm?

Uh-huh.

They have chosen to use it for self-gain.

Yes.

You hear? Now, those, those minds of earth and of mental substance and all, very few so-called great scientists—

Uh-huh.

—understand the infrared. They cannot control it.

Yes.

But they have more understanding than others.

Uh-huh.

The infas are all present. Why shouldn't they be? They are speaking of their work.

Yes.

We are speaking of their work.

Uh-huh.

Do you understand?

Yes.

Yes. Now, a little question time. Remove that, ah, can't take the temperature increase generated by the presence.

Uh-huh.

Yes.

Now in the process of developing the image—

Uh-huh.

—the photograph, the infrared is an essential ingredient.

Indeed, to all—infrared, the action of infinity is indispensable to all illusion—radio, transmitter, photograph.

Yes. Now the image of the photograph is a reproduction of the vehicle through which it's viewed.

Yes. May I say one thing at this moment, child?

Yes.

If you take a photograph of, let's say—well, I'd rather choose an oak tree than a willow.

Uh-huh. Yes.

Let's say you've taken many phototrees of an oak tree. *[The teacher said "phototrees."]*

Yes.

Many photographs.

Uh-huh.

I want you to think. In the development here.

Uh-huh.

There are chemicals required.

Yes.

Now those chemicals are necessary for the developing process through the infrared.

Uh-huh.

For the illusion to take form.

Yes.

You hear?

Uh-huh.

Now, try to understand this—and I'm sure you will—about an object of illusion.

Uh-huh.

The chemicals, though all the same—

Uh-huh.

—in the actual development process, whether it's an oak tree or a willow.

Uh-huh.

You hear?

Uh-huh.

That which is an oak tree, when you completely analyze the chemical process—

Uh-huh.

—uses certain amounts of the chemicals for the oak tree that it may or may not use for the willow. Do you understand that?

Yes. Yes.

In the actual chemicals.

Uh-huh.

In the process of—to create the image.

Uh-huh.

Well, if you take photographs of many oak trees—

Uh-huh.

You hear?

Uh-huh.

—then the accessibility, the easiness of access to those particular chemicals within the consciousness of the physical body—

Uh-huh.

—is where it's taken from.

Uh-huh.

Through frequency of use—

Uh-huh.

See? Da-da-da-da-da. *[The teacher makes a series of sounds that suggest rapid production.]*

Yes.

Photographs.

Uh-huh.

Rise up predominantly.

Yes.

Because they, they slip through easier.

Uh-huh.

Do, do, do you follow me on that?

More readily available.

Indeed. Do you follow me on that?

I do.

Well now, this is what we're talking about in your own evolution of how this is—

*****

Yes.

In the acceptance of similarity man moves to totality and in that movement awakens to the Light that is the All. For the principle, not the limit called personality, is the freedom, the soul, the being *is*, known as truth, just be. Remember, the full acceptance of similarity, totality is dependent upon.

Yes.

MARCH 11, 1983

Class March 13, 1983

[The following teachings may have been given to a very small group of advanced students.]

The desire to control, under the guise of love, is indispensable to the glory of the throne of self.

*****

Man's greatest love is the need to control.

*****

No forms do I see,
for I just be!
The view for you,
The view for thee,
The joy of life,
Be, be, be
Free, ever free.
Free, the you, the thee, the view, the joy
Ever, ever, ever be.

*****

[The following teachings were given to the larger group of Sunday night students.]

We know, clearly, that our souls instruct, and it is something else that dictates. Now what do you feel it is that dictates?

*****

Now, why does the mind dictate? Doing absolutely contrary of what the true being [does], known as our soul, which instructs. Why does the mind dictate?
Because it goes on—strictly on—

*****

So?

And it wants control.

It wants control, which reveals that which wants control does not have control. Is that correct? Which, then, further reveals—would you say security or insecurity?

Very insecure.

All right. Now that which is temporal, does it have a sense of the security of continuity? Or does it have a sense of insecurity, not knowing when something shall begin or end? What would you say?

Insecurity.

So, we see clearly, from living demonstrations, that mental substance, which we awaken within our consciousness, is an experience, a feeling of insecurity. Does insecurity offer to us faith or fear?

[If the student responded, it is difficult to transcribe her response.]

Does it offer to us fullness or need?

Need.

Does it offer to us want or joy?

Want.

Now we can clearly see from our own lives what the thought of I, which opens the door to mental substance or mind, truly offers. We can see clearly the principle. It offers us insecurity. It offers us fear. It offers to us need. It offers to us—does it offer acceptance? [*After a short pause, the teacher continues.*] Anyone? Does the mind offer acceptance? But we do see it does offer destiny to those who believe in it, because, you see, it offers to us denial. And denials are destinies. Remember this: denials are destinies to those who believe they are the thought.

*****

In the belief that you are the thought is the Law of Denial established.

*****

It is our belief that we are the thought that offers to us the want, the need, the denial, for they are all one in the same. Want, need *is* denial. You can't want and you cannot need until you first deny. And what is it you deny? You deny that you are the whole, complete, and perfect being, the Truth, the Light that you are. You must first deny that by belief. You only deny that by belief: by believing you are the thought that is passing on the river of your consciousness. By that belief do you deny that which you are. And from the denial of that which you are, are you destined to that which you shall never be.

*****

The command of God is "shall." And many things will the command be; the wills to be and have been.
[The above teaching is accurately transcribed, but it may not be punctuated in a way that correctly reflects the meaning the teacher wished to convey.]

*****

In other words, will and wish away, shall and do today.

*****

Wise men have faith, even the faith of the mustard seed. Fools have belief. For *believing*, the meaning of the word is leaving the be. Be-leaving: leaving the Light, the Truth that you are. And so those who believe cloak themselves, from their closets of infinity, in many garments many times in the great evolution of eternity in infinity.

*****

Our belief is its fullest and its greatest with all that has been.

*****

Belief is the chain that binds the soul to illusion, delusion, self-deception. Faith is power that frees it to the heavenly heights, its true home, eternally in infinity.

*****

Infinity is freedom, the effect of eternity, which is truth.

*****

The Law of Gravity is not partial to the apple.

*****

To-bes hope, and has-beens despair.

*****

So just be a be and repair the repairable.

*****

That designed to shine must be kept polished.

*****

Dictates tarnish. Ah, but instruction polishes.

*****

Repetition, frequency, continuity is indispensable to the divine principle of instruction.

*****

Wise ones rest and rejuvenate. Fools sleep and regurgitate.

*****

May your tombstone ever read "Rest"—not sleep—"in Peace."

*****

Only a fallen be knows need to control the me.

*****

That's the me of another be.

*****

What you wear is telling you where you are at the moment of your choice.

*****

There's no problem in knowing at any moment what our motive is.

*****

The problem appears, in your world, to be getting to the closet on time.

*****

Illusion is time. Delusion is form. Awaken, truth just be.

*****

As I have said before, time is dependent upon reference. Reference is form. Therefore, there is no time when there is no form. There is no form when there is no time. So there, my friends, be! Just be, be, be.

*****

The tick of the clock is the want, and the tock of the clock is the need. So, want need, tick tock away. You'll never be in the light of day.

*****

No one experiences satisfaction without service. And there is no service unless there's servants. So, the higher you rise, the more servants you have to order and dictate to serve you.

*****

So, irritate yourself and awaken. Satisfy yourself and sleep.

*****

Best to be a good friend to yourself, a little ant, than a cow that chews away in the valley.

*****

Satisfaction is Lucifer's efforts to build a throne greater than the one he left.

*****

Dictate and satisfy. Instruct and enjoy. Life is a beauty to behold.

*****

And don't forget, it's *be*-hold, not hold.

*****

Behold is being the observer of form which holds. So, behold and have all the goodness the joy of life has to offer.

*****

The slide is the thought of I. The grease is the need of the deception.

*****

[The following teachings were likely given to a very small group of advanced students.]

Whoever loves principle shall live abundant joy.

*****

Yes.

Each thought you think is a step on the path of eternity. Look at the length of your journey. Indeed, the steps are many. Now method is the servant of principle.

Yes.

Ahh, device, the servant of personality. Whoever flows in principle *is* Truth, Light, the joy abundant of life. And whoever trickles in deception drowns in their own river in the illusion called time.

End. *[The teacher may be instructing the recording technician to stop recording.]*

*****

Only the power of faith will overcome the force of belief.

*****

—called joy is an inside job. Hear?

Yes.

And in keeping with the law that reveals joy is an inside job, we get out of a thing what we put into the thing and not one iota more. Hmm?

Yes.

Now, for example, if you go to do something and, of course, you have mental substance to work through and you believe that this may well be your one and only chance—

Uh-huh.

—it's amazing how much you get out, isn't it?

Yes.

Because isn't it amazing how much you put in.

Yes.

And depending on that law, do you experience what you call fullness and joy.

Uh-huh.

Hmm?

Yes.

Now, shut it off. *[The teacher refers to the microcassette recorder.]*

MARCH 13, 1983

Class March 15, 1983

[The following teachings were likely given to the larger group of students who volunteered Tuesday nights at the temple.]

Our faith is greater than the force of belief shall ever be.

*****

For the love of God is freedom and the love of self is bondage.

*****

When you love self more than you love God, you forget the purpose for which the human mind has been designed.

*****

Whoever, whoever forgets the purpose of design is destined to despair.

*****

Each time you dictate, you deny. And each time you deny, you forget the purpose for which the human mind has been designed.

*****

The battle hymn of has-beens is dictate, dictate, dictate.

*****

Marching to the tune, "O bondage, I love you so."

*****

You better record it. *[The teacher addresses the recording technician.]*

Every thought is a step on the path of eternity.

*****

View clearly the long, long, long journey.

*****

Loss of value is the Law of Abuse. Show me your tools and I'll show you your value.

*****

Record.
Familiarity breeds contempt.

*****

No respect? No freedom. No freedom? No good. No good? No God, no joy of life.

*****

Friends, that is what self-love has to offer.

*****

Hearts share. Minds compare. Unfortunately, most of us think we're sharing, but it's a pointed heart; and therefore, it's a mind dictate.

*****

Failure is the fresh breeze of reason that whispers, "O thought of I, you're not infallible and cannot be God."

*****

Compare stimulates the ego and establishes competition.

*****

Now we must conclude. Whoever competes is destined to defeat.

*****

For only God, in the final analysis, is the infallible winner.

*****

So forget your losses; enjoy your gains. Good night.

*****

[The following teaching may have been given only to a very small group of advanced students.]
Temptation is the teasing of one's self-love.

MARCH 15, 1983

Class March 16, 1983

[The following teachings were given to a very small group of advanced students.]

Remember, child, that belief makes you the victim: puts you in the trap of bondage. Ah, but faith, faith is the power, the power that frees you, the power to use and never abuse. So, whatever it is you choose to do, use the power which is faith. Now what is faith? Faith is total acceptance of [that] the choice of your desire is already fulfilling itself, whatever it is. Ah, but belief is dependent. And because belief is dependent, it is bondage. And belief is the trap.

*****

Friend.

Yes.

Now you remember that I stated that understanding, the pillars of the Great Rotunda?

Yes.

That the roof is wisdom?

Yes.

And do you recall what I said the floor is?

I've forgotten the floor.

Shame. Truth rests. Understanding rests on truth. Does not understanding rest in truth?

Yes, it does.

And does it not rise to wisdom?

Yes.

And is not the understanding of the temple of your soul the great triangle? Pause and view again.

*****

The freedom of the flow is dependent upon the passivity of the form. The greater the flow, the more passive the form, the less resistance, the more defenseless. So, the brighter the Light and the flow thereof, the more defenseless the forms in the night.

*****

Less Light is more defense in the night for the fool doesn't know his bondage.

*****

My friend, it's not eagles that fly at night.

*****

One should not think of a workload when one desires to sail. There's always time for rest.

*****

My good friend, what kind of a sailboat bucks like a bronco?

MARCH 16, 1983

Class March 18, 1983

[The following teachings were given to the larger group of students who volunteered at the temple Friday nights.]

Remember, has-beens frown while bes smile.

*****

The ears of ego hear many things for they conceive ever in keeping with the has-beens in control. But the ears of perception, the soul awakens and responds in the light of reason.

*****

All parts of the temple of God, called human anatomy, are functions or faculties depending on our willingness to listen or our laziness to hear.

*****

Has-beens order. Bes instruct.

*****

Has-beens destroy. Bes construct.

*****

The goodness known as the joy of life.

*****

All functions are balanced and faculties when we be we're free. All functions, faculties are bound when we have been.

*****

Has-beens are the throne on which self-love glorifies itself. And the battle between has-beens, the functions, and the be, the soul, is bound within the throne until the light of reason, through suffering and struggle, finally rises with its lamp of honesty.

*****

So, children, eliminate, and don't forget to pull the chain.

*****

It's known as giving.

*****

Some people take ex-lax when they're bound.

*****

Wise men, they take understanding and wisdom with their little lamp of honesty.

*****

There are no corners in the Light for everything is round.

*****

Show me a square universe and I'll show you a blockhead.

*****

Made, made of solid concrete.

*****

Seamen sail concrete boats. *[A more accurate transcription might be "See men sail concrete boats."]*

*****

[Lazy men sail concrete boats.[1]] They're molded with little effort.

*****

When you finally awaken to the fact that the getting has gotcha, it's time to give.

*****

Lucifer lost his wings because they turned into claws that he may clutch and hold and, therefore, glorify in the need to control.

*****

The wings of freedom only fly on the honesty of motive.

*****

Truth is greater than science fiction. Why, of course, it's beyond belief!

*****

Just start recording. *[The teacher addresses the recording technician.]*

An uneducated ego is the clutches of Lucifer himself.

*****

The holes of hell are filled with the tears of sorrow.

*****

So, shift to reason; stop holding the clutch.

*****

And don't forget, to been—to-bes grin from ear to ear.

*****

For they don't yet see what's got them by the you know what.

*****

What is it inside of us that, under the guise of politeness, courtesy, care, kindness, and consideration, what is it inside of us that prompts what is in truth faculties? *[The teacher may have intended to say "functions" instead of "faculties."]*

*****

It is the fear, unfortunately, of not getting what we think we must have, for we accept it not from God, but from man.

*****

It is indeed talent, an ability to study the weaknesses of others. Ah, but it's technique to apply the law and gain the glory of control over them.

*****

Glory, recorded in mental substance, is an insatiable need to be served. It's called, by mental substance, satisfaction.

*****

In other words, "Bind me tighter. I'm still able to breathe."

*****

The word *recorded* clearly reveals copy.

*****

Our need to bind reveals our lack of security, for that which is on the throne of God is called the little self.

*****

The throne is too big and we just can never seem to fill it.

*****

Truth is not bound by form. That includes language.

*****

Whoever refuses to change form is bound to the armies of has-beens in the great eternity and evolution of the being, the Light we are.

*****

"O belief, I love you so. You bind so tightly."

*****

So cut the ropes of bondage and fly to heaven's heights, for that is the paradise of peace.

*****

The isle of harmony in the sea of confusion.

*****

The waters of regret.

*****

Be a better fisherman for there's a hole in your net.

*****

Man believes what he knows and, in the belief, loses wisdom.

*****

We lounge in the front yard and soon forget there's a back one.

*****

Until the weeds have made a jungle of our little paradise.

*****

Awake in the beautiful Light of Truth, man has no need to wander for he knows everything. His isle of paradise is right where he is. It is when that great truth enters the I, the thought, the I enters the form, that he looks, has knowledge, and begins to wander. Losing what he has, he seeks what someone else, he thinks, might have.

*****

In many philosophies throughout the world, there's always been the teaching of lost souls. There are no lost souls, only in the sense of wandering souls.

Good night.

*****

[The following teachings may have been given only to a very small group of advanced students.]

Truth is the wise use of understanding.

*****

Yes.

Whoever awakens to the divinity of design and, through understanding that truth, applies the wisdom of use is destined to joy, feeling goodness, and all the love that life has to offer.

*****

Has-been, total control, your days are numbered. Forget your goal.

*****

Yes.
Record.
Uh-huh.
Keep faith with reason; she will transfigure thee.
Yes.
Reason is a great magnet. It transforms everything that enters its sphere of action.
Yes.
Reason is the child born from the intercourse of understanding and truth. And so, whoever keeps faith with the child known as reason shall be transfigured, of course, transformed.

Yes.

Thought you would like that little tidbit.

Yes!

*****

OK.

Temptation is the romance of self-love in its challenge to control others.

*****

Yes.

Divinity, the Divine expression, the expression of Divinity man knows as desire. Impinged upon mental substance, it is recorded by the mind—hear?—

Yes.

—as need. Now that awakening in mental substance is the need of the source that it is being impinged by. In other words, the need is recognition of mental substance—hear?—

Yes.

—of the Divine which sustains it.

Ah.

Now that is the need.

Ah.

Now, when man, in his descent, became aware of the thought of the I—

Uh-huh.

—man lost the I through a divided house.

Uh-huh.

It's known as the Garden of Eden.

Yes.

Hmm?

Uh-huh.

Now, the rib of Adam—

Yes.
—you understand?—
Uh-huh.
—is the reason.
Right.
Now when man loses reason—
Uh-huh.
—the impingement in consciousness of the divine expression—
Yes.
—known as need, without the light of reason—
Uh-huh.
—you hear?—
Yes.
—man awakens to the thought of I, to the romance of self, the challenge to control everything it sees, hears, senses, feels, and touch[es].
Ahh.
Man has done that by a house divided.
Uh-huh.
And he has done that because he looks down instead of up.
Ah.
So, man sees—
Uh-huh.
—and does not view. Man hears and does not listen.
Yes.
Hmm?
Uh-huh.
Man senses and loses wisdom, for he knows what he senses. And his knowledge is much. And with his great knowledge, he loses his humble wisdom. Hmm? So, man touches and reacts. Man no longer touches and be-comes.
Ah.

So therefore, man is now the victim of that that he touches, that which he hears, that which he sees, that which he senses, that which he smells.

So when, with faith—you hear?

Yes.

Faith, we return.

Yes.

The upward climb.

Uh-huh.

You see? For that which is sustaining us is above. Authority is above.

Yes.

Bondage is below.

Yes.

You see, freedom is above.

Yes.

The bird flies.

Uh-huh.

Ah, the snake crawls.

Yes.

Hmm?

Yes.

And so, in the beak of the great eagle—

Uh-huh.

—is the snake of deception.

Yes.

And it takes the snake that crawls upon the ground—you hear?—

Uh-huh.

—in its beak and flies to heaven to return it to the Source.

Yes.

That it may awaken—

Uh-huh.

—in the Light. And be transformed by reason.

Uh-huh.

For she, reason, transfigures thee...

*****

Whoever holds high the lamp of honesty is in the flow of reason.

Yes.

And when they touch, the awakening within is the sensation [and] is within their own being, is not dependent upon the touch. But one is [has] permitted themself to be receptive to what they touch. And because they are awakened, to they alone can open or close the door. Hmm? That it is not touching that is doing it.

Ahh.

But that it is in truth a conscious choice. "I touch. Ah, now I feel."

Uh-huh.

"The feeling is good."

Uh-huh.

"I touch and now I feel. And I have judged the feeling not good."

Yes.

"Therefore, I no longer touch."

Uh-huh.

So, you see, my friend, that's how we view instead of see. Go right through it. Go beyond it.

Uh-huh.

And there we are.

Yes.

The observer, no longer the observed.

Uh-huh.

Hmm? So, learn to touch. "Ah, that feels good." Learn to touch. "Ah, that feels good."

Uh-huh.

Learn to touch. "Ah, that feels good."
Uh-huh.
For that is taking place within your consciousness and you alone are the captain of the ship. And you alone make that decision. You see, we are no longer aware that we alone make the decision because, through habit, abuse—
Uh-huh.
—we lost the awareness.
Yes.
Hmm?
Uh-huh.
But that that is lost shall be found.
Right.
And you are in the process of finding that which has been lost.
Yes.
Hmm?
Yes.
So, when you look, you begin to view. You go beyond. Right on in and through.
Uh-huh.
Ah. And it's beautiful. You touch; you go beyond. Beyond the illusion.
Uh-huh.
For there is where it really is. That's where the captain you are.
Uh-huh.
Beyond the illusion.
Hmm.
Shut [it] off.

*****

Ready?
Yeah.

Everything is God when *we* let it be. The sadness is we don't let it be. We bind it to what has been.

Yes.

We do that to our self. Therefore, that is what we offer everything.

Thank you.

You're welcome, child.

*****

Ready?

Yes.

The insertion of understanding in truth is rhythm in reason. Now, child, I gave you this truth many years ago. Rhythm harmony balance peace. Rhythm harmony balance peace. Hold release, hold release. Thank you, God, I am—

At peace.

—at peace. Rhythm, the transformation reason. Good day.

Thank you.

*****

OK.

Self-pity is the harvest moon of self-love.

MARCH 18, 1983

Class March 22, 1983

[The following teachings were given to the larger group of students who volunteered at the temple Tuesday nights.]

"The Lord's Prayer," "The Law's Be." Now the Lord of the universe is the law of the universe. And so, the truth is revealed: "The Law's Be," that is, "The Lord's Prayer," the law's declaration.

[Please see the appendix for "The Law's Be" affirmation.]

*****

"Our Father which art in being—Our Father which art in heaven," our consciousness, our being, consciousness, truth. Now think about that. "Our Father which art in heaven." "Our being [is the] consciousness, truth." That is the father, the creator of all of our experiences, everything in our life, within our self.

*****

"Hallowed be thy name." "Holy be the identity." "Holy be the identity" is the goodness, the holiness of the I as it dents the illusion. It's not the dent. It is the process. The dent is the thought of I. And that's what binds us.

*****

"Thy kingdom come." "The joy of life" is ever subject to what follows. So, the kingdom come is ever dependent upon the will of God, which is subject to, within our consciousness, our own choice.

*****

"Thy will be done." The divine will, the will of God, you already understand, *is* total acceptance. There is nothing that is not sustained by the will of God. And so, you clearly see "Thy will be done" *is* the totality of acceptance in your consciousness.

*****

"On earth,"—mind, mental substance—"As it is in heaven." The consciousness of God which you are, the Truth. So, it simply reveals "On earth as it is in heaven," in the mind, the Light in the mind as it is in the heart, for heart is the vehicle through which your soul speaks.

*****

"Give us this day." "Grant us the Light." We are able to see in the day, but we stumble in the night. And so, it simply declares: "Grant us the Light" or "Give us the day." Nothing lives in the night, in the depth of the darkness.

*****

No one can possibly live without their daily sustenance, which man calls his daily bread. The sadness is, by calling it "Our daily bread," we look without to get it. Instead of the demonstrable truth "our daily sustenance": that it is inside of us waiting for us to partake of it.

*****

"And forgive us our trespasses." "And forgive us our has-beens." In order to free, one must give forth. So that which trespasses crosses the consciousness, the Light of the truth that we are. If we do not forgive it, we do not free our self from it. So, you do not free yourself from a has-been, from things that are passed, by simply demanding and dictating that that is gone: you forgive it; you free yourself from its trespassing from the shadow in front of your view by giving it forth. And who does one give it forth to but the source from whence we have called it up.

*****

"As we forgive those who trespass against us." "As we forgive those has-beens who" *we tempt*, who we tempt to steal our joy. We tempt them through our ignorance from our love of self, for it is our love of self that is temptation. No one tempts anything that they do not love. No one teases anything that they do not love. They love it inside themself. It is the self-love. You see, our minds clearly reveal to us if we tease something, we get a reaction from it. Depending on the tempting and the teasing how much reaction that we receive, how much energy is returned unto us, that is a revelation of the degree of the need of the love of self for the throne of glory. Is there any question on the demonstrable truth of temptation or teasing?

*****

The statement is, in the change of the copyists, "Lead us not into temptation." It is not the Light, you understand, that romances with self-love. It is the lack of the Light that romances with self-love. And the romancing of self-love is the insatiable need to tempt and to tease.

*****

"Deliver us from evil." "Deliver us from the false king—the service to the false king of shadows." Now, that which has no true substance is a shadow. It is a shadow of that which is real. And so, it is clearly revealing to free us from our service to that which is not real. Now, illusion, we all know, is a reflection. That that reflects is not real. It is only a shadow of the genuine. So, shadows reflect, you understand?

Now, for example, the sun shines brightly and a tree casts a shadow. It is an obstruction in front of the Light. But the shadow that you see is not the tree, but it is a reflection of the tree, for the tree itself is obstructing the Light and you see the shadow. And so, this illusion, that you call form, is not a reality; it is not true substance, but it is a reflection inside of yourself. It is an illusion. It is a shadow. And it's clearly telling you that who controls the shadows, the illusions in life, is the king of darkness. For that's what he has as his domain: the shadows, the illusions of life, not the truth, not the substance, not Life itself, but only the reflection. That which obstructs the Light reflects itself, called form. Any—

*****

"For thine is the kingdom." And what is a kingdom? A kingdom is a domain. Now there are many kingdoms, but the Light is the kingdom. Thine is the *thee*, the true be. That is the kingdom. That is available to you to enter at any moment of your choice. Any moment. But it must be entered moment by moment. For if you do not enter the Light moment by moment, it is one moment later there's a shadow and you *think* that is the kingdom.

*****

"The power and the glory forever" is demonstrably revealed. That *is* what you are. That is not the illusion. That is not the shadow. But it's what you truly are. You cannot be aware of what you are until you free yourself from need, for need is the reaction of the illusion to the truth that impinges upon it.

*****

And that reaction of the illusion, the shadow, is known to man as belief. And so, man believes many things and is bound by all of them in the service to the king of shadows.

*****

The "Amens" change from the truth that is revealed, are simply a recognition of a power, of a light, of a truth that is greater than the thought, which is a form in mental substance. So, all minds know beyond a shadow of any doubt there is a power that is sustaining it. But because of the nature of mental substance—to gather and to garner—it wishes to gather and garner the very Power that sustains it. And in its great effort to gather that which sustains it, man believes and is bound; and power, for him, becomes force. Now force returns to the sender. Ah, but power, it ever goes on the circle of the divine, infinite, eternal circle of truth, without beginning, without ending. So, whoever in honesty and in the light of reason is the receptive vehicle of the Power that is shall ever be filled and never be in lack. It is force that goes out into the universe and returns unto the sender. Sometimes it returns in ways the sender never desired nor designed for it to return.

*****

Slow death of anything is a painful birth of everything.

*****

Fools will what they want and weep in their dependence on others for fulfillment. Ah, but wise men will what is the divine right of their domain—personal responsibility—and are fulfilled with the spirit of joy and the abundant good of life, for the Light returns unto them the right on the divine circle of return.

*****

In other words, blow your own nose and free your reason.

*****

Ready? *[The teacher confirms that the recording technician is ready to record.]*
Yes.
On the throne of self-love sits the prince of piece. Whoever enters his domain must be willing to share whatever piece the prince decides to take.

*****

Knowledge is the reflection of understanding and, of course, is a shadow.

*****

Sleep is the land of shadows. We enter it to serve. Therefore, wise men rest, but never sleep. Therefore, wise men are rejuvenated by the Light of Truth.

*****

Fools seek the glory of a throne. Wise men know that thrones are designed to be sat on. So, fools are sat on frequently.

*****

A clutch is designed to be stepped on in order that you may shift and go. So, learn to be; just be the shift and the go, and not the clutch you know.

*****

In other words, hold and destroy; free and unfold.

*****

The only way to enter the salt mines of hell is through the open door of the thought of I. And whenever we open the door known as the thought of I, we must rejoice in our service below.

*****

For we are getting what we think we need.

*****

Therefore, my good friends, know need, know greed in service below. Awaken in the moment which is the freedom, the joy, and abundant good.

*****

Just be. Free is no past can I see. No future do I plea. Just be. God is the moment of your conscious choice.

*****

All has-beens watch and wait for all to-bes, for their armies to grow and to prosper for you to serve without end until the moment you just be.

*****

Coming events forecast their shadows, for man lives in self 90 percent; and therefore, forecasting is 90 percent accurate.

*****

The Light views and clearly reveals the coming of the has-beens. Be of good cheer for 10 percent is one-aught. And one is God in the circle of Infinite Intelligence. The power is ever greater than the force of belief, for belief, the child of need, is dependent upon.

*****

Be one in your universe. Then, just be. For that's the I, eternity. Good night.

*****

[The following teachings may have been given to a very small group of advanced students.]
Whoever faces the Light is aware the shadow they cast is behind them. Therefore, they are free from service to the realms, the salt mines below.

*****

Whoever shall view will rise anew. Only the fool looks back and is bound. So, rise anew and learn to view.

*****

Look back, move forward, and enjoy the hole which you fall in.

*****

All things are believed possible to a mind in the glory of self-love.

*****

Humor is the upliftment of our understanding and, of course, is at no one's expense, for it's an inside job called joy. And when we just be, humor shall we see: upliftment, joy, and the abundant good. It's the job we're doing inside. Be a good builder, not a flake in the field.

MARCH 22, 1983

Class March 26, 1983

Energy or vitality is ever dependent upon the lack of self-love.

*****

[The following teachings may have been given to a very small group of advanced students.]
Go.
Understanding truth frees us from the knowledge of belief. And that process, to man, is known as wisdom.
OK.
And so whenever this takes place—you hear?—
Yes.
—man frees himself in the fullness of being.
Uh-huh.
You hear? Now, mist is ever before the thought of I.
Yes.
And homeland, fullness, joy of life, abundant good is ever before the being of reason.
Hmm.
You hear?
Uh-huh.
Your planet offers faith.
Yes.
Moment by moment you choose between thought—
Uh-huh.
—form—
Uh-huh.
—I—
Yes.
—freedom.
Uh-huh.
You choose this moment by moment. Thoughts, forms; ideas—

Uh-huh.
—Light. You hear?
Uh-huh.
So when you look at a thought—
Uh-huh.
—you are bound by its form.
Yes.
Ah, but when you *view* a thought—
Uh-huh.
—you pierce the veil—
Uh-huh.
—and are freed by the vehicle of use designed for the purpose of expression.
Uh-huh.
Hear?
Yes.

*****

Yes.

Form is the effect of thought. Thought is the servant of force. Force is dependent upon belief. So, man knows much *[After a short pause, the teacher continues.]* and wisdom ever knows better.

*****

A wise man views. Then he be. For a wise man awakens to view that he may see and, in so doing, ever be the fullness, the joy, the life that be. Remember to view; then you may see.

*****

For then you go beyond the me.

Doctor Bronson. Hello.

Hello.

[Dr. Bronson is a spirit who would occasionally share his understanding through Mr. Goodwin's mediumship. He would sometimes identify himself.]

*****

It is the me that needs to see. So be the I; view eternity.

*****

Yes.

The purpose of design, called form. Now, you see in your world many forms. Of course, they are dependent upon belief, force, what you know as mental substance or mind.

Yes.

They exist and have continuous effect upon what is known as the temple of God, the form through which the Light expresses itself.

Uh-huh.

Ever in keeping with need, which of course is dependent on "me," which is, of course, the thought of I or the form of the indent—

Yes.

—identification, identity. Hmm? Now, for example, you have the temple of the Light, called God.

Uh-huh.

And a soul animates it, moves it, causes it to speak, sense, feel, etc., etc., etc. Hmm?

Yes.

Now the soul, of course, is aware that it is not the house.

Yes.

But that it lives in the house.

Uh-huh.

That there are many houses that it has lived in before.

Uh-huh.

That there are many houses or vehicles that it will use again.
Yes.

Now, the soul, in its evolution, of course, in entering the form, absorbs, ah, vibration of form—

Uh-huh.

—mental substance, in the sense that a sponge will absorb the water in which it is placed.

Yes.

Hmm? Now, the very nature of the sponge does not change.

Uh-huh.

It appears to change because it's now absorbed the water. Is that not correct?

Yes.

Now, appearance is the covering or the individualization—

Uh-huh.

—of the soul. Now that's what it is, is the covering, you see. You talk about a soul identity, well, you're talking, then, about what it has absorbed.

Yes.

Hmm? But it has not changed the soul.

Uh-huh.

It has not changed the Light.

Uh-huh.

For it is lesser than the Light.

Yes.

It is the lesser light. It is what it has absorbed. Hmm? Now, in keeping with its absorption in evolution does it, through the Law of Like Attract Like, enter that type of form.

Yes.

You hear? You follow me, child?

Yes.

Fine. And so, here we have these many, many souls and they're in many different forms throughout their evolution.

Uh-huh.

And now we'll enter your little world, your peanut world.
Uh-huh.
And we will see the forms ever in keeping with the "me" that we believe.
Uh-huh.
That is the thought of I. And, we see that, of course, in keeping with what we see within ourselves.
Uh-huh.
For like attracts like and becomes the Law of Attachment.
Yes.
Correct?
Uh-huh.
Yeah. But we want to go beyond and we want to begin to view.
Yes.
Once again!
Yes.
You see? And so, we view the form and we see that it's basically this type of form or that type of form.
Uh-huh.
We call that man and we call that woman.
Yes.
We see, in the difference between the two, there is something there that we believe we need.
Yes.
For we have identified with form within our self. We are aware, we know—
Uh-huh.
—that we have such and such and such and such. Our house is made a certain way. And that this house here is made a certain way. And that when these two houses or vehicles come together—
Uh-huh.
—there is an exchange of what is really, in truth, energy.

Yes.

Ah, the purity or contamination of the energy, which is energy—

Uh-huh.

—is dependent on what it has absorbed—you understand?—

Uh-huh.

—through its own exposures in what you call life.

Yes.

And so, if the sponge—which never changes its basic nature, of course. A sponge is always a sponge.

Yes.

A rose is always a rose.

Yes.

Though roses have many thorns and sponges don't. And there is a difference there, you see.

Uh-huh.

Now, and so we are attracted within our self for a release, if we are an electric being, for we must be dutiful to the purpose of our being.

Yes.

Therefore, the principle reveals to us that we are destined, by our nature, to release and, through the release, to experience.

Yes.

And, through the experience, to fulfill the purpose of our being.

Yes.

You follow me?

I do.

However, by the illusion of the thought of I or form, we then become the victims of the illusion in order to fulfill the principle.

Yes.

Now that takes place through, of course, our beliefs.

Uh-huh.

That, of course, is dependent upon the force, which, of course, mental substance is a vehicle thereof.

Yes.

All right. Now, so we've now, we've now lost the principle of it.

Uh-huh.

And we have entered the personality of it.

Yes.

In other words, we've lost the I in consciousness; we've now entered the form or thought of I, you hear?

Yes. Uh-huh.

And therefore, by entering the thought or form, we've entered the limit and we are dependent there upon.

Yes.

Hmm. Now, we begin to awaken and we begin to view. And we see this person seems to be this way one moment and that way another moment. And they keep on changing, and they never know just who they are or when they are, and etc.

Uh-huh.

Well, the house is a temple of the Light.

Uh-huh.

And the soul—you hear?—

Uh-huh.

—is visiting in the temple. It belongs to the Divine.

Yes.

And it's used for a time.

Uh-huh.

Well, in keeping with our evolution, in keeping with our little sponge and what it has absorbed and etc., and in keeping with the laws of evolution, we are ever with the divine right—

Uh-huh.

—of choice.

Yes.

Now we may choose, through our own evolution, that, what form or the illusion has to offer, that it calls power, that it has control over creation—

Uh-huh.

—you hear?—

Yes.

—which is the twist and abuse of a divine law.

Uh-huh.

For the I, indeed, has the divine right and charge and control over all its own creations.

Yes.

All thoughts.

Uh-huh.

All feelings. All emotions.

Yes.

That is the Divinity, the right that you *are*.

Uh-huh.

When it gets twisted, it expands out to control everything.

Yes.

And the need becomes greater.

Uh-huh.

You see? For it has denied, and through the Law of Denial, it has destined itself to delusion and deception.

Yes.

And it takes place within our consciousness.

Uh-huh.

You hear?

Yes.

And so anyway, we involve our self in these many things. And we begin to view a tiny bit.

Uh-huh.

We become aware of these varying changes.

Uh-huh.

Well, you see, because it's only a house, a vehicle—

Uh-huh.

—because it belongs to the Divinity—

Uh-huh.

—and its purpose is simply for a place to reside in order to animate the illusion—you hear?—we ofttimes, at times in evolution, we make our agreements if you can say—

Uh-huh.

—to have power.

Yes.

We are tempted—

Uh-huh.

—to control and to feel this God that is, yea, even greater than we ever have before.

Uh-huh.

There's a great temptation.

Yes.

And so, what happens? We sell out.

Uh-huh.

Is the proper word. We sell out. Not sell out, you see. Our being—

Uh-huh.

—which has earned that particular little house to reside in—

Uh-huh.

—it moves out.

Yes.

And these souls, you see, that have also sold out that are working in the various salt mines—

Uh-huh.

—of creation in those realms, they get to enter—

Uh-huh.

—for they are earth-bound. Still bound to the temptation of form—

Uh-huh.

—you hear?—

Yes.

—and its sensations, you see. Losing the principle, which would grant them both—

Uh-huh.

—in balance and harmony. And so, the ruler of the realm—

Uh-huh.

—you see? The greatest of the servants to the ruler—

Uh-huh.

—you see?—they get sent off to flesh and to the house that is vacated—

Uh-huh.

—to reexperience the sensations, you see.

Yes.

And to, once again, get this great charge of energy. You hear?

Uh-huh.

And they're sent in and they have their moments and times.

Yes.

Then the next one is sent in.

Uh-huh.

And the next one and the next one and the next one. Whatever the ruler, you know, in his little payments and his rewards—you see?

Yes.

—to ever get them to do more.

Uh-huh.

Ever more. Because it's never enough, you see. It's never enough to that realm, child.

No, no.

You see? And so, you have forms that are used in that way.

Uh-huh.

You see? Now, then there's a law involved there that is also—the law is available to the Light.

Uh-huh.

And then the forms of those who are serving the Light—
Uh-huh.
—are receptive to that, you see? There are beings, souls—
Uh-huh.
—that enter it, use it for a time, and leave it.
Yes.
And always, you see, the difference is they leave it encouraged and uplifted, you see.
Better than they found it.
Better than they found it, for they respect it. They know who it belongs to.
Yes.
So, they've come. They enter. They visit in the temple.
Uh-huh.
And they leave.
Uh-huh.
You hear? And—because, you see, they have something to offer and not something to gain.
Yes.
You see, there's the difference.
Uh-huh.
You see, blessed are those who give—
Yes.
—for their receiving is not of this world.
Yes.
Do you understand?
Yes.
Woe to those who take—
Uh-huh.
—for dependence upon form shall increase in [to] an insatiable need. So, those of the darkness, you see, they enter—and they're all lined up—
Uh-huh.

—waiting to get through, to get that what you would call in your world a charge—

Yes.

—a stimulation, you see.

Uh-huh.

And so, they, of course, receive energy.

Uh-huh.

You see? They receive it from other forms. They pull it, you see.

Yes.

And so, you have the experiences [and you] never know what is going to happen with . . .

Uh-huh.

Hmm?

Uh-huh.

Really? And you find ever serving and serving and serving the energy, you see?

Uh-huh.

It's always hungry. [It] has to have more and more. And in other words, it always has to be bigger and better.

Yes.

It's totally dependent upon that process. Because when you see the lineup, you'd understand.

Uh-huh.

Hmm. Yes. Now, are there any questions on that part of the design?

Yes. Now how much control does—do those souls have over the vehicle when they enter to get their charge?

Well, now that—it depends in [on] how much belief the form in mental substance has over the need. You see, the greater the belief—

Uh-huh.

—that they need this for, whatever they need it for—

Uh-huh.

—in the mental substance—
Yes.
—that is deposited there—
Uh-huh.
—you see, then that's how much control they have.
Well, evidently—I'm—we're speaking of a specific one now.
Indeed, yes.
And evidently the need there is quite great.
Well then, if you see the lineup, then you'd understand the need.
Yes.
Now, if you've got—for example, say if you have 2,000 soldiers that haven't had breakfast, lunch, or dinner—
Uh-huh.
—for a week, then you would understand, wouldn't you?
Uh-huh.
They're quite hungry.
Yes.
Hmm? There's never enough. I think in your world you call it the great clutch.
Yes.
Hmm.
All right. Now how much control over—what I'm asking is, who decides when they will go out and get more energy from someone else's river?
Well, the ruler decides.
OK. Now the one who is assigned charge over that form, he stands—
That's the prince.
Yes, the prince. He stands and he regulates how often this form will be used to gather energy or to get—
Why, of course, ever in keeping with the lineup.
Yes.
Now, of course, you see, he also is subject to a ruler.

Yes.

Hmm.

Yes.

The king himself.

Uh-huh.

And if he doesn't do a good job, well, then you know where he ends up.

Oh, yes.

Well.

Yes.

And so, you see, then what you have, you see, there's mental substance that has to be worked with.

Yes.

And sometimes, you see, in mental substance they start—the mind starts to register, "I'm exhausted."

Uh-huh.

"I'm just so tired." And then what happens—that's when the rul—the one in charge—

Uh-huh.

—impinges on the consciousness, "Well, you need da-da-da" *[The teacher seems to be suggesting a list.]*

Yes.

And then they send them on, you see.

Uh-huh. So how much control does the mental substance have over what will be done?

Depends the—it depends on the usage by the one in charge.

Uh-huh.

You see. For example, how many years, it is not dependent. It is dependent on the frequencies, you see.

Yes.

And it also depends upon the belief in the mental substance of the temple itself.

Uh-huh.

You see.

OK.

You see, if there is great belief that the—for example, now say that there is a specific purpose that the ruler in charge of the form—

Uh-huh.

—the direct one, you see. But they are a prince, for example—

Uh-huh.

—you see, they are termed "princes." For example, if they have something that they are determined that must be done—

Yes.

—then they will impinge with their force—

Uh-huh.

—in the consciousness, the mental substance—

Uh-huh.

—that that's—they must have that.

Yes.

That is absolutely indispensable. And they will keep impinging that.

Uh-huh.

Don't you see what I mean?

Yes.

Until they get it.

Uh-huh.

Of course, they don't always get it, for Light and Power that sustains thought is greater than the thought, you see.

Yes.

And, of course—but they will do almost anything to get it.

Uh-huh. And in the meantime, the other work has to be done to satisfy those who have merited some charge or some opportunity to use the house.

Oh, absolutely. You see, so that has to be considered.

Yeah.

You see, because there's the lineup that has to be served.

Yes.

An endless line, child.

Yeah, yeah.

Now, you see, how does this—how do these doors open up? It opens up, you see, when the great Power is directed to mental substance, known as belief or the force.

Uh-huh.

And, you see, it's called overidentification with the self or the thought of I.

Yes.

The more overidentification [there] is—

Uh-huh.

—the more openness there is to this.

Yeah.

Now, shut it off. *[The teacher refers to the microcassette recorder.]*

MARCH 26, 1983

Class March 29, 1983

[The following teachings were given to the larger group of students who volunteered at the temple Tuesday nights.]

Now the question is, creation doesn't do you in; it is your belief in it that does you in. Well, for example, whatever we believe in, by the Law of Believing, we become. So, it is our belief in creation, which is form, which is limit, that, so to speak, does it in, for it is our belief in it that limits us through the Law of Identification with it. We become the limit of our own belief through the Law of Identity.

*****

Eternity, is it beyond time, the illusion? Infinity is beyond space, the limit. So, when you go beyond time and space, you find truth.

*****

To go beyond the illusion of time and space, one must be the I that they are and stop being the thought of the I that they are.

*****

Man finds the love of self when he loses the love of God.

*****

Without need, man is not tempted. Man experiences need at the loss of God. And that, of course, we all know, is by finding the self.

*****

Lucifer, in truth, *is* the thought of I.

*****

His throne *is* the throne of self. It is sustained by the power of God, known as love. Man makes the conscious choice moment by moment.

*****

Without the totality of acceptance, which is the will of God, there is no faith in the Power that is.

*****

When you believe you are, you no longer are. That's when you lose truth.

*****

Of course, man asks the question, "What would I do if I didn't have all these other things?" When you have freedom—what is freedom? Why, it is not only the absence of bondage, it is the flow of the being that you are, not limited and restricted in the prison house of the senses.

*****

Believers sleep and feed the masses of forms that they believe they are in keeping with their own self-love. Wise men rest and are rejuvenated, for they know beyond a shadow of any doubt the Light within *is* what they are. It is not what they become. It is not what they have been. But it is what they are. So, rest; don't sleep. Rejuvenate; don't weep.

*****

Whenever we experience need, be stilled. Accept the demonstrable truth: we are experiencing the effects of the transgressions of divine, immutable law! Be of good cheer for change is ever your opportunity of the moment.

*****

[The following teaching may have been given to a very small group of advanced students.]
The intercourse between time in space is the freedom from the bondage of form, the illusion of self.

MARCH 29, 1983

Class April 1, 1983

[The following teaching may have been given to a very small group of advanced students.]

Whoever understands their need and applies the light of reason is guaranteed fulfillment, the joy of life.

*****

[The following teachings were given to the larger group of students who volunteered at the temple on Friday nights.]

The original sense is the sense of feeling, from the amoeba to man, from the microcosm to the macrocosm. So, man feels, thinks, forms, and acts. That is what man knows. What man is, is his own ability to awaken that all feeling is sound or vibration and is the very instrument through which man sees and, therefore, is bound by what he sees because man believes what he feels.

*****

So, when we hear a sound, we see a form. And when we see a form, we believe what we see, for it is based upon what we feel. And because of that, we become. Man has lost, because of self-thought, of self-feeling, man has lost, temporarily, that awareness and, because of that loss, pays the price and binds himself to what is known as the love of self for the glory of God.

*****

All feeling is principle. All thought is dependent upon the interpretation of the feeling, which is also dependent upon the identification with the limits of what is known as self. That is what all judgments are based upon.

*****

Sadness or joy is an interpretation that is created by our identification with what we call self.

*****

When you understand that creation is a dual sight—it sees, and it doesn't see; it knows, and it doesn't know. For everything that it knows guarantees everything it doesn't know that it needs to know. And so, man is constantly flowing between fullness and need.

*****

The thought of I is the form that we make in our own interpretation of what we are. It is not what we are. It is the form, the image that we make. Our interpretation of what we are is not what we are.

*****

Without movement, there is no form. Therefore, we are not form, thought. We are that which moves form, thought. That's why we are not what we think we are. We are bound by the form of what we think we are, and that is our suffering in life.

*****

You see, you hear a sound and you *feel* that it is beautiful. But you don't *see* that it is beautiful; you *feel* that it is beautiful. Because, you see, you're looking from a very small, little periscope. You're seeing; you're not viewing. The subconscious or inner mind is a language of form; it is a language of pictures. The subconscious mind does not know words. It reacts to feeling because it is viewing form, the forms that the sounds, which are the feelings, which are the forms, which are controlling your being.

*****

So, you hear some music and you don't like it. But you don't know why you don't like it. You just don't like it. You hear other music and you feel wonderful. You love it, but you don't know why you love it. Because the overidentification with self has closed the door of the Light within you.

*****

You see, whether we like or dislike a piece of music has absolutely nothing whatsoever to do with the painting that has been painted by the artist in what we call sound. It has everything to do, moment by moment, with our own overidentification with self. For there are times, we love a certain piece of music. Then there are other times, we don't like it quite as much. So, it reveals to us where we are in consciousness with overidentification with the self. For it is the self that limits it, distorts it, and gives an incorrect interpretation of the true picture, the true painting that the artist is, is painting for us, you see.

*****

Many people are receptive to the great paintings called the classics. Through man's own narrowing or limitation and that music to them is called jazz, popular, ragtime. But if you trace its root, you will find it's taken from the great inspiration of what you call the classics.

*****

It has become tailor-made to the limits that people have put on themselves through their own self-thought.

*****

[That is[2]] why a wise person chooses wisely what their ears will be receptive to. Because if they don't choose wisely, they don't know what is binding them.

*****

Identification with the self is the open door to discord, for our thoughts that fill the house of self are most discordant.

For every yes, there is a no. For every go, there is a stop. For every night, there is a day. And so it is, anyone who insists upon thinking of self cannot and is not receptive to what is called the divine principle of harmony and, not being receptive to it, cannot *be*, can only have been and hope to be.

*****

This is why harmony, the principle, harmony, is the health of man. It is the wealth of man. It is the joy of life.

*****

Harmony unites. Discord divides. When our ears are the ears of ego, they hear discord. When they are the ears of perception, we listen and we receive harmony. And it's all taking place by our choice inside of our self.

*****

Whenever we understand need, our need, we enter the divine Law of Just Return and are filled.

*****

It's not what goes into the mouth that defiles the temple of God; it's what comes out of it.

*****

Spiritual is the expression of Spirit. Therefore, the question is, What is Spirit? Well, Spirit *is*. What *is*? Truth *is*. That what [which] you are.

*****

Go right to it.

[Student O], you are principle; or are you the thought of principle? *[After a very short pause, the teacher continues.]* I asked a question. Which are you?

Ah, I'm principle.
Therefore, there is no thought. Thank you.

*****

That which you are needs no defense. It's what you think you are that needs all the defense in the whole wide world. And that defense comes from down there. Take a look. Authority is above you. Thank you.

*****

The difference between music is—music is harmonious. And that which is not music is discordant. Now man calls discord music, and then there are times that he calls harmony music. And because man doesn't know the difference—because man is dependent upon mental substance, he suffers between discord and harmony. When man just is, he is no longer dependent upon reference. And not being dependent upon reference, man experiences the great beauty of the art that came from the realms of inspiration. For man in the be, the just be, is *in* God and there, in God, *is* inspiration.

*****

The receptivity to what man knows as divine love is through the path, and the patience on the path, of unbearable suffering of the senses, for the gain of the soul is the loss of the senses.

*****

Science is art. It holds true in all great art. The Law of Divine Love is the law of the six. There'll always be six of them.

*****

The cycle of greatness, of what you call greatness, the cycle of great art, whether it's science, literature, music, singing, whatever, is the cycle of 150 Earth years.

*****

Move arou—The law is. The law is not something you can go under, to the left, or to the right. There's no way out of the law. There's only the way in the law. Man has the choice to move in the law and, once having done so, cannot get out until the law fulfills itself. For the law *is*. It's not subject to the minds of men. Now you want to know about the Law of Frequency?

Yes.

Then, the Law of Frequency is the child of the Law of Motion. What is the Law of Motion? The Law of Motion is the child of the Law of Impulse. What is the Law of Impulse? The Law of Impulse is what you call beginning.

*****

Beginning of what? The beginning of what you call determines. Thank—

*****

Really.

Sorry. [The recording technician may be apologizing for an error in operating the microcassette recorder.]

Man confines; the law designs.

*****

The purpose of the design of a house, the temple of God, is for the service of good.

*****

So, the purpose of design of all form is for the service of the Light, for heaven on earth.

*****

[The following teaching was given to a very small group of advanced students.]

Whoever loves the shadow denies the Light and struggles in the pain and suffering of life.

APRIL 1, 1983

Class April 3, 1983

[The following teachings were likely given to the larger group of students who volunteered at the temple Sunday nights.]

That which is unbearable is that which is not born or carried. Therefore, be grateful to what you call unbearable.

*****

Divine love is the totality of love; therefore, cannot be known by the limit, what man calls thought, form.

*****

All cycles reveal to man the divine Law of Just Return.

*****

From the great halls of infinity, far beyond the conception of the human mind, graduates are sent out into the universe from these great halls of inspiration. They enter form in order that the service to the Light, which you call inspiration, God, harmony, may be revealed to these planets of forms.

And you ask the question, Why do they seem to be so emotional? That which is unbearable is that which is limit or form. And because they are inspiration and are graduates of the halls of inspiration, form is unbearable or not borne; and you witness that as suffering and struggle, for form you see, for form you identify with.

*****

Whatever we view we free, for we can only view when we be. Whatever we see we bind, for the seeing is what has been and what's to be. That's the difference between inspiration and perspiration.

*****

When you understand and apply the principle of the infrared, you'll be free in form and not of form.

*****

Learn to be an intelligent camera and you won't have to worry about bondage.

*****

As above, so below is never dependent on what you know.

APRIL 3, 1983

Class April 5, 1983

[The following teachings were likely given to a very small group of advanced students.]

Laziness is a state of exhaustion one experiences from their lack of effort to control what has been. And the forms of what has been are having a daily Thanksgiving dinner. The problem is, there's no thanks and a lot of getting. So it, in truth, it is a greed day of filling.

*****

It's now on.

Well, that's fine. Yes, I'm not afraid of it. Are you afraid of it?

No, of course not.

Not afraid at all. Now what were we talking about, child?

Belief.

Oh, yes, the bondage of belief. Oh, yes. And so we move through many things. We believe and we bind. And we know and we free. Now how simple it is to know things. To know—because, you see, whoever knows—the knowers are viewers. And the believers are seers. And so, you see, you have this great attraction. And, of course, you find attraction, attachment, and bondage to forms—

Yes.

—because you believe.

Uh-huh.

And you believe form. Well, whoever believes form serves form. And whoever serves form is bound by what they serve. Ah, now, then we move on in our expanding consciousness to knowing. So we know and we view, and we see forms. Oh, yes, there's a mist. That's all that is, is a mist. Well, of what benefit is a mist if you're not inside to see that the mist is what you move? You're not the mist. But because you believe you're the mist, you can't move the mist. Because you're bound by what you believe and you believe you're the mist. And therefore, the illusion, it holds you and you cannot [be], and are not, free.

Yes.

Because, you see, you believe.

Yes.

Well, one, in time, gets tired of believing, doesn't one, child?

Yes. Really.

One gets very weary of all that foolishness. Now we're talking about the salt. We're talking about the salt of, the salt of, of, of the world—

Uh-huh.

You see. You see, the salt of life. Yes. The salt of Earth and the salt of this and the salt of that. Well, you see, the Light uses salt as a means of purification.

Yes.

The darkness uses salt as the means of solidification. For the fools, it serves to bind through what you call belief.

Yes.

And for the wise men, it serves to purify and is known as transformation.

Uh-huh.

So, you see, Light, your faith, your absolute knowing, you see—

Yes.

The Light that is, that sustains everything, you see, it transforms all forms. Because what it does, it moves you from solidification in consciousness—

Uh-huh.

—to purification, for there you are. Now where's all your questions? Well, you know?

Now.

Yes?

There is a form that we have out in the garden. It's called a snail.

That's true. There are many.

Yes. And we had an abundance of them this year.

Well, you should have, considering what's been happening.

And there seems to be a direct relationship—their characteristic is one of something of the realms of darkness.

Well, this is where they multiply, grow, and prosper. And what does salt do to them?

It disintegrates them.

Indeed. Indeed. It disintegrates. It does not solidify, does it?

No, it doesn't.

It purifies and returns—returns the illusion to its substance.

Yes.

Now there's a living demonstration. Now, you see, if you don't do that purification—

Uh-huh.

—with those particular little, little, little forms—

Uh-huh.

—they do a number on you. Now, do you notice that they chew away and live off the living plants?

Yes.

They, as far as, looking, they—it makes them look very ratty.

Yeah.

And it takes away the very life essence of what the plant itself is thriving on.

Yes, it is.

Yes. And, you see, you notice that a plant, you see, it's leaf and it grows and it prospers, ever turning to the light—

Uh-huh.

—you know, in varying degrees.

Yes.

And they come and they attack the part of the form or the vehicle that turns toward the light, you see.

Yes. Uh-huh.

Don't they?

They do.

And they especially go for new growth.

Yes.

Now, what does new growth have that more mature growth does not? Well, new growth, don't you see, child, it has more vitality.

Yes.

Or energy.

Uh-huh.

Like you would say of youth of form, you see.

Yes.

It's filled with vitality. It's filled with life. And, of course, that's where those things go for. Because those are the most choice morsels because they are receptive to more light.

Yes.

Receptive to more energy and, therefore, contain more energy. Yes.

Less dense.

That is correct. It is less dense. It is less solidified.

Yes.

You see, it is flexible, moving—

Uh-huh.

—growing, prospering.

Yes.

And that's what it seeks and that's what it searches.

Uh-huh.

Oh, yes, there are a lot of snail-heads in your world.

Yes.

And we all know what they do.

Yes.

[The teacher laughs.] Yes. Yes. This is yours. This is yours.

Yes.

Yes. Yes. And because, you know, someday you're going to say, "Well, I don't feel like watching that picture-box [television].

I've spent enough of my energy on these forms called beliefs. I think I'll listen now for a little bit, a little while. I [will] sit down, just relax and listen."

Uh-huh.

There you are.

Good.

Well, one of your great men, used to be on your planet—fine soul, fine soul's over here—been over here quite a while now. He used to have a fireside chat with all of you. Yes. And he helped a lot of people and brought a prosperity and goodness to your particular country.

That was a Mr. Roosevelt.

Yes, indeed. Yes, indeed. Yes, yes. Loved his fireside chats. That's because, you see, he had a great love of humanity.

Uh-huh.

All right. Well, we'll have our armchair chat. You go ahead.

OK. [Student R laughs as he responds.] *Ah, no. OK—*

Snails. You have an interest in snails. There's a good example, you see. You notice they flooded the temple this year.

They did.

Oh, yes.

The vibration was what attracted them.

Oh, of course, of course, child, they're out there by the billions.

Uh-huh.

You should see their multiplications.

Yes.

Going to have to have another snail hunt soon.

Yes.

Very soon. Going to have to stay on top of it—

Uh-huh.

—because otherwise you're going to be very unhappy, you children.

Yes.

You see, it takes diligent effort. You can't quit.

Uh-huh.

Every day you look. Is that one? Phsst![3] *[The teacher makes a sound that is difficult to transcribe.]*

Yeah.

Every day. You walk out in the garden of the temple—

Uh-huh.

—and you look. Open your eyes. Oh, there's one over there. Oh, there's a big snail over there! Phsst!

Yes.

Because, you see, that will help you awaken to see what it takes.

Uh-huh.

To see what it takes to free yourself from that realm of bondage called belief.

Yes.

To the freedom that you are.

Uh-huh.

To see what it takes, no matter how, how tired you think you are—

Uh-huh.

—which is a bondage of a form created within your consciousness, you see.

Yes.

That's all it is. Yes. It's nothing more and it's nothing less. Yes, you go ahead.

Now the seventy-two is the mist of creation.

Well, you see, it is the attraction. You see, it is the attraction to the duality.

Uh-huh.

You see, you are attracted to, to comparison.

Uh-huh.

You see, that's one thing a comparison offers: "Oh, that's better than that."

Uh-huh.

"I'll take that." You see?

Yes.

And so, it offers—seventy-two—offers that to you.

Uh-huh.

Ah, but eighty-one, what does eighty-one offer to you? It offers you . . .

God and infinity.

God and infinity. It offers you movement. It offers you harmony. Take a look at it, you see.

Uh-huh.

You see—ah, what do you call it? A sideway[s] eight. It's just like a perfect movement, you see. And if you look at it, you go up, down, up on the other side, up, in there, and down and back up again, don't you see? You see, God above and God below.

Yes.

There is one.

Uh-huh.

When all you know.

Yes.

You see, God above and God below is truly one.

Yes.

When we know.

Uh-huh.

You see?

Yes.

It's your view.

Uh-huh.

You see, there are no opposites. There are no comparisons. That's all dependent upon your bondage, which is dependent upon your belief. That's not principle, but that is personality. There's only one.

Yes.

Everything else is dependent upon your illusion.

Uh-huh.
Totally dependent upon your illusion, child.
Uh-huh.
One is one. It'll never be two.
Yes. There could be no God below without the God above.
That's correct. It's all is one.
So, it is just one.
That's right. And above and below, you see, is ever dependent upon your view.
Yes. That's right. Perspective.
Yes. I think you ought to study the snail a little bit more.
Yeah.
Yeah— *[The teacher coughs.]*
Yes, they have a very strong relationship. What is it—it—many of the students have asked the spiritual significance—
Look at those big ears they have. Everyone else—
Antenna. Yeah.
Well, those are ears.
Their eyes are on the end, aren't they?
Why, yes. Well, take a look. Take a good look at them and try to understand them.
Yes.
Try to perceive. Because, you see, you perceive how they are.
Uh-huh.
And, you know, you look at them, you see.
Yes.
You study them. Well, then you get to understand—
Uh-huh.
—when you see those things that live in the mist.
Uh-huh.
And the characteristics, you see, and how they worked.
Uh-huh.
Yes. You see?

Slow moving, but diligent.

Only slow moving to your view.

Uh-huh.

But you take a good look and you'll see how—slow moving? Put them on a choice new leaf all loaded with energy—

Yes.

—and you'll see them go phssst! *[The teacher makes a sound that is difficult to transcribe, but suggests speed.]* You wouldn't believe how fast they are consuming.

Hmm.

In a matter of seeming seconds—

Uh-huh.

—it's a nice big hole.

Yes.

They appear to be slow moving.

Uh-huh.

And you'll see they are very clever in that respect.

Uh-huh.

Very clever. And multiplication?

Yes.

Unbelievable.

Yes. I've seen the evidence of that.

Well, now I want you to personally take it upon your . . . whenever you walk around— *[It is difficult to transcribe one word.]*

Uh-huh.

—to open your eyes.

Uh-huh.

You see? And to free each one. Choo! Choo! Choo![4]

Yes.

When you step aside, move over and lift your, lift your hand and pick up a few.

Uh-huh.

They're everywhere.
Yes.
You see, within days there'll be millions more.
Uh-huh. Yes.
Think of it. Think of it.
Yes.
You have been given charge all over all of that.
Uh-huh.
Exercise the authority that you are.
Yes. Now, as the vibration raises, they will diminish.
Indeed. And in the process of raising the vibration, you must be diligent and do your part. Choo! Choo! Choo!
Yes.
Never before has the temple here been under such attack.
That's right.
Never before, child—
That's right.
—has anyplace on your planet, has it been under such attack as it is.
Uh-huh.
. . . the garden of the temple. . . *[It is difficult to transcribe a couple of words.]*
Yes.
And I'm right on top—just like with those snails, I'm on top of you.
Uh-huh. Yes.
Because, you see, you are designed by the Great Architect to reside in a temple that's far greater than a snail. Now I'm not going to walk around here calling you a snail-head.
No, no.
You're supposed to be on duty . . . *[It is difficult to transcribe a few words.]* Don't you see, they're like clutches: they're designed to be stepped on.

Yes, yes.

And, my good friend—

Uh-huh.

—never forget that.

Yes.

What's designed to be stepped on, step on it.

Yes.

Don't play with it.

Uh-huh.

So, that's your new duty.

Uh-huh.

You're out there, open your eyes. Look. Then view.

Yes.

And start stepping.

Uh-huh.

You have to reach a few times. They're not always right in front of you. You have to look to the left and to the right as you're moving forwards.

And a little underneath.

And a little bit underneath, which you haven't—you're not used to doing.

Yes.

Belief always just wants to look down. Oh, yes. But look what's underneath. *[The teacher laughs.]* More than once you've looked down and never bothered to look what was underneath and look what you got.

Yes. Yes.

Have you forgotten so soon . . .

*****

A fool loves himself for he believes what his self is. A wise man loves what he is for he knows what he is. I am I and thou art thee. All is one and one is me. Therefore, yes, indeed, a wise man knows who he is, what he is, where he is. And because he knows, he opens to the will of God, total acceptance, and loves everything and everyone. For everything and everyone *is* one, and that's what he is. And so, a wise man does love himself, for "himself" is everyone.

APRIL 5, 1983

Class April 10, 1983

[The following teachings were given to the larger group of students who volunteered at the temple Sunday nights.]

—thing about what you have: reject—

Uh-huh.

—resent, and retaliate. And so, you now know that reject is . . .

Discord.

Discord.

Resent is disease.

Resent—disease.

And retaliate is destroy.

And retaliate is to destroy. Do we not destroy what we retaliate against?

Uh-huh.

Hmm? Now what do we do with the other two?

Well, when we resent, we have that condition in our throat.

And what does it say there? *[The teacher may be referring to a student's notes.]*

Resent is disease.

Well, we're diseased by whatever we resent. Hmm? And what happens when we reject?

Ah . . .

What does it say there?

When we reject, well, we're in discord.

That's right. We reject; we are discordant. The will of God is not discordant. The will of God is a harmonious flow. So, whenever we go against the will of God, we are discordant; we are out of sync. That's what you call it: out of sync. We're not in harmony. And when we're not in harmony, we're in whatever the opposite is. The opposite is discord. Now that's how we get discordant. That's how things start breaking down in our life.

All we have to do is to reject. That's all we have to do. All we have to do is go against the divine Law of Abundant Good.

Now you [have] already been given the joy of life is the totality of acceptance. You already got that in "The Law's Be." And there's no way you're going to change "The Law's Be," because the Law's be.

Do you understand that? *[After a short pause, the teacher continues.]*

Save the tape. *[The teacher instructs the recording technician to shut off the microcassette recorder.]*

*****

Yes, we see clearly that a rejection is a discord. That means, it's not harmony, right? And, tell me, what is it that needs defense, truth or falsehood?

Falsehood.

So, we see that rejection requires defending. Why does rejection require defense? *[After a short pause, the teacher continues.]* Because that's how it protects itself. And what is it that rises to do all the protecting? Is it your be, which is truth and free, or is it your has-been?

Has-been.

Well, any questions on that simple truth?

*****

Do you fear what you accept or do you fear what you reject? Tell me something: which do you fear: what you reject or what you accept? What is it you fear? Hmm? Tell me.

What you reject.

We fear what we reject. And why do we fear what we reject? *[After a short pause, the teacher continues.]* Would that not be our way of defending it?

Yes.

Defending our self from it? You cannot fear what you accept. You can only fear what you reject. A person takes a look around and says, "Oh God, I hope I never become like that." Well, what do they mean when they say, "Oh God, I hope I never become like that"? What do they mean? They tell the world, the law, "I reject that. I hope I never become like that." And so, they build up a wall, you understand? A wall of what? A wall of rejection. Which is a wall of what else?

Judgments and defense.

Yeah, but what is it tied in—what is—of the three *D*s, what is it connected to? Come on, [Student H], start relating.

Discord. A wall of discord.

[You] build up a wall of discord, don't you?

Yeah.

You reject that. And what is that wall of discord? Would you call it attachment or an adversity?

Adversity.

So, you build your own wall of adversity. And you move along in the stream of consciousness and it becomes your what? *[After a short pause, the teacher continues.]* What does adversity—what does the wall of adversity become?

Your attachment.

Aha. You become attached. You become totally attached to what you rejected and built up a wall of adversity [to]. Because you built the wall and it's yours. Ta-dum!

Is it the continued defense of the rejection that turns it in—the continued defense of the adversity which turns it into the attachment?

Absolutely, because it's the directed energy thereto. And so, we all know coming events forecast their shadows. And there's plenty of shadows from the walls of adversity. So, we clearly see what we are not yet attached to we are guaranteeing to be. Because we're spending so much of our energy directing towards it. Uh-huh.

Discord, disease, and disaster. That's what we have. Reject, resent, and retaliate.

Now the only thing that frees us from all of that, from all those experiences is the Law of Harmony. And what is it that's indispensable to the Law of Harmony? [Student R], what is indispensable to the Law of Harmony?

Acceptance.

Acceptance. What kind of acceptance?

Total acceptance.

Total acceptance. The totality of acceptance is the joy of life because it is the Law of Harmony. That's how it's the joy of life.

Now an indispensable ingredient in the joy of life, which is revealed in the totality of acceptance, is what man calls possibility.

*****

We teach, of course, to God all things are possible. The God inside of you, not some God you're looking outside for. *[After a short pause, the teacher continues.]* OK?

You can shut that off, [Student R], and not waste—

*****

Yes, [Student H].

Yes. Recently I was listening to a tape in which they were saying that one of the things that fear does is that it cons you into believing that you're not afraid of what you're fearing.

Absolutely.

Could you explain that, because I had problems with that.

All right. Now what, what is your question?

Well, my question is, I feel that I am clear in my mind as to the things that I fear. I know what I fear. They may be unfounded, true, but I, I know what I fear.

Oh, do you?

Well, I feel I do. I mean, there may—

Yes.

—be some things that I'm not aware of fearing yet. But I do have a list of things that I—

Well, may I say one thing? Anyone who has the totality of awareness of what they fear is a person who has had the fullness of experiences that life has to offer. Perhaps that will help you with your question. Does it?

Thank you.

Yes. Well, I see the light's still on there. *[The teacher may be referring to the light that indicates that the microcassette tape recorder is recording.]*

There is a time delay. [The recording technician responds.]

Oh, there's a time lapse. OK. Fine. Just let it play then.[5]

*****

Now you see clearly how that works, don't you? I can see how this is not working. *[The teacher may be referring to the recorder.]*

I mean, [Student H], if you knew all things that life has to offer, then you could say, "I know everything I fear."

Uh-huh.

But there's no way possible—

Right.

—that you could say you know everything you fear, because you don't know everything yet.

Right.

And neither does I or anyone else that's on the planet here. Not yet. But life will offer, in keeping with the laws that we establish, the golden opportunity to see "Oh, I feared that and knew it not."

That's why knowledge knows much but wisdom knows better. See, wisdom knows we don't know it all. We don't know that, but wisdom knows that. That's why it knows better.

There is always a better way to do anything and everything. There is always a better way. If there is not a better way for us, then be rest assured we must totally forget possibility. And we must become aware that we are bound to fatalism. When we say something won't work, we establish the Law of Obstruction. And then we feed off the very law we have established. When we have fed our full, it starts to feed off of us. Now that process is known as growing pains. [Any] questions? [Student G]?

Not at this moment. Thank you.

Good, then we can just finish our coffee. Excuse me. *[After a short pause, the teacher continues.]* Yes, [Student H]. [Student H] has a question.

Well, I'd like to know how, how it is that that process then starts to feed off of us.

Well, you have to understand that whatever you feed off of, you become dependent upon for your sustenance. And when you have fed your full, that very sustenance that you are dependent upon, in the process of your dependence, becomes dependent upon you. And as every dog has his day in court and every devil has his dues, so what comes from a thing returns to the thing from whence it came. That is the demonstrable Law of the Divine Circle of Just Return. Does that help with your question?

Yes. Thank you.

Seems fair, doesn't it?

Uh-huh.

Well, that's how it works. Yes, [Student G]. Now you [have a] question? No question?

No. Will we have an opportunity to get some of this . . . [The student may be referring to getting a written transcription of these teachings.]

Well, hopefully someday.

That went a bit fast.

It gets really . . . Yes, that went a little bit fast?

Yes, that last part.

Well, why don't you just do that—⁶

*****

There's a question here.

Well, we were discussing about this statement here, when we cannot do something, we then feed the obstruction. I was playing the piano after [Student Q] left—

Uh-huh.

—the house. And there was a particular passage that I played years ago. And I've always had difficulty with it.

Uh-huh.

And I thought, "My goodness, here's a judgment that was born years ago and it's still with me." And so, I tried to say, well, light of reason, you know, let me cast some light on it. This is this moment. And yet I continued—even I did worse after that.

Uh-huh. Because, you see, all has-beens retaliate. You see, when you cast light—you see, you say, "Keep faith with reason; she will transfigure you." That's the Light. And when you cast light on any obstruction, what you do is shock and blind the has-beens that you serve. When you do that, they retaliate. And as you make the effort, you find yourself doing even worse. Things always get worse before they get better because you must pass through the has-beens. So, you see, that's why we've always taught, just before the victory are the hissing hounds of hell. Well, the hissing hounds of hell are the has-beens that we have been serving. That's all that they are. So, you see, a person must pass through things getting worse in order to enjoy things getting better.

And if they're not willing to demonstrate the Law of Continuity, which guarantees success, for only the Law of Continuity of Effort will bring them through the armies of has-beens.

Nothing else will work. It's that law of the continuity of effort. If it takes ten thousand times, well, it takes ten thousand times. If it takes ten million, it takes ten million. But one can be rest assured the law, the law will not fail. Has-beens will not go easily depending on whether or not we identify with what we call our beliefs. The more we identify with the self of belief, the more difficult is our struggle. Now that's just the way that it is, for all of us.

The person who awakens from their sleep of satisfaction and tells themselves the truth, "What a beautiful world it is. And how fortunate I am," establishes the law for that in their consciousness. Now the has-beens don't like it and they immediately look around and say look at this and look at that. And they show you all the obstructions. But time, through this great illusion, proves, beyond a shadow of any doubt, whoever makes the daily, moment-by-moment effort to demonstrate the divine Law of Gratitude shall move in the flow of the Law of Harmony. Because no one can enter the Law of Harmony without passing through the soul faculty of gratitude. There is no possible way to experience the Law of Harmony without passing through the faculty of gratitude. It's called being grateful for the crumb. For the gratitude of the crumb is the very seed that is necessary to experience the abundant good that the Law of Harmony has to offer.

Does that help with your question, [Student V]?

Very much. Thank you very much.

Yes, [Student S].

Could you please explain this, what you mean by that which has, is and that which is, has?

Yes, in contents [context] of the devil?

Right.

Well, that which we believe we have is that which we are, or is, at that moment. And that which we are, or is, is that which we believe we have. So *has* and *is,* in that sense, is one and the same. For example, a person says, "Well, I feel good. I have goodness in my life." And then you ask the person, "Well, who are you?" "Well, I'm me." "How are you?" "Why, I'm good." Because you believe you have goodness; therefore, you are goodness. You believe you have hell; therefore, you are hell. So *has* and *is,* in that sense, is one and the same thing. Because man still identifies with self, so man still believes: man still has or has not; therefore, man still is or is not. And that's called the duality of creation.

"So, I have this; I'm happy. I have not that; I'm unhappy." So *has* and *is* is one and the same thing for those who believe that they are the limit that they seem, at times, to enjoy. Does that help with your question?

Yes. Thank you.

You're welcome. Has is and is has.

For example, nature shows us that truth. The cloud cries when the sun wants to shine. If you don't understand that, study something about atmospheric conditions. OK? Any more questions? *[After a short pause, the teacher continues.]* No more questions. We got has is all settled? And is has? A very important part of the philosophy: has is and is has. You have to remember, there's no be in has is and is has. But there are has-beens and there are to-bes. Yes, [Student Z].

Richard, would it be possible to hear that part?

Which part would you like?

About the has is?

Oh, yes. Did they get that? OK.[7]

*****

We believe that we are what we have and have not. That is the greatest bondage, called self-deception.

*****

When we are the same person when we have that we are when we have not, then we are free because only then are we true unto our self.

APRIL 10, 1983

Class April 11, 1983

[The following teachings were likely given to a very small group of advanced students.]
Truth is the consciousness of being.

*****

Truth is the consciousness of being. Be, the Light made manifest in the order of Divinity.

*****

No has-beens can conquer me for I just be eternity.

*****

All that has been cannot be.
That's not God and I'm not free
Until I give, then I be
The joy of life that sets me free.

*****

Beyond a shadow of any doubt is the revelation that all doubts are has-beens. And when we go beyond has been, we be!

*****

Bound is he who believes, for be-lieves is leaving the be. And when we leave the be, we have been. Bound is our eternity. Lost is the spirit that is free.

APRIL 11, 1983

Class April 12, 1983

[The following teachings were likely given to the larger group of students who volunteered at the temple Tuesday nights.]

Whoever believes leaves the be of truth for the love of what has been and enjoys the bondage thereof.

*****

To be is to free. To believe is to bind.

*****

So just be.

*****

Beyond a shadow of any doubt is beyond the has-beens of belief.

*****

That, of course, is where truth is.

*****

Faith is beyond all conscience because faith *is* the path of peace, the passivity, the Truth that is. All other things are necessary for form, be they physical, mental, or spiritual.

*****

Be grateful when you lose, for your gain is beyond the forms of bondage.

*****

Forms of bondage known as desire demands.

*****

Beyond satisfaction is the freedom known as the joy of life.

*****

It is not possible to satisfy the senses without the thought of I.

*****

And the thought of I, like a panting dog, is ever thirsty.

*****

There are only two types of thoughts: the ones that bind and the ones that free. They're known as good and not so good.

*****

They make you smile or make you frown. Take your pick.

*****

I give it to you again. When you have given everything, what then is left?

*****

If you want to know where you're going, look at where you have been. Then make an intelligent choice: either the I or something greater; where you've been or a new beginning.

APRIL 12, 1983

Class April 17, 1983

[The following teachings were likely given to the larger group of students who volunteered at the temple Sunday nights.]

When we identify with creation, we divide from that which we are and then strive to become what we are, instead of being what we are.

*****

We are whole, complete, and perfect until we believe.

*****

Man believes and fears. Man fears and knows need.

*****

It is not possible to need until you first believe.

*****

For we must first *leave* the *be* or *be-ing* that we are.

*****

Whenever we leave what we are, we strive to become what we were. Man calls that the good old days.

*****

Known as, "Just one more time."

*****

For the good times.

*****

Whoever tries to be, has been.

*****

It is the darkness that tries to be the Light; it's not the Light that is the Light.

*****

There's no trying in Light. There just is.

*****

Whoever tries to be is the veneer of fear, never knowing when it's going to peel.

*****

—that's right. Man's security is ever dependent on the temperature of his judgments.

*****

As long as he insists on being identified with self.

*****

Remember, veneer is that which covers. And so, self-image is that which covers. It is not that which is. It is that which we hope to be.

*****

Stand on the rock of principle, your right of being, and you'll never again be concerned about what anyone thinks, let alone does.

*****

For being is the Law of Total Consideration, the love of God, the Light made manifest.

*****

We shine the brightest when the veneer is gone.

*****

For what's, for what's underneath is the substance, our foundation.

*****

Whoever works diligently inside is surrounded by beauty, harmony, and goodness outside.

*****

That which is susceptible to control is controlled. That which we desire to control in truth controls us.

*****

It's known as divine justice.

*****

Whoever permits the deception of need is destined to be controlled.

*****

For they deny the be that they are.

*****

The joy of practice is the love of being.

*****

Talent is beyond a shadow of a doubt for talent *is* that which *is*.

*****

Talent is never dependent on what someone else thinks, but it is restricted by what *we* think.

*****

Man lives in love and dies in despair. So, change your thought and breathe fresh air.

*****

All forms color the principle, for they cast their own shadow.

*****

[The following teaching was given to a very small group of advanced students.]

A man who needs to defend is a man who justifies his own devices and deception for the sake of the glory of his ego, to which his love is totally attached.

APRIL 17, 1983

Class April 19, 1983

[The following teachings were given to the larger group of students who volunteered at the temple on Tuesday nights.]

I wouldn't worry about notes because it's—unless you want to take notes.

Now I think everyone, hopefully, most everyone—I guess the ones in the cabinet shop may not have been aware that we have a very serious disease that is permeating the temple and the students in it. A very serious disease. And that disease is called the lack of communication. Now the lack of communication is nothing more and nothing less than presumption, which is the Law of Descent. That's exactly what it is.[8]

Now we presume, and therefore do not communicate with others. The reason that we presume and do not communicate with others is quite simple: we are overcommunicating with our self. We are so filled with self-thought and self-interest we are overcommunicating with our self and presuming that others are facing their responsibility. And through that presumption, we are not facing our own responsibility.

Now tonight's fiasco here in this temple, which sacrificed our harmony—the organ had to be shut down. We had no harmony time here at all because discord, disease was the predominate love in the temple.

Now I want you to bring that—hand that chart there to [Student H]. So he can show everyone. Now many months ago, the Spirit Council, the authority of this church, approved this chart. For years we've been going through this mental crap on this *[Serenity] Sentinel* magazine, the Light to the world—the only purpose that we came here. And each month we've been playing with our self, having one problem after another from the lack of organization. So, this was brought about and brought to the Council for approval by the board of directors. This was approved. What month was that approved, [Student S]?

It was last summer.

Last summer it was approved. When was the last month that it was used by you, who are responsible?

We used it February. [Student H responds.]

[Student H] used it in February. Now you haven't used it since February. Is that correct?

Yes.

Now what happened to you in February that you went against the organization, that you went against the authority of this church? Now tell the students—set it down. Tell the students what happened to you in your consciousness that you went against the authority of this organization.

Well—

Now, please, tell all of us, considering this fiasco that developed out of this. Yes, there they are. There's your co-students. And you're a director.

Well, I was finishing shooting the Sentinel *one night. And I was trying to make my deadline with it. And I finished. I was trying to clean up on time and I didn't do it. And so, I forgot to come back and fill it in.*

That was last February.

That was in February. And the next month, I just broke the habit. And the next month, I just didn't do it.

Do you consider personal responsibility a habit, [Student H]? Is that what you consider personal responsibility to be, a habit?

Well, it's, to the mind, I feel it is because the mind has to have a routine.

Do you come here for the superiority of your mind or do you come here to be freed from that trap?

To be freed from it.

Then that's contradictory. A house divided cannot stand. You come here for one thing and demonstrate the opposite. How can you get what you [have] come for? Did you report to the board of directors that you had neglected and failed to do that?

Did the board of directors come to you and check to see whether or not you had done it?

No.

So, all this money spent—thousands of dollars for music and the Law of Harmony means that much to you. *[The teacher makes a sound suggesting that money and the Law of Harmony have no value.]* Is that what it means? What's the demonstration here? *[After a pause, the teacher continues.]*

That's what your problems are, friends. Face it. That's your problem. Do you see that, [Student Z]? *[After another pause, the teacher continues.]* Is [Student Z] present?

I'm here.

Oh, I thought you [were] over there. You see that, [Student Z]?

Uh-huh.

Self! Overcommunication with self is absolute zero communication with anyone else. And so, the thing that you come here and the responsibilities that you have to get the Light out to the world with a humble little magazine gets that. And then you wonder what I'm doing racing around here straightening things out. I don't see anybody else doing it, do you?

No, I don't.

Well, the new system is the scheduled work will be done regardless of the hour. Now I have a report from the board of directors that the scheduled worked for this night has been done. That is the report you gave me, isn't it?

Do the rest agree? [After a short pause, Student S responds.] *I don't want to speak for them without . . .*

I can attest to the Sentinel. *That's done.* [Student H responds.]

But your responsibility as a director is not limited to the *Sentinel*. My good friends, that's where the problems are. So [Student G] typesets the *Sentinel*. So that's [Student G's] thing. So [Student Q] does the books. So that's [Student Q's] thing. So each one has their thing. So [Student Q] is the choir director.

Supposedly I have no responsibility. I have nothing to say about that, for the angels who founded this organization. That's the problem, child. That is the problem. Everyone's got their own separate, little empire, doing their own separate, little thing. [Student Q] doesn't have an empire with the choir. If the Council decides that song is not going to be sung, it's *not* going to be sung. Do you understand?[9]

Uh-huh.

You have a responsibility as a director. That's not limited to an empire of the [photographic] plates down there. You've done a lousy job with that: since last February, you didn't even follow the chart. You went absolutely against—you transgressed the rights of the temple that you come here, as a director, to support. You blatantly transgressed it!

Now you think you're going to get away with something like that as long as I'm around? Maybe when I'm gone, you'll get away with your transgressions. You may glorify in your transgressions when I'm gone, but not while I'm here you won't. No matter what energy it takes out of me. Now what makes you think that you can go against the authority of this church and just shove that aside? Whatever—what makes your head think like that?

Well, it didn't think. I, I didn't, I didn't do it to go against the authority.

Since last February you've been doing it.

Well, I don't believe it was my motive to go against the authority.

What was the demonstration?

That was the demonstration.

The demonstration is the revelation. Do you deny the very philosophy that you're learning and in hopes to apply? Do you mean to tell me that now, because it doesn't fit your own selfish thought, that the philosophy that is demonstrable truth, that teaches the demonstration is the revelation, is now a falsehood? Is that what you're trying to tell me?

No.

Well, the demonstration *is* the revelation. Now to deny that the demonstration is not the revelation, then forget the Law of Personal Responsibility. Just totally forget the Law of Personal Responsibility. And forget the effect of personal responsibility, known as freedom.

Now, [Student H], something happened to you last February. That's rather obvious. *[After a short pause, the teacher continues.]* How dare you sit there and tell me that the demonstration is not the revelation! That's no philosophy taught in this organization. That's totally contrary to the demonstrable truth.

Do you believe that there are no accidents in the universe?

No, I don't believe that.

You don't believe that there are accidents, do you?

No.

They are effects of laws we are yet—

Right.

—to awaken to.

Right.

Hmm?

I believe that.

Do you believe that we forget what has value in our life?

Uh-huh.

You believe that you forget—that people forget what is valuable to them?

I know I forget what's valuable to me quite often.

No, child, we never forget what's valuable to us. Oh, no. We change from moment to moment, and there are different values in our different levels of consciousness. Good God, man, you've had the philosophy for years. What's happened? *[After a short pause, the teacher continues.]* From the lack of effort, which is the lack of self-control, our values change! And that's the obvious demonstration. Where were you?!

You transgressed the authority of this church! Blatantly! Demonstrably! Since last February. And *you* are a director, responsible to enforce the rights and rules and regulations of this temple, not to transgress them!

Justifications. Defenses. What do you think they are? What do you think a justification is defending, child? Our own devices for the glory of our self! That's what justification defends! That's why truth needs no defense. It's deception that needs defending, devices that need defending, from the laziness and lack of effort.

Your only problem—that *thing* you were serving at that time couldn't see the payments. It wasn't interested in any payments! *[After another short pause, the teacher continues.]* Well, it's your turn to speak.

Well, I see that clearly. What I was serving wasn't interested in any payments.

Then just what were you serving?

Well, I really don't remember that, at that time.

Since last February, you don't remember?

Well, obviously self-interest, but I don't remember specifically what I was serving at that—

You don't remember what part of self you were serving, is that what you're telling me?

Yeah.

That's pretty sad, isn't it?

Yeah.

Don't you think that's pretty sad?

Yeah. Yeah.

We go around the world doing things and we don't even know what we're doing or why we're doing them. We just do them. Well, if you're not in control, who is in control? Someone has to be in control. You can't move a vehicle, a body without some *thing* or someone being in control. And if you're not in control, then something is in control. By God, if it was me, I'd damn soon find out what that thing or someone was or is.[10]

If you don't know what's controlling you, my God! God help you because only God can help you. It's your responsibility to know who's in control of you. That's *your* responsibility, your personal responsibility. *[After a short pause, the teacher continues.]* Does the demonstration reveal that you were in control?

Uh-uh.

Then it does reveal that something was in control.

Right.

Well, don't you think that reason alone reveals that you should make some effort to find out what that thing is that controls you—

Uh-huh.

—that you don't know? I'd damn soon find out what thing was controlling me if I didn't know what it was. Damn soon. I wouldn't even want to take the next breath until I found out.

Well, I'm trying to think back [to] that time.

Just going to have to face the truth: if you're not in control, something else is.

Uh-huh.

Because your mind doesn't move, nor your thoughts, nor your body, or anything else without something being in control. Hopefully, it's your soul. But if it's your soul, it's light and it's reason and it's wisdom and it faces personal responsibility because it knows the effect thereof is freedom. And because it is free, that is its main purpose. Freedom, not bondage. Your soul comes here and is welcome. That's freedom. Not bondage. Now if you're in bondage doing those shenanigans, then it's your responsibility to find out what got ahold of you—what you allowed to get ahold of you. Then you'll know what you're serving. Because you can't do a thing about what you're serving until you find out who you're serving. *[After a long pause, the teacher continues.]*

I would suggest that you start thinking and have something to say about it.

Well, I am thinking.

Considering whatever that thing was, he deprived all the rest of us of our rights of harmony, was an instrument of that deprivation. You don't have so much force that you're capable of depriving all of us. Just one of the instruments. Takes 51 percent for that to happen.

Do you value the Light to the world?

I do.

Do you think the *Sentinel* magazine is a light to the world?

Sure.

Then that thing that got ahold of you, child, doesn't have your values. Therefore, it only proves that it's not you.

Hmm.

That it's something else. You have a responsibility, a personal responsibility to find out what that something else is. Is it a *thing*? Is it a being? What is it? *[After a short pause, the teacher continues.]* You have a personal responsibility.

Well, can I ask the Friends for a clue?

Well, I think you should first make some effort. What were you doing? What were you thinking during those times?

That's what I'm trying to remember.

February's not that far off.

Well, I'm trying to remember that last evening I was shooting those plates and finishing up.

Last February.

Yeah.

[Student H], you can't expect to get freedom from this philosophy, let alone truth, if you don't start applying it.

Uh-huh.

You're wasting your time, your efforts, your energies, your money.

Uh-huh.

You're wasting it: throwing it right down the river. That's like going out for singing lessons and never once practice. Once a week go to the teacher, maybe even twice a week, maybe three times a week. Teacher tells you to go home, "Yes. Here, this is what you practice." You go home and you go do your thing. What kind of singer do you think you're going to be?

Lousy.

Well, do you think this teaching is any different? It's the same law and the same principle. It's called practice. I'm not spending my energies and time for you to write a book. You already got a book.[11] *[After a short pause, the teacher continues.]*

Well, does anybody have anything to say about who's controlling you? Yes, [Student B].

As a proofreader, [Student Z] and I use that chart.

Yes.

And I know that we stopped using it, when the transformation took place from single galleys that are one-page long to the long galleys—

Uh-huh.

—because there were no page markings on those long galleys.

Uh-huh.

And so, we couldn't write down page 2, 3, 4.

Uh-huh.

Because it didn't say it.

Uh-huh. Did you report that?

No, we just stopped.

All right.

And because the person who goes ahead of us didn't enter anything, we didn't enter anything.

I see, and you didn't question it.

And we didn't question it.

Uh-huh.

Because there were no pages and that chart was based on pages—

Uh-huh.

—so we thought we couldn't use it.

Uh-huh. Thank you, [Student B]. And [Student Z], did you question it? Did you report it?

It seems to me I vaguely remember that we did, sort of, talk about it. And then it seems to me that [Student G] did put a little marker down on it. She would divide and mark the pages on it—am I correct? [Student Z addresses Student G.]

Uhm— [Student G begins.]

No? [Student Z questions.]

After we saw it the first time. [Student G remarks.]

After we saw it the first time. [Student Z restates.]

There was not . . . [It is difficult to transcribe Student Z's last few words.]

Now, [Student Z], do you see where the problem is? Everybody's doing their own thing: building their own empire. That's your real problem! That is the problem! That *is* the lack of communication. That *is* presumption, the Law of Descent. That's the empire! That *is* the problem.

Why did not the directors report it? [Student S]? What authority does [Student G] have to delete page numbers?

She doesn't.

What authority does she [have] and who gave her that authority?

She doesn't. But had the directors been checking on the list, we would have picked up it wasn't being used.

Then the directors didn't check.

Right. And we would have questioned why it wasn't being used.

No communication?

Right.

How can there be? Presumption, the Law of Descent, the lack of communication, the building of empires. Yes, [Student G].

I did not presume that pages could not or should not be numbered. There's no way, really, of doing this accurately until the galley has been proofread because sometimes there are whole sentences—

Did you bring that to the authority of the Council?

I didn't. But month after month—

Why didn't you? Why didn't you? Why did you not report that? Why did you presume? Why did you not report a change in the system, that you could not put page numbers on? Why did you not report that in responsibility as a member of this church?

I don't know because—

Well, this is what we're—this is what we're discussing.

Well—

Why is everybody doing these things? Why is this one presuming this and that one presuming that and building their own separate empires? Is that why we came here, to build empires or have truth and freedom? Why are we here?!

When there is a change, you have a responsibility! I have a board of directors to face that responsibility! That is the problem. If there's a change in the choir, [Student Q] has a responsibility to inform me. She's choir director; she's not a separate empire. Is there a change in the financial system? She has a responsibility! She is not the empire of the treasury. You are not the empire of the *Sentinel* typesetting. There's a change; you have a responsibility. Proofreaders have a responsibility. These are not separate empires.

And I want you directors to see that it's corrected.

That's how empires get built! That's how the truth gets torn to smithereens and crushed to earth. That's the Law of Descent!

You want energy so you can have the truth you came for? Stop building separate empires! Because that takes energy to crash back down again their false, ugly heads that rise up from the depth of self-interest.

Anyone else have anything to say about this separate empire building, this lack of communication with others because we're so overcommunicating with our self and our interest with our separate little empires? [Student S], you're a director. [Student H] is unable to speak right now.

Well, I think we're just going to have to take more time. What, what happens every time, like, we go through this—we've gone through this so many times about looking at that chart. And—

Well, it, evidently, has not been looked at since February.

Right. But see, like, when we went through this huge siege before, whenever it came through—last summer I think it was.

It was a year ago.

OK. Everyone vowed that they were definitely going to look at it all the time.

Everyone made the promise.

Right.

It must be all in the bakery. It's all piecrust.

That's right. And, and what happens—then for a time we do, but then we move on. And the emphasis shifts and we don't remember—

What do we—what do you mean, move on? We move on from personal responsibility? How can we move on from personal responsibility?

Right. Well, that's it, though, because as we get our attention placed somewhere else, then we're not remembering all our responsibilities—

My attention is everywhere, child.

I real—

And I am not some separate incarnation! It takes practice and a little bit of self-control! You mean to tell me that you're working ten times harder than I am?

No, I'm not saying that at all. But I'm, I'm saying that as time goes on, then we get sloppy and we do not cover all the bases that we're supposed to be—

Now you see what sloppiness offers?

Uh-huh.

Paper empires! They collapse in the breeze! How long does it take with all the time you're here to walk in and see if a chart has been properly filled or even filled at all? How many seconds does that actually take?

Doesn't take long at all. And it should be—

Now I could have continued to do it.

Uh-huh.

And then you could just continue on with your crutches. That isn't why you came here (to be a cripple), is it? *[After a pause, the teacher continues.]*

Then, what does it reveal? The directors are going to have to have a book, a list of responsibilities to check. And I have mentioned it more than once. Because their memories are not infallible. And the demonstration of that is constantly being revealed. Their memories are not infallible. You will have to accept that sooner or later. You do not have infallible memories as directors. You will have to make a list. You do not have infallible memories.

Where's the list? How many times must I mention that you must make a list of your responsibilities because you are proving repeatedly that your memories are fallible from the lack of self-control. Something else is in control. Yes, [Student S].

Also, we then should ask the Friends their advice on this because it's no long—half of it's no longer applicable under the new system.

That's right.

And that's never been advised.

Are you now asking?

Yeah, I'd like to ask—

Why, certainly.

—their recommendations.

Then you've got to make the necessary changes, yes.

There's only two top lines that are not applicable. If that was just changed to percent, then the whole thing would work. [Student R remarks.]

There you are.

But we have to get permission to do that. [Student S responds.]

You now have permission. When is it going to be done?

The set-proof, if that was changed to percent, then it would work. [Student R remarks.]

And I want page numbers on those things so that these proofreaders can check that. I want that system worked out. Do you have any problems with that? Yes, [Student B].

Is there some reason why it can't be in order 2, 3 ,4, 5, 6, instead of jumping around? It, it's probably—

[Student G] has that problem.

It's, it's very time consuming. [Student B continues.]

Extremely time consuming.

I mean, is there a good reason for that?

Well, we'll let [Student S] speak as a director, and [Student Q] who worked with [Student G] on that. [Student S], you have first turn. [Student B] has asked a question that requires an answer.

I'm not—

An intelligent answer.

Yeah, I'm not sure I can really explain it. [Student S begins.]

Well, then if you can't, [Student Q] should be able to. Because you both spent untold hours with it.

OK, she should do much better with it than I.

[Student S] feels [Student Q] can do much better with answering [Student B's] question.

Well, I think if you look in any magazine, you always start an article on 1 and 2 and continue on 32 and 42, and another article comes. You can't have, at least in most papers, you don't have one article from page 1 to 20 and then another article from 21 to 42, because they jump all the time. You have a few pages and it's continuous. And you have a few more pages and you continue it. I don't think the Sentinel *would look pretty good if you had a lecture of 20 pages following each other and then you have the rest of it.* [Student Q explains.]

I think you best get a *Sentinel* magazine. It's called layout. Get a *Sentinel* magazine, would you, [Student Q]?

Sure.

So that [Student B] can understand, in the typesetting processing, how it has to be fitted in.

I understand that. But I don't understand why the chart has to be based upon that principle. That's my question. [Student B clarifies.]

Because [Student G] turns her plates in that way. She turns in her typesetting that way.

Ah. In other— [Student B continues.]

[Student G] works down at the newspaper.

In other words, it's a convenience for one person out of all the people that are working on that? Is that it?

[Student G], you answer the question.

I don't understand the question.

Well, the chart. I'm just talking about the chart. [Student B clarifies.]

Yes.

I understand the principle of you can't have pages—

Yes.

—but on the chart, it goes 2, 42, 6, 45.

That's how she turns it in.

You know, it jumps around. [Student B continues.]

Oh.

At, at, at the top of the chart.

OK.

And I'm just wondering why. [Student B clarifies.]

It jumps around. [Student G offers.]

For whose benefit is that? For whose— [Student B continues.]

Whose convenience.

What is the reason for it? [Student B asks.]

It is not for my convenience. It is very difficult to find those numbers when you go to—

[Student R] wishes to speak. He's worked on this.

Those numbers are the way the one piece of paper is numbered as it goes through the press. [Student R explains.]

Yeah. Now—

The one piece of paper— [Student R continues.]

Yeah, I understand that. [Student B interjects.]

It has—

It has a back and— [Student B speaks.]

It has a back and a front.

I understand that. Yeah. [Student B acknowledges.]

And a one side and the other side.

Right.

That's, that's the way this was laid out. It was laid out for the press.

Oh, it's for the press.

It was laid out for the press and for the—

No other way.

—for the, the, photo-setting. [Student R clarifies.]

Uh-huh.

That's what it was laid out for, because the typesetting and the press work on that principle, the page numbers—and it's side one and side two because—

Yeah.

—you can't print one side of the page and then flop it over—
Yeah.
—and print the other.
That's not the problem. The problem is the chart. And that's why I wondered— [Student B continues.]
Well, the chart, the chart was made by—
[Both Student R and Student B speak at the same time, which makes transcription difficult.]
. . . the chart set up for. And obviously, for the press. OK. [Student B continues.]
It was made for that.
That's the reason it's set up that way because my students are unwilling to put in more time to get the printing and the plate work and the layout done. And there's no other way we can operate and get the magazine out, [Student B].
Yeah.
But I wanted all the directors to understand, because your question is an intelligent question, and they should have full understanding of why it operates that way. That's why the Council approved the chart that way. Because otherwise, there's no possible way, with the time that is spent on the—
[Side A of the microcassette tape recording this class ends at this point, but the class continues. Several minutes later, the tape is flipped and recording on side B begins.]
[Student A] speaks over an intercom on all these speakers and tells the director of the church to come up here—yes, [Student A]?[12]
I'm very sorry. It's my lack of projection. I'm extremely sorry. I . . . [It is difficult to transcribe several of Student A's words.]
No, you can't take all the credit because he heard you. But he heard you his way.
OK.
He heard you—because you were not that specific.

I know—

You see, had you said what I had said to you, "Tell [Student R] to come up here now, please."

Oh.

Now, [Student R]—that's exactly what I told you.

Uh-huh.

But you heard, you see, you heard according to the thing that was in control of you at the moment.

Uh-huh.

You said to him to come up here. You did not say come up here [to the east wing]. He did not ask where you were. Therefore, it was your responsibility to say, "Come up here to the east wing. Mr. Goodwin wishes to see you now." That's not what you told him.[13]

No.

Because, you see, something else entered into your brain. That something else was you don't want to put up with his forces and his flak. Therefore, you will censor this and you will present that in ways that you judge are acceptable to him. That's how those things work in our brain. They're called has-beens. Because we don't want to put up with the flak.

I don't have no [any] problem putting up with your flak. I'll let you know. I give you the flak right back. Just give me more and you'll get that much more back. Multiplied a thousand times. And if you feel bad about it, all you got to do is stop bringing it to me. Because I'm only returning unto you what you give me. Because I'm not selfish. So, if you give all that to me, I give it all back to you. And I add unto it. *[A few students laugh.]* I've never considered myself selfish that way. So, all that you send me, I shall return. May it—God will multiply it. *[A few more students laugh.]* Bring me the good and the good shall return. Multiplied. For that's the law. I didn't make it. It's the way the law works.

Now you understand, [Student A], if you didn't allow those has-beens to take control, then you would communicate and you wouldn't have this fear: "Oh, I don't want him to get mad at me." See, they don't say it consciously because it's gone way back here in the subconscious. They're way back here, the has-beens.

Uh-huh.

And they react. Instead of act, they react. "Oops!" They go in the depths of the dark, they say, "Oops, the last time I spoke up like that I had to listen to his raving—or her raving." *[A few students laugh.]* "Nope, I'm not going to do that." And so, all this censorship, all this distortion, all this falsehood, all this mist rises up. And so, you speak according to that censorship. Think of that.

And how does that work? It's called fear. And we don't have fear unless we're in the thought of I, for that's where fear reigns supreme. The queen of fear is the thought of I.

You cannot have truth and fear, too. If I had fear, I would not speak the truth to [Student H] and his shenanigans. Oh, no. Oh, hell no. My has-beens would say, "He's very sensitive. He could get sick. Why, he could just ball. He could break down. He could be gone for a week. He just can't make it because he's sick—maybe even a month." And all that has-been crap could all come in, couldn't it?

Uh-huh. [Student H acknowledges.]

Yeah. I notice you drive, don't you?

Yeah.

I remember that day you wouldn't. That should be encouraging.

Yeah, it is.

You didn't get there by me feeding your has-beens. They kept you out.

Yeah.

Fear does it. So, just remember as we conclude, [if] you insist on thinking of yourself, then be the eternal servants of fear, the bondage of life, for fear is bondage. Of course, it is. It has to have a protectorameter; it has to be defended. It has to have a protection. So, keep on fearing. The only way you fear is through your thought of I. The love of self is your fear. [If] you have something to defend, you [have] got to protect it and defend it. Why, of course. Why not? You're a little island unto yourself. You [have] got to protect it from being drowned.

Now that's not what you come here for. And that isn't what I'm about to offer you.

So, you see, [Student A], you served [Student R] very well; your has-beens [served him]. He almost got his way. Almost. [Student R wanted the students to] close up and get out of here. No, no, no. [That's] what you offered him. *[Many students laugh.]*

I see. Where am I? [Student A replies.]

Yeah, where are you? I mean, you're not even married to him. Why did you serve him so well?

That's a good question.

That's a damn good question. Since when are you his downstairs maid or upstairs maid?

Or anything at all?

Well, there you are! There you are. But what's the demonstration? You weren't serving the Light. The Light had revealed to you exactly what to say. You twisted and distorted and turned it all around in keeping with your has-beens of his forces.

I'm sorry.

Oh, don't be sorry. Just wake up.

Excuse me, please.

Yes.

Why do you think . . . again . . . I asked . . . one little thing . . . [Student A speaks softly; so, it is difficult to transcribe several of her words.]

Go ahead, [Student A]. Put your head up and speak up. Because we're closing up.

I made the effort, the conscious effort to listen to the Spirit. [Student A continues.]

[Student A]—

I would like to—

Just a minute. Now you stop and let me speak. Because I know what your has-beens are saying.

OK.

You made the conscious effort and you had some results. You at least told him to come up here. You didn't tell him where you were. So, they didn't have as much control as they used to have. Isn't that right? Now that's encouraging, isn't it?!

It is.

Tell your has-beens to go back to hell. Hallelujah. You hear?

OK.

I know how those bastards work—the pool of pity.

Oh boy, don't they.

Self-pity and rejection, that's how they work! And that's how they keep you bound down to hell. That's their devices. They're not limited to you. That's their devices.

That's right.

So, you start encouraging yourself.

OK.

Truth is encouraging. It's how we interpret the truth that is discouraging.

That's right.

You see? Now you should be very grateful to be aware, [Student A]. Your effort is not in vain. You had partial results. After all, [Student A], you merited being corrected, didn't you?

Yes, I did.

Well, you could have been in the bondage; [the] Friends [could have] just let it go. Everybody closed up hours ago and the job's not done. Then no game tomorrow and we have to come over here to do the work.

Now let's conclude and don't forget the duties you're supposed to do.[14]

APRIL 19, 1983

Class April 22, 1983

[The following teaching was likely given to a very small group of advanced students.]

Unto God, the Goodness, the Light, the Love, the Light, all has wandered. Therefore, all is in the process of return to God, the Light, the Love, the Light. It is the divine circle of return.

Be still, my child, and view and you shall know beyond the shadows of doubt you are returning. Be not weary of the journey. See not the obstruction[s] which are shadows of the past and your path shall be clear, straight, and beautiful. That is the law, the joy of life.

APRIL 22, 1983

Class April 28, 1983

[The following teaching was likely given to a very small group of advanced students.]

The good I know is where I go. And where I go is what I show. Hallelujah, has-beens. I am the goodness that I know for I am the one who makes it so. And when I'm told that I must go, I choose to be because I know that I am the good that makes it so.

APRIL 28, 1983

Class April 29, 1983

[The following teaching was likely given to a very small group of advanced students.]

When you're living day by day and find that things don't go your way, declare the truth and be the good, for then you see a brighter day. When thoughts, they think and don't have their way, you, the be, shall know the way, for you're the good, the joy, the love that makes the way day by day.

APRIL 29, 1983

Class May 15, 1983

[The following teachings were given to the larger group of students that volunteered at the temple Sunday nights.]

—that this group is not something that is advertised with their friends or anyone else because that's just what's kept this group going for many, many years, [Student O]. We all have our different duties here. And you'll learn those as you go along and the directors will all help you there.

And sometimes, some Sunday nights we have class. And some Sunday nights we just have coffee. Some Sunday nights we have harmony time, and some Sunday nights we don't.

Now, does anyone have any questions in reference to all the notes they've already received—because pretty soon we'll just turn the recorder on. Now what we're going to do, rather than keep you up 'til 1:00 o'clock in the morning—and many a time the Sunday night group has had to go to 12:00 or something like that—rather than—is this already on? *[The teacher refers to the microcassette recorder.]*

Yes.

Well, leave it on. Rather than do all of that, you have permission, if you have a volunteer who, on their own time—I cannot let the tape out. It's the only one we have and they're not allowed to be rerecorded—anyone who wants to, on their time, come over—I have a headset—and wishes to take down the dictation and share with the others, that's fine. Rather than take all the time. But you're allowed to take notes during whatever the questions and answers are. All right? But we will not stop and rewind the tapes to play back because we won't get anywheres near as much in and it'll be very, very late for all of us. OK?

So, anyone, after class is completed this evening, who wants to volunteer on their time—can't be in the time they're already giving, because they'll just carve into our workload and won't be able to keep things going—but anyone that wants to put on—put in an extra hour, half hour, whatever it takes to get the transcription done, then they can share that—handwriting—for the rest of them. OK? Good. Any questions about that? *[After a very short pause, the teacher continues.]*

All right. So, if—when you're through, ah—what are you doing?

I'm just making little labels. [Student R responds.]

Labels? Well, when you're through making labels, then we can go—

I'm through.

Are you finished?

Yeah.

Oh, I thought I heard something move in there. OK. Well, now let's see. Whoever has their hand up, that's the ones we'll try to get to. *[After a short pause, the teacher continues.]* No hands up? No go—oops, there goes the hands. OK, well, [Student S's] hand rose up here. What is the question in reference to all these notes you got?

OK. In a class, it was stated whenever we understand need, our need, we enter the divine Law of Just Return and are filled. And I'd like to ask if you could speak a little bit more on understanding our need and how it affects the Law of Just Return. And, also, is this related to the karmic wheel?

Well, in reference, first, to the karmic wheel, the karmic wheel of cause and effect, now, you're asking, Is it related to the karmic wheel? No, it's not in that respect. The karmic wheel is dealing with the mental substance of identification. Now you know you cannot be affected by a mental world until you first identify with a mental world. Now we're speaking on the just law of divine—the divine Law of Just Return. For example, in reference to all your thoughts, acts, activities, in reference to the lessons in evolution that you have passed, the lessons in evolution that you did not pass, those laws fulfill themselves repeatedly until each and every lesson you have to learn, as the necessary steps to your own freedom are repeated, until they are accepted.

Now, for example, you've already received the teaching, the understanding that your adversity becomes your attachment. That's the law that works for all of us. So, whenever we are adverse—we've already given that teaching—that is the direction of energy.

Now energy is absolutely impartial. It has no personality. It has no concern. It has no interest. It is subject only to direction. You are the one who directs the energy. So therefore, if you choose, at any time, to direct that energy to your unwillingness to learn a lesson that is in keeping with your own freedom, that law, on the divine circle of just return, will repeatedly spin in your universe. It'll keep coming back again and again and again and again until the change in consciousness is made.

Now when the change in consciousness is made, what happens, you move to the next step on your evolution in your process of return. See, because the Source, that which we are, [which] we wandered from, we have to return to it to be free. This is why freedom and all the things that you seek do not exist outward. They only exist inward. And therefore, it is the journey inward, the return to the Source, that is the fulfillment on the divine circle of just return.

Now we teach repeatedly inside, inside. It is the most difficult place to go. The reason that it is difficult to go within is because of fear. We fear going within. We fear being alone. We fear the stillness. Therefore, we are constantly making great effort for distraction. Because we fear because we *know* there are lessons, whether we like them or not, that we have got to pass. Does that help with your question?

Yes. Thank you.

You're welcome. Now [Student M] had her hand up next.

Uh-huh.

Yes.

What is the difference between planning and organization and setting yourself up for the to-be cons—

Plant—planting?

Planning and organization rather than the to-bes. You know, you say do not . . . to-bes because— [It is difficult to transcribe a word or two.]

Oh. I see. Oh, I see. Yes, of course. Because to-bes are merely forthcoming has-beens because they can only fit into the parameters that the has-beens will allow. So, what is the difference between that and organization?

Uh-huh.

All right. Well, it's the same thing as the difference between a decision and a judgment. Now a judgment is a rigidity based upon what has been. It has a total consideration of what it dictates. That is a judgment. A decision has a total consideration of the possibility of expansion, change, or growth. Never losing its principle upon which it is based, but it contains within itself the possibility of another way. Now a judgment does not contain the possibility of another way. Therefore, it is restricted and it is limited and it is based upon what has been and guarantees the continuity of the past in a to-be.

But a decision, like organization—whoever organizes is a person who pauses in consciousness, weighs out all possibilities and all variables in order to bring about that which they choose to accomplish. They do not permit the mind to dictate that it shall be—it has to be this way, because there are 20,000 other possibilities in which the principle may be fulfilled. Does that help with your question?

Yes, it does. Thank you.

Fine. Yes, [Student G].

In one of the early classes, it is stated that intelligence is a soul faculty.

Indeed, it is.

And I wonder, if that's the case, how we can expand or unfold our intelligence?

Well, you see, it is the mental intelligence that's asking the question. It's not the intelligence that is the soul faculty. You see, there is a vast difference. The intelligence asking the question is prompted from mental substance, How can it expand it? Well, they have a multitude of schools that build the boxes even bigger, and there we sit. But the intelligence which is a soul faculty is the Infinite Intelligence that flows through the faculty of reason. See, all faculties are triune. And many of those triune faculties you have been given. Well, there is no reason in existence—or possible—without intelligence. But not the intelligence of the limits of the human mind. That is not the intelligence that is the soul faculty. Does that help with your question?

Oh, yes.

You see, when the teaching says keep faith with reason; she will transfigure thee—Now, that that is magnetic attracts, doesn't it?

Uh-huh.

And that that is electric does the opposite, doesn't it?

Yes.

All right. Well, what does it teach you in those simple statement[s]? Keep faith with reason; *she*—not he—*she* will transfigure thee. Because reason is a magnet that attracts. All right? That help with your question?

Yes. Thank you.

You see? It's not something that's sent out. It is something that is attracted. OK? Yes, [Student V] has a question and then [Student H].

In church today, you gave somebody a message or you told, in closing, someone about opening your heart.

Yes?

And we all know that the heart is the soul, which is the—and it is also the universal consciousness. Can you—how do you open your heart, Richard?

Well, the opening of the heart—you see, the heart in its expression, you understand, is subject to what the mind will or will not permit. Now, to open the heart—now, that is a closed heart. Therefore, the heart may express itself only through the avenues through which the mental world has permitted its expression. Now, for example, some people say, "Well, now I love this little, this little rabbit," for example; maybe they have a bunny rabbit or a cat or a dog or a bird. And they love that. And then they look at another little creature, but they don't have the same feeling. Because, you see, the mental substance has only had an avenue open for the heart to flow in that particular channel. All right. Now that is a restricted or closed heart because it is subject to what the mind will permit.

An open heart, you understand, is not subject to this, but this here is stilled by the very power within you. You see, there are times when we can still our mind. There are times when our mind is extremely active and it absolutely refuses to be still, you see. However, when our mind is extremely active and it refuses to be still, there is always something contained within the mind that may distract it long enough for that, the soul, to rise up and still the mind completely. There is—to all of us there is within the mental substance an area through which, wisely used, we can calm our own mind down: to stop its broadcasting, to stop its beating and [it is] within our head, you see.

So, to open the heart, the mind must be absolutely still.

Then, you see, the same feeling that you have, for example, for a dog, you'll have the same feeling for another dog or any dog. Because, you see, the principle of that is equal. It's not limited by what the mind says, "I can love this dog because this is the dog that I feed and I care for," and all these variables that the human mind offers.

Now. Then you can walk down the street—say you love a cat—and you'll have identically the same feeling because without the mental substance activated, the principle of the cat is a cat, you see, whether the cat is gray, black, brown, cream, or white has absolutely nothing to do with the principle of the cat being a cat. You see, it's not the form, but it is what is flowing through the form that you love. Because what is flowing through the form is the same thing that's flowing through your form. It's identically the same.

So, there's a part of us that loves that which is our life. And our life is that pure, intelligent Energy that flows through us. And it is identically the same that's flowing through the cat. The only thing is, that the human mind restricts it, limits it, and will only experience it through the various dictates that it offers by the mind. Does that help with your question?

Very much. Thank you.

But it's still—remember, it is still a vehicle through which our mind has permitted God to express to us. Now [for] someone else, [it] could be a plant. [For] someone else, it's another human being. And then there's all these variables: that's all dependent on what—our own minds—we permit our minds to do, you see. But that does not change that God is working or flowing through man, cats, dogs, insects, and everything else. Because the intelligent Energy that sustains the plant is identically the same as the Energy [or] Intelligence that sustains us. There is no difference, you see.

The difference exists in the human mind or mental world. It exists no place else. Because, you see—and the human mind, the mental world is sustained by this intelligent Energy. And that's the great trap. That *is* the great trap.

The mental world serves a purpose when we awaken that it has been designed so that man may experience God through *all* form. But it, in its own ignorance, has narrowed it down that it has to be this, that, that, that, and that. And that's our great suffering. Yes, [Student V].

So, say, whenever we get into personality and then we, we're blinded by, say, by our active mind—

Well, now let me explain something about personality: personality dictates that God or Goodness is flowing through a form or forms that we, at any given moment, are receptive to. You see, Goodness is not a luxury; it is a necessity because it is God. Now, when we say, well, we have personality, that means that our minds do not permit us to experience Goodness or God flowing through that particular dog, for example, or that particular person at a certain particular moment. The restriction and obstruction is in the mental substance. We can change that; we have that power within us because it is our mind and our world in which we have created these images. Do you understand? You see? It's our mind. We did it.

Now, we didn't consciously, in our awareness, sit down and say, "This person has this image. Therefore, they do such and such and I feel good. Now *that* person I like." But, you see, that's that image there. Time passes and there's another image and another one and another one and another one until there's hundreds of image[s] in the mental substance in which we identify. Now, if a[n] image rises up there that is not like that image, then we say, "That person's changed! That's terrible!" The person has not changed. *We* are now on a different image that has been plucked out of our own computer, so to say. Do you understand that?

Now, in the next instant, something takes place within our consciousness, and we move from this image to that image; the person's the same and we feel better. And we say to our self, "Well, they finally woke up." But that's not what happened at all. *We* moved along the river of consciousness, plucked out a different image on the river, and the person is still the same.

So, the only way that we're ever going to be free and enjoy life and have the goodness of life is to recognize, "Let's see, that's that person. I got 782 images of that so-and-so. Oops, I don't like that image. I go pluck one that says what a nice person they are." But, you see, that image exists within my consciousness and I have the right, the divine right, to pluck which image that I choose—you understand?—at any given moment.

Now, if we are wise, we'll pluck up all of the images, set them in front of us and say, "Oh, yes, that's not the person, but that 782 images in my head that try to tell me that that is the person—because this image doesn't correspond to that image and I can't believe the person could be so diverse. Perhaps they're a split personality." And go through all that foolishness. That's not the person at all, but that is an image in mental substance of the person that we have. That's what it is.

Now we enter that world of images inside of our self the instant that we identify with the self. That's the only way you can enter. There's no other possible way to enter the world of images in our consciousness.

But, you see, a wise person, using reason, says, "All right. I'm going down into this world to enter this realm of images. Let me not forget, God, that it is images. Let me never forget it is not the soul, the be." But one must remember [remind] themselves: "This is not me. It is a thought in this moment and it is a feeling, but it is not me. But it is what I am using." And if you ever remember that, then you'll always be with a person, place, or thing, never a part of a person, place, or thing and will not have all of the suffering and payments that the world of images has to offer to everyone, you see. Because for every beautiful image, there's an ugly one. For every bright image, there is a very dark one. And whether it's an animal, a flower, a plant—it doesn't matter what it is, for that's the world of duality and its law is opposites. That is the world of creation.

That's why we teach separate truth from creation, for without that separation, you can never be free. You cannot permit yourself to believe in images and not have the faith in the truth that you are, which will recognize: "Yes, these are images. Yes, they support my belief. And my belief changes with each image. Let me keep control." You see? Recognize it is belief. It is a mental world. "I have identified with it. But I have consciously choose[n] to identify with it for a purpose. That purpose is to use it like I use an automobile to go where I need to go. I am not deceived by it. Therefore, I'm free from the effects of it within my own consciousness."

That's freedom. That's joy. That's happiness. But one must talk to themselves frequently. Because in a world of creation, you're filled with a multitude of images. And they're constantly changing, etc. Some are strong images, because there's been much repetition, you understand. Some are weaker images. They're all images. They have no substance at all. Does that help with your question, [Student V]?

Oh, wonderful. Thank you.

Yes, [Student Q] has a question. Oh, I'm sorry. [Student Z] was next. I'll come right to you. She had her hand up before. Thank you, [Student Q]. Yes, [Student Z].

You spoke the other night about—that to educate is to cast the light of reason.

That is correct.

My question is, Is there a way we can practice casting the light of reason or is that something that just comes with growth?

No, it isn't something that just comes with growth. Growth—reason, the light of reason, you see, there is a magnetic attraction. Keep faith with reason; she will transfigure: that's the great magnet. Now, it's a practice, like playing a piano—

Uh-huh.

—singing or anything else; it's practice. Each time, whether you're out there in that jungle working or you're here, no matter where you are, the instant something doesn't feel good to you, declare in your mind, "Thank you, God. This is an image. I don't like it. It doesn't feel good. But it is an image. Now in this area," you see, "I have more than one image. Now let me look at all the images that I have in my consciousness. Let me see one governing this same situation that is good. Now if I can't—if I haven't yet created an image there that is good, then let me create it because I have the power within my mind to do so. Because this is how I created all those other images."

Uh-huh.

So, you see, it's a constant process. When someone, for example, is not happy with you, you say hello and they [say], "Ugh!" And you immediately pull an image out of your consciousness—that's where it comes from. You alone pull it up out of your consciousness. It's not a pleasant one, but you have the power to put another image there. And if you are diligent and strong with your right to pluck your own images up, no matter what other images are just popping up by themselves, seemingly—they don't pop up by themselves. They're pulled up, but they're so quick, *[The teacher snaps his fingers.]* you see, from habit. You create one, if you don't have it there, that is a good image in reference to the same situation, and if you're diligent and you are strong—remember the law that like attracts like [and] becomes the Law of Attachment—all things around you will have to respond to your image.

Didn't I speak to you about that, [Student G], in reference to marriage and your home—many years ago?

Yes. [Student G responds.]

You see, because the law reveals herself: what is around you will grow in keeping with your faith in the Light that you are, the true Light, or it will go. It does one of two things. Because there's—you're in a world of creation. In a world of images, it will grow or it will go. But you have to be diligent daily, constantly with what image *you* will permit to control your mind. Because our minds, all our minds, are controlled by images. Thoughts are forms; they are images. We're controlled by thoughts, feelings, attitudes, patterns of mind is what... *[The teacher speaks a few words that are difficult to transcribe.]*

What is a pattern of mind? It's a multitude of images. We have created them from varied thoughts. What are varied thoughts? They are varied images. That's what they are. That's all that they are. They have no substance. They live off of the intelligent energy that we direct to them. You see? And they are not stronger than us. It is not possible. They live off of us. How can they be stronger than us?

See, now if you go to work and someone disturbs you and you've had, say, months or years of that experience, you have to understand that those images within your consciousness are very strong. But they're subject to your will. Don't ever forget they are subject to your will. And you can will any image you choose because the power of the will is the Lord or the law of your universe. So, you are never left hopeless or helpless. You alone can bring that change about. That's your right. That is your absolute right at any moment. Did that help with your question?

Very much. Thank you.

Yes. Now, [Student Q], I think, had a question.

I had one, but I wasn't really thinking of this one here.

Yes!

OK. What do you, then, in a situation, like, when a person is stronger, not mentally, but verbally than you are?

Yes.

When, when they constantly are on top of you and providing you with, in your, with your images, [is] nastiness—

Uh-huh.

Do you swallow it and say—

No.

They, they don't, they don't know better.

No.

Ah, if you speak up now, it's going to cause disharmony. Do you work on you? Or do you wait until a moment later, when you are calm and, speaking up, then you say now this and this bothered me when—do you wait or do you flare up when you are angry? Or do you have to wait?

No. You don't have to do anything. But it depends on many factors. For example, say that you are experiencing that which is registered—because it's all registered within our consciousness—

Right.

—an image that is not pleasant; [it is] discordant and etc. Now, you have in that moment the wisdom of the universe because it's constantly flowing through us, all right? You have the light of reason. It is there. It is available to us in that very instant. You can do one of many things. You can, at that moment, looking at your images that are of this particular person or situation, you can see: "Ah, ha! This image, it's ready to go full swing." And you can take a look and see if that image, within the consciousness, has returned unto you any good. All right. Now, to say, "Oh, image number 27—no, it didn't bring me any good. That image rose up before and I went through hell on that image." You take a look at all these other images and you take a look and you say, "Now this image here was very calm and very peaceful and it was very patient. And when it saw the timing was right, it spoke and said what it had to say. From the experience with this image, I see clearly this was the best image for me to use in this particular situation at this particular time."

So, it is extremely varied. It isn't that a person turns the other cheek or anything like that. You see, it's all taking place within consciousness and you have literally hundreds upon thousands of images in which to use. The wisest thing, of course, to do is to be—pause for an instant that you may view all the images within consciousness that are available to you, be aware of what their return was from past experiences, and use the image that the light of reason within you shows to you returned unto you the goodness, which is the very thing we all seek.

But all those images are constantly available.

So, the situation, of course, is—has many, many variables. And there are many different images that one can use. But one should take that second to pause to see which image they themselves know from their own life will bring them the best good. Because those images do not fail. They go right out and bring back, you see. Because that's, that's the job they have to perform. They are created for that purpose. We alone have created them to serve that purpose.

This is why when [Student G] said to me something about the subconscious—ah, what did you say? "It's where the soul goes?" Good God almighty sakes alive, the subconscious is all these images—that's where all these images are stored. Those are vehicles that we've created to use. Ha! I don't care to have my soul down there playing around all the time.

[Student G says something that is difficult to transcribe.]

And I don't think anyone else would appreciate it. Does that help with your question, [Student Q]?

Yes, yes.

Because there is never an instant [in] which we are denied, by the divine law, the right to stop and look at all the images, because there are thousands that we can choose from any time we want to choose, no matter what the situation is and no matter how disastrous it seems to be.

And now, sometimes—and a person knows from experiences—when they don't use, perhaps, an aggressive image, then they're down there in the depths. Sometimes they take a look at their images and say, "Well, this is going to cost me." And they try to cast the light of reason around it and say, "Yes, well, I'm willing to pay this much because this is what my experience, etc., etc., etc." Reason shines a light on all those images, and then we choose which one we know—because we will know inside—that's the one to use at that moment.

Thank you.

OK? [Any other] questions? *[A glitch in the recording makes a complete transcription difficult.]* [Student H].

Then would I have to, to image or choose an image if I wanted to be courageous in a situation?

Yes. You have, under the category of courage, hundreds of thousands of images. Some very strong and some very weak, but they're still under that category called courage. Now, you see, they're strong and weak according to somebody else's view. But to you that may be—they may be very strong. Someone else looks with their images and says, "That's courage?! Ugh!" Do you understand?

Yes.

But, you see, this is—all these images exist individually in our own evolution.

All right. So, you want to use an image of courage. Do you want an image that shows courage to someone else or an image that's courage to you?

Hmm.

You see, that's the question that you [have] got to ask yourself. Under the category of courage, are you interested strictly in a principle of courage or are you interested in impressing someone else with your courage? You must ask—reason tells you that. It says, "Now let's see, courage? You want to impress this person with your courage? You want to impress yourself with your courage, or do you just want courage?" Because, see, all these images are there. But you must ask them the question. You alone. Only you can do that inside. Does that help with your question?

It does. Thank you.

Of course, sometimes, you know, in a situation a person says, "Well, I've got to be courageous here. I [have] got to be aggressive." Because with many people, courage and aggression are the same. But courage and aggression are not the same. Courage may or may not be aggressive. Ofttimes the greatest courage is passive. Very passive.

It's just like a song. You like all this energy and this fast singing, you know. This vibration is just wonderful. Well, oh, it's much easier to sing that. Ask any singer. Try singing the slow songs—"Silver Threads Among the Gold"—and sing it properly. It's a slow piece. They're much more difficult. Do you know why? It takes more control; it takes more effort to sing a slow song. And the listening ear can hear, "Oops, they're off again." You understand? It takes much more effort. It takes more practice to sing a slow song than a fast song. Does that help with your question?

Yes. Thank you very much.

Yes. Courage just is. And if there's someone you're trying to impress, usually it goes under the guise of aggression. But not always. Not always, of course. It takes great courage to be passive, great courage, true courage. Indeed, it does, for it takes great courage to be patient. It takes phenomenal courage to be patient because it takes courage to control those images that are not impatient [patient] at all. They want what they want and they want it now! And now means "the moment that just passed," of course.

Yes, [Student Q].

I . . . [It is difficult to transcribe a few of her words.]

Certainly.

. . . my first question. If, if you want to give somebody a thought on the other side, like, like his birthday or something like that, should we give them a thought on the birthday that they were born on this planet or the birthday that they passed on?

No, the birth to their new world. That's their birth. Because, by doing that, you see, you put them into the present, into the world in which they truly are. Otherwise, what it does, it rather calls them down here to this world of ours. You see, their birthday, their true birthday is the day that they entered the other world. That's their birthday. That's the world they live in. Yes.

Yes. Thank you.

That is their true birthday. Because, you see, they're no longer here. Now, you see, that would be like us celebrating a birthday before we got here. I mean, in principle it would be the same thing. *[A few students laugh.]* So—but they are happy and [they] rejoice that you are celebrating their birth to that world in which they now live that you are destined to go. Yes.

[Thank you.]

[You're] welcome. Yes, [Student G].

What happens or what takes place in the mind with all these images and what not, when one takes tranquilizers?

Well, do you have... *[Several words are difficult to transcribe.]* All right. Now what does tranquilizers or any of these things actually do? Now, what they actually do—look, they slow down the mental substance. Now, nature does that herself, too, you know. You see, a person can go out to the ocean—I mean, we are limited by how we will slow down these images spinning in our consciousness. Some people can go to the mountains and they feel so relaxed and beautiful and peaceful. Some people can go to the seashore. Some people can do all kinds of different things. They can go to the symphony or they can listen to certain music and there's a calmness that comes over them. They start to feel good. Well, what is actually taking place [is] the spin, which takes place—which is the mental substance activity, it starts slowing down.

Now, as it slows down, you understand, these images, instead of being superimposed all over each other and all jammed up, you see, with activity—multitudes of them—they start to take their little slots, you see, like in a computer. See? And they take their slots, and now there is the harmony or the balance and they're all in their proper slots in which we had created them. Well now, there are times when we, going under different pressures, the images get speeded up, and they stay speeded up because, you see, they don't have within them the intelligence that they're supposed to be in a proper slot. They get pulled out of that slot and they go brrrrrr! *[The teacher makes a sound that is difficult to transcribe, but it suggests a very rapid movement.]*

And so, sometimes we'll take a tranquilizer or something, and it slows down this activity. The images get into their slots. And the light of reason starts to be cast. But then there's always these varying dangers. Tranquilizers serve their purpose as long as we do not permit our self to become dependent upon them. As long as they are wisely used and we understand their purpose, their temporary purpose—very temporary—that when we have made the effort, through our varying channels that are open to us to do this or to do that or etc., etc., etc., which gives this calmness.

Now, for tranquilizers, there's nothing better, you know, than pure celery juice. Fresh celery juice. That's nature's tranquilizer for our food, a drink. Now some people don't like celery, but I can assure you it contains natural chemicals, when it is used, that help to slow down the mental activity, you see. You see, nature and her natural foods do contain all these various things. Now the body reacts more harmoniously to nature's natural chemicals than it does to the synthetic chemicals. Because, you see, the synthetic chemicals—most all of them—contain minerals; they're from the mineral kingdom. They are not composed of the chemicals that are contained in the plant kingdom, you see.

So therefore, it is very beneficial to use the varying calming chemicals that are contained in certain types of, of foods and plants, you see. Now the plants contain such strong chemicals—and they're properly combined—that the strongest tranquilizer that man can create from synthetic substance cannot compare with the effects. But one does not go overboard.

Celery, our good doctor has recommended for years: take a glass of fresh celery juice [and] you go to bed. Because, you see, nature's chemicals, they work slower, but they work more natural and are more effective, you see? You don't get a change that quick, but over a period of time you bring about a balance in that, you see. Does that help with your question?

Yes. Thank you.

Pause it for a minute. Shut it off. I— *[The teacher refers to the microcassette recorder.]*

*****

You have a little more understanding on that.

Now what happens here with the images, you see, for an image in the mental world to be activated, in other words, it's moved out of its particular slot, [that] requires energy for that process to take place. Now this energy flows through the temple, through your, the body, through what you call the nerves or nervous system. They're like wires: all connected. So, an image pops up and it drains, over the nerve, like electrical wires, energy in order for it to be activated. Now if you have these coming up, you see—and there are many of them—then there's a drain of the voltage, through the wires, you understand, for them to be activated.

Now if they get overactivated, then the next thing you know, they're vibrating and they pop right out of their little slots. And you have hundreds, thousands of them in movement. All right? Now, when that happens, this energy, being pulled through the nervous system, through all these wires, it becomes overheated. You understand that? Now when it becomes overheated, just like electrical wire to your light, it starts to burn the insulation that is protecting it. Do you understand that? So everything isn't short-circuited.

Now, in time, it'll burn off all of the insulation. And in the body and in the mind, in the consciousness, you won't feel right; you won't feel good at all. Now, when that happens, you understand, there are many ways, of course, to correct it. You don't say, "Images, stop," and they stop. Because there's this phenomenal flow of energy, electrical power flowing through, activating all of those things, and it doesn't just work by saying stop. There are many ways, when this starts in, to work with. The most important way—and I have given that to you before—is the breath of life.

You see, in the breath of life is the control of the images of the human mind. So, it is the breath of life that the light of reason must be cast upon. For example, a person says, "I'm furious. I'm angry!" All right? Now, if you will have that person start instantly with a very deep breathing, a cleansing breath, and you will keep repeating that and repeating that and repeating that, those particular images, overactivated, will start slowing down, slowing down, and they'll go right back into their slots.

Now, you see, there's pros and cons of using artificial or synthetic ways of doing this. The dangers—and that should only be used very temporarily because [of it] involving many things and using synthetic process or artificial process. What happens is this: there's a slowing process, by slowing down the energy, the vital body, where—from which this energy, this electrical power, is coming to activate the images. So, the very vital body is being slowed down in its motion. Therefore, you see a person starts to slow down with physical movement. You see, "Yes, they're under sedation or they're under tranquilization or etc." And this is a great danger because the person feels good. The reason they feel good is not because of a particular chemical; it's the effect of the chemical: the images have slowed down, gone into the slots, and, once again, God or Goodness is reigning more supreme within the consciousness.

But, you see, there's much better ways of attaining that and having reliability within your own self. Everything necessary is within there, you see. And if it is necessary to slow that down, then there's nature's natural way, such as celery juice. But the breathing is where it is. It's called the cleansing breath, which was given to you long, long ago. The cleansing breath religiously practiced—because, you see, the breath and the thought process are inseparable. Because, you see, the vital body is no longer vital if there's no longer any breath. Do you understand that? And the energy that activates the images comes through the nervous system, through the wires, from the vital body.

Now a person—Are you ready to turn it over? Ah, better turn it— *[The teacher refers to the microcassette tape. The discussion on side A of that tape ends at this point. The discussion on side B follows.]*

*****

Now, where was I? The vital body. Ah—
The purpose.
Yes. Well, you see, the vital body—the purpose—it is the vitality, which is dependent upon the breath of life for its own vitality. So, when you slow down, from control of the breath, the vital body, which is like a dynamo—just brrrrrr!—you see, and all these images are using it all up—you start to gain control and you start to feel good. Because you take a person that has been overactive in mental activity, images, and when they stop, there's this, "Ugh." *[The teacher makes a sound that is difficult to transcribe, but conveys being very tired.]* They're exhausted. Why, of course, because you, once again, become aware of your vital body and it's totally drained, like a prune. Do you understand that?

Because this is where all the—the images are draining all of that vitality from the vital body. The breath of life, that's where it is. Control of the breath of life, see? Something is disturbing to you? It is an image in consciousness. Usually a multitude. Stop. Be perfectly—just stop in that instant. And start your cleansing breath. Keep doing it. Be seated when you do it. Keep your spine upright. Relaxed. And continue on, like I showed you many years ago.

[The teacher demonstrates the cleansing breath, which takes about thirty seconds, during which, there is no conversation. The quality of the audio recording does not allow an estimation of the inhale, holding, or exhale portions of his breath. Please see Volume 14 for additional guidance on the cleansing breath.]

You will feel a strange sensation in your head, because that's the images starting to slow down. That's the sensation.

Now everybody stop for a moment and try that. And when you're taking your cleansing breath, do it slowly, rhythmically. The peace, you see—yes, you may shut it off. *[The teacher instructs the recording technician to pause the recorder.]*

*****

I find the difficulty here is, [for] some of the students, is sufficient oxygen is not being taken in. You see, your chest doesn't hurt. Your chest must hurt from expansion. You must have that feeling in your chest. The oxygen that's taken in, through the cleansing, it must hurt your chest. You must feel it, and even at that moment even take more air in. And it must flow out in the same rhythm in which you took it in, you see. Now—and it is more difficult, I note, in your exhale than your inhale, which reveals the lack of control. Do you understand that? So, you see, the practice of this—can be practiced several times a day and night. Should be seated, when it's done properly, like this, you see. But, you see, your chest is not hurting. Your chest is not going to explode. You must remove all foolishness like that. Your chest will not explode. But you are not taking in sufficient air and it is not being exhaled in the same flow that it is inhaled, which reveals images [are] still active.

You should feel, after taking in all of this air, you should feel a hurt in your chest. You should feel, as you hold it for a few moments, you understand—and the more you do it, you'll be able to hold that air longer, which is the control of your vital body, which is the slowing down of the multitudes of images within the consciousness, put back in their proper slot, you see, waiting for you to pluck them out by the light of reason—and you will feel this strange sensation across, throughout your head. Now that should increase and *that* is what controls the images.

Now that's the best calmness, the best cleansing you'll ever know. And it's in the very air that you breathe. Because they are dependent upon your vital body for their movement. Totally dependent upon it. Yes, [Student G].

How should this be done in terms of a rhythm with the pulse?

Well, you shouldn't move to that yet—and the power breath—until you've got the absolute cleansing [breath] under control so that your vital body, you, once again, have just and rightful control over it, and the images don't just drain it until you're blah! Do you understand?

Uh-huh.

But I would definitely recommend, for anyone, the celery juice, which is a wonderful calming, chemically, for the body and the system, be used in conjunction with the cleansing breath, but never at the sacrifice of the cleansing breath. Absolutely not.

Now I realize celery juice is an effect of freshly—what do you call it?—"osterized" celery and not everyone has one of those things. But it is certainly—now, that's something else. The enzymes, which they are, you know, that are contained within that vegetable, must be done fresh. It should never be refrigerated. In other words, you may refrigerate the celery—hopefully not for a week or two. But the fresh celery, you understand, as fresh as you can get it, placed into one of those machines and then drank at that time, immediately—because the enzymes will only be alive so long, you do understand that, don't you? Those must enter *live* into the system to do their jobs with the chemicals. So, in other words, you don't make it and set it in the refrigerator and drink it two hours later or an hour later. Yes.

For those who do not have an Osterizer, would it be advantageous to just chew it a lot?

Yes, that's true. The only trouble is, it would take a lot of those stalks to benefit from one glass—the standard water glass—of the juice itself. That's the only thing. It'd be more difficult for them to eat—ah, let's see, it'd require one bunch of celery, you see. Almost a bunch. So in that respect, it would take a lot of celery to chew on. *[A few students laugh.]* Now, if you—no, seriously—but if you take a whole day and when you feel a little hungry or something, you chew another stalk of celery, it's a much slower process. It's the live enzymes which do the work on the chemicals in the system and bring about that benefit, is what they are. Yes, [Student V].

How much water should you put in with a stalk of celery?

You don't put any water in at all.

Not at all to mix the—

Oh, no, no, no. You see, in one of those machines, you have nothing but the pure juice of the celery itself. That's where all the enzymes are. Don't add no [any] water or ice or anything like that. Yes.

But we couldn't chop it, when it was just plain celery. And the Friends said to use water for the gravy.

Yes, that was for the gravy. That was not for drinking.

Yeah, well, we tried to chop it and we couldn't chop it.

We don't have an Osterizer.

[A student makes a comment that is difficult to transcribe.]

Yeah, but not a juicer type of thing. If you have one of those regular vegetable type of things that strictly turn vegetables into juice—

Oh, I see.

—you wouldn't use any water at all. It just goes in there and goes phhhsssst! And nothing but water [juice] comes out and the pulp gets thrown away. Because that's what it is: pulp. It has nothing in it, you see?

I see. Thank you.

But, you see, with the proper machine—this is not really—*Osterizer* is not the proper word. That's not the proper machine. There's a special little machine which does nothing but make juice out of vegetables, you see.

OK.

Now, there's certain vegetables you have to be careful of, such as things as carrots—which are, are excellent, of course, and I don't mean just for the eye sight, but they activate the system. You have to know something about chemicals. And not only do they activate the system, they have an effect upon the skin. And if you're not careful, you kind of get kind of a strange looking tan. *[Many students laugh.]* I don't think you'll appreciate it. It's more on the yellowing side. Yes.

What [would] be happening when we be doing the cleansing breath and we be exhaling and you have to swallow?

There's total lack of control. That's an image that's popped in there demanding its energy, and you are gaining control over the very dynamo that feeds its energy. It takes control, control of the breath. Without control of the breath, you can forget about life, for you're only the victim of circumstances, you see? I've taught that for many, many years. It is the breath of life. But you must understand, surely, that is not God's fault, for it is revealed to all beings, even animals: control the breath, you see? Because that's life. That makes you captain of your ship.

But if you don't control your breath, then you cannot be captain of your ship.

[When] you awaken in the morning, you cleanse your little ship. Clean it all up. Put your house in order before confusion sets in. The breath of life—the most precious thing that you have, hmm? Otherwise, you're going to burn out all those wires and you're not going to be too happy.

Yes, do you have a question, [Student H]?

No, I . . .

Yes. But, you see, you don't need the juice unless it's an emergency situation and you need the chemical as quickly as possible combined with your effort—you see, you do your cleansing breath all day. Especially do your cleansing breath—you see, from experience you say, "Oops, now let's see, I'm going to meet that son of a gun. Oh, I better be prepared." Well, you prepare yourself. And even if you're in front of them, you can delicately do your cleansing breath without them particularly noticing it, you understand. You see? Right in the midst of a conversation, you can do your cleansing breath. No matter where you are or where you go, the air, there's no charge for it. There's no one [who] can keep it from you, you understand? And so, you do your cleansing breath anywhere and everywhere. Because without control of the breath, which is your life, you are the victim of creation. And that's not what you come to Earth for. Yes.

What is hyperventilation?

Oh, hyperventilation—take a look at these things they call joggers. *[The teacher demonstrates panting, as though he were running.]* And then they get a high. They call that, I think, in your world a jogger high. Well, I can assure you the doctor certainly doesn't recommend that foolishness. They get a strange sensation. They might as well go take some shots someplace. That's what that does. Yes, that is not what we're talking about. Absolutely not.

We're not talking about—you know, you can sit here and you go *[The teacher again demonstrates panting.]* and hyperventilate until the point you get all these strange feelings and sensations. The next thing you know—blah! *[The teacher makes a sound that suggests complete exhaustion.]* Oh, yes. My God, don't try that. That's real bad on the heart. And that's not the only thing it's bad on. Because it calls up images, you see, that are pulling that and pulling it and pulling it and pulling it right out of your vital body. No, that's not the way. I think you call it jogger highs. Yes.

But when the, when the people in the choir started doing the cleansing breath, some of them got very woozy.

Yes, because there's [they're] not doing [it] properly. That is true. That is true. They're not doing it properly.

And, you see, another thing you must remember: you know there's such a thing as what you call—there's other factors involved, too. There's what you call the *r* and *r*: reject-retaliate. Images in control at the moment were being rejected and they retaliated against the system. And because they are draining through the nervous system, through the wires, they put an extra *[The teacher makes the sound of slurping.]* charge, you understand, an extra draw upon the dynamo, which is the vital body. Now, when they put that *[The teacher again makes the sound of slurping.]* like that, real quick like, you [feel] blah! And you get what you—you have an experience, a sensation: dizzy. So those are other factors that are involved.

Now, some people [say], "Oh, I can't do that because I get real dizzy and I think I'm going to faint." But they [have] got to work on two factors: improperly doing the cleansing breath, but especially the image at the moment in control. Now some people, at sometimes, they do it and there's no problem. And at other times all of a sudden, they get dizzy. What is happening? They're doing it properly. The image in control at the moment is giving them what you call the shaft. It's rejected. It is in the process of draining the energies from the vital body. You're interfering because you are now slowing down the dynamo. You slow down the dynamo, and all of a sudden, they feel this, this lowering of the voltage. And they immediately pull it over your nervous system. Instantly. Because, you see, they are created from mental substance and they fear. The slightest change registers fear. And so, they control your body.

So, those in the choir that are not here and not a part of this, well, you just let them be. They don't have to do it if it makes them dizzy, etc. Because they haven't yet earned what's really going on. They've earned much. That's fine. Leave those images in control if that's what they need. But you will notice that with different people at different times—you notice that, [Student G]? Sometimes you feel a little woozy. Sometimes you just feel great. But that depends on the images in control at that moment that you're—this is why it's so advisable to do your cleansing breath many times a day. And sometimes you're, "Oh my God, look!" You see? That's why I recommend you sit down. But that'll tell you what images are in control. And that's it!

And you will learn very soon—because you do have your own awareness: "Uh-oh, this is what I was feeling and thinking about." And that image is determined. "I do my cleansing breath again. I consciously call this image up," through your thought process, "to face that I'm gaining control of my own vital body." And slowly but surely, what happens, you become the captain of your ship and the master of your destiny. It doesn't happen overnight, but it certainly does happen. Yes. Any other questions? Yes.

Yes. When they have surgery and they cut all the nerve endings and what not—

Yes.

—how long does that take before that all heals up? Or do they heal up? Or—

They will heal. They'll heal much quicker with a cleansing breath. The nerves have been cut. They'll heal much, much faster with the cleansing breath. But you have to understand that when nerves are cut like that, they take a minimum, in your world, of at least one year. A minimum. Now that's a minimum. Now with daily usage of a cleansing breath, which is really controlling the vital body and the energy flowing through the nerves, giving, once again, conscious control to an individual, then, you see, instead of all of this energy being pulled through—and those nerve endings are cut, you understand and they're just wearing [down] the insulations until there's no insulation left, because there's been an interference, you understand—with the daily cleansing breath, the time could be shortened anywheres from 50 to 75 percent. But normally, what you would call normally, it takes a minimum, a minimum of one year. Minimum. Yes.

Thank you.

You're welcome. Yes.

What is the insulation and how long does it take to regenerate it if we burn it off?

Well, you see, for example, now what it is—electricity, you have it in what you call an insulation. Now what is the purpose of insulating that? So, it doesn't burn down the house, right? So, the purpose of nature—she has her tissues and things that cover these nerves, you understand?

Uh-huh.

And they're all protected, like a wire. Now, you see, the purpose of that is so those nerves, the energy flowing through those, don't burn down all the tissues—

Uh-huh.

—in your house, the house of God, you see. Now, an overcharge of energy or electricity going through those nerves burns off its coating. Do you understand that?

Uh-huh.

But Nature, when this, this pull of energy through those nerves, Nature herself will start to rebuild her insulation, for it is the design of nature to keep it coated, these nerves, these wires, you see, just like with a house. And so, this is what you have to do. Does this help with your question?

I—

You see, when you're calm and when you're peaceful, then these tissues gradually, slowly but surely, they start to recoat the nerves, the wires that go through your house. Yes.

Well, like, can this be, like, a momentary thing, like when we feel upset and all our wires feel exposed and then we get calm in a matter of, say, minutes—

Yes, but you have, what you have is a band-aid treatment.

I see.

Why, sure, I mean, it gets coated, but, you see, it's not—it doesn't have endurance. It doesn't have the, the *real* insulation—

Uh-huh.

—that it originally had. That takes time and that takes practice. That's what is required. Oh, certainly. You can give—now, for example, you get a band-aid coating, what—in the sense—what happens is, you see, your vital body starts slowing down. And it slows and it slows down and slows down. And then there isn't as much as [of] this electricity going through those wires. And not being as much, it doesn't burn through what little coating is left, you see? So in that respect, you gave it a band-aid coating. But God help you when other images start popping up in your head, and they require energy to be activated and stay activated, then they pull more current through. And as they pull more current through, you're well aware of it. *[A few students laugh.]* Does that help with your question?

Yes. Thank you.

Now that's the band-aid treatment. Yes.

What is the spiritual counterpart of the nervous system?

Well, now, you have been given that in about forty different ways. Now, perhaps someone around here, after all these years, can tell me what the spiritual counterpart—because I've already given it to you in many ways—of the nervous system is.

Could I venture a, a guess?

Yes, I want everyone to *venture* their understanding—not adventure. Don't add to it. *[Some students laugh.]* Just venture their understanding. All right?

I would say it's a communication.

That the nerve system is a communication. All right. Now, anyone else—because I'm going to ask all of you. What is the spiritual counterpart of nerves? *[After a short pause, the teacher continues.]* Well, what does the nervous system serve? I mean, that's the question to ask yourself. I mean, I just got through trying to explain it: how it's connected to the vital body, where the dynamo is, which is totally dependent and controlled by your breath. By your breath. See, your breath controls your thought. You have that choice because your thought is dependent upon your vital body. It requires energy to be activated. Yes, [Student S].

Well, we understand that reason is the air. So, would it be related to reason?

Well, now that's a good thing to consider. Yes. Reason is a breeze of fresh air. It certainly is. It is the element air. Reason is the element air. Now stop and think. You've been given these things. And air, control, your vital body. And your vital body is in charge, depending upon how much it's going to release or not release at the demands of these images. Stop and think of the connections. Yes, [Student O] has—what is your understanding of that. What is the spiritual counterpart of the nervous system?

Of the nervous system? I'd say understanding.

[Student O] says understanding. Anyone else? Yes, [Student V].

Well, we also have that water stan—water center.

Yes, we know what controls the water center.

Well, that's also part of the nervous system, which are emotions.

Oh, yes. And what our emotions are, are what our images our doing. See, because e-motion is moving the *e*. You see? Why, sure. But how does it move? It's totally dependent upon what the images are doing: which ones have popped out of their slots. It's totally dependent upon that. *[After a short pause, the teacher continues.]*

Now, you had all of this wonderful philosophy on has-beens. Now, we're moving to see what the has-beens really are: they're the images in these slots and their parameters. *[The teacher laughs.]* La de di, de di. You understand?

All right. Now let's get to this nervous system, the spiritual counterpart. Anyone else? [Student R], you've been around a long time. What do you have in mind? [Student S] has given her explanation—[Student O] and [Student G]. And we have several [others] to go through. What is the spiritual counterpart or, let's put it more, perhaps, in shorter words: What is the balance of the nervous system? Because that which is a faculty balances out [that] which is a function. They're both necessary in a world of creation. It's a matter of balance. What is balance?

Harmony.

But isn't that neutrality?

Neutrality?

Not dependent upon images. See, God is not dependent on images. Your goodness isn't dependent on images. Your goodness is dependent upon the control of images, not *on* images. Your discord is dependent on images. Your harmony's not dependent on images. Only discord, disaster, despair, despondency; those are dependent on images, for those are contrary to the Law of Life. Those are illusion, delusion, and deception.

We all know we're not the image. So why work so hard to present one? *[The teacher laughs.]* When we know we're not them at all. Isn't that true, [Student G]? Why work so hard? Why waste that vital body, that vital energy, which is in truth our most precious commodity?

Yes. What balances the nervous system? What lets God in, [Student R]? What lets goodness in? Yes, [Student V] has an answer here.

The heart.

[Student V] says the heart. Yes, [Student G].

Acceptance.

[Student G] says acceptance. Yes.

I was going to say the same thing: acceptance.

Well, tell me something: Is the will of God good? Well, we have to ask the question, is God good?

Yes.

Could it—could God's will be anything but good? It would have to be true to itself, wouldn't it? Well, there you are. The divine will of God, which is, we understand is total acceptance—think of that—is the balance to the nervous system [and] restores harmony, health, wealth, and happiness to all beings.

Now remember this: that which we deny we destine. So, if we deny the truth that we are good, that that is our true being, then we are destined for the images that are the contrary to truth. And we are destined to be their victim, and we are destined to the inability to do anything about them. And ask yourself the question if that's what you want in life.

Now I have taught repeatedly that the spoken word is life-giving energy. Can you speak a word without the breath of life? My goodness, when will you do your cleansing breath religiously and be that which you truly are? And not the images that you insist—that tell you, you are them, for they change all the time. Hmm?

On that, I'll have a cup of coffee, please. Here.

Shall I stop it? [Student R asks about stopping the recorder.]

Oh, might as well.

*****

Put it on there. *[The teacher may be referring to the microcassette recorder.]*

How can you speak your word forth into the universe knowing that it shall not return unto you void but accomplish that which you send it to do if you have no control over life? Because you refuse to control the breath of life. It's not possible. You have to be on the other side [that is, have control of your breath or you are] the victim of it by denying your divinity. Whoever denies their divinity must pay the price of its opposite. And we all know what the opposite of divinity is, of course.

Desire is the expression of the Divinity. Man's dictate of desire is known as the demons of desire. And so, it's the demons that we work diligently to drive out, because that's not good; that's not God. It is, however, that which is supported by God, for God sustains all things. So, man, moment by moment, has the choice: serve the images by the lack of controlling the breath, which controls the dynamo, which controls the energy, which flows through the wires, the nervous system, and pops them up into the consciousness.

And one moment you think you're that image only in the next moment to think you're *that* image and act accordingly. You see, that's not acting. That is reacting. So life is a stage on which many actors and actresses are placed. Not reactors and reactresses. No. Actors and actresses. Then life is beautiful. Because that's the way life *really* is. Life is not the image that pops up into the consciousness. That is not life. Life is the breath.

Why, the Bible teaches you clearly: into the nostrils God breathed the breath of life—you see?—and the great dynamo, the vital body, moved and you be. From that moment on, what you do with that is up to you. But it is moment by moment, and you're never left without the moment of your own choice. I am simply revealing to you a way so that your choice can be fully expressed within your own consciousness. What great effort is it to breathe properly and to control the breath? What effort of practice is it every day?

And moment by moment you have this golden opportunity: there's always some image popped up that is not a good feeling. You have in that instant that wonderful opportunity in knowing the way—that's it! *[The teacher snaps his fingers.]* And go right into the control of your breath, which, of course, takes care of the dynamo which serves the image, you see.

Of course, there are times the old image will be so strong it'll retaliate on you. Then another image will rise. You'll either get disgusted, discouraged, angry—hopefully you'll get angry, because that's a good image that you can use wisely inside yourself. "That's it! That thing thinks it's going to control me?! No!" Inside of you!

So, you see, you have all these images. You can use this image to straighten out that image, and that image to straighten out *that* image. *[Many students laugh.]* You're not short [of images]. I haven't met any student, yet, of mine that's short.

Yes. You want to—anyone who wants a coffee break can have a coffee break. Then we'll have a coffee break. If there's any other questions, you go ahead.

No, I just wanted to be excused to go to the bathroom.

Certainly. You go right ahead. Absolutely.

*****

All things are controlled by the breath of life. No matter what your need, [what] you think it may be, the breath of life controls it. It is the breath of life that brings it to you. It is the breath of life that sends it from you. And when you gain control, through the proper cleansing breath, you too will know how that works because for you it works like it works for all of us. It's the breath of life.

All great philosophies have taught you that in their own way. In the final analysis in the bottom line, it's the breath of life. The thing we give such little consideration to. Unfortunately.

*****

—of an image that you don't like. Well, do your cleansing breath and gain control. You got other images; knock that one out. But, you see, you first slow down the dynamo. Otherwise, you're going to be very exhausted when those images get through with you.

*****

—teachings, a teaching of positive thinking and etc. But what good does that do if it does not reveal a way to control that so there can be those images, you see? You see, for every time you want to be—you want to encourage yourself; you got other images that rise up immediately. And they go pop, pop, pop! *[The teacher makes a sound that is difficult to transcribe, but is poorly transcribed as "pop."]* They shoot them down.

But it doesn't have to be that way. It's your breath. It's your life. It's up to you if you want to have more goodness in it because it's ever available to you. You must remember, it's not dependent on anyone out there, but it is totally dependent on what you're doing about your own images. But, you see, you have the breath of life and you can control that because that is the div—the design; that's the true design. You alone have that control.

Well, look, in your world and in the Far East, they still have people who can do many things. How do they do that? They do it by the control of their breath. They walk upon fire by the control of their breath. They control the images. That's how they do all those seemingly miraculous things. They do it by their practice of the control of their breath. Certainly. Because they control the images of the consciousness, the stream of consciousness. Yes.

It seems that when we're enthused that we have more energy. Is this true and why?

Well, it's quite simple. You see, when you're enthused—did you ever know a person [who was] enthused that didn't feel good?

No, you have to.

Yes. You're enthused when you feel good, right? You're enthused about this and you feel good about that. Well, what is that revealing to you? There are not contrary images fighting for energy, pulling it out of your vital body. There are images there, of course. And you feel good about that because those images are right up front and they're in control, you understand? And they're very happy, those images, because they're getting a nice—full energies from your vital body. And it's amazing how much you can do in those moments that you're enthused because you feel good. Because, you see, this is nice and clear, and it has certain images right there. And that's the only ones there. Do you understand that?

Uh-huh.

And you're enthused. And God is there. And you feel good.

Thank you.

And we can be enthused *[The teacher snaps his fingers.]* any moment of our choice. I choose to be enthused. I got a cup of coffee and I'm more enthused now. I'll have a little drink right now. *[The teacher takes a sip of coffee and a few students laugh.]* And I feel good. But that's dependent on the daily practice— whether it's a hundred times a day or a thousand, it doesn't matter—of your own breath. Not someone else's breath. Your breath. Because their breath does not matter. Unless you're too close, then sometimes it matters. *[Many students laugh.]* Yes, [Student M].

Is that why—and they have come to—it's probably not very new—but in natural child birth, they've been giving all these breathing exercises for, like, to go easier, it's the same—

Well, it's to control the images.

Uh-huh.

It's the images that cause the struggle.

Uh-huh.

Your muscles tighten according to images.

Uh-huh.

Because, you see, your muscles are controlled by your nerves. You do know that, don't you?

Right.

Hmm?

Uh-huh.

See, it's all controlled by your, by your nerves.

Uh-huh.

Because that's how they—all this takes place and gets the energy from your vital body. Remember, it's a *vital* body. Without it, you don't exist in this realm.

Uh-huh.

That's why it's called vital.

Uh-huh.

That that is vital is indispensable, would you not agree? Well, let your vital body go and you'll see. You'll be gone with it.

You see, all stimulation of mental substance means a mass of contradictory images. It's very detrimental. It's extremely detrimental. And I am sure we'll all agree. You like going to the seashore? Go to the seashore. You have a few images. You feel great. If there are two kids there throwing a ball and one hits you in the back of your head, then you don't feel so great. Because another image just popped up. You understand? Probably a hundred of them. And then you say to yourself in your mind, "Why do the kids have to be here?!" But it's not a private beach, you see. But then, another image comes up and [it says] they've never been here before at this time on this day. You see how that works? Those are all images. Yes, [Student G].

So, when a person is frustrated, they can't decide which image they want to . . .

There's no control of the images. There's no control. There's thousands of them and they're battling, you see. And they're draining all of the energy through the nervous system. They're overloading the wires. The insulation's burning off. That's what's happening. And then you know what happens then, when the insulation gets burns [burned] off? There's no sensibility with our sensitivity, for there's no insulation. Don't you understand that? So, you see, you drop a pin and phsst! *[The teacher again makes a sound that is difficult to transcribe.]* It registers immediately. An image—many images pop up into the consciousness. Because there's no insulation. Now in your world you call that thin-skinned, don't you? Well, sometimes we're thick-skinned and sometimes we're thin-skinned. Well, that depends on if there's any insulation there, you see? That's how we burn out. We burn out.

But it's wonderful. It's like *a, b, c*, one, two, three. We know what to do. Now, it's just a matter of breathing. And using it when you need it the most. But you've got to have the practice. You can't just sit down and play like Paderewski on the piano, when you haven't gone through year after year of practice, practice, practice seven days a week. But, you see, the world offers you [a] wonderful opportunity for practice: something always make[s] you mad. *[Many students laugh.]* If not, the weather will do it for you. *[Again, students laugh.]* Isn't that true?

So, I choose to feel enthused. So those are the images that I allow. If something else pops up, I do my cleansing breath again. But, you see, you don't know when I do my cleansing breath. When you practice, then a person doesn't know, do they? Because it doesn't show. But that takes daily practice. Then—what I've said to you—you can go down there, use those realms. Get a rapport and communicate. And come back up again. Because you pull those images out of their slots. Use them, you see, for the purpose to be served. Put them back into their slots and get your other images up.

Now, you have to admit that when you come to that point, that's control, isn't it? That's when you're captain of your ship. That's when you're master of your destiny. Until that time, you'll always be victim of what you call circumstances. That is not the design of life at all. Never was the design of life. Yes, [Student G].

So, if you really do this, then the atlas vertebrate would stay perfectly in alignment.

Ah, you wouldn't have any problem, because that's controlled by the nervous system.

Uh-huh.

That's true.

Well, why—this is why it's so important to balance credulity with suspicion.

You've already had that wonderful teaching. Because those are all images. For every yes, there's a no. You want neutrality. And that's how you gain it: control the breath; bring it into balance.

When you see the good in all things—don't you see? So, we have so many images of *everything*. They're beyond limit. The mind is constantly active. Images constantly popping, jumping all over the place, like a jitterbug in the, on the stream of the consciousness, you know. Some do a waltz. Some do a jitterbug. Some do a square dance. Go on down the list of how they act.

Well, you want to call up those—you see?—through your will, which is the lord and the law of your own universe—you cannot exercise the lord of your universe until you gain control of the breath of life. It's impossible. It's contrary to natural, demonstrable law.

[After a short pause, the teacher continues.]

Well, [does] that take care of *all* of our questions for tonight's class? I think so. We can finish our coffee. If there's any [that] come up during coffee time, just speak them up.

*****

All right.
So that, ah . . .
Are you afraid of that?
Ah . . .
For your notes? You don't even know what the answer might be.
Oh, I just wanted to say I think this is the most important class that we've had. And I would like to volunteer to transcribe it. And—
Very well. Then we'll make arrangements so that you can come, because that's the only little tape we have, and share it with the others, who will hand write it, of course, you know. Because, you can't be typing it up and passing it out, you know. That, that eliminates the Law of Effort and value for what is, you see.
Uh-huh.
See? So, it's most certainly accepted. Then you will have all of the notes and then those who want any can make arrangements on their time and yours to get those notes from you.
Uh-huh.
Certainly. Or if anyone else wants to make arrangements on their time, they, too, can listen to it and get their own notes. But whoever has the notes will share it only with the group and the people who ask, you see. All right?
Now you can shut it off. Are there any other quest—

*****

—what—you give what you have to give; you care less what they do with it. Because if you care what they do with what you have given, that shows you very clearly that images that you have not chosen are popping up taking control within *you*! For they are the reactors and you've lost the act, you see. You are a rising star that has fallen. Do you understand? Don't be a falling star. Yes, [Student G].

So, when you're attached to something, these are simply the images that pop up with the greatest frequency.

Why, of course! Absolutely. You are therefore the total victim. You've lost control of your own ship. What is the attachment? The attachment is a dependence upon another person's images. That's the attachment. That's the bondage. You sold your soul. La di. For your image is dependent for its very survival on another person's head and *their* image. And you are the helpless victim. Is that what life is designed to be?

That's not what I choose it to be for me. Not when there's a better way: just by controlling my breath.

Well, look at attachment. Say you're attached to this person. When this person does certain things, you are very happy. When this person does other things, you are very unhappy. Now what does that tell you? That tells you that your images are dependent upon their images. That's the bridge. That's the chain of bondage that you have stepped into. And that is your right, but whatever is attached, by the divine Law of Freedom, shall be detached.

Now that doesn't mean that two people are going to separate physically, but it does mean all people awaken. Where there is a thickening, there is destined a thinning, for that, too, is the law.

So, be not attached and be not bound. Be with a person, place, or thing; be not bound by them. That depends on your willingness and your effort to gain control over the breath of life. Without it, there is no life. There's survival, but not life. There is a difference. A vast difference.

*****

Accept from God; you'll never have to pay man. Because, you see, that has to deal with the images in your consciousness.

You go to the Source; it is within you. And then you won't have to pay the price of what someone else's images do or don't do, for their images are very fickle for they're not making the effort to gain control over their own life. Now that's what's to be considered.

God flows through man, not to man. Therefore, a fool permits themself the delusion that their goodness is dependent upon another person's images.

*****

When we awaken that our goodness is dependent upon *our* control of our own images and we choose not to have our images dependent upon someone else's images, then we have joy of life, the true joy of life, the true being, the true freedom, the abundant good that is the design of God or Goodness.

*****

—and what are you giving? You're simply giving those images that are the obstructions to the goodness and the joy that is the design of the Divine. What are you giving him—giving them? You're giving them back to the slots where you want them to be. That's what you're doing. Yes. The joy of life is the art of giving.

And that takes a giving, believe me, when they rise up and *demand* what they have now considered their right to their expression. But the light of reason cast upon them, says, "Just a minute. You, this image here, served me at a certain time in a certain circumstance and condition. Now, under the light of reason, [that light] shows me that you, *you*, image, you will not serve me well. You have proven to me, in these circumstances, you don't serve me well. I have other images over here, rather new ones, that serve me very well. You go back into the slot." You understand that? You give that image back to the slot here that you have in the computer in your, of your mind. That's the art of giving. Then, you're an open or what you call a free channel, you see? And that's your joy. It's all inside of you. That's called the totality of acceptance, the will of God.

God is good and we have the right to be receptive—

[Side B of the microcassette runs out of tape at this moment. At some point later in the discussion, a new tape is placed in the recorder and the recording of the class continues.]

*****

—because that's just the way it is. You don't have that much time left. Well, it's your nerves. It's your life. If it's something you want to do, well, you do it. It's within your universe to do any moment you choose. But remember, if it's dependent upon another, then your image that you're serving—oh, the poor thing, God help it; you don't know how fickle somebody else's images can be. Well, maybe you already know. *[The teacher laughs joyfully.]* I don't know; maybe you know. I'm sure some of us know, from time to time. The problem is, the images rise up and we forget. Yes.

But we should be of good cheer: at least we know the way. We really know the way.

Did you ever know of an image that could move by itself, of its own volition? An image? No, it's totally dependent upon a source of energy. You're that source of energy. And you have the right to turn down the voltage or turn it up. That's the power that you have. And that little knob, there, inside of you, that's called the knob of choice. You turn it this way (down) because there's too many of them and they're not bringing any happiness. Or you turn it up a little bit. And you do that any moment of your choice, because that's your choice knob.

And if it doesn't feel good, then it can't be God. Sometimes a person will have an image: they're out in the garden and they see a flower. They just feel wonderful! Just one little flower—for a moment, they take a look and say, "My God, it's beautiful." That image in their consciousness, you see, brings them goodness: they become receptive to God in that instant.

Now, our work is to be receptive to God in *all* instants.

So, if you're wise—and wise I know you are—you will practice your breath of life and you will gain control over your vital body, upon which all images are dependent. All of them. Good ones, bad ones, all kinds of them.

When you feel good whether a person does or does not do, whether a person says or does not say, when you still feel good, you know then, in those moments, that you, once again, have returned home to God and goodness. You are no longer dependent. That's a wonderful feeling: not to be dependent. And that's what controlled breathing, the breath of life, has to offer you.

Freedom is something that is moment by moment because, you see, it's a long path to gain that much control over the breath. But even moments, when they are needed, are the most precious thing we could possibly ask for.

Some of you admire the yogas [yogis], what they're able to do. They do that from proper breathing. Controlled breathing is proper breathing. Don't you know that your images, whatever they are in consciousness at any moment, are controlling your breath of life? They cause you to breathe slow, to breathe fast, to breathe discordant, and your body reacts. Because, don't you understand, you see, your images are draining the voltage from your vital body. And your vital body is sustained and supported by the air, your breath of life. So, if there are images up there demanding more energy, then your dynamo moves faster and you breathe more [and] faster. And ofttimes you're not even aware of the change in your breath.

Take a person that starts singing. They want to sing and they get real nervous. You see, they get real nervous—and a little bit of fear. And all these images rise up. Their breath changes, you understand? *[The teacher pants for a few breaths.]* You see? The dynamo moves faster. And they don't sing anywheres near as well as a person that's very peaceful and very calm. And then the voice just flows. It's the images. Once you control the images before they go to speak—before they go to sing, and then when they sing, the effect of that is a good feeling, for God is there, because the images aren't.

Then, like water through a pipe that deposits its own minerals, that [that is] flowing through you from your vital body, you understand, by your breath, which is receiving that, you have that effect of a good feeling. You just finished your song, you just finished your words, and you just feel great! Do you understand that?

Don't forget, you are the song you sing and the words you speak. That's what you are.

Well, look at that simple truth, "I speak my word forth into the universe knowing that it shall not come back to me void but accomplish that which I send it to do." You have spoken forth the word, the breath of life. The image is exactly the word you speak. The forked tongue has become one. The power is. So, you speak to the mountain, "Mountain, move," and the mountain moves, for there's one image, there's one word, *[It sounds as though the teacher slaps his hands once at this moment.]* and that's the power. For that's God. But there's only one, only one.

I also gave you the truth: Concentration is the key to all power. Well, what is it? Here's the image. Here's the word. The forming of the breath of life, life itself.

[We] must conclude. Now you know these so-called secrets of materialization. OK. But then it's getting late. Classes carry on.

MAY 15, 1983

Class May 18, 1983

[The following teachings were likely given to a very small group of advanced students.]

Thought force is the absolute supremacy of mental substance registered in consciousness with the divine desire known as God's expression. Now this desire, the fulfillment thereof, dictated by mental substance, is formed and is directed to its fulfillment regardless of any and all consequences, for consideration is in its totality in the supremacy of the dictate of the human mind. Therefore, any form and all form that is registered within the consciousness of mental substance that is known to mental substance as an obstruction to the fulfillment of the dictate of the desire becomes the victim of what you know in your world as thought force.

For example, one chooses to fulfill a desire to have an ice-cream cone. Mental substance registers its supremacy of having the ice-cream cone. It sees, in its world, that there are two, three, or more obstructions to the attainment of its desire. And in seeing those obstructions, it consumes, through identification, for the ice-cream cone, it consumes the forms that it sees as an obstruction. In other words, it takes those forms which are not ice-cream cones and it simply, by its absolute supremacy and belief in its own force, it transforms them into instruments of movement that bring forth into their consciousness their ice-cream cone.

*****

Now that is known as thought force. There are no limits, only in the sense of what the mental substance can conceive. Now a person who is the victim of this force of thought becomes possessed and registers within their mind a compulsion to do or to have a certain thing. For example, one who is expert in thought force, registering another person as an obstruction to their desire, would register within their consciousness an absolute compulsion and be possessed by the desire to have an ice-cream cone. And therefore, in that moment, if they would but pause and they would be honest and sincere with themselves, then they would know beyond shadows of all doubts, for they would go beyond mental substance, beyond thought force, and they would clearly view this desire to have an ice-cream cone is simply the registration in their consciousness, for they are, in the consciousness of another, an obstruction to the other's desire. I do hope that's helped with your question.

*****

Yes, how does one, using thought force, transform what they register as an obstruction form to the fulfillment of their desire? Because the one who is registered as an obstruction to another's desire is living in a mental world in which identification with the world, the mental world known as self, places them in the principle of belief. Because they are now the victim of belief and because they have registered within their consciousness a rapport with the one who is now using the thought force against them, it is belief that is the instrument that is used by the manipulator of thought force that transforms them and they become absolutely possessed.

*****

The only defense against thought force is a removal from the realm in which mental substance and belief reign supreme. Now the removal from that realm by any individual is what is called redirection. The first thing that must be eliminated is the thought of I, not the I, but the thought of I. The self-thought must be removed from the consciousness. This can be done in many ways. This can be done from distraction. Usually, the way that it is done is to drive out what is known as the demons of desire. Now driving them out takes a great amount, you understand, of counteracting force. And so it is a phenomenal drain upon the, ah, what you would call, the exorcist. It is a phenomenal drain upon the energy from their vital body. And therefore, they must restore that energy through rising above the mental realm, after they have used the mental realm and all the force they could possibly muster and [that was] available to them. That's known as driving out the demons. That's known as freeing the soul from possession. Does that help—I hope—with your question?

*****

For example, I have many, many times, many times used the mental force to counteract and drive out the possessing demons. And other demons have risen under cleverness and cunningness; that, what you call foul language, is not necessary. It's always, you see, the cleverness of the mental world. Their best defense is an offense. You understand that principle?

Yes.

It is the principle in which they truly work. In other words, cry foul ball in order that you can be more foul.

Yes.

MAY 18, 1983

Class May 24, 1983

[The following teachings were given to the larger group of students who volunteered at the temple Tuesday nights.]

Promise is a contract between a giver and a receiver and is subject to the conditions or laws of the contractual agreement at the time of signature or commitment.

*****

Our egos are revealed when our judgments are threatened.

*****

We permit our self to be disappointed when people do not do what they promise to do. And the reason that we're disappointed is because we are dependent upon our mind and, therefore, are disappointed by theirs.

*****

Whoever sees the good in *all* things is freed from the bondage of *any* thing.

*****

So fools fear to be the blade of grass.

*****

It is not possible to believe without judgment. And it is not possible to judge without denial. And it is not possible to deny without the destiny to free our soul.

*****

Man believes what he knows and is bound by the judgments of his limited experiences. That is why knowledge knows much and wisdom knows better.

*****

Whoever believes in God experiences goodness ever subject to the experiences that have been. But he who has faith in God is freed from the bondage of self.

*****

The god of clay feet is the god of belief. And clearly, we see there is a God greater than the one that we believe in.

*****

How quickly our understanding crumbles when the God in which we believe doesn't do according to our belief.

MAY 24, 1983

Class August 16, 1983

[The following teachings were given to the larger group of students who volunteered at the temple Tuesday nights.]

Tonight's class, as I said, is Why do ex-students cry? Now the question has to be asked, What is an ex-student? An ex-student is a student who never applied the lessons they studied. That is what makes them an ex-student. For example, we set the law into motion, through our own desires, to study any particular subject. We do not complete our study until we apply what we have studied, and that incompletion is a student that's an ex-student.

The reason that we don't apply what we study is because we do not maintain the self-discipline or control of our mind that is necessary to move in consciousness from receiving to giving. Now the reason that we don't move in consciousness from our need to receive to the fullness to give is because, from the lack of application of what we receive, we continue to experience need. Now that lack of application or movement in consciousness is known as the denial of personal responsibility.

*****

Whenever we permit our mind to justify, to excuse our self rather than to face honestly transgressions of natural, divine law, we are not only a house divided, but are in truth self-destructive.

*****

Laziness is ignorance. And ignorance is laziness. Whenever we permit our mind to blame outside for our experiences, we are not only ignorant, we are lazy. We're [too] lazy in consciousness to make the effort to awaken to the Law of Personal Responsibility; and therefore, in honesty, see clearly the error, the ignorance of our own thought. Without laziness, there is no ignorance. And the law is no respecter of ignorance, for the law *is*. The Law of Life is the Light of life.

Whether or not, from our laziness, we choose to be ignorant of the demonstrable truth, we are not exempt from the effect of the law that we transgress. Our efforts to blame outside for what we're doing inside reveals clearly to us our laziness to make the changes that are inevitable: our own ignorance to think for a moment that we can bypass the natural, divine laws of life.

*****

The refusal to make changes in consciousness that the light of reason within us reveals to us is necessary for our own good, the refusal to make those changes clearly shows us personally our own immaturity. Whoever, in the light of reason, makes changes instantly is free from the darkness of their own subconscious mind. Those who refuse to make changes that the light of reason within them dictates know, in those moments, they are controlled by a child that must have its own way. Now some people call that type of a mind a spoiled brat. Some people call it something unrecordable.

Shut it off.

AUGUST 16, 1983

Class May 20, 1984

[The following teachings were given to the larger group of students who volunteered at the temple Sunday nights.]
 This is the . . . [A director whispers to the teacher.]
 That's what it's supposed to be doing. Yep, that's the proper way, I think.
 I've got the power center in the laundry room. [Student P informs the teacher.]
 Go ahead, [Student P].
 Would that be OK?
 Certainly. Are—you need to take care of that?
 It'll go off if I don't.
 OK. That'll be fine. *[After a short pause, the teacher continues.]* All right. Now we had—what was the final count on the reservations?
 One hundred seventy-eight.
 One hundred seventy-eight. All right. And last month?
 I don't know exactly. [Student S responds.]
 The final count on reservations last month? [Student R responds.]
 Yes. Not this dinner, but the one—the dinner before.
 [It] was less than that. It was . . . [Student R continues.]
 [The teacher speaks, but a few words are difficult to transcribe.] All right now this is—yes, [Student G].
 I thought it was 172.
 All right. Well, you see, this is where we want to clean these things up. First of all, the dinners bring in a supply to your church and your school, which you would not have, a church or a school, if it wasn't for that, unless you came up with the difference. However, the demonstration is the revelation is showing that the interest is not there. If the interest was there, then the directors, setting the example, would, would know beyond a shadow of any doubt what the reservations are, how

many there are. Because that's your responsibility. Otherwise, we should get new directors.

Now, you are allowed these things in this school in order that you can grow. You see, it's like a child. You tell the child, "If you take and strike that match, there is the potential danger of burning down the very house in which you live." Now the child—some, depending on their evolution, they will listen. They will not doubt that that will happen. But then there are many children—the majority of which—[who] will strike the match so that their egos can prove to themselves, "Yes, that is true." Now anyone that has raised children certainly is aware of that, wouldn't you agree, [Student B]?

All right. So, you're in a school, a nursery school. You are allowed—you are told what will happen. And then you are allowed to do what your minds demand of you to do that you may prove to yourself that the Light knew exactly what it was talking about. Would you not agree, [Student S]?

Uh-huh.

And [Student R]?

Yes.

And so consequently whether or not it is streusel cakes that are [have] totally bypassed the authority of the organization by a director or whether it is [Student O] who is given permission to take a child, [Student E] in this case, into the healing room, you are given these opportunities to wake up and use the faculties of consideration.[15]

Now, when [Student O] asked me if [Student E's] playpen could be taken into the healing room, I was very unhappy, personally, with the Spirit. Because I saw that [Student O] would not question or consider that the church accounting was being done and he should wait until the church business is cared for before he did that. But, you see, I had to—and I didn't appreciate it, because I knew what was going to happen. I'm in the midst of recording upstairs. I've shut the whole recording down and [have] got to redo it. So I can come down here to straighten [you] out—to help you people grow.

Now, [Student O] was granted permission to take [Student E's] playpen into the healing room. But [Student O]—and I saw it very clearly, just like I see anything else—did not say, "Can I interfere with the church accounting?" If the church business doesn't come first, there's no church. So, it was [Student O's] opportunity to grow. If that was not allowed, [Student O] could not grow. If [Student R] had not been allowed his shenanigans over these past twelve years, [Student R] could not grow. If [Student S] had not been allowed to go against the Light's guidance, she could not grow. Could you?

No. [Student S replies.]

So, you see, as I said to [Student R] today when the report came in of the upset over our accounting, I said, "Now just a moment." Because, you see, coming in from a mental world, there's not the total consideration: the soul isn't even included. Now, [Student R] knows after twelve years—and I told you right out front, didn't I? I said, "Now just a minute, [Student R]. You want to interfere and deny [Student O's] soul the right to awaken and grow up. Did the Spirit in your titanic shenanigan against the Light, did they interfere? No! They allowed you to have your number and go against the right of the Light. They allowed [Student O] to do the same thing because he did not show consideration of the Spirit and the work that is to be." Do you understand?

Now if that system did not operate here, you could not possibly grow. Do you understand that, [Student B]? How can you grow if you're not given the opportunity? If [Student Y] is not given the opportunity to support [Student G's] judgment based on [Student G's] prejudice of the moment over streusel cakes, then [Student Y] cannot grow.[16]

Now as recent as last evening, I mentioned to [Student Y]—for [Student Y's] good—that her presentation is not professional. I spoke to her very kindly. I give her credit. She managed to gain control over 40 percent of her ego forces. Because, you see, anyone who is singing who hunches over a microphone is not professional and everybody and his brother knows it. Now she's interested in doing better. So, I helped her with that at the guidance of the Spirit.

I am working with [Student E]. I have worked for eight months as I have watched the ever-increasing attachment of the child to his mother. The mother didn't listen. The father didn't listen. They heard, but did not listen, because if they had listened, corrective measures would have been taken. And we wouldn't have the problem today, would we, [Student O]?

No.

No, we would not have the problem. So, we've got to clean that up because it affects the church, and [Student O] has spoken to the Friends in reference to that.

But, you see, you're allowed to get away with certain shenanigans so that you can grow. Because if you're not allowed that, then you be rest assured you are not growing; you are simply suppressing those levels of consciousness. And this is where all the cost is to your school and to your church. Those levels must be allowed their expression, but never to the point where they will destroy that which God has ordained.

[Student S] has been allowed to do her numbers. [Student R] has been allowed to do his. And we are still here. What [Student R] and [Student S] do not realize, if the Spirit, in its divine right to its own rules and regulations in its own church and school, if it had not stood up on the rock of principle, either [Student S] or [Student R] would not be sitting at this table this evening. And that's the truth of the matter. One of them would have been gone, but not both of them. [As a result of] the Spirit, impartial and working totally in principle, they're both here today. Do you understand?

Now it's the same thing, you see—I have asked the secretary of the church to make great effort to help [Student G] in her temptation in her weakness to go against the right of the Light to establish its rules and regulations and to enforce them. Is that not correct, [Student S]?

That's right.

Because I am aware, as [Student G] is aware, that she has that temptation, she has that weakness. She is not alone with her weaknesses and her temptations.

Now, [Student O], I am well aware that you were upset today with [Student M] and the situation with [Student E]. And I have been working on that all afternoon. You're going to have to do *your* part. Do you understand? The thing is, that I do hope if you don't see by now, you should see that when you ask the Spirit something, you will be given the opportunity to do your thing that you may awaken that there's more to be considered than your selfish desires, whether it's a streusel cake or it's [Student E] being placed in the healing room and not stopping and pausing to think, "Yes, the Spirit has granted permission. Do I go by the spirit of the law or do I go by the letter of the law that killeth? Did I ask the Spirit can I interfere with the accounting? Or shall I wait 'til the church business is done?" You see?

Those opportunities must be given [to] you. Just like they're given [to] [Student S] and they're given [to] [Student R]. Now, corrective measures have to be taken because the church cannot subject—subject itself—the Light cannot be the victim of creation. You see, you see, for the church and the Council to allow [Student O] or [Student M] or [Student E] to interfere with the spiritual work would mean that the Light is becoming the slave of creation. That will never be allowed. It wasn't allowed for [Student S]. It wasn't allowed for anyone else at this table or that has been in or out of the organization. It shall never be allowed as long as I'm on Earth.

So, it's [Student O] and [Student M's] responsibility to ask for the recommendation and not to interfere with the right, the divine right of the church to its rules and regulations that consider everyone. See? All right.

Now, that's where your problems are. Your problems are—and, of course, things are getting better because the Friends have really put their foot down—that you don't take control of your mind.

Today, I went to the brunch and I had my brunch and here was a potato as big as my cigarette lighter in the potato salad. At least that size. And that's not exaggerating, you received it. It was wider than this, but it was that large. Now I checked with the secretary of the church to see who had made that potato salad. Now I want you to listen carefully to these justifications that are not allowed. She investigated, and it was [Student P]. I had [Student P]—I had her bring it back, set it at my table, that huge potato salad. It was not made according to the recipe. At least my taste buds, I can rely on in that respect. And I told [Student S] that this was not up to the quality standards of this organization, but that it did not taste proper and something was wrong in reference to that recipe. Something was missing. It did not have the proper flavor. All right.[17]

So, we called over [Student P] and she immediately started the con game of self-pity belligerence. "It was real late when I got to work on this and I really tried to put God in it." I sat there and I listened for a moment to this self-pity belligerence. And the Spirit said, "Oh, yes, she tried real hard to put God in it—to put the god of her ego in it." And I said to the Spirit, "Exactly, specifically what do you mean?" She never once made the effort to play the tape with the music that she had spent the money to buy here. Of course, she only paid for the tape, like the rest of you. She never listened to that. She listened to the ego, which has access to every single affirmation your mind ever gets. There's a vast difference. And so, her ego did her in. Do we yet perceive this simple truth, [Student B]? *[After a short pause, the teacher continues.]* Does anybody perceive that simple law?[18]

When you speak an affirmation, do you know what level it comes from? *[After a short pause, the teacher continues.]* Well, has the demonstration of the years you've been in this church—when the Spirit speaks an affirmation, what has been the results?

Spirit . . . [Several words are difficult to transcribe.]

That's right. What's been your experience? Is there a change for the better?

Yes. There's always a change.

Look, I spent untold hours recording an affirmation for you people. I didn't have to do it. No, I didn't have to do it. It was my personal request to the Spirit that you people may benefit as I benefit from it. And so, I made that personal request to the Spirit for *your* benefit. What do I get back as the result? I get back the frustrations from some: from [Student G], she could only hear the message, couldn't hear the music. From [Student P], I get back something else because there's a part of it that really bugs her, although at first, she really liked it. But when it came to the time of great need to use it, it was never used.

Think about it. With other students, I get the upset that that part that really bugs them is "the purpose of being is freedom from what has been." *[For the complete text of the "Controlled Spiritual Environment" affirmation, please see the appendix.]* You see, if you don't want to be free from the shadows of your life—don't you understand?—you're in the wrong school. You're in the *wrong* school. You must get that through your brain. If you do not want to be free from the shadows of your life, you are in the wrong school. Make an intelligent choice, and don't live a life of frustration.

If the shadows of your life mean more to you than the Light that frees you, for goodness' sakes, make a change and make a move. I have no chains upon you. That's not my purpose of being. Is there anyone who doesn't understand that? Anyone who doesn't understand?

You don't seem to be relating that you are given these mountains of opportunities at phenomenal expense, *phenomenal* expense in order that you can make intelligent decisions. What has greater value to [Student S] in over ten years of service here to the Light? What has greater value? Stop and think. The shadows, *shadows* of life or the Light? That's the question. Which has greater value? Isn't that a question? What do you feel? What has greater value?

I feel very strongly the Light.

That's right! Therefore, you're still sitting here. Is that not correct?

Absolutely.

Because, you see, if [Student S] could not free herself from the shadows of her life, she could not sit here today. Don't you understand that? So, if you don't make the effort to free yourself from the shadows of your life, you can't make it, you see?

Now, [Student O] and [Student M] have a problem, a domestic problem. All problems contain within them a solution. The domestic problem, unfortunately, is dumped on little [Student E], another student of mine. But it's a domestic problem. I have yet to counsel a man and his wife, in forty-three years of my effort, that the wife, the mother doesn't spend 90 percent of the time with the child. The father wants to take care of the child when the father wants to take care of the child. I mean, this is just the way it is in the good old U.S.A. And show me any difference to that. [Student B], you're a married woman. Wasn't it that way in your upbringing of your children?

Yes.

Wasn't all of that dumped onto the mother?

Yes.

Wasn't the father there? Is [has] that not been your experience as a mother? *[After a short pause, the teacher continues.]* And has that not been your experience as a mother? *[The teacher now addresses Student M.]*

Pretty much. Not totally.

Yes, because you're fortunate: [Student O] is a student of the Light.

Exactly.

And has a responsibility.

Uh-huh.

But, you see, as I spoke to [Student O] today, and I will speak to you: you've got to release him in your ego.

OK. [Student M continues to respond.]

Because it's your ego that's created a problem. Isn't that right, [Student O]? And I've explained that for eight long months. Now I can't spend all of my energy on your problem with [Student E] because I don't have any problem at all with [Student E]. [Student E] and I have no problem at all. He got along real fine this morning, didn't he, [Student O]?[19]

Sure did.

Just fine. Just as happy [as] can be. Looking out at the trees. Looked at the dog. See [saw] the flowers. There's no problem at all because I don't have an ego need to control his soul, [Student M]. All right.

Now, do you understand, like with [Student P]; oh, she said that she—"I did work real hard to put God in." Well, that should give you the message that as hard as you worked, don't work with that level because the result was a disaster. An intelligent person will say, "I'm not going to work my butt off like that again; look at the results I got."

[Student P], you stop and think. Stop and think. Why did you bother to spend $2 or $3 for a tape and not use it? Why bother? To please me? You didn't please me at all. It doesn't matter to me whether you get it or you don't get it. I asked that you may benefit for [from] it. The Council gave an approval that—yes, you may—I may make one for you. That's what they told me. I didn't have to make one for anyone. I'm making them for myself.

But I'm a practical person. I don't believe in waste. Well, what's your answer with this fiasco? Number one: you didn't put the pickle juice into the potato salad. More important than that the chunks were cut for a giant. What is that supposed to be all about?

I got the recipe and it is incorrect. So, I'm going to— [Student P responds.]

Well, it's your responsibility to see that you have a correct recipe.

Right. So, I . . . to get changed. [It is difficult to transcribe a few words.]

Yes. Now, [Student G], this is a very serious offense, no matter who it happens to. When—and, and try to relate in your consciousness—when you are working and you believe that you're working for your soul, for the Light, and for your spirit, when you believe that and then demonstrate the opposite, you have no divine grace. There's no deposit. Try to understand that, whether it's you or [Student O] or anyone else. You have no spiritual deposit.

Now, you can relate to the bank and to taking money out and being overdrawn. You can relate to that. And you can relate to the penalties you pay. The law[s] that applies [apply] in a material world is [are] identically the same laws that apply in mental worlds and the same laws that apply in spiritual worlds. Can you relate to that, [Student B], as a lawyer?

Yes.

The law doesn't change. Its expression is different, but the law itself remains the same. You work—and work is a direction of energy—you understand that?—through the Law of Attention. Now the return of that in a material world is dollars and cents. Now you all can relate to that, can't you? *[After a short pause, the teacher continues.]* Pardon?

Yes. [Several students respond.]

All right. Now you work and you tell yourself, "I'm working for the freedom of my soul. I'm working for peace and harmony. I'm working for the goodness in my life. And that work, I understand, being done for God, returns that to me." Can you relate to that? *[After a short pause, the teacher continues.]* Fine. Now, as you work in a material, physical job and Friday comes or whatever day you get paid, you get your little paycheck and you go back home. *[The buzzer of a timer goes off.]*

Go ahead, [Student P]. *[The teacher instructs a student to attend to the task associated with the timer.]*

You relate to that? And from your paycheck, you do the things that you want to do in keeping with the laws you have established. Correct? Fine. All right.

Now you go to work to do something for God. Hmm? To make a deposit in a spiritual bank account, your work—so that in your time of need there's something in a bank account for you to draw out. Do you understand? You don't even think of it that way. That's just the way it is. The same law works in the physical world.

Now while you are working, if you permit your prejudice, your prejudgments—do you understand?—to interfere and to dictate the way the work is to be done, then your belief that you're working for God, for the goodness to return, is a total self-deception, for that energy and that attention—energy following attention—is going to a mental world. Do you understand that?

Consequently, your deposit from your efforts, under the guise of building up a deposit in a spiritual bank of goodness, is built in a mental bank of creation. So, in your time of need, you experience what a mental bank of creation has to offer: temptation and total frustration.

That's where the deposits have been going—too much of them.

Now when you ask for help from the Council, from the Spirit, what takes place is they take a look at the law; they look at your deposit, you understand, how much is there. How much it's going to withdraw from the deposit to grant unto you, in keeping with the law, what's called divine grace. Because divine grace is not some partial thing you just dump out and they got it. In your time of need, when your health cannot be restored by any mental deposit, by any physical money deposit in a material bank, there's only one bank account to draw from for the restoration of your health.

Now, the angels take a look at your deposit. They see your needs. They see what you insist, by establishing laws that are yet coming back to you, how much, in the best interest, can be drawn to help you through your great time of need. Do you understand? Now some people, though their physical bodies were present, their mental bodies were present, the deposits were all going into a mental bank account. And so, the day finally came when withdrawals from the bank account could not meet the need for them to remain in the Light and no longer could it be drawn from someone else's bank account.

Now can we all relate? For the law does not change. It's only a different world of consciousness. That's all it is. That's what's happening here. When you are physically present and your prejudice is being fed, you are making deposits, through the Law of Attention that energy follows, you are making deposits in mental bank accounts. Mental bank accounts will not keep you in the Light. They will, however, bind you deeper and closer to creation, but they will *not* keep you in the Light.

Now are there any questions over that very simple system that has always been? Are there any questions on that? Yes, [Student U].

Is there some sort of measuring thing that we can ask ourselves?

Why, certainly. All you've got to do is to pause and be beware: Who's in charge in your consciousness? That's all you have to do. You see, it's very simple: and when you're talking to people, if you get all frustrated when you don't have your way, you know right where your deposits are going. It's going into a mental bank account and you are experiencing the deposits, which are frustrations and unfulfilled desires. Just loaded with them. You see, if we didn't have such huge mental bank accounts, we wouldn't have so much unfulfilled desires and so much temptations and so much frustrations.

Energy follows attention. My God, you've got to relate to the law that you know beyond a shadow of any doubt: Energy follows attention. Money is the effect of directed energy. You have a responsibility as a chairman over a dinner, over a brunch, and if you are directing, through attention, the divine Energy to mental realms of consciousness, we shall not get the goodness, the return to keep the Light shining. Do you understand that?

Yes.

Well, that's how simple it is. It's not a matter of numbers. It's a matter of quality. You're baking something in the kitchen: your ego prejudices—you start putting your attention upon your prejudices and interfering with the spiritual work, then the results are fiascoes. And that's just the way that it is.

Where are you when you're working for God? Where are *you*? Because if you're not there in the goodness in the moment you're working, then the energy is going to something else. Where are you? That's the question. We see your physical body and we know the results. But where are you?

How many times I've spoken to the secretary—"Just where *are* you? Where are *you*? I see your physical body, but where are you?" Because I see the energy, at times, going to mental realms where no good shall return. Then, when the health goes, there's only so much deposit. The law will not allow me to use [my energy] to [go beyond] the point [where] energies that are required for my vital body [are used] for someone else. I have my responsibilities as a teacher, but not beyond that point. *Not* beyond that point. You know the law. And it's up to you to apply it and bring the changes in your consciousness.

I'd like some hot coffee, please.

Now do you see how you've benefited today in awakening, hopefully, [Student O], your faculty of total consideration, which is God's love? *[After a short pause, the teacher continues.]* See? We must pause to think. When we are bombarded with a desire, which is mental substance, we must say, "Now God, I have asked and received permission, what is my responsibility, the letter of the law that shall kill me or the spirit of the law which shall free me?" There's the spirit of the law [that] contains total consideration, but the letter of the law—that's it!—and it killeth. Even the Bible teaches us that. Good.

Now, perhaps you understand why we have the system that we have. You see, you have choices to make. You come to me; you're going to get an answer from the Spirit and you're going to get the experience, right [Student S]?

Right.

And you had plenty of that. *[A student laughs.]* You come to the director, you come under a different law. Didn't I reveal that to you last evening over trunks, [Student B]?

Yes, you did.

You see? Now you come directly to the Light and you're going to pay the price of the law you establish. You come through a director and you're getting censored in reference to the law, for there's more than one law now involved. Do you understand the difference? All right.

Now, you see what would happen—let me explain this to you, [Student O]. This is important for you. Because [Student E] is coming along just fine. As I say, it's vibration. [Student E] come [came] out this morning, wasn't he in wonderful shape? Didn't he do just beautiful? Stopped his bawling and screaming and everything. Didn't he, [Student O]?

Sure did.

He looked around at the trees and he was smiling, just as happy as can be. Because he's a little baby, totally like a sponge of the vibrations that are closest to him. See? And all those forms, whether it's his mother's or his father's, it doesn't matter. He is affected by that which he identifies with, [Student O]. He identifies with his mother. He identifies with his father. Do you understand?

Right.

So, when you bring him to me, I go to work to free him from the forms that he is responding to. And I've told you, show him the trees and the leaves and the things of nature and he will be freed from that. Do you see what I mean?

Uh-huh.

And he did. He was, wasn't he?

Right.

And he was entirely different. See? Those are forms. Just—

[At this moment, side A of the microcassette tape on which the class was being recorded ends. The class continues and at some point, the tape is turned over and recording on side B begins.]

*****

—for. Are we doing these streusels for that mental realm down there or are we doing them for God and his ministering angels and the Light to free our soul? That's the question. Because the results that finally came out of all of that was that the Spirit Council had granted authority, [Student B], for dark brown sugar. Well, how do you expect them to be light and serve your prejudice? This is a very serious transgression. I mean, the principle of it. It's not a streusel cake. Worse than that—[Student G], I'm trying to help you—you had the audacity, without checking [with] the authority of the Light, to buy those streusels, denying the Light that service. So that all went for mental substance and frustration. You see?

It did. [Student G responds.][20]

See? So those are the things you've got to consider, [Student O], whether it's you, [Student G], [Student B], [Student P], [Student R], or anyone else. Those are the things to start waking up to. Where is all your energy going? And you can know right away: where is your attention going? What are you thinking about? Because that's where the divine Energy is being directed.

You see, I know what [Student P] was thinking about. I'm not interested in this business that she was saying her affirmation trying—what affirmation were you saying? Because the ego sure got locked onto that one.

Well, I was lying to myself, [saying,] "I'm doing this for God." [Student P responds.]

It doesn't do any good. It created the opposite results. Can you image that? Can you imagine your mind telling you you're doing this for God and have the opposite results? When you look, the results show you: you did it for that thing down there. I mean, can you imagine that, [Student B]? Can you imagine working, making potato salad, telling yourself you're doing it for God and have the opposite results? I would make a change in my head, wouldn't you?

Better make a change in your head. And you better listen to an affirmation that didn't come from the ego in the first place.

Yes, [Student G]. The spoken word—just a moment—is life-giving energy. So, the spoken word that you used at that time, "I'm doing this for God," being life-giving energy, the result, the demonstration revealed who has control of that affirmation in your consciousness. Do you see that, [Student B], as a lawyer?

Yes. [Student B responds.]

Yes, that's important, I think. Yes, [Student G].

I was just going to say if you don't feel good—

Then God's not there.

—you know very well how many affirmations you say and it's just a lot of baloney.

Because, you see, the mental realm has access to the mind. Of course, it does. They can use anything that is recorded in your memory and in your mind. Any and every experience. Anything that is there they can use against you. And don't think they don't, like they did [to] [Student P] last night. They used it against her.

When you hear the Spirit speak the affirmation, of course there's irritations that rise up. Those are the things that are in control at the moment. Now, most of my students there, [Student B], they thought it was just beautiful at first. After hearing it a while something else came up to speak. *[The teacher laughs.]* So, but that is an inner awakening, don't you see? That's an inner awakening to face these things. Because if you don't face them, you can't work with them. There's no way possible. No possible way.

All right, are there any questions? [Student G], did you have a question?

No, I did—

Oh, you help[ed] there [with] [Student P]. If you're not feeling good, then you can be rest assured your energy, through the Law of Attention, is going to something that is discordant and is therefore not God. God is not discord. God is not disease.

And even—any doctor with any intelligence will tell you he cannot heal. He may put something together, but that is dependent on something else. The healing, the cure is dependent on something else. Isn't that right, [Student B]? Look, the same medicine works for one, [but] doesn't work for another. The identical same treatment. For some it works and some it don't [doesn't] work. Because, [Student B], where's their bank account? That's what's at stake. That's what's at stake. There's not a sufficient amount to withdraw. Do you understand?

Yes.

That's where it is. Some people, they listen to the Spirit and follow the direction of the Spirit, have a positive result. Some people listen to the Spirit; they go about to do what they are guided to do [and] they have a disastrous result. Where's their deposit? Because it costs to have the experience, see? Where is it? If it is not deposited, you cannot withdraw it.

Now some people, they have experiences where they're feeling real good and then they expose themselves in an over-identified way with another person and the next thing you know, they feel terrible and their health starts breaking down. Then, the time comes, they no longer identify with the person, their health is totally restored. Well, what the hell do you think is taking place? It's energy! You see, there's the zappers and there's the producers. Some are constantly draining your energy. Some are producing. Do you see? There is a difference. Some are making spiritual deposits. And some are doing nothing but making withdrawals.

And I expect deposits around here. In no uncertain terms or I'll let you know. You, you don't have any more to withdraw. You've with—you're overdrawn.

But, you see, what causes that? Why are some people zappers and other people producers of energy in a spiritual way?

Well, it's quite simple. *[In another room, Student E begins to cry.]* They all have—go ahead, you're excused, [Student M]—they all have attention and they're all directing divine Energy. Some are sending it down and some are sending it up. The ones who are sending it down—that's a hollow hole down there; that's a bottomless pit. And so, they drain everything they can drain. Show me a person overidentified with self and I'll show you the greatest zapper you will ever meet. A total zapper. All the energy, they're, they're sucking it; [they will] suck your blood dry and they're all sending it down there.

I will not have that around me because it will kill me off. And I know it. It's called survival. Because, you see, they'll zap not only what energy you have in reserve, if you have any, but they'll even zap the energy that is needed for your vital body. Then your health will break down. And everything will start to go blah! That's what happens. That's overidentification with self to a mental world. And all of the energy, no matter how hard you work, is being drained for that mental world.

So, when you think you're tired and you think you're exhausted, you [have] got to pause and think, "My God, where is my attention?" You [have] got to go to work. I'm grateful to God that no matter how, how far down, through overexposure, I have gone, with God's help, I have always rejuvenated. Because, you see, [Student J], here, a student of mine for fourteen, fifteen years or more, he was the first one. And he said in that garage at the Sunday meeting last week—it was last week, wasn't it? He said, "Mr. Goodwin, I cannot understand how you can expend as much energy as you do and still survive." I . . . that I have had to expend. *[It is difficult to transcribe a few words.]* But those days have come to a screeching halt.

I cannot expend this energy to dissipate the mental forms that people's prejudice insists on creating when they're supposed to be here serving God. Because the deposits are going to mental realms. Now, not all the time. It is getting better. So in that respect, I'm encouraged. But this fiasco at church today, this fiasco on the streusel, this fiasco on all those things, that is not why you're here. You have to make effort. The effort has got to be made.

I realize that you're tempted in that world of creation and your minds are going lickety-split and the energy's being siphoned off for that realm down below. That's what that world has to offer. You come here for rejuvenation. But not at my expense. *You* have to put in your share, not just your physical bodies. Your physical bodies are nothing. They're present. But where is your consciousness? That's what I'm interested in, because you're making deposits down there or up there.

Now, are there any questions on that very simple process that's absolutely demonstrable? And besides, let's clean our act up because [Student R] had to take a call today from that—what was her name?

Ah, what was her name? [Student R asks.]

You know.

Yes.

[A different student offers another name.]

No. The other one.

No. The one that we had— [Student R offers.]

[A last name] or something.

Yeah.

Oh. [Student S interjects.]

[A last name.] What the hell is [her first name?] [Student R questions.]

Oh! [A complete name]! [Student S interjects.]

It is not—no, [a first name], I think.

[A complete name.][21] [Student R remarks.]

Let's not deny the Law of Personal Responsibility. Mental substance rising again [and] the calls come in. See? So, let's clean it up. We had a nice dinner. I want the work really poured in on this next dinner because that's the survival of your school. Otherwise, you have no right being here.

Now there are very few members left. And fringe members are all working themselves out, no matter who they are. Because it is contrary to the law here. Absolutely contrary to the law, [Student G]. I don't give a—my own sister, a fringe member, is long gone. She's no longer a member. I guess you realize that, don't you? It's contrary to the law. The church is moving on; the fringe members are going their way.

And, in fact, we don't deny anyone membership or the right to stay as a member, but we have the right to increase the dues proportionately to balance out the cost of what everybody else is putting in. Now that's just the way it is. And I want everyone to know. Do you have any problems with that? I have it recorded on tape. Do you want to support those who cannot make up their mind, sitting on the fence? Now it's their right; and I don't care whether it's my sister or anyone else, the day has to come and the day has come. The membership is getting smaller; the church is growing beautiful. And that is a law, and it means changes.

Now I don't care who they are, I'm interested in the law. I've gone through my own thing with my sister on the fence and this and that. She's no longer a member. And that's the way it is. I am not running, nor did I come to Earth to operate, St. Anthony's kitchen.[22] That's not my purpose for being here. For anyone. Now if our minds don't like it, then just step into my shoes and see what it's really like.

You not only have a very unique school, but I will no longer tolerate this emotional self-interest over the light of this organization, and I'm not interested in who it is. I think we understand that, don't we? I will not. The day has come. I've earned that law.

You have an opportunity to evolve and grow with the school, and you also have the opportunity to turn your back on it and say, "It's not for me." That's your choice. No matter who you are. I have no emotional attachments to any of you. I want it very clear. I've gone through all the emotional attachments with my own family. They are long gone. Because the Bible teaches you very clearly: your mother, your father, your brother, your sister, your son, your daughter must go to follow the Light of eternal Truth. What does that mean? Your ego must be educated that God and God alone is what your value truly is. And if you're not ready for that, then you're certainly not ready for the evolution of this school. You're not ready for this school. Uh-uh. No, no, no. Go to one of those other schools.

I tell you that ego attachments shall take you out of the Light. That's why ego attachments are not allowed in the Light. You see that, don't you, [Student S]?

Sure do.

Ego attachments are not allowed in the Light. You come in here as a man and a wife, that's fine. But be rest assured don't mix it with the Light because you'll never make it. Ego attachments are not allowed in the Light.

And any school of Light does not allow it. They won't even let you in. Did you know that? *[After a very short pause, the teacher continues.]* You won't even get to the door in a temple of Light with ego attachments. They know better. They know exactly what it offers. That's why you have monasteries.

Yes, come right ahead here. *[The teacher addresses Student M, the mother of Student E.]* Hello, [Student E]. How are you doing?

[As an eight-month-old child, Student E was unable to reply.]

You cannot have ego attachments and the Light, too, because you cannot mix water and oil. So, you separate truth from creation when you're in a school of truth, for creation can never be allowed to enter, no matter how much you're tempted. In a school of Light, they do not mix, and they cannot be allowed to enter. And as long as I'm on Earth, they shall not enter! Because it guarantees the students [are] on their way out.

Now, [Student B], as a mother, haven't you had to go through that process?

Three times.

Three times. That's manifestation, [Student B]. Manifestation. Now, are there any other questions? *[After a short pause, the teacher continues.]*

No, I remember and I took a look and I said—my mother says, "Richard, God is more important than your sister." I said, "Well, she's your daughter, Mother." She says, "Oh, how well I know that. You don't have to remind me." *[The teacher laughs loudly and joyfully.]* How well she knows that. But we also have another sister over there, you know. Been there a long time. My mother also reminded me of that, you know. "I," she says, "I also have another daughter." I said, "Oh, yes, I know."

No. No, when it came time when my sister held on to the fringes and the day came, that was it.

Because, you see, it's just like with [Student E's] opportunity to have his playpen [moved] into the healing chapel. Don't you see? You're always given the opportunity. Now if [Student R] hadn't been given the opportunity to do his ego numbers in over these twelve years, don't you understand, he would not be here today? For, you see, his ego would constantly tell him he's under duress, you see? And that *thing*—those ego things—would feel suppressed, constantly suppressed. He would not be sitting here today if he hadn't been given the opportunity—don't you see, [Student O]?—the opportunity to express his ego and see what a fiasco he'd make of his life. Do you see that? They must give the ego the opportunity to the point that it shall never ever interfere with the rights of the organization and its continuous, harmonious organization.

Now, time and again, the Spirit will say, "Oh, yes, yes. They can go right ahead." I'm furious for the moment because I see what's coming out of it. But, then again, I have to take a look: if the ego isn't given the opportunity, it will never learn the lesson no matter whose ego it is, whether it's [Student S's] ego or [Student R's] ego or [Student P's] or someone else's.

You see, I could have called late last night and said, "[Student P], you're in terrible space. Be alert. Be awake. Be aware. Be alert." She could have played that [tape] and she wouldn't have had this fiasco today. I saw that: "Oh, no! Look at this fiasco." No, I've got to put on my best bib and tucker. I [have] got to be totally ignorant and innocent—"What happened to this potato salad?!" *[Many students laugh.]* You see?

What's the matter with people? I talk a lot, but I know how to keep a secret because they're never given to the blabbermouths. Maybe from that you benefit therefrom. Here, the games are not hidden. It is only an ego deception that they are hidden. That's all it is. You are in a school of Light. You are very fortunate. You have earned that in your evolution. It's coming along nicely. And we just have to make the necessary changes in our consciousness. There are very few members and there are very few being allowed. Be rest assured of that. Because God's angels are not dependent on numbers for their work. There are very few being allowed.

Like my own sister, no one will be holding on to the fringes because those are transgressions, and they only serve that thing down there. They serve nothing else. And therefore, like my mother said, "It's in the best interest, Richard. It's for her own good." Now, she [can] come and go with all her games when she wants to come and go. She'd call [Student R] repeatedly, "I have to work. I won't be able to make it. Oh, I'm definitely coming to the next dinner. Oh, yes, I'm going to do this and I'm going to do that." Total self-deception. Hell, the streets of hell are paved with good intentions and broken promises, and they are crowned with justifications and presumptions! It's just one titanic con game. And the only one being conned is our self.

OK. What does everyone have to say? *[Student E makes a rather loud sound; it is not a cry, but it is not a happy sound either.]* [Student E], what's the problem here? You want to come up here and sit down? What's the matter with you? Or you want to sit with your daddy? *[Student E makes another sound.]* Now just a minute there, he wants to sit with his daddy. Let's see how [Student O's] vibration is; [Student M] gets nothing but whining. *[The teacher laughs. Student E, who had been sitting on his mother's lap, had been whining before he loudly cried out. Student M passes the child to Student O.]* [Student E], yeah, you feel better? Huh? He feels much better there with you, [Student O].

OK. [Student O responds.]

Isn't that nice? Well, *[Student E quietly coos.]* yes, he wants to be with his daddy for a while. What [are] you going to do with him, [Student O]?

[Student O responds, but it is difficult to transcribe his response.]

Oh, yes, so he can sit up. Very good. I think you're a little sleepy, myself. But you'll, you'll get—you'll fall asleep. Yeah. *[Student E again makes a rather loud sound.]* What's the problem, [Student E]? We're having class. What's the problem? You feel better now? Do you feel better? I think you do. I think you feel a little bit better. Mr. Reddy's looking for you. *[Reddy is the church's dog.]* Reddy, [Student E's] here. *[The teacher and several students laugh.]*

All right. Now let's discuss these laws and what we're doing with them. I think it's time that you people poured in some energy, spiritual energy, right at this table, instead of me all the time. We'll start with you, [Student S]. What is your space in awakening? *[After a short pause, the teacher continues.]*

Now let's, let's—I'll give you something so that you can start it, because, you know, you always feel real nervous if you have to make a speech. You're not making a speech. I said last night, "Oh God, I've got to make a speech. God save me." And I just—I'll tell you, my temperature went up thirty degrees. This is ridiculous. Absolutely ridiculous. *[Several students laugh.]* I'm no good at making speeches at all. If the Spirit's working, that's different. But if I got to go up and make a speech at a birthday or something, oh God, that's just too much.[23]

All right, go ahead, [Student S]. Now, why don't we start with this affirmation and how you permitted it to affect you or the entities inside of you. We'll start with you on that. Have you been playing it every day?

Yes.

Good. And what was your early experiences? And what is your later experiences? Because I'm recording this so it's very soft and subtle, as you people learn it. *[The teacher refers to the tape of the "Controlled Spiritual Environment Affirmation" that was recorded with music of the student's choice.]*

Well, when I first heard it, I realized that it was a very important time or the Spirit wouldn't go to those lengths to bring it through, to record it, and have it on when we came in [to the temple].[24]

They sure did.

And I liked it very much because it sounded—the futuristic part—

Very positive.

And—right—and it was—you feel more a close sense with the Source.

Uh-huh.

And then when you hear the words . . . [A few words are difficult to transcribe.]

Purpose of being . . .

Purpose of being.

. . . is freedom from what has been.

Right.

That's why we're here, isn't it?

And then the part—and I also mentioned this, too—the part about freedom from self, then that brings home again that any entertainment of the has-beens [means] you're in self.

You're not in God. God doesn't entertain the shadows of life. *[The teacher laughs.]* [A] beautiful truth of the philosophy in a little capsule there. Go ahead, [Student S].

So, then you hear it or I heard it, I was working, cleaning away, felt real good. And then I really have, in these several months, been paying attention to what, what . . . I can hear in my head— [It is difficult to transcribe a few words.]

Uh-huh.

—once again. Then you realize . . . because here you are at the temple in self. [Again, it is difficult to transcribe a few words.]

That's right. That's what's going on: the pollution. That's what I've been working on all these years.

OK. And . . . [It is difficult to transcribe a few words.]

But, you see, isn't it important? You see, that's an instrument through which you awaken that the percentage of time, of energy going to self, to a mental bank account is unbelievable. You see? Go ahead, [Student S].

OK. And then the, I mentioned to you about the song today.

Which song?

"Just a Closer Walk [with Thee]"

Oh, yes, a beautiful song!

OK, that really tied it all in for me. If anybody examines those words—

Uh-huh.

—there're very special.

It's in the words.

And if it can be that I'm, if I'm paying attention to my duty in the Light and, and the Light is the only thing that I really have, at all, in this whole life and it's just . . . the Light, then I don't have to worry about anything else. [It is difficult to transcribe a few words.]

That's true.

I don't have to worry about me. I don't have to worry about that, that . . . [Student S laughs.]

That's right. But, you see, that takes the effort of controlling the mind.

Right.

Now, the affirmation, when it registers in the mental substance, is an instrument of Light shining the Light over those realms of consciousness that have such control that we're not even aware that we're thinking about our self. Don't you think that's important, [Student B]? Because, you see, as you hear that, all of a sudden you become aware, "I'm thinking of myself again!" You're not even consciously aware that you're thinking of yourself. Here you're working so hard for the freedom of your soul and something else is taking place all the time, like [Student P] and her potato salad.

She said, "I want to put God in it. I want to put God in it. I want to put God in this. I want to put God in this." And what she was saying and what was taking place was feeding that other—the opposite. Yes, [Student S].

Well, I'd like to know what to do with this part. It's, like, whenever the—because it's all tied in the computer, everything's going together—whenever I even hear the word has-been—

Uh-huh.

OK. [Student S sighs and then laughs. Many students also laugh.] *The computer flashes up all the has-beens.*

That's right. Because you can never control what you're not aware of. Now here's your philosophy. Freedom is the effect of self-control. If those things are not brought forward, you cannot control them. You cannot control what you are not aware of. This school is extremely unique: it is an instrument through which the Light is shining to make you aware of those things. Because if you don't deal with them, they're dealing a great number with you. Now that's your alternative and that's your choice. They say that ignorance is bliss. They never said that ignorance was truth, did they? Well, now there you are. There's a vast difference between bliss and truth.

What does *bliss* mean to you? *[After a short pause, the teacher continues.]* Did anyone ever see any part of this philosophy where blissful was a faculty of the soul? Hmm? I think that's in other philosophies. Bliss. Now what does *bliss* mean to you? Anyone have an answer? Yes, [Student B].

It's sort of a euphoric state.

A euphoric state. Thank you. What does *bliss* mean to you, [Student H]?

It's, it's euphoric to me in the sense that, that I feel satisfied without having to make any effort at all. Even to sustain it or get it.

That's right. Very euphoric. [Student G], what does *bliss* mean to you?

Well, I would say what [Student H] said and without any awareness.

Uh-huh. The totality of satisfaction, which is the fullness of the entertainment of the senses, is known, in this philosophy, as a state of bliss. Try to remember, even a bird lands sometime. And in this school, you've landed. *[Several students laugh.]* [Student H] summed it up very well: a state of satisfaction of euphoria with no effort. Is that in keeping with the demonstrable truth of this philosophy, [Student B]?

No.

Damn right. It is, as the Spirit has explained, the fullness, the absolute totality fullness of the senses! But, you know, the minute it's filled, it's emptied. Only to demand another fullness. So, it's a constant process of filling a bottomless hole. Did you ever get enough for the senses, [Student P]?

[The response of Student P is not audible on the recorded tape.]

[The teacher laughs loudly.] Do you know anyone that ever got enough? It's never long enough. It's never big enough. The timing isn't enough. Go on down the list. It is never enough.

You see, [when] you enter these states of, of so-called time-pressure, there's never enough. It's not enough. There's not enough time. There's so many desires screaming, like demons, in the consciousness because the energy, the deposits have been made in mental bank accounts. You people with the bombardment of unfulfilled desires are going to have to wake up and face the truth: you have titanic deposits in mental bank accounts from the Law of Attention of where you're sending the energy. So they all rise up—"Oh, I'm under such time-pressure!" And there's all these unfulfilled desires, you see? The bank opened its doors and you're getting your deposit back. The chickens [have] come home to roost. It's *your* deposit. *[The teacher laughs.]*

Look, if I didn't make some effort, I could not have left it shut off and rewound and took out cassettes of a recording that I wanted for me. I shut it down after almost thirty minutes. It was ready for side two. The Spirit says go now. So I came down. So? I'm not going to ruin my recording. I just rewind the whole thing and redo it over again. But I didn't put myself through a mountain of frustration. You want to know how come? Because I don't have a mountain of mental deposits that hit me. Got the message? Hmm? I'm not perfect. There are some there or I wouldn't have been PO'ed [pissed off] when I had to tell [Student O], "Yes, you have approval to put the playpen in the healing chapel," seeing what his ego was going to do with that opportunity. But then again, how does he grow up and be a man? Hmm? He must, like [Student R]—and then [Student R] was upset.

And you got the message about the opportunity you had been given to do your numbers.

That's right. [Student R responds.]

Isn't that true?

Yes.

Well, there you are. Because—

[At this moment, side B of the microcassette tape ends. Class continues as another tape is put into the recorder and recording begins.]

*****

Yes, go ahead.

Ah . . . [Student S pauses.]

So, you've been gaining an awareness of the constant bombardment of identifying with self.

Uh-huh.

Through the affirmation, is that it?

Right. It calls up all my has-beens.

But isn't that a wonderful opportunity? *[Student S laughs.]* Look, stop and think. If they don't call up the has-beens for you to face to see what's happening to your life, to see who's in control of your body, your mind, and is running your little soul around in its numbers, if those are not called up, how are you ever going to face them and gain control? If you don't have them called up—you can't control what isn't called up. Can you see that? *[After a short pause, the teacher continues.]*

This is not a school for daisies and pantywaists. That's not the kind of school this is. Hmm? So, when they're called up, do you take a look at them?

Uh-huh. [Student S continues.]

And what do you tell them? Is that you or is that something of creation that your mind's created?

Well, I look at it that way and I also try to put the whole thing into perspective . . . have real value in my life and what the purpose is, and then examine the law and I know it's true. . . [Certain parts of her response are difficult to transcribe.]

—is right. Not what the ego dictates.[25]

Right.

Is that the difference?

Uh-huh.

Do you see? *[After a short pause, the teacher continues.]* That's the difference. What is in—what is good comes from God. Everything else comes from the ego. What is good comes from God. So, if God is in it, you can only experience the good. And if your titanic egos are in it, you can only experience the opposite. So, put your ego in, have your frustrations, your unfulfilled desires, and every—all the other numbers that mental bank accounts have to offer. Do you see that, [Student O]?

Yes, sir.

Or put God in it and experience the good. Now if you put mental dictates and all your prejudice in, you're going to have the opposite. So, if you want good, then you must have value for truth more than anything else. All right, thank you, [Student S]. Now it's your chance, [Student O].

. . . tape very much. Ah— [A few words are difficult to transcribe.]

What was your experiences with it? Are you playing it daily, [Student O]?

Constantly.

Good for you.

Right now.

Good.

The tape, the tape, kind of, well, more than likely, it fits everything else that I have been receiving here. And the only immediate effect that I've, I feel, from the tape, playing the tape, is that, kind of, the forms, the mental forms that want to take control, because they had control so long, they kind of just lie back and let you go off in a trance or, so to speak, they let . . . some other forms have their way. And then they lie back and the minute that you are not directing your thoughts constantly, they sneak in and do their number.

They sure do, don't they, [Student O]? *[The teacher laughs as he responds.]*

Right.

They've been doing it all along anyway to everyone; so don't feel bad. Go ahead, [Student O].

But because of the light that's on them, that's shined up on them now, they're, they're more subtle. And they're, they're more . . . [The recorder may have shut off.]

Now don't you find that that section, "Your purpose of being is freedom from what has been"—how do they like that section?

The "freedom from what has been"?

Yeah, like, like the thought a minute ago. Or the experience at church or go down the list. *[The teacher laughs.]* How do they like that part?

Ah, they—well, I, I tell them like this—

What do they say to you?

What do they say?

Yes.

They don't say anything.

They don't say anything. What do they do to you?

They just sit and wait. [Many students laugh loudly.]

Waiting there for their opportunity to do their number, right? Ah, see? Oh, how clever. They [are] clever little things, aren't they?

Very much.

Uh-huh. Then, when they get a chance, all hell breaks loose, doesn't it?

Yes, sir.

Then you feel all frustrated and all mad and angry and upset and disturbed and discordant and brrrrrr! Everything bad's happening outside, right?

Well, everything, the things [that] are happening, that, it's more or less—well, I'd like to speak about today right after church.

That's good because that's a has-been. That's wonderful, [Student O]. Let's, let's take care of that has-been.

OK.

But let's not forget our purpose of being is freedom from that which has been, as we're discussing it. Go right ahead, [Student O].

Right.

Good.

I was aware that, that I should have asked you—or what—the thought did come to my mind that I should have asked you. But I also was aware that, that you knew that the thought came to my mind.

I was. That's why I was so furious I couldn't do anything. *[The teacher laughs.]* Because the Spirit had to grant you—don't you see, [Student O], you are not treated any different than [Student R]. Now [Student R] was allowed to do his numbers in twelve plus years in this organization, but not to the point of ever causing this ship to sink. He was allowed to do his numbers. He was allowed to go against the light of reason in his consciousness. He *was* allowed that. He was granted that right, you see?

So, I informed him today when he was upset over your upset at church, I said—when it was reported—I said, "Now just a minute, who is running this organization? Your ego? My ego? [Student O's] ego? Whose ego is running it? No ego is running it. You were granted the right to do your ego number. [Student O] is granted the same right. Because if [Student O] is not granted that right, then we have partiality. [Student O] will not grow. He must be given the opportunity that the Light states he shall be given. And no more. But he must be given the opportunity." You saw that, didn't you? Because, you see, how you help a person is to relate with the numbers they have done: to see if they have grown in tolerance to understand the way this school really operates. Don't you see that, [Student B]?

We have ex-students that were allowed to do their numbers. The Spirit is very well aware of it. I personally don't appreciate a lot of the tolerance that the Spirit has, but *my* duty is to go along with it because I've made that agreement, you see?[26]

So, I know you had the thought, [Student O], but you didn't speak. Go ahead. Go ahead. *[After a short pause, the teacher continues.]* Yes, it's my job to be aware.

Yes.

It is not my job to go against the Light. And that's one thing I can say in all honesty I have not done, and I'm not about to do. Go ahead, [Student O].

So—

You went ahead.

I went ahead. And I, I done what I did. And—

No problem.

I realized what level I was in. And, and the level that was in control that was doing what it was doing.

Yeah, those things were doing their number with you.

Yeah. Retaliation and revenge. [The teacher laughs.] *I realized when I, when it, when it was happening.*

You're quite human, [Student O].

Right.

That's what they call human.

Uh-huh.

Ahh. *[The teacher sighs.]*

And—

But didn't you, from the experience, gain a little bit of growth, [Student O]?

From the experience?

Yeah.

Yes, I, I, yes, I gained some experience.

No, growth, [Student O]. *[The teacher and many of the students laugh loudly.]* We all know you had the experience, [Student O]. I'm talking about growth, the effect of the effort.

You have—don't you feel you've grown a little bit? I know you have. You demonstrate it. You're able to discuss it without collapsing there. Go ahead, [Student O].

OK. I gained some growth from the experience.

Uh-huh.

I probably—well, tolerance, gaining tolerance is growth.

Tolerance of yourself, right, [Student O]?

Yeah, that's what it is. And—

Isn't that encouraging?

Yes, but I have, the outlook I have about it is the Light, the Light is going [to] accomplish its purpose because—

Definitely. Absolutely. Absolutely.

—I mean, you can, you can make it easier or you can make it—

On yourself.

Right.

Right, [Student O]. *[The teacher laughs joyfully.]*

And—

You got the message, [Student O], in that respect.

Yes, I don't, I don't have any problem with the Light. I mean, in, in that in accepting what it has to say or—

What's the demonstration, [Student O]? You been with us quite a while now.

What's the demonstration?

Yes.

Ah—

Do you feel in any way that the Light operates in a prejudicial way?

No. If I did, I wouldn't be here.

Good for you.

As a matter of fact, I know it, I know it doesn't. And it has demonstrated that repeatedly. That's why the, the Light—I wouldn't say I love the Light. I say I have the utmost respect for the Light because it has demonstrated repeatedly that there's no prejudice. And if there's anybody that knows prejudice, I do know it.

I do, too, [Student O]. Believe me.

I know you do. And that's—yeah, without a doubt, I mean, I have no problem with that, I mean, in so far as, I mean, it has made me believe, you know, in the law and stop and realize, you know, just what law is. And the, the main thing I have been working with recently is the direction of my energy in, in so far as the things I really key in, in so far as what's manifested in my life every day. And, and—

I'd like to ask one thing, [Student O]. Very important.

Yes.

Is your car a '56 or '57?

It's a '58.

Oh, it's a '58? Is that so? Then those fins must have come prior to that car. You know, the fins they used to have on the sides. Those sharp fins.

Fifty-seven.

Was—when did the fins come up?

I remember them coming in after that car, Richard. [Student H offers.]

The fins came *after* that.

I can draw it for you. [Student H continues.]

No, that's all right. I know exactly what it looks like. *[Many students laugh.]* You don't have to draw it. I see it very clearly in front of me. So that's a '58.

Right. [Student O responds.]

So, the fins came in '59?

Right. [Student H confirms.]

Ah, ha! OK. That settles that. Fine. OK. All right, [Student O]. *[Again, many students laugh loudly.]* Nice car. Yes, it's a very nice car, [Student O].

Uh-huh.

Give it a nice polish job.

Yes, sir.

Yeah.

So—

It's treating you well, isn't it? The automobile, I mean.

So far.

[The teacher laughs loudly.] How about being a little positive, [Student O]? Good God, it's your car. All right, go ahead, [Student O].

OK.

[The teacher laughs loudly again.] Huh?

What—

Nice-looking car, [Student O].

As, as you all know, I just accepted that car the other day.

I understand that, [Student O]. I—why, of course, I understand that. Nice-looking car.

Thank you.

Has a little class.

Thank you.

Take care of it; so it'll take care of you. Yes, go ahead, [Student O].

Right. So, as I said, I'm working on, well, I'm working with . . .

Energy.

. . . energy. And that's, that's, I mean, that's probably—all of it—the direction of energy and it has repeatedly shown itself time after time. And now it's just a matter of, for us, trying to gain some kind of control over your—over the, over the . . .

Mind.

. . . mind.

[Student O], I guarantee you: you listen to your affirmation—let it play constantly—and you be rest assured, it is an instrument of Light through which you will pause [and say], "Oh, no." And you will say, "What is this foolishness in my head?" And then you will grow and say, "This is my head. No good comes from this. What's the matter with me? That, I'm not going to have in my consciousness. I am in control of this mind of mine. This mind is a vehicle. It is not me. I have no good coming from these dictates from that realm." You see? You talk to yourself. You see? You become aware. And then you feel real clean for a few moments. Whoops! There it goes again. And then, you keep hearing it—ah! And you get the reminder. You see? It's called repetition is the law through which change is made possible.

Now, here we've come to a school of Light. Without change, there's no evolution; the purpose of being here is not served. So, change is guaranteed. The only upset that we have is not making the effort to be consciously aware of where the attention is, for that's where the energy is going, and we are making deposits in mental banks that return unto us with nothing but unfulfilled desires and frustrations. Now, that's not the purpose of being here, is it?

No, it's not.

See? So, you're very wise, [Student O]. And try to tell yourself this great truth: it's your mind; there is no problem in controlling it. It is a matter of constant awareness of it. See? Because, you see, they wait and do their number when you're off guard. Isn't that true?

Yes, sir.

Now, when [Student O] gets off guard and he's not aware of his thoughts, like anyone else, they do their number. The thing is, the purposes of this great affirmation is to so reprogram [the mind] that they don't even get a chance to do their number. See? They can wait 'til hell freezes over because hell will be freezing by the time they get to do their number on you if you stay on guard. Hmm? OK?

Very much.

And [Student M], how was your experience? Thank you, [Student O].

Thank you.

Uh-huh.

Well, at first, it was real nice hearing it all the time. [Student M begins.]

Yes?

And then it started being increasingly irritating.

Irritation wakes the soul. That's critically important that you have those irritation experiences. Yes.

Because it will be playing in the house and it would be playing in the car. [A few students laugh.] *And playing in the house and playing in the car. And everywhere I went, it would be playing.*

Yes.

But what I realized is when I get to work, I would be so aware of how much I'd be in self that—like, everyone around me would be talking about themselves . . . [It is difficult to transcribe her last few words.]

It's constant. The bombardment's unreal.

I thought, "My God, is that what I'm like?"

Yes, yes, [Student M]. That's why you're here.

I thought—

You become aware.

I know.

The first thing we're able to see is something outside.

Yes.

Then we can see it nice and clear.

Yeah.

Every other word is self.

Yeah, it's true.

Every other thought is self. To the point—it gets to the point that every thought is self; every word is self. Isn't it a wonderful awakening?

It's wonderful!

That's what I deal with here. *[Some students laugh.]* It's not pleasant to be around, is it, [Student M]?

No, it really isn't.
It isn't pleasant, is it?
No.
You don't like to be around a person that can think [of] nothing but themself. Self, self, self, self, self, self, self. Everything's self-related. Isn't that true?
It's true.
It's repulsive to be around, isn't it?
It really was no fun.
[The teacher laughs loudly.] You're waking up. You're waking up, [Student M]. Your self is terribly irritated that you've got to listen to somebody else's constant self-tape! Nobody wants to be around it. All right. Because—don't you understand?—that's tempting their self [and their self] isn't getting a chance to express. And it's very irritating. *[Student M laughs.]* And sooner or later, the soul wakes up. Thank you, [Student M]. A wonderful experience. *[A few students laugh.]*

The first thing with some, you see, you must realize, it'll just shut it off. It [the form in control] won't listen to it anymore. That's when it needs it the most, because the thing that's controlling the mind is really doing its number. Go ahead, [Student G], you're next.

Well, I found a recorder at home that played the music.
And the message, [Student G]?
And the message.
Good. Good for you, [Student G].
And I listened to it all day yesterday.
And how'd you feel?
Well, I felt not too good. [Many students laugh.]
Was that when you broke the cake, [Student G]?
Ah, no, the cake, ah . . .
Did you—didn't you have to replace the cake?
I had to do one layer over because it just would not—I couldn't find my timer. [The teacher laughs joyfully and very loudly.] *It*

was absolutely—when I got to a higher level [of consciousness] later, it could have bitten me. It was just sitting right there. I could not find it, and I let one layer just totally over bake.

Ahh . . .

And had to go out and—

[Again, the teacher laughs loudly and joyfully.] All the way from Forest Knolls?

[I] had go to three stores.

Three stores!? *[The teacher speaks as he laughs.]*

Yes.

They did their number; they were so furious with you.

They did.

Go ahead, [Student G].

The interesting thing was—

It's wonderful. Are you listening to your tape?

It didn't bother me about the purpose of being. That was very soothing. But when I tried to learn the affirmation, I could never remember the line about self-thought.

Oh. *[Some students laugh.]*

[Student G says something, but it is difficult to transcribe.]

Hold the conversation, [Student G]. I'm going to the bathroom. I definitely want to hear this. *[The teacher laughs.]*

*****

"Foreign to this environment," it refused to accept. Go ahead. That was the point that you were at. *[The teacher laughs again.]*

. . . calmly. And I, I had it playing constantly and then I would [The teacher laughs as Student G speaks and it is difficult to transcribe a few of her words.] *. . . it wasn't—I, I didn't even hear the music at times. And would bring myself back and I would, I did talk to myself, that these are only forms of creation—*

[The microcassette recorder paused because it did not register Student G's words.]

—true. It isn't, [Student G].

It really—

It isn't.

And then, after I ruined that layer— [The teacher laughs again and it is difficult to transcribe a few words.] *I said, "OK, now look, it, it just—I have to give it to God. I just have to at this point because I won't finish."*

That's true. That's very true. [And] on the anniversary of your church, [Student G].

And it's got to be right. So, I guess at that point, I started coming up [from lower levels of consciousness]. And then, after I did my . . . affirmation along with you—

[The microcassette recorder again paused because it did not register the student's words.]

"You are in a controlled spiritual environment." You see, that's the thing, [Student G]. That word, "controlled," that really bugs some of our levels of consciousness. But you [have] got to understand: it's inside of you that is—Go ahead, [Student G].

Ah . . .

And you tried saying the affirmation?

And I did. And, and that helped me to concentrate on it and it helped a great deal.

Yes, because, you see, you gave life-giving energy within your consciousness to it. You gave life-giving energy.

Now [Student R] knows, I play it when I take my walk in the morning after breakfast. And I say it to myself as it's playing on the tape. Don't I, [Student R]? I just keep on saying [it]. And it's amaz—because, you see, it will free you from those realms. It will—it literally frees you from those realms if you will stick with it. Then there are times you could, "Oh!" You see, you could just phsst! *[The teacher makes a sound that is difficult to transcribe, but seems to suggest throwing the tape of the affirmation away.]*

The thing is, this is why I'm recording—you see, first of all, you've got to get it into your conscious[ness] [until] you know it by heart. Then the next step is to play the music with a more subtle—I've been recording it much softer, [the volume of the spoken affirmation], see? So then the time comes where the message comes through, but the physical ears don't hear it. But you will find that the mind will be working with it and if you turn the volume up, you're right on queue. See? That's the phases to go through. But *first* you must get it into your consciousness so when the music plays, you be rest assured, you'll even have the pauses because the mind will relate through the laws of association. And so, as you're hearing the music only, the other is taking place within the consciousness and you're keeping yourself freed from that stuff.

It's wonderful that we have evolved to this point to be able to have that, [Student B]. It is. And everyone. But, [Student G], you see what those things can do, like [Student O] is becoming aware. That's a wonderful step. It's only a painful step to so-called creation. But we're not here for creation. We have not come to the Light for creation, see? And to permit our minds to dictate, from demonstration, that we have come here for creation is absolutely a house divided, and we can't make it, you see? You see, we guarantee the day, if we permit our minds to demonstrate that we have come here for creation, we have established the law that guarantees we shall leave for creation. That's what's at stake. *[After a short pause, the teacher repeats himself.]* That's what's at stake.

This is why temples of Light, they will not allow any of that. They will not allow any creation attachments in the temples, you see? You see how critical that is? Because they know the law. They *know* that a person is going against their purpose of being in the Light. And when you go against your purpose for being in the Light, you guarantee to lose the Light for you! See? That's how come I have ex-students: because they tempted to go against their purpose for being in the school of truth. They have creation out there. That's where it always must be kept. It does not work in the Light, for they go against the Light in their consciousness. Does anybody not understand that? Is there anyone who doesn't understand that, [Student S] and everyone? You go against your purpose of being here and you guarantee your exit.

Now, you spend most of your time in creation; that's where you have to make your separation. You have to talk to yourself: "I'm going to the temple of Truth and Light. I'm going there for the purpose of freeing myself from creation. I got to work my tail off in consciousness because I'm totally loaded with that stuff. I'm spending so many of my hours in creation." See? It's like—[Student M] says she's just waking up that those people she works with, the only conversation they carry on is self. Well, the only way she's become aware of it, is [by] becoming aware of what her mind's doing to her. See? Then she looks around [and says], "Oh, my God, this is disgusting." Isn't it rather disgusting?

Uh-huh. [Student M replies.]

That they can think about nothing but themself? That the world is so small and they're so prejudiced that the only thing they can think about is themself? Oh, my God. Well, [Student G], I'm glad you had that experience.

Oh, it was divine. [Student G replies.]

Well, I guarantee you, the more you play that tape, the more you're going to wake up, in spite of your own creation. It's guaranteed. I play it daily! Go ahead, [Student H].

When I was playing it this week...

Yes.

... I found myself reacting to the part where it says, "Be alert."

Be, be, be alert.

Yeah.

Be awake.
Be awake.
Got to be awake first. "Be awake, be aware, be alert."
Right.
And what did that number do to you?
It sounded like, like I was sitting in a classroom and a real strict teacher was using a yardstick, you know—
Discipline.
Yes.
[Student H] doesn't like discipline. Those things that control [Student H] don't want any discipline.
That's right.
Better license then, [Student H]? *[Student H and other students laugh.]* Uh-huh. Uh-huh. Go ahead, [Student H].
And I guess I found myself continuously reacting to that, to that line.
To the "Be awake?"
Right.
"Be awake, be aware, be alert." Uh-huh.
And then . . .
What is it you don't like about discipline, those things? Do you know?
What, what it tells me is—
What does it tell your mind?
It, it says that, "Oh, I'll be disciplined, but on my time, when I choose to be. Don't you tell me when." That's, that's the tone.
Uh-huh. Uh-huh.
And my way or not at all.
And when those things say your way, you already have the experience that that's a very fickle level of consciousness.
Right.
For "our way" is dependent upon the forms that rise up to take control at any given moment in keeping with our own weaknesses. See, a person, they look around and they decide or

judge, "I'm going to do that. That's what I want to do." Well, that's *that* level at that moment. And after it does its number or sometimes even during the process of doing its number, some other level takes control. *[The teacher laughs joyfully.]* So, is that truly us?

Life teaches us already—and demonstrates—that's not us at all. One minute this thing is in control of our mouth and our mind; and the next moment, that thing is in control. And we don't know because we haven't made the effort, and we're trying to make the effort to consciously make a decision and therefore stick with it. So, you find people to be good starters and terrible finishers.

People who are good starters and poor finishers reveal to the whole world they have no control of the forms that are using them. They are total victims of these things that rise up. Wouldn't you agree, [Student O]?

Sure would.

So, they start on something and you see they don't finish it. And they don't get it finished unless someone is standing over them with a sledge hammer to make sure that they do finish it. And what that someone has to do is to pay the price of all those different forms and levels of consciousness that are screaming to do their number. You see?

Now this is why people, supposedly, have adversity to responsibility. What they're really telling you, very simply, is, "I have no control over my mind. I sold out long ago to anything that rises up to take control of me. I am the lackey and the victim of those things. And I don't know when they're going to rise up. I don't know what they're going to do. Therefore, responsibility, I don't want anything to do with." Do you understand that, [Student H]?

Yes.

OK. And God forbid if it's called *personal* responsibility. Go ahead, [Student H]. *[After a short pause, the teacher continues.]*

So, those things that have been in control, which is not you, they don't like, "Be awake, be aware, be alert."

As a matter of fact, I was—one time when I was listening to the tape, I happened to be working on a project which I alone had chosen to work on—

One of your levels, yes.

One of my levels, which was really gung ho on this project.

Yes.

Really couldn't wait to get started.

Uh-huh.

And so, here I found myself listening to this tape and being bored with this project, wishing it was over with, you see? I mean, no longer wanting it around.

That proves to you a different level is in control. Does this sound familiar to you, [Student R]? Pardon?

Oh, yes. [Student R responds and Student H laughs.]

Thank you, [Student H]. You're continuing to listen so you can awaken?

Oh, yes.

[Student P].

When I first heard it, I was, like . . .

[The microcassette recorder again paused because it did not register the student's words.]

—you are. You are in a different space. Go ahead—at those times, yes.

And then, what happened was, I went off and started working on—

[At this moment side A of the second microcassette ends. The conversation continues as the tape is flipped to record on side B.]

*****

—*that level rose up.*

Yes.

And I thought of every self-thought I could think of. [Many students laugh.] *And I just kept telling it to shut up [and] go back to hell. And, and I started saying the affirmation out loud and that worked real well. And I calmed down. And then after about a half hour [or] an hour I finally came—*

An hour later. Uh-huh.

Yeah. And then I come up here and I was pretty peaceful.

Yes.

And it's been great when I'm here. And when I listen to it ... [Again, the microcassette recorder paused.] ... *something inspired me and I left it off. And I just totally sabotaged myself. When I'm listening* ...

Do you know what that reveals to you?

Well, that I don't have that much control over my forms when I'm not here.

Yes, but don't you know what that reveals to you? *[After a short pause, the teacher continues.]* What do you suppose happens that when you're here listening to it, you don't have all those problems and when you're away from here listening to it, you do have those problems? What does that tell you, [Student P]?

Well, I'm in a controlled environment here.

Thank you. What does it tell you, [Student S]? *[After a short pause, the teacher continues.]* Does it not tell you that the forms themselves have made a choice based upon past experiences? [Student R], what does it tell you?

It says they've come to an understanding that while she's here, they will cool it, while they're there, they're in charge.

Uh-huh. Uh-huh. But, don't you see, you can't be here all the time. You see? But then, [Student P's] been with us ten years, hasn't she? So, after ten years, it's very rare they dare cross the line. Because they've had so many experiences of what happens to them if they dare. You see, it takes a lot of experience and a lot of energy. That's what happens, [Student P]. So, you see, you must realize they've made a judgment. They're very prejudiced. *[Student P and others laugh.]* They've made a judgment that when you're not here, you'll do any number that they want to do. You are totally their lackey, completely and wholly. See? And if you don't do what you've always done for them, they'll leave your gas cap [at the gas station] and they'll do whatever other numbers they want to do. But we're in this school to be free. That's our purpose, you see? Now don't you find that helpful, [Student P]?

Yeah, I really do.

Hmm?

But I did have one of the best weeks I've ever had . . . I felt, I mean . . . [Again, the microcassette recorder paused.]

Because of your effort *[Student P continues to talk, but it is difficult to transcribe her words.]* to gain control over them. That's why you had such a good week. Because of your effort, [Student P]. See? It's a constant effort.

Your mind is in a constant process of broadcasting and dictating. That's the way the mind is. So, you have an intelligent choice to make: either you program something in there that is beneficial to you or you just continue to lie down and be lazy and serve them, see? That's the choice to make. OK, thank you, [Student P].

[Student B], I'm glad you're smiling. *[The teacher laughs loudly and joyfully.]* No problem, [Student B], you got to hear all of the others. The experiences are rather similar.

Yeah.

So, you—

I got my tape Thursday night.

That's right. Yes, I remember.

Well—

And you liked it. I remember.

I loved it.

Yes, you did.

I, I took it home and I decided, well, I'll play—I want to learn this and memorize this . . . put it in the computer [of my mind] in the program. And I put it on—all night I played it, you know. [A few words are difficult to transcribe.]

Wonderful, [Student B]!

So, Friday, I went to work. [I] typed it. Really worked hard trying to get it into the program.

Because the Light inside of you has great value for it. Just like everyone who's here, really.

I, I really liked it.

Something happened inside, [Student B].

Yeah.

Go ahead.

Well, Friday was an unusual day. My last attachment left home.[27]

Uh-huh. I know, [Student B]. It's all right.

Ah—

You're getting free.

I thought, "Boy, I got this great tape." [After a short pause, Student B continues.] *I wouldn't listen to it.* [Many students laugh.]

They wouldn't let you, [Student B].

But part of it, I realize, that first line, "You are in a controlled spiritual environment," I would say that fifty thousand times. Just over and over. Couldn't remember the rest of it.

It's all right.

But that part I could remember. And the part, "thoughts of self are foreign to this environment."

You got the essence of it, [Student B]!

It would come up and I would just, you know—they sure are cornered. [The teacher laughs loudly.] *Then I realized that every time I thought of my attachment, I was really thinking of me.*

That's true.

And it was the first time I ever realized that.

But isn't that a phenomenal freedom, that truth?
Yeah.
It isn't—
It was—
The attachment is [to] [Student B].
Yes, it was.
It's got a different hangar on it. You put a tag on it. But it's not the person. It's [Student B].
It was! Yes!
I know. I know. I'm trying to teach—
And so, every time I thought "Thoughts of self," thoughts of self have won . . . saying over and over. And it did help me. [A few words are difficult to transcribe.]
You got through it, didn't you, [Student B]?
I got through it. I had a hell of a day.
But you got through it! *[Student B continues to speak, but her words are difficult to transcribe.]* They battled you.
Yeah.
But you had something to work with so that you—you see, the thing is, the battle isn't a week or a month. Oh, they'll try again.
Sure.
Sure. Now, see, this is how they operate: whenever, through the laws of association, anything that triggers the computer to open the door of that attachment, they'll swarm in by the thousands because they're really PO'ed. Do you understand that, [Student B]?
I do.
So you can be at work, you can be walking down the street, you can be doing anything that in any way is associated with that and those things—you [have] got to be on guard. Because—phssst! See? It's like [Student S]—when she hears the tape and it says, "The purpose of being is freedom from what has been," she has them all come to the front. But then, you see, if you

don't have that, you can never control them. Either you declare your divinity and you are greater than that which you have created or you're the lackey of it. And that's the simple choice to make in life.

So, the attachment—and that's a wonderful freedom, that awakening—the attachment is not something out there. It never was. It's the attachment to self. It's the self-love. You know, it's very difficult. I work with students trying to get them to see over these years: "This has nothing to do with that person. That has nothing to do out there." My God, open your eyes! It's your love of self! You've got a name tag on it, but the only thing you're talking about is your own love of your self. That's a hard awakening to make. But once you make it, you be absolutely free from it because it's totally in your control. It's entirely within your consciousness. And you can eliminate it or you can continue to serve it.

That's where it is, [Student G]. It's not the child. It's not the wife. It's not the husband. It's nothing, it's no thing out there. The door is opened through your love of self. It's in your consciousness. You've given it a name. And your love of self demands and orders you to serve it. See? There's where the problem really is. To think any other way is nothing but to deny the demonstrable truth of personal responsibility. Wouldn't you agree, [Student B]?

[There is no audible response from Student B.]

I tell you it works. And it works beyond a shadow of any doubt. You see, when we awaken that it is nothing more and nothing less than our love of self, that we call by some name, the first thing the self-love forms do is go discouraged, you see, heart-broken. Because that's their number, don't you see? That's how they stay in control. Because, you see, what is really happening is they are feeding the entity of self-pity. The pity of self is the love of self. Good God Almighty!

So, thoughts that bring discouragement, thoughts that bring pity, do nothing but feed the love of self. So, if you've got a name for it, you say, "Oh, my attachment. Oh, my heartbreak." All you're doing is loving your self. That's all it is. Now you know I've taught that for years, [Student S].

Uh-huh.

The same truth. It's just this great love of self. And I've tried to teach students, "Wake up. Put God where this love of self is and you'll be totally free. And the goodness of life you will experience." That wonderful experience of joy will be yours any moment that *you* permit it to be. That's, that's a real step, [Student B]. That awakening is a real step. And it's a hard step to make, but it's the demonstrable truth. And your freedom will reveal that and has revealed it, your moments of freedom.

[Student B makes a comment that is difficult to transcribe.]
Pardon?
Saturday was better. Sunday was good.
You see? And tonight is good.
Yes.

Now you [have] got to remember, in this school these things are revealed: the Light is cast upon them. So, they're right up front there, see? They're waiting to do their number. So, you better stay on guard. See? You better stay awake, aware, and alert because, in this school, the purpose of the Light is to shine.

You see, look, we talk about the shadows. That which has passed is a shadow. All right. Now what is a shadow? A shadow is an obstruction to the flow of the Light of the goodness of life. That's what it is; it is a reflection. A shadow is a reflection of an obstruction to the Light. Now does everybody understand that? Because take a look, and the Light shines [and] you see the shadow of that which is in front of it. All right? So, when you permit your mind to place its attention and its energy upon the shadow, which is the reflection of an obstruction that *you* have created in consciousness, through your self-love, then you must pay the price and the suffering thereof. It is a terrible waste of life. A terrible waste of life.

Just think, you're playing with a reflection of an obstruction. You're not even playing with the obstruction! If you were playing with the obstruction, you could move it out of the way of the Light! But, don't you understand, you're not even—you don't even have your hands on the obstruction. You've only got your hands on the shadow. Did you ever try to grab a shadow? *[In another room, Student E begins to cry.]* Go ahead—sure, [Student O]. Did you ever try to move a shadow, [Student B]?

You see, don't you understand, by entertaining, which is your love of self, these shadows of life, events that have passed, you are trying to manipulate and to move the unmanipulatable, the unmovable. Because it is only a shadow, which is a reflection of an obstruction to the Light—your own Light. You don't even have the obstruction; so how can you move it? Think of that! And they call that—I don't want to say that—they call those things attachments. Oh, oh, oh! Yes, [Student S]. Oh!

If it's only a reflection, what is the actual obstruction and where does it go?

First of all, you have permitted within your consciousness the entrance of an obstruction to the Light of the Divine. That's called creation. You have created an obstruction, all right? Now you have permitted this in your consciousness. For example, you say—let's take an example. You look around in a store and suddenly you see an object that you desire, right? In your senses, you have created possession of that object, all right? You've created that in your consciousness. Now, through that process of creation in your consciousness, you now move the physical body and you go through what is necessary to pay the price to get that object, all right? Now this object in a physical world, you now move into *your* physical world. And you set it—say, it's a cup that you desire. And there's the cup. *[The teacher moves his coffee cup.]* All right? Now your mind now possesses this cup. It has made the judgment you paid for it and you own it. All right? First mistake. Man owns nothing. He is loaned everything, but he owns nothing. But the—that mind—you can't tell the mind that. The mind has made its judgment: it now owns the cup. All right?

Now something happens and the cup is destroyed, but not by your judgments or conscious choice, all right? You've established laws—but that takes personal responsibility, another whole ballpark—and the cup becomes destroyed. You then experience various emotional reactions. Is that not correct?

[There is no audible response.]

Fine. Now those various emotional reactions to the destruction of your cup, you will experience every time you see a cup that's similar. Every time, through the laws of association, that you think of your cup, you will continue throughout eternity to experience that frustration, that upset, that anger, and everything that the water center has to offer, for that's where it comes from, you see.

You see, without water, there's no creation. That is the law. That is not only a spiritual law, that's a physical law. See, that which is a spiritual law is a mental law and a physical law. They have different expression. For there is only one law that governs body, mind, and soul. There is only one law. That law is the Law of God. It is infallible.

Now, so here in this school of Light, we, in our ignorance, forgetting temporarily our purpose of being here, attach our self. And when we do that, through our self-love and our desires, we guarantee the Light to shine over that in keeping with the laws we have established so we can see what our love of self is doing to us.

Now, anyone would say, "Now, that's really stupid for a person to be upset over a cup that they once owned, years later." But a cup is a form. And form is creation. And creation, we are controlled by through our love of self. Now without the love of self, creation has no control over you. Only through your love of self are you the victim of creation. Without the love of self, creation becomes your servant, that which it has been designed for.

But you have made, some of you, at sometimes, now and then, you have made creation your master and must pay the price. When you free yourself from the love of self, you will no longer be the victim of creation. Creation is a playpen; choose wisely when you enter.

You see, if you come in from a realm of reason and light, you say, "All right. So, I am now tempted. This is a weakness of mine. I want to play with creation." Well, at least you'd have enough sense to play with the creation, the obstruction to the Light, that is something you can handle. You wouldn't say, "I am now tempted. I will play with creation, that is, the shadow of creation." And try to manipulate or to hold a shadow. How can you hold a shadow? You go right through it. That's not possible to hold a shadow. And so, people who, through self-love, are trying to hold shadows, that is, obstructions that no longer exist, only the shadow thereof, are really ruining their lives. Does anybody not see that?

Now say, for example, you're attached to—say a mother is attached to her daughter. All right. Well, the daughter, she's moved. All right? So, the mother can no longer physically sit her down or physically do anything with her. But what does a mother do? Some mothers, in their stupidity, they play with the shadow, the shadow! The obstruction no longer exists, but the shadow is there. And so, they try to sit the shadow down. They try to talk to the shadow. I mean, it is pure insanity. Would you not agree?

Yes. [Several students respond.]

Oh! The obstruction has gone out of the light of your consciousness. Only the shadow remains. And you're trying to manipulate and to control a shadow. You don't even have the obstruction itself anymore. For your duty has been completed.

Do you understand that, [Student B], as a mother attached—past attached?

[If Student B responded, it is difficult to transcribe her response.]

Now, then those forms that control that realm, working through the obstruction that is now only a shadow in a person's consciousness, they start doing their number. They have desires. And they look in the universe in the mental realm. They have access to everything the mind has to offer: all the experiences and etc. They call on the telephone and they do their little number. And the mother or the parent starts playing with the shadow again, only the shadow. And they pull the strings to fill their selfish desires. Tell me if that's freedom, let alone truth.

There we are. How simple life is. Those who play with the shadow must ever suffer the price. And it's very high, because it's only a shadow they're playing with.

It's just like, say that something enters our life, through the laws we've established, and something leaves our life, but we don't want it to leave. Well, we have a conscious choice: we have the shadow; we can play with it; we can go crazy by it, through our self-love, or we can free our self from it. That's the choice we have to make. Yes.

If, if life really isn't real, a reality, like, if it's an illusion anyway, just taking place in our own head, what's the difference between a physical cup and a shadow of the cup— [Student S remarks.]

It's all the diff—

Does it really matter?

Yes, it does matter because we make it matter through the laws of identification and self-love. See, we make it matter. You see, that's like telling [Student G] [her daughter] doesn't exist. Try to tell her that and see what your answer will be.

She really doesn't exist, does she?

She exists to the realm of illusion that you identify with.
OK.
Yes.
Isn't it belief that gives it form? [Student R asks.]
Of course, it is. Look, why can some people pass through the wall? How does this work? How are they able to dematerialize? How are they—how is the Spirit able to materialize? I have all of those experiences in my computer.[28] Why, it's very simple: through the Law of Identification. Look, that which you place your attention upon you have a tendency to become. Now that that you truly are is the Divine Life Power itself. So, if you direct, through your identification, through your attention, this divine life Energy, then, through that direction, shall it be made manifest. That is the law of all creation. Do you understand that, [Student B] and [Student S] and everyone? That's how the law works.

So, as you, here, place your attention upon self-love and all that it has to offer, the shadows take control—that which you cannot use constructively.

This is a very valuable school.

Yes. Belief is the instrument that you use, when faith is the power of God. Faith. You see? Look, haven't you noticed a change in the church in the past couple of Sundays? Well, let's keep it that way.

You see, as this self-love, through an awakening of the affirmation, as you gain more control over where your consciousness is while you're here, then I have available to me more energy to do more work to keep your church and school open. That's the simple, mathematical facts. So, as you gain more—make more effort, consciously, to gain more control over your love of self and all that it has to offer—those shadows—then the energy that I have been using this past year to keep those things under control so there's any school for you at all, I can now, once again, use to keep the church, the supply, and the doors open. Now it's that simple. It works for the church, and it'll work for your own lives, but you have to make the effort.

You can do nothing but play with a shadow. You can't lift it! You can't push it! You can't do *anything* with it but dissipate beautiful, intelligent life Energy! That's all you can do with a shadow. And the only thing that keeps a shadow in our consciousness is the degree and extent of our love of self. That's the only thing that keeps it there.

You're very fortunate, [Student B], to have that awakening.

Thank you.

And that tape—I've told you people right in the beginning—that tape and that affirmation is so important. Some of you will awaken and know the great importance of that, no matter what your head is telling you while you're listening and speaking it. It'll tell you. Because it came from the Light to serve the Light. And you are the Light, not the shadow.

So, you just switch around these crazy beliefs. You are not the shadow. You are the Light. That's why you're able to do something with your life. If you were but the shadow, you could do nothing with your life because no one can move a shadow. You are the Light. You are not the shadow.

Now between you and the Light is the obstruction that is created by the love of self. That's all. See, if you look at your skin and you love your skin, then your skin receives all this energy flowing through you. [If] you see a blemish there, you guarantee another one there. [If] you see two now, you guarantee a third up here. You now see three, the next thing you know, there's thirty thousand. For you are directing divine, intelligent Energy just to your skin. Now, if you take another part of your anatomy, maybe your toe, and you start thinking about your toe. Well, then you take a look and say, "It's too big a toe. No, it's too small a toe. How come I merited a crooked toe?" And go on down the list. You see, it's insanity. You see, it's pure insanity.

And yet we are here to wake up and stop playing with these shadows and this foolishness. It's up to us. [Student U]—thank you, [Student B]—it's your turn.

I, personally, really like the tape.

Uh-huh.

And I just got it yesterday. And I listened to it from the house to Guasco's [grocery store]. And until, apparently, a German opera came on.

How did that get on if you were listening to the tape? *[A student laughs.]*

It's on the tape, I believe.

Oh, that's interesting. How'd that ever get there? Well, bring the tape back. That's really interesting. Go ahead.

The second half is even more interesting.

What else is on the tape?

The assassination of JFK.

Oh, in the equipment, the radio must have got in. The assassination of JKF?

Yes.

Well, why would they have that on the radio? That's interesting. Bring the tape back.

That started it off that— [Many students laugh loudly.]

That's really interesting. [More students laugh loudly.]

Like [Student G's]! [A different student observes.]

That's much better than [Student G's]. Hers just didn't play the music. *[Laughter from the students continues.]* Go ahead. Are you sure it's a tape that I gave you?

I think it is. I mean, I, I—

Well, if you have it here with you—

Yes, I do.

Well, I'm going to have to hear that. Go ahead, [Student O]. I mean, [Student O]. *[Many students laugh.]* Go ahead, [Student U]. Whoo! Go ahead, [Student U].

That, that started— [Students continue to laugh.]

All these strange things happening, [Student O]. *[The students' laughter continues.]* The assassination of JFK. That's a brand-new tape, man. Go ahead. *[There is more laughter from the students.]* A blank tape! Go ahead.

Well, I didn't listen to it while I prepared my brunch [item for the church's Sunday brunch].

Oh, my God. [Another student exclaims.]

I, I left it in the car and—

Ahh.

I said to myself, "Ah, it's just too much work to go out to the car and [it's parked] a block away—

Isn't this interesting.

So, I started it first thing in the morning, when I was driving—well, not the first thing—when I was driving to church.

And what did you hear?

The assassination. [All the students explode with laughter, but Mr. Goodwin does not seem to laugh.] *And I said, "This is incredible! I don't want to listen to this." But I listened to it a little more and then the music came on and the affirmation came on.* [More laughter from the students.] *And I listened to it 'til it ran out. And I was recently having trouble with the control. While I was here [at the temple], listening to it, I was having trouble with the word* control.

Ah, I knew someone was destined to have trouble with the word *control*.

And my brain said, "That's brainwashing!" And I—

That's right. That's right. Talk to [Student R]. Go ahead. He wouldn't dare say it to me, but I know what he said to himself.

I said, "Shit, man, your brain needs washing. [Everyone laughs.]

[The teacher laughs loudly.] Good answer! Good answer, [Student U]. You're waking up. It does need washing. It's pretty dirty.

And that's, really—I haven't listened to it that much that it could—that they've only just started to rise.

Is it on the second part or the first part, this JFK—

The German opera—oh, the JKF is on the beginning of the second side.

And this German opera?

Is on the tail end of the first side.

This is incredible. I—you have it with you?

Shall I get it now?

Yes, you're excused to get it. I'll put it on the system. How in the name of God could the assassination of J.F. Kennedy get on to that new tape? *[Student U leaves to go to his car to retrieve the cassette tape.]* We have the best system in the world.

[Student S makes a comment that is difficult to transcribe.]

I tested the beginning of it. I don't test the endings. Christ, I'd never give you a tape if I had to test the whole damn thing.[29] That's incredible! How could the assassination of J.F. Kennedy get on to a brand-new tape? Isn't that interesting, [Student H]? And he had problems getting his, because he wanted the Nut Cracker Suite. And he finally got it on the Great Classics. Yes, go ahead, [Student S]. Because [Student U] was late getting his. He was the last one to get one because he wanted the full Nut Cracker Suite, if you remember. And I looked up there and I said, "Oh, no, I'm not going to go ahead and record a whole record, then on to tape, then another tape on to another tape, and then do another tape and the other tape and then make him, finally, a tape. I'll never get my work done."[30]

MAY 20, 1984

Class September 27, 1984

[The following teachings were given to the larger group of students who volunteered at the temple Thursday nights.]

All right. We'll start this class here right now.

Oh, that should have come on over there? Fine.

All right. Now perhaps we can get this situation here underway. The reason that this class is being called, for your benefit, is because over 51 percent of the students are proving their need at this time.

Now how does a person prove their spiritual need? And how do they demonstrate it? Well, they prove it and they demonstrate it through a lack of applying the laws that they have already learned. And so, we've reached that point where a sufficient number of our students are demonstrating their great need by not applying the spiritual laws they've already learned.

Now duty, gratitude, and tolerance is the first soul faculty. When we permit our self to place our attention upon the obstructions, there is no possible way of finding the way. So, when we permit our self to establish the Law of Ingratitude, we guarantee the effect of that law. Now how do we demonstrate the Law of Ingratitude? We fail to give life-giving energy to the law through which we can experience the continuity of goodness and supply in our life.

Now let us stop and let us think.

We had a choice example here last Sunday and it granted me a wonderful opportunity, because last Sunday and again on Tuesday, I was sorely tempted by the trap of disappointment.[31] Now I'm sure that you will all agree that disappointment is a terrible trap, considering that one must be in the realm of overidentification with self in order to experience disappointment. Now you think about that. *[After a short pause, the teacher continues.]* And you already know from your own personal experiences, as well as the teachings of this beautiful philosophy, that overidentification with one's self is the most destructive force you will ever, ever encounter; it's known as self-pity. We also know that one cannot experience disappointment unless one directs life-giving, intelligent energy to a judgment. And so, knowing that great truth, I made great effort and did not fall to that weakness known as temptation.

One, at times in their life, finds themself expecting from someone what they have no right to expect, for the only thing that grants us the right to expect anything from anyone is attachment to the fruits of action. And so, when I found myself being tempted by that terrible trap of disappointment on Sunday and, once again, being tempted on Tuesday, I filled my consciousness with the truth that I have spent my life sharing with you as students.

Now specifically what was the disappointment? Now that I have made the effort and I am not tempted by that judgment—because a disappointment can only come from the effects of a judgment. The judgment can only come from an attachment to an experience. Temporarily, for a moment, forgetting that a teacher must give what they have to give and to care less what the student does with it, for to care with what one does with one's efforts in life, to care what someone else does with one's efforts in life is a terrible, terrible path. A terrible path. Brings no good into one's life. And so, I reminded myself, you give what you have to give, you care less what they do with it. Specifically, the situation was, after God and his ministering angels had saved you people over three hundred and thirty some dollars at a bake sale on Sunday morning church, there was not one student of mine that expressed in any way, shape, or form gratitude for all of the effort of God's ministering angels, which I had to work on myself not to enter the trap of disappointment. Because, you see, I realize it's nothing but an error of ignorance. That's all that it is.

Because sometimes we don't seem to understand the angels that bring you this beautiful philosophy have no interest, time, or energy for material substance. They do not live in the Bank of London. They are not interested in any way, shape, or form with the gold of earth. It is the gold of heaven for which they work. And the gold of heaven is known as wisdom. Now that's why we're having this special class because we are losing, at times, our perspective for our purpose of being here.

Now, all of us know that we get out of anything in life exactly what we put into it. And when we permit our mind to think we're getting nothing out of what we think we're putting something into, then pause and ask yourself, What is the Law of Life that is demonstrable?

Now many times you have been given the opportunity to democratically vote on whether or not you would like to have this particular, unique spiritual school available for you. And each time you have voted, your request for it to be open has been honored. Now, you cannot, in life, look at failure and expect success. The Law of Success is dependent upon the first soul faculty, the very first: duty, gratitude, and tolerance. That class, I urge all of you to study again. For whenever you permit your minds to demonstrate the opposite of the Law of Gratitude, you guarantee struggle in your life.

Now we all accept, I'm sure, that God, what we call God, is goodness. The reflection of goodness is known to man as love. So, we permit the experience of love in our consciousness by what we permit ourselves to reflect. Now, for example, a person says they have experienced love and they feel wonderful. Well, what has a person done? A person has permitted their mind to reflect the Goodness or God in themself. You can look at the flower and permit your mind, through control of your mind, to reflect the God or Goodness that is in you; that is known as love. You can look at the dawn, you can look at the sunset, and you can permit your mind, through control of your mind, to reflect the God or Goodness that is in you. To a person who makes the daily effort to control their mind, whatever they view, they will experience love, for through the control of their own mind they reflect the Goodness that is in them by viewing an object in the world around them.

Unfortunately, because, through our ignorance, we have created this reflection of Goodness, reflection of God within us, through a lack of our effort through an error of our own ignorance we experience what we call love, the reflection of the Goodness within us, in very limited ways dictated by early experiences in our life. And unfortunately, we so often now call what is truly lust, we now call love. Now the difference between lust and love is very simple: lust is the experience of the senses from a temporal satisfaction, an excitement of our nervous system, known as a thrill. Unfortunately, through our ignorance, we often now call that lust "love."

Therefore, in this stage of evolution of this student body—and I have mentioned to a few of you students that if you wish, sincerely, to continue to broaden your horizons and to brighten the Light that exists within you, to be the free Spirit that you truly are, to separate what you are from what you think you are, for there is no freedom until you separate you (truth) from creation. And to separate you (truth) from creation, you must first accept that you are not the thought that temporarily rises in your mind. You are not that thought. You are not that emotion. You are not that attitude. You are the creator of that attitude. You are the creator of that experience. You are not that thought. You are not that experience.

Now, where the effort is sorely needed with the students at this time is the separation of truth from creation by making the constant effort to declare the truth: that you are not the thought; that you have, through ignorance, through lack of effort—because lack of effort is true ignorance—through lack of effort, [something] has taken control of your mind. And in so doing you are not experiencing love. You are not experiencing harmony. You are not experiencing the divine abundant flow of Goodness in your life. Because, for a moment of ignorance, the effort is not being made to separate truth from creation.

Now I'm going to give you a few moments for your questions. If you have any, please raise your hand. If you don't, I will continue on. *[After a short pause, the teacher continues.]*

In reference to your school, I would like to say this: no matter what we desire in life, whether it is a school staying open that we may have the privilege and the honor of attending or whether it's a desire for anything else, there are certain requirements to fulfill any desire that we have. And so, in the desire for the school to remain open for us, there are certain requirements; there are certain responsibilities that you, making the request, are duty bound to demonstrate. And it is only right, proper, and fair that you know what is required of *you* in order for *you* to have *your* desire fulfilled. Would you not agree? Therefore, one of the most important requirements is to refrain from demonstrating, within the school, the blatant denials of the very laws that you are learning to apply.

You don't get a graduation certificate from this school. You have no piece of paper when you finish with this school, for this is a school that has no finish. It doesn't have any graduates. For a person to graduate from a school of life would imply that the student is greater than life. We can never be greater than the Light. We can only be an inseparable part of the Light. And whatever is [an] inseparable part of anything is never greater than the thing of which it is an inseparable part. So, there is [are] no diplomas. There is no graduation. There is the continuity and the expansion of one's consciousness.

Now while we're having this class, I know that some of you have stated that you have many questions. I give you, now, that opportunity to ask the many questions that you have. *[After a short pause, the teacher continues.]* Those of you who have many questions, please be kind to ask your questions while we have the moments for them. If you do not feel that you want to ask them at the time allotted, then we will continue on. Yes.

When one is feeling—I believe this is experiencing oneself as creation instead of truth—the feeling of failure, what is most helpful at that time when you, it feels like you failed? And for myself, it's hard to not experience the failure.

Thank you so very much in reference to feeling like a failure or feeling that you failed in anything. It is not possible to experience failure without attachment to the fruits of action. And so, attachment to the fruits of action, known as bondage, offers to us the wonderful, wonderful gift of the emotional trauma known as failure. Now, first of all, a person must be attached to their fruits of action in order to establish in consciousness the judgment that they have failed. A mother ofttimes finds herself attached to the fruit of her womb and experiences, throughout her life, what she calls failure in the rearing of her children. Therefore, to be freed from these experiences of failure, one must make the effort to free themselves from their own attachment to their fruits of action.

One must learn in life to give what you have to give and to care less what the world does with it. If you permit yourself to constantly strive and work to be what someone else wants you to be, then you will find that you have lost yourself and gained only passing images of creation. Does that help with your question?

Now, we all know that, of course, we can't experience that feeling without the attachment, without the judgment from the experience of the attachment, and that is the bondage that it has to offer. When you find yourself entering the realms of overidentification with the self, then all you have to do is to remind yourself what it was like the last time. If the impact was sufficient on your consciousness, then you won't go back down there. You'll put the brake on, and you will redirect your energy, through a control of your mind, to something that will bring you joy. Does that help with your question?

Thank you.

Certainly. You see, it's just like I said to you a little bit earlier. I was sorely tempted by the trap of disappointment. But what would it offer to me? I know what it offers, and I know how the law works; so, I chose not to enter that trap of disappointment, for it offers the judgment of failure and this judgment [and] that judgment; it offers nothing but the panorama of judgments and prejudices and prejudgments. That's all that it offers. There's no good there. And if we will only make the effort to remind our self what it was like the last time and we will take control of our own mind in those moments, we will know that we have come to Earth for a purpose; that it is up to us to fulfill that purpose. And that we have a responsibility to our true being to demonstrate the law through which the world will lighten from the joy of expression. That help with your question?

[Thank you.]

You're welcome. Now we can pause for just a moment. *[The microcassette recorder is paused.]*

*****

Honesty takes a lot longer than three minutes. Now, a person, all people have this type of thinking: wanting to know what their tomorrows are going to be like, whether they're going to be successful in their endeavors, whether or not their marriages are going to work out, whether or not their love affairs are in their best interest and whether or not they're going to express their talents and when will the day come and how long will it be and all these mountains of questions that all minds have.

Everyone has the right to know what tomorrow is going to be for them. That is their right. It is a total deception of the human mind to believe that if God wanted you to know what your tomorrow was to be like, God would reveal it. Because God has already revealed your tomorrow. God has revealed your tomorrow when the lamp of honesty lights your consciousness; because when the light goes on in your consciousness, the effect of honesty with yourself, then what happens [is] you see clearly the laws that you are establishing. And by seeing clearly the laws that you are establishing, you know beyond a shadow of any doubt what the effect of those laws, for you, will be.

Now we can turn it over. *[The teacher instructs the recording technician to turn over the microcassette tape and begin to record on side B.]*

*****

I'll let you watch it because you're quite interested in it. *[The teacher may be speaking specifically to the recording technician regarding the tape recorder.]*

Now, how does one know what the experience will be? How does one know the law? One has to know themself. And one knows themself by being honest with themself. One knows what thoughts are in their mind. One does know how they think they feel. One does know what their attitude about anything really is. But we spend so much of our time presenting an image that we believe will be our best face to the person or the persons that we want something out of. Unfortunately, that is a luxury to a man of reason; a luxury that a man of reason cannot afford, for it comes at the sacrifice of honesty. And the sacrifice of honesty is the blindness to what the next moment will bring you, for you cannot see clearly the law. *[Reddy, the church's dog, begins to bark loudly. It sounds as though Reddy is some distance from the microcassette recorder.]*

He may come into class as long as he sits and is quiet. *[The teacher informs a director to get Reddy and bring him to the room where the class is being held.]*

You cannot see the law. You can only see a mist of images that you are creating because a judgment has been made, early in life, that someone else can fill your desires; therefore, you find that all the desires that enter your mind are dependent on what someone else will do when you solicit fulfillment of your desire. Does anyone not understand that yet?

And because early in life you have made the judgment that your desires (the fulfillment of them) is dependent on what someone else will do, you spend your days and nights in constant manipulation of what you judge that person wants you to be like and spend the time and the effort to present yourself in keeping with how you judge they want you to be. Because you want something from them, that's the reason the mind does that. That is an absolute guarantee of failure in life because you are depending upon a law of duality that guarantees opposites. And the law that you are depending upon will only temporarily bring you what you desire and is guaranteed to finally bring you the opposite of your desire. And we sacrifice the lamp of honesty for that type of mental activity. And by so doing, we are blinded to what tomorrow shall be.

We no longer pause in the moment, clearly establish the law, and experience the return of the law that we have established. Our purpose of being in the school of Light is to awaken our consciousness that we may clearly see the law, to choose wisely the law we wish to establish, and to have the wisdom of patience for the return of that law into our experiences.

Now as a person, as I have said before, as a person continues to grow in the spiritual Light, as their consciousness brightens within them, they establish the law and it returns unto them quickly. Sometimes in a matter of days, weeks, hours, or minutes. The quicker the return of the law, the more awakened in that particular area is the consciousness of the individual. When the law takes some time to return, it only reveals that it has to pass through a mountain, [an] absolute mountain, mountain of mist created by untold thousands of images that the sender has sent out in their life. That's what takes the law so long to return: is passing through the density of all of that mist.

So, here you are. You're in a school; you desire it to be successful. The Law of Success is very clear: the goodness of life is the absence of mental activity; to free oneself from the attachment of the fruits of action while on spiritual duty. To be attached to the fruits of action while on spiritual duty, there is no spiritual duty. It is nonexistent. You cannot permit your mind to attach to whatever effort you are making in life and call that spiritual, for there's nothing spiritual about it. Absolutely nothing.

Now are there any questions during this next pause that we have? Yes.

If, in setting certain laws, where one's suffered, in motion and there is a great deal of patience in its return, but somewhere in between you recognize that one of the things that had to be done with that law was governed by some old judgments and you noticed that immediately that you've already goofed or, at least, it feels like you have. By releasing that, can that—and not concern oneself with it—can that reestablish the good law?

The good law of life, in other words, I accept when you refer to the good law, is that you desire to experience some goodness in your life. Is that correct?

Yes.

Therefore, to desire to experience goodness in one's life, there is no dictate of how it shall come. Is that correct?

Correct.

And because there is no dictate of how one shall experience the goodness that they seek, there is no reliance or dependence upon a past event. Is that correct?

Correct.

Therefore, one who desires the goodness cannot permit themself to be concerned about the goofs that they judge was a goof in their days of ignorance. Does that help with your question?

Yes.

You see, goodness is goodness and is not subject to, nor dependent upon, any dictate of the human mind. For Goodness is God, and God is not subject to the minds of men. Therefore, for a person to say, "I wish goodness," and then to speak forth the word how the goodness shall come to them is a house divided. And a house divided is guaranteed to fail.

You see, when a person awakens inside themself, they stop and they think, "My God, my God, I have put my God into such a narrow place in my consciousness that I can only experience my God and goodness and love through this dinky, little peashooter that I permit to be open in my consciousness?" That is a very sad day for any human being, any intelligent being with any ounce of reason being expressed to put their goodness, which is their God, into such a narrow, narrow place in consciousness. That is heartbreaking, truly heartbreaking: that we would permit our self, as individualized souls, to be such a victim, to be the puppet that some other hand may pull whenever they choose to pull the strings. That's not what this school is all about. And that is certainly not what this philosophy is about. Because the first teaching of this philosophy is "Broaden your horizons." I do not consider that anyone who permits God or Goodness to enter their consciousness through a peashooter has a very broad horizon. Do you?

No.

I hope that's helped with your question. Yes. Yes.

How does one know when to move on from a particular job?

How does one know when to move on from a particular job? It's a wonderful question and a very important question. Honesty reveals to a person asking that question their original motive or motivation. Honesty reveals that. Now many people go into many types of jobs for many different motivations or reasons. When a person is honest with themself, their original motive of entering the job is revealed to them. Do you follow me?

When they leave, want to leave the job, their original motive is . . .

Is revealed to them when they are honest with themself. Now a person, being honest with themself, will see clearly the motive or reason that they went on a particular job was to fulfill a certain desire that they had at the moment or a combination of desires. Do you understand that?

Yes.

Now people, it has been often said that people are like gypsies. Well, people involve themself in many, with many things in life: jobs, religions, churches, schools. Go down the list of the things that people involve themself with. When the motivation, the original motivation, is satisfied, that is, the desires that motivated them to go on the job in the first place, when those desires are filled, a person begins to experience moving on. They begin to justify they've been there too long. They begin to justify they're not really getting out of it what they should be getting out of it. But honesty will reveal to the person, "My motive for coming here were these combinations of desires. The years have now passed and I now have a new combination of desires. And this new combination of desires that I, in my mind, have created are not being satisfied here. These old desires I had, they're all satisfied. So why am I here?" Is that not a good question?

Yes.

And so, if a person isn't honest with themself and sit[s] down and talk[s] to themself and look[s] at it as an intelligent being, they begin to find they [have] got to move on. They begin to find a million things wrong with the job that they have. So, all you have to do to know if it's time to move on is: number one, be honest with yourself, take a look at the desires that motivated you to take the job in the first place, see if they got fulfilled;

and if they didn't get fulfilled, then you made a judgment they won't be fulfilled there. Do you understand? And then you work intelligently with that panorama of mental substance.

You know, you see, this school is a unique school. Many people enter it with a mountain of different desires. They're motivated by different desires. Now, if the student remains in this school, they slowly but surely begin to be honest with themself and they say, "Ah, well, several of these desires that motivated me to come to Serenity have been filled. Now there's another batch over there that haven't got fulfilled. And time has passed and I have judged that they're not going to get filled there." And you're honest with yourself. And you slow—because, you see, that's creation—and you slowly but surely begin to awaken, begin to take control of your mind, begin to be honest with yourself because you cannot treat the spiritual path as you treat a material job, for one is eternal and the other is temporal. Does that help with your question? *[After a short pause, the teacher continues.]*

How do you know if it's time to move on? By being honest with yourself. Does that help with your question?

Yes. [The student responds only after a significant pause.]

Pardon? It doesn't satisfy you. But the answer to your question is not to satisfy your senses, but to free your soul. Honesty reveals to you what your original desires are. Honesty reveals to you if they've been filled and you're having this, this feeling of moving on. Honesty reveals to you if some of them haven't been filled and you have judged there they are not going to get filled. Then you begin to learn about what's controlling you. That doesn't mean you go on a job and you stay there the rest of your life, but at least be honest with yourself.

So, if you could change the judgments, you could make it work? Or . . .

Anyone can make anything work for them if that's what they want to do. Anyone can make anything work for them, for that is the power that is within you. But that takes honesty in order to gain self-control.

Then where would the wisdom come in, of, of . . .

Wisdom is not dependent upon creation. You see, you are discussing creation and being the victim of it. You were motivated by desires to take the job. Correct? The job has either filled your desires and you now have other desires—

[The microcassette recorder seems to have stopped recording for a moment.]

*****

—faculty. All right. Now you can just take an assessment of the desires that motivated you. Have they all been filled in that job? If they have not all been filled and you feel like moving on, it simply reveals that you judge very quickly and you didn't get your desire fulfilled as quickly as you judge the desire would be fulfilled in that particular circumstance and situation. Now do you understand?

Yes, I do.

That does not mean that you should not move on, and it does not mean that you should not move on. *[The teacher may have intended to say "should move on."]* It does reveal to you that you are very impatient when you judge your desire will be fulfilled. Do you understand that?

Yes, I do.

You see, you know, don't take it personally that you're the only one impatient with a desire because most everyone I ever met is very impatient with a desire.

Yes.

They are so impatient with a desire that they experience a bombardment of time-pressure. It's what they call time-pressure. The bombardment of the things because the desires are so impatient. You see, it only reveals that the moment man steals the divine expression known as desire. How does man steal the divine expression known as desire? Man forms it; man limits it. And the moment man limits it, he has stolen it because that is not its original expression. Do we understand that? You see, what we steal—stealing is a process of forming. We understand that, don't you [we]? It's a possession. Do you understand that stealing is a possessing of something without the effort...

Ah, yes.

... of attaining it?

Yes, yes.

Do you understand that? That's what we steal. See, we steal the divine expression. We take this formless free substance in the universe and we steal it by forming it, dictating and then going through the frustration because it doesn't work the way we have formed and dictated it. Do you understand? So, it simply reveals that we, being motivated by stealing desire, pay the price of the impatience of the limits that we alone have created.

You see, when you turn to Goodness or God in consciousness for the fulfillment of your life, whatever it is, then you will not experience moving from one situation to another and ending up frustrated because the desires were not fulfilled. Does that help with your question? *[After a short pause, the teacher continues.]* Because, you see, what you desire, man cannot fill.

Right.

However, what you desire is already filled when you change your dependence. Does that help with your question?

Yes.

So, if you, in putting the lamp of honesty over the situation, if you see that clearly, then you can move on and be more aware of the next thing that motivates you, see?

Even if it's within the same situation?

Oh, absolutely! Certainly! You see, it's just like here at the school. I find students motivated in different ways at different times. Do you understand that?

Yes.

Now stop and think. You've been here long enough to know that I stand not in the way of anyone coming to the Light and I do not stand in the way of their going from the Light. Now do you understand a little bit more why I don't stand in the way? Someone has to pay for the theft. I'm not about to. You see—

Oh, I—

—the theft or the stealing of the divine expression, limiting and forming it, to come here or to leave here, someone must pay for.

So that applies to anything in—

That's their payment and I, I work diligently not to interfere with the divine right of their return. Do you understand that?

Yes.

So, if a person wants to come and is not honest with themself, looking at the many desires that have brought them, or if a person wants to go, looking at the many desires that is [are] taking them, somebody must pay for desire. Would you not agree? Why should I pay for it? That's their right to pay for their own desires. I have my own to pay for. Why should I add on top of myself the payment of someone else's? If that's what they want to do, I share with them the Light that I have to share. If they, controlled by temporal desire forms, want to move on or want to come to, they alone shall pay the price.

The grass, as they say, is always greener on the other side of the fence. Would not everyone agree with that? That the grass seems to be greener on the other side of the fence. We are only tempted by what we judge is either unobtainable or difficult to obtain. We are especially, especially desirable of that which we judge is unobtainable. Do we not know that about the human mind yet? Because what we judge is unobtainable, we desire with a great thirst, known as lust. For that which we judge is difficult to obtain or unobtainable is a greater challenge that we may prove to our self how great we are. That reveals, that need to prove to our self how great we are, reveals to us that we are bound by belief, the supremacy of mental substance, instead of freed by faith, the Divine Spirit which we are. Yes.

Three minutes. [The recording technician reports the amount of time remaining on the microcassette tape.]

That's fine. Then you can keep an eye on three minutes and take care of that thing. All right? We had one question before we conclude. It's already been an hour. Yes.

Regarding the mist in which the law returns.

Yes.

I understand that the thought forms that we send out are part of that mist. How—so we could prevent more forms by changing our thought. What do we do about the forms that are there that are keeping a law from returning?

As we gain control over the vehicle, which is our mind, as we move from the belief that we are the thought into the acceptance that we are the mover or creator of the thought, we need not be concerned of what has been, because not to be concerned of what has been is to free oneself in consciousness to a realm where the Light, Eternal Light, removes the shadow. In other words, if you establish a law while in the Light, and you remain in the Light to experience its return, you don't have the—the law sent from the Light does not pass through the shadowland to return, unless you descend, after establishing the law, to the shadowland, where it will take time for its return.

So many people are so interested in healing. Well, healing, that depends on your effort to enter those realms of consciousness where the healing can take place. You have mountains of demonstrations here, day in and day out, when you're here, and you do not see them. The only reason you do not see them is because you are identified with the mist and, therefore, cannot see them, for by seeing the mist, that which is taking place you are not aware of.

Be not concerned by what has been, and therefore you will be what you truly are. That help with your question?

Yes.

You see, it's just like, whether it's, it's our Light to the World Committee, it is our bake sale, it is our dinners, it is our brunches, or anything else, if you will face life the way life truly is, not the way we believe it is, the way it truly is, then you'll speak your word forth into the universe from that realm of consciousness and it shall manifest ever in keeping with the first soul faculty and how open you have it in your consciousness. Duty, gratitude, and tolerance. So often, you see, we have these seeming problems with supply. The Law of Gratitude is the Law of Supply. We're not pausing to think that we are demonstrating the opposite of the very Law of Supply by the things that we say, the things that we think, and the things that we do.

Now in keeping with that, I—my time is up. And I'm going to conclude this class. We have some refreshments. And I want to say this: in keeping with this, there will be no charge for this class. However, the microcassettes will be available to those who want them simply at our own cost, as soon as I can get them. We've ordered them; they haven't come in yet. I might have to go to the store and buy some, though. But they will be available on microcassette at that 2.4.[32] And I also want to say this—let it run itself out—the, the school that you enjoy, because I know you do enjoy it. I'm not interested in what this temporary rollercoaster of mental substance has to offer. I'm well aware that that's not you. If I thought that was you, I would not be sitting here; I can rest assure you of that, because I got a temper like all of you combined! And—but I have that wonderful opportunity to declare the truth of an absolute, complete unity in reference to these reservations [for the monthly dinner] and a

complete unity on our bake sales and things. You see, I am not concerned that there are only two shopping centers in which we are presently going to [to hold bake sales]. I am interested in—
[The recording ends.]

SEPTEMBER 27, 1984

Class September 28, 1984
Desire by Default

Well now, tonight's little class and lesson, here, to learn is desire by default. Now we spoke on this last evening in reference to motivation. If you recall, a question was asked on—or reference was made to motivation. Well, the only thing that motivates the physical and mental form is desire. Now when you understand and accept that desire is the expression of the Divine, the expression of God or Goodness, then you will understand that that is what moves the mental form of which the physical form reacts.

Now specifically tonight's class is on desire by default. Say, for example, we just take a hypothetical case here, that a girl, having many desires, motivates herself to becoming involved with a boy and judges, in the process of the involvement, that there is the possibility or at least the potential of fulfilling this particular group of desires. Now we can take it as a boy gets involved with a girl because it's—we're speaking of the human form, you understand. So, the girl decides—we'll take the case of the girl—the girl decides that there's a possibility of this group of desires that has motivated her to meet the boy can be fulfilled. And so, the judgments are made. The desires begin to sense a possibility of their fulfillment. And the next step is, as part of the group of desires and their fulfillment, the girl has a baby. Right?

Now, we now see in this particular case that the motivation for having the baby is a part of the original motive for the fulfillment of this various group of desires. Time passes on. The child is born. The child represents to the motivating force of the person, now, the mother, of fulfillment not of one desire but a whole group of desires.

And so the mind, looking at the avenue, the child, which is the avenue that the mind judges shall be instrumental in fulfilling this group of desires, fears and, by fearing, controls and protects, in keeping with the original motive or group of desires, the child. Therefore, to that level of consciousness there must be, under no circumstances, any interference in any way, shape, or form, for the preservation of the group of desires, the original motive, is what is at stake.

Now many people will look at their child as an extension of their ego, and of course, that is what it is. As long as a person continues to believe that they are the desire of their mind, they cannot help but believe that the motive, that which moves them, they are. And because of that false belief, there is, within the consciousness of the individual of which we are speaking in this particular case, there is this constant fear, constant fear of losing control.

That is the blindness of desire. If you understand the cause of it, then you'll have no problem in casting the light over it and educating it.

Now, are there any questions on desire by default? *[After a short pause, the teacher continues.]* Yes, there are still questions because some of you do not understand how the desire is fulfilled by the default. *[After another short pause, the teacher again continues.]* When you ask the question, perhaps you'll receive the answer. What is the default?

We have clearly presented a hypothetical case of motivation of desire. Now where is the default? Where is the default of desire? *[After another short pause, the teacher again continues.]* Let's first explain what we mean by the word *default*. Does someone have an understanding of the word *default, to default?* A person has defaulted on something. What does that mean to you? Yes. What does that mean to you, [Student U]?

To fail in your responsibilities.

To fail in your responsibilities—a person has defaulted on something. [Student B], what does *default* mean to you? I'm going to go around to each one and get their understanding of to default, default.

As for me, it means a sport challenge, where you lose because of a technicality.

You lose because of a technicality. Would you then agree that you lose because of a lack of responsibility in understanding all the components of the particular situation in which you find yourself involved?

Yes.

That's just exactly what we want to discuss. Because of a technicality you default. Because of a lack of facing personal responsibility for what you have set into motion, you default. Would you not agree? Because when someone involves themselves in anything, by the process of involvement, they bear the responsibility to thoroughly investigate, would you not agree? So, losing by a technicality is the responsibility of the loser, would you not agree?

[The student's response is difficult to transcribe.]

Ah! The law is very clear. It is the responsibility of whoever chooses to establish the law to understand all of its technicalities, would you not agree?

[A student may have responded, but their response was not audible on the tape.]

Thank you very much. Now, [Student S], you had a question.

Oh—

In reference to default.

I was—since the word says de-fault, *it's like blaming the fault outside rather than the personal responsibility. Although you're making it very clear that no matter what, it's the person that's still personally responsible for understanding since they're playing the game.*

If you—yes—if you sign your—if you commit yourself by signature to a contract and you do not thoroughly study and understand the contract and you are called into court at a later date for default, who is responsible, [Student B]?

You are.

Do you understand? *[The teacher addresses Student S.]*

Yes.

For *you* have chosen voluntarily to commit yourself to the contract unless you can prove that you committed under duress. Is that not correct? *[The teacher addresses Student B.]*

Yes.

There! If you cannot prove that, in your commitments in life, you have committed under duress, then in the court of justice, divine, you bear full, total, whole, and complete responsibility for the default.

Now do you remember what the name of this class was when we opened a few minutes ago? Was it not desire by default? Now, are we getting somewhere—a little headway now in our understanding? Desire by default. The fulfillment of desire absent of personal responsibility establishes the Law of Default. Does it shine a little brighter—the Light—now? Legally and reasonably.

Now what have you written on those notes, [Student S]?

Ah . . .

This [Those] last words.

The fulfillment of desire absent of personal responsibility establishes the Law of Default.

And that is known as desire by default. Are there any questions on that? *[After a pause, the teacher continues.]* Yes, [Student G]. In other words, putting it in terms, perhaps, we would more quickly relate to, there is no possible way to get some *thing* for no *thing* or something for nothing. Now can we relate to it? Yes, [Student G].

I guess what bothers me is the term "the fulfillment." Why isn't it "the satisfaction"?

Because we are deluded by terminology. You see, satisfaction to the human mind, based upon the shadows of the past, known as experiences, clearly reveals it's temporary. Therefore, the human mind, in its desires, chooses, regardless of truth, to fulfill its desires, [Student G], not satisfy them. Therefore, it is important to understand what the human mind will accept. A person's mind will accept the fulfillment of a desire a thousand times more readily than the satisfaction of a desire.

A cup of coffee satisfies you for a time. It does not fulfill you. To the human mind, when a desire is a priority, then it will only accept fulfillment; it will not accept satisfaction. Does that help with your question, [Student G]? All you have to do is relate to desire and you'll see, "I satisfy this desire. I've had something to eat. I am now satisfied." Ah, "I desire to be"—you will not accept the word *satisfaction* in what you desire to be. You will accept the word *fulfillment* in what you desire to be. Not satisfaction. Is that not true?

[The student responds, but it is difficult to transcribe.]

And it's true with everybody else's mind. OK? Yes, [Student S].

Why then, if we always get what we really want, is there so little fulfillment in life with the mind in control only giving satisfaction?

Because there is no fulfillment to desire to the human mind. It is nonexistent. And although a person may be aware of that, it is a process of growth and evolution to grow through it. Many people are aware that desire does nothing more and nothing less but satisfy the senses for a time. It always leaves the senses thirsty. It always will. Because you cannot fill the unfillable. There's no way possible. Yes.

But am I correct in understanding that the mind is always questing to fulfill?

The mind is always thirsty. Because, you see, if you understand—and we've discussed it before. The human mind is a combination of these many levels of consciousness. You have forty soul func—faculties and forty sense functions. Combined, you have eighty with this intelligent, infinite Energy being the eighty-first.

Now, to the human mind, it desires—it steals the divine expression—forms and desires many things. So, as you desire something on level of consciousness, say, twenty-two, and level twenty-two is satisfied, you understand, in the moment—and ofttimes prior to the satisfaction, and sometimes during and sometimes after—from lack of control of this vehicle of the mind, you find yourself now on level of consciousness fourteen. Well, level of consciousness fourteen doesn't have the desire forms that sought for the satisfaction. Therefore, while you are on level fourteen, you are not satisfied. If you, in turn, move back up to level twenty-two, you will experience the satisfaction. What life is revealing to you [is] you are unable to maintain, for any duration of time, a certain level of consciousness. So, a person begins something that they desire, while they are part way through it, ofttimes, from lack of control of their mind, they move to a different level of consciousness and are no longer interested in the job that they are in process of completing. That simply reveals a lack of control of the human mind.

Whereas concentration is the key to all power, concentration reveals, to those who apply it, a maintaining on any object of your choice. When you grow to the point in consciousness where, first, you are aware of the level that you are serving, [and] second, you are able to control the level by your conscious decision of how long you will remain on the level to serve it and you will consciously choose when you desire to move to another level of consciousness and how long you will stay there, you will know yourself, you will know the truth, and you will be free.

Are there any questions in that respect?

[After a short pause, the teacher continues.] Look at the many times we've discussed frustration. What are the—what

is frustration? We've discussed it a mountain [of] times—and time-pressure. The bombardment of desires! Look, show me a person in time-pressure and I will show you a person who is zipping through the levels of consciousness at such a rapid speed, from the lack of control of their mind, that they are at the verge of a nervous breakdown. At the verge of a nervous breakdown. For what is happening, through a lack of conscious effort, their little soul is moving so rapidly through the levels of consciousness, there is a phenomenal bombardment of desire forms! That's what's happening.

I've discussed with you before that time-pressure is the effect of the hailstorm of desire forms. Now this hailstorm does not exist just on one level of consciousness, but a combination of many levels of consciousness. And if a person's lack of effort to control their mind and their soul [is] moving rapidly through the various levels of consciousness, you experience a hailstorm of desire forms. And you're under phenomenal time-pressure! You have an anxiety that's rising up; you cannot control it. Because you have this bombardment of all these things you think you must do, you want to do; and nothing gets accomplished. Is that not true, [Student P]?

It is.

And because you find yourself with this phenomenal anxiety with—right at the verge of a nervous breakdown and you sit down in a chair and you watch the picture tube for the next six hours. And go to sleep. I've seen too many students do that. That is the cause of it. The total lack of controlling this, the soul's movement, you understand, through the various levels of consciousness, [and then] one goes berserk.

Now, are there any other questions? Do you have a question, [Student S], on that? Time-pressure? Frustration? Desire forms? Desire by default? *[After a short pause, the teacher continues.]* Yes, did you have a question, [Student M]?

Yes.

Yes.

OK. If desire is, is from the soul—

No, I didn't—I never said that desire was from the soul. I said the desire *is*—isn't from anything—desire *is* the divine expression. Desire *is* the divine expression. The expression of the Divinity, that's what desire is. Man steals it when he limits it. And he limits it by forming it with his judgments of how it shall fulfill itself. Go ahead now with your question.

Uhm—

We must clear this up very clearly.

So, the mind is constantly grabbing it to dictate it, to form it, and to tell it what to do.

No, to tell the person who is serving it how it will fulfill itself.

Uh-huh.

You see, desire tells the mind it will fulfill itself in this way and that way. Desire forms do not tell the mind, "I will satisfy you." *[The teacher laughs joyfully and loudly.]* They never tell—I've yet to meet a mind where a desire entity said, "I'll satisfy you." It never says, "I'll satisfy you." It tells you, "I will fulfill you." *[The teacher laughs loudly again.]* For the ego that has created the formation of the desire, the forming of it, will *not* accept a satisfaction. It will only accept what it says is a fulfillment, not a satisfaction. Yes, go ahead, [Student M].

Did you feel satisfied when you conceived [Student E] or did you feel nine months of fulfillment? *[After a short pause, the teacher continues.]* Yes?

I felt both.

That's nice. You got it on all levels. Go ahead with your question. *[The teacher laughs.]* But satisfaction didn't last.

No.

But what is judged as fulfillment.

Excuse me.

What is judged as fulfillment, now that's lasting, isn't it?

Yes.

All right. Good. Go ahead, [Student M]. [Student M] got both. She got the satisfaction plus the fulfillment. Now go ahead with your question in reference to desire.

All the energy—

And motivation, yes.

—of this divine expression—

You have put into a peashooter, like anyone else does.

Right.

Go ahead.

And basically, to help that just expand your horizons, meaning create new desire forms, is—

I wouldn't recommend that when you got twenty million in the basement to pull up at any moment! In fact, they'll pluck themselves up any time. No. The question is, you're saying, is an expanding of your consciousness. One does not expand their consciousness, one does not broaden their horizons by creating new desire forms when they already have available to them[selves] multitudes of them.

The broadening of one's horizons is the effect of conscious effort to think of something besides oneself.

Anyone who permits themself to be the victim of a peashooter desire, that is, a limited desire, the divine expression put into a limit, like a peashooter, anyone who permits themself to be a victim of [a] peashooter desire is destined to suffer. They will blow themself apart every time they identify with the area of consciousness where the peashooter desire was first created.

So, because we all have untold numbers of peashooter desires in the consciousness, which is controlled by the throne of the thought of I, known as self, wisdom reveals the path to follow is to broaden one's horizon by stopping the overidentification with oneself. In other words, think of something—think of the tree or the sky or the stars—think of something that is not limited. Think of the air. It moves everywhere. Think of the freedom of the bird in flight. Think of something besides yourself, and you'll free yourself from your peashooter desire.

Now you know from experiences that every time you think of your peashooter desire, in this case, your baby, you become frustrated, you feel bad, sorry for yourself, problems with your husband, and every negative thing that can enter your consciousness [does]. All of that exists within your own mind. And you may have those experiences any moment you choose to think about yourself. Now, on the positive side, it serves a beautiful purpose: sooner or later it will drive you to something besides constant self-thought.

It's a slow path, however. For most people, it requires untold years of suffering. It requires that long of time because people who they find themself associating with, they don't want to hear about it; they're not interested; they got their own self-trips that they're thinking about. Therefore, they—either they walk away from you or let you rattle on. They don't tell you the truth: you're totally locked into overidentifying with yourself. If they were true friends, they [would say], "That's enough self-pity. I will not tolerate it around me." They would do you the greatest favor they possibly could. They'd tell you the truth: "Stop thinking about yourself. Start thinking of something besides yourself and all your self-related garbage can." And you might get angry, but you are the one who will benefit and feel as though you just took a clean shower. Is that not true? We all know that from experiences, right, [Student U]?

Yes, sir.

But unfortunately, out there in that jungle, usually, people just walk away or what they call nowadays tune you out. They tune in their own radio as they turn off yours in their consciousness. They don't want to hear it. But they don't have enough care, kindness, or consideration for you to tell you the truth: "You're back in that rut again? That's all I ever hear you talk about. Aren't you tired of talking about that?" You see, if they'd tell you the truth, you'd soon get out of the trip and see how beautiful life is. But they won't tell you the truth because they want something out of you. That's why they won't tell you the truth. If they didn't want something out of you, they'd tell you the truth: they'd say, "You're back in that rut again? I'm tired of hearing about that. Move on to something else because I'm not going to have it around me." No, they want something out of you. That's why they won't tell you the truth. Does that help with your question?

It does. Thank you.

Uh-huh. *[After a short pause, the teacher continues.]* Any other questions while we have a cup of coffee and finish up? Yes, [Student G].

Desire always promises, does it [or] does it not?

It cannot exist without promise.

Then, what—

It promises whatever—you see, say that you have a desire in your mind. It will promise you the fulfillment of that and along with the fulfillment of that are a mountain of other little desires that are hiding behind it. You see? Say that you desire to, ah—well, we'll make it more [one] that you can relate to—say that you desire to be a painter, all right?[33] And it will promise you all of the things that will come: if you will do such and such, you can be the painter. But it will promise you all these things that are hiding behind the initial desire. It'll promise you success. It will promise you luxury. It will promise you leisure time, especially leisure time. So, what it is doing [is] it is the mask for a mountain of other desires that are suppressed.

You see, it won't tell you, "You're already a painter." Therefore, what can it promise you? You already are a painter. No, no, no, no. It promises you that you will be such and such a painter, and by being such and such a painter, all these other desires hiding behind it all get filled. That's the con game of the formations of desires. You see, that's why I say, a person's motivation—there isn't just one desire. There's the upfront facade presenting itself, but there's all these other things behind there. There's a whole army of other desires that are hiding behind the mask up front. *[The teacher laughs.]*

You see, if a desire rises in the consciousness and tells you, you'll be a painter, that's fine. Then you can say to the desire, "What are you talking to me [about]? What are you promising me? I'm already a painter." Then you pause and you will hear all those other ones hiding behind the mask. They'll say, "You can have all this time to yourself. You can do this. You can go there. You da, da, da." And it'll go right down a whole list. You just be quiet with it and you'll pierce the veil and you'll see what's behind it: it promises you the fulfillment of all of the other ones that have been suppressed.

See, with every mask of desire—behind every mask of desire are the armies of suppressed desires. That's what's behind them, see? We can all relate to that—can't we?—in honesty. So, when a desire pops into your consciousness, say, "Just a minute. You are promising me what? No, no, no. I already have that." Then it will have to let some of the suppressed ones peek through so you can see them. See? Like, "Oh, you won't have to get up 'til 10 in the morning, maybe 10:30." "You'll be able to have breakfast in bed someday." "Work? Don't worry about going to work. You won't have to work at all. Just when you feel like it. Maybe a couple of hours a day, two days a week. You can stay home and take care of the baby. You can spend all of your time controlling your desire package. You can manipulate it and have a perfect, malleable mold." Uh-huh.

Well, look at [Student M]. [Student M] well knows desire by default. You see—and, and she's honest enough in her conscious[ness] to know that. If she can set up the situation sufficiently, like this evening allowing [Student E] to pull the tablecloth, knowing the rights of the organization and the school, she will fulfill her desire by default. She will—therefore, [Student E] will not be allowed into school. So, someone will have to be with [Student E]. So, she will be able to be home with [Student E]. Of course, she'll have to quit her job, later down the road. But she will be able to be home with him. She won't be able to be here Sunday, Saturday, Friday, Tuesday, or any of the work days because [Student E] is destroying things. And she's allowing it to happen in order that, by default, she can fulfill her desire [and] have [Student E] to herself at home and totally control him.[34]

You see how it works? It's called desire by default.

Because, you see, first of all, you have to understand the mind first knows that the Spirit and the Council will allow so much destruction. And then that's it. And before the child was even born, she was informed repeatedly, "He's not allowed to run loose." And it was left up to the parents' discretion whether they have him by the hand or he has a harness. Remember? So, unless you correct that, unless you go back to the original motivation, the—a person who does not control their desires, you understand, will fulfill them, in the respect, by default. You understand that? That's how you get desire by default.

Don't you find that interesting? Yes. *[The teacher calls upon Student S.]*

You were speaking in regard to the law, unless you can prove that, you know, like, you entered this contract under duress—

Unless you can prove it to your conscience. Because it's your conscience that's at stake. Each person's conscience. Yes.

Wouldn't, as we understand the Law of Personal Responsibility, though, cover the fact that the person set laws into motion to merit being under duress?

Why, certainly, certainly. Absolutely, [Student S]. But you have to understand that there are different levels of awakening of the person in gaining control of their mind. So, if we're speaking to some levels, then you have to say, "Unless the person can prove that it was done under duress." But then we move to the next step: the person had to establish the Law of Duress. But that's an awakening consciousness.

OK.

There's no way to escape personal responsibility. The law is the law. It's like a person saying, "Well, I had an accident. I'm not at fault at all." Now we all know differently. We all know there are no accidents in the universe. Now that would be like, what, telling [your friend, Friend A], "Now, [Friend A]"—now, maybe you can tell him—you say, "Look, we merited this."[35] But you tell the average person that and they'll probably slug you. *[Student S laughs.]*

You have to say, "Why was I at that spot at that time? What law did I set into motion? I didn't have to be at that spot at that time, but laws I set into motion placed me there. And that's the experience I had."

That's like with [Student M], who's constantly getting in trouble, as you—are you not able to see the setup, [Student O] and everyone? You see, by [Student E] destroying things or being allowed to do so, the mind already knows he won't be allowed in school. That was made very clear, wasn't it, [Student O]?

Yes, sir.

And by him not being allowed in school, his mother will have to be with him, right? And by his mother being with him—you understand?—the desire and the motivation will have its way. So, the desire's being accomplished by default—a total denial of personal responsibility.

So, unless one is honest with oneself and says, "Just a minute. I'm an intelligent being. Why am I repeatedly permitting and allowing laws to be established to sacrifice my child's right to the Light?" See, you have to be honest with yourself. You [have] got to take a look at that desire to see how compelling it is to have total control and have him right out of the way. Do you see that, [Student B]? How that works? And everybody? That's desire by default.

And it's not just limited to [Student M] setting it up. But, you see—don't worry, this tape isn't going to anyone. But, you know, I'll just keep on speaking. There's nothing to worry about that. I have no fear. Hopefully, you don't, being students of mine. I'm very outspoken and if you don't know it after five, ten years around me, then it's too late, I guess. The thing is, would you call that consideration or selfishness? What would you call it?

Selfishness. [Student M replies.]

Then, when you experience, as you said you did the other night and you were crying in the kitchen, that he threatens to take the little fellow and leave, don't you consider that selfishness on his part?

Yes.

Like attracts like and becomes the Law of Attachment.

Uh-huh.

Doesn't it? So, myself, looking at the situation, I look at it as a very selfish thing to allow the little fellow, only being thirteen months old, to do the things that will sacrifice his little soul's right to the school and to the Light. That's how I see it. How do you see it, [Student B]?

The same.

I see it as a very selfish thing, [Student O]. Very selfish.

So when, [Student M], you experience this hurt feeling, rejection, and selfishness on [Student O's] part, try to remember that's a very selfish thing to do to a little thirteen-month-old, who cannot speak up for himself and say, "Just a minute. I don't want my right to the Light sacrificed by anyone." He's not old enough to speak up and say that. You understand that, don't you?

[Student O responds but it is difficult to transcribe his response.]

OK. So, what we are looking at here in this desire by default, what we're looking at is what these desire forms, created by our mind, what they're like: totally selfish. Not an ounce of consideration for another soul, for the spiritual Light, for God, for goodness, [but it is] absolutely and completely selfish. Would you not agree, [Student O]?

Totally.

So selfish that they will sacrifice—think how selfish they are. See, I know that's not [Student M's] soul. But I also know it's a compelling possession-obsession desire entity. So selfish is the formation of desire, so greedy and selfish it is, that it would sacrifice a little thirteen-month-old baby's right to God's light. That's how selfish desire is in our mind! Now we know it's called the *theft* of life. How selfish!

See, that's not you that wants total manipulation and control over a little baby. But take a look at how greedy and selfish it is. Wouldn't you agree, [Student O]?

Yes, sir. It's, it's blindness.

Total blindness. Desire is absolute blindness.

Yes, sir.

See? Desire has no light. Have we not spoken on that for many years? Desire is absolute blindness. That a little baby would be sacrificed. The slaughter of the lamb for the creation of insane desire. That's what desire is: totally blind! Absolute sacrificial lamb. Uh-huh. Yeah. Think of it. Think of it. Because that's the growth steps that we're making. And how important.

And on that, [Student P], I'd like a cup of coffee, please. You can empty that out. It's cold. And then we'll conclude this nice, little class.

Think of that. Think of—that's what almost breaks my heart. Take that, [Student P]. And don't forget that paper on the floor. I don't know how it got there.

You see, I know that [Student M] does not sit around thinking, "How can I fill this greedy, selfish desire? How can I sacrifice my son in order that my desire may have its way of total control over this little piece of meat here?" She doesn't sit around thinking like that. But that's how that thing thinks! For the demonstrations are the revelations. See?

And it's a wonderful thing because it will help us all to see the greed and selfishness of desire of the human mind. It cares for nothing and for no one, for it is a servant of self-love. Try to understand that. And then you will understand its selfishness and its greediness. That's all that it serves.

You see, the light of reason reveals that, [for] little [Student E], for example, sacrificing his right to the Light because someone has other desires for his life and that it manipulates and works in those ways to accomplish it, there's no love for a child. But that, I understand. You have to look at it, [Student M].

Oh, I am.

Take a good look at it.

I will.

Because you're the one that's been doing the number and he's the one that's suffering. Because, you see, first of all, the mind has to make the judgment that he will be booted out, because that's part of the whole panorama of the desire by default. You see? Now, I've had many people do all kinds of numbers so I would kick them out of the school. I have yet to do so. I've never been ordered to do so. But we had [Student D2]. She stolen [stole] the table cloths and everything else. That's outright theft. But she did. You know, the napkins and things. And did all kinds of numbers. And some of the ex-students. They did not get desire by default at my expense. And for that, I'm very grateful. I know a little bit of something about the law. But they sure did beautiful numbers trying to get desire by default. Yes.

Now, don't you think it's important to see how desire works? Do you think there's an ounce of selflessness in it? Look at its greed. Whether it possesses [Student M] temporarily—her mind—or anyone else, look at its *unbelievable* greed and selfishness. A little thirteen-month-old boy, [it would] sacrifice his little Light because he can't speak up for himself.

Yes, does anyone have any questions? Yes, [Student S].

You wouldn't do it, like, you said incur the payment, by having anyone leave.

No, no, I didn't say that. I would not incur the payment *by* being the instrument through which they could default. *[The teacher laughs.]*

Why, I'd like to ask—

They will not default at my expense.

In, in other examples, like in our own lives—

Uh-huh.

—what kind of payment is incurred if we, if we were to do that on a personal level?

Well, you see, for example, when you're on a personal level, you can't relate it to an entire school organization which involves many people, you understand, because the whole must be considered. That depends on the blindness of the attachment. It will be ever in keeping with the blindness of the attachment, the payment, therefore, shall be.

The blindness of who's attachment?

The one— *[The teacher laughs loudly.]* Ask [Student O]. [Student O] will tell you. [Student O]. [Student S] has a question for you, [Student O]. Now, I pick [Student O] because [Student O] is in a situation like that, and little [Student E] is in the middle. So [Student O] can easily relate to that. [Student O], there's a question for you. *[The teacher laughs.]* It's in keeping with the blindness of the attachment. *[The teacher laughs again.]* Yes, [Student O].

I'd like to try to answer the question, maybe I could help some—

Yes. I'd like you to. Thank you.

First of all, if a person, if Mr. Goodwin should do, with the— this is the way I understand it—if Mr. Goodwin had kicked those people out, and they constantly, to me, seem like they would feel that they be done won, that the level would be done won. And not only would that level feel that it be done won, he would be sending out to the whole . . .

To that realm.

. . . to the whole realm. And then he would become trapped by that realm. And we *would become trapped by that realm. And the school would be out. The Light would be out. That's the way I see it. I don't know, but that's* . . .

You cannot be attached to creation and serve God. Yes. *[The teacher calls upon Student S.]*

Could you repeat what you said? I couldn't understand what you said. The level would be what?

The, the level of consciousness that's perpetrating all this, if Mr. Goodwin had kicked them out, they would, in their consciousness, they would feel like they be done won. [Student O repeats.]

They won.

Yeah, they won. [Student O remarks.]

Won. That they won it. [Student S confirms.]

Yeah, they won. [Student O remarks again.]

OK. Thank you.

They got just what they set up to get.

Yes—

That's what makes them so furious with me because they don't get what they set up to get because there's someone that sees the setup before they are even consciously aware of it. *[The teacher laughs joyfully.]*

The whole school, the whole school and the whole organization would be jeopardized because Mr. Goodwin would have to be— [Student O continues.]

He sees. *[The teacher says this almost as an aside.]*

—on call by that realm and controlled by that realm. Yeah.

Good perceptive [perception]. You've got good perception, [Student O]. There are moments when you have absolute clear perception. There are those moments, [Student O]. Even the most titanic ego *[Another student laughs.]* is right at moments. Yes, [Student O]. That's true. Be grateful for a titanic ego. It can serve you very well under the light of reason, under the light of reason. I don't consider that I have any peashooter ego. Go ahead. Yes, [Student S]. *[The teacher laughs again.]*

[Student B] is thinking very deeply.

Am I correct in understanding, then, that, that the principles of the Light, then, are to operate—that they're all accepting, where the way that the other side, the darkness, is run, they would establish, like, denial? [Student S asks.]

Well, let me put it another way: the Light does not respond to temptation. The forces of darkness work only on temptation. The Light does not respond to temptation. So, you see the setup of those who set up their numbers, you understand, are to tempt you into their ballpark. Don't you under—do you see that, [Student B]?

[If Student B responds, her response is difficult to transcribe.]

So, if you remain in the Light, that is, God, in this situation, is at the helm, you do not react to temptation. Temptation is the weapon of the realms of darkness. Truth is the sword of Light. Not temptation.

Well, if you want to know about weapons, angels of Light have the sword of truth. The tempters and temptresses of darkness, the soldiers from below, have the three-pronged fork of temptation. Now the devil isn't depicted with a three-pronged fork just because of some fairy tale. At some future time, be it in divine order, I will reveal to you his weapon: what the three-pronged fork really means. *[After a short pause, the teacher continues.]* Well, the Friends will give you this much and no more and we'll close this meeting. There are three parts of the temple of the soul, the house of clay, through which the forces of darkness can tempt you.

Good night.

*****

Won't take that long to answer the question on Neptune. First of all, in reference to the question you have asked on Neptune, what is it that Neptune holds? What weapon does he hold in his hand? Yes, [Student U].

Trident. [Several students respond.]

And what does it look like?

Three-pronged.

It's three-pronged. And what does Nep—what, what element of nature does Neptune represent?

Water.

The water center. You can only be reached through the emotions by that weapon.

Thank you and good night.

SEPTEMBER 28, 1984

Class September 30, 1984

All right. I want you to know I had no intention of coming out here this evening, but your needs have demonstrated—some of you—that they are so great—and either your lack of understanding your purpose of being here or your lack of understanding the laws involved with your rights to be here [have required it].[36]

Specifically, this evening, we have to go through this law that you received years ago, known as hell is paved with good intentions and broken promises. Anything that you permit to interfere with your spiritual duties cannot possibly be spiritual, for if they were spiritual, they would not interfere with spiritual duties.

Now you are very fortunate being here, for you have a very unique situation. You do not have the weight of responsibility of the mountains of decisions that must be made, daily, in order to operate a school of Light in a world of creation. You have that unique opportunity. When you do not take advantage of that unique opportunity and you sacrifice your spiritual opportunities by brain judgments because you don't know what to do and your mind judges what you should do, then you are not in any way, shape, or form on a spiritual duty.

Now earlier today I spoke to [Student O] to help him in reference to his sacrificing his spiritual duty in this church—one of his many spiritual duties, as one of the ushers, is taking up the offertory at offertory time.[37] He sacrificed that spiritual duty today, and for the sake of his own good in life, I spoke to him, even though *he* is the one that has the spiritual duty and responsibility to ask what to do when his spiritual opportunity is being interfered with, with any brain judgments. Specifically, the case was that he sacrificed his spiritual duty of taking up the offertory, with all of the people in the angel world waiting, caring for the service to be done, and took care, by making a mental judgment, of his son, who chose to go into his number at the exact timing when his father had the opportunity for a spiritual duty.

Now, [Student U], you will not be receiving your tape this evening simply because—not that it is not here and available, but the authority of your church was transgressed and bypassed for your order to be filled. The authority that founded the school, through which you benefit, was totally ignored and bypassed by the directors of this church, specifically [Student G]. Therefore, you will receive your tape when the Council decides, for this school is not here to be run by [Student G's] ego, [Student O's] ego, or anybody else's ego. And if it's going to be run by someone's ego, I know several of my students who won't even be here the moment it starts to take control. Because I know my own students. And I know they have a hard enough struggle not constantly serving their own uneducated egos without going and being a lackey for somebody else's uneducated ego.

I want you to know that I do not appreciate those games. And I also want you all to know that I am very capable of playing them back, if that's the only way you're going to stop them. *[After a short pause, the teacher continues.]* I do know how to stop them: fight fire with fire.

Now we'll start with you, [Student G], for what *you* have to say in overstepping your authority in this church.

Well, I certainly do apologize because consciously it did rise that I should check and immediately . . . check went on by. The desire tape came that—there was some extra tapes. And I had made the labels not realizing that there would be an extra one because I was just looking at the— [Several words are difficult to transcribe.][38]

When did you report that [Student C2] had changed her mind about pay—of purchasing the tape?

She was just simply—I wrote her name on the order form Thursday and she immediately told me that, when I asked for her check, that she did not have any checks with her. And I scratched it out right then and there.

Well, just, now—yes, when did you report all of this game going on?

Well, actually, there was nothing to report because—

How many orders did you turn in?

What I did—

Just a moment, please, [Student G]. How many orders did you turn in? Nine or ten?

I turned in—there were ten.

That is correct. You turned in five standard cassettes and five microcassettes. Now let's go on from that point.

And I was incorrect in that—

When did you report that you were incorrect? *[After a short pause, the teacher continues.]* When did you report to the only authority this organization has that you were incorrect? When did you report your error to the Council?

I just realized tonight that there were six micros and four regular, because I had not scratched all . . . [A few words are difficult to transcribe.]

You mean to tell me that you gave me an order, as hard as I've worked to make microcassettes for you, for five. Now I've got to make another one. Plus, you turned around and you sold one to [Student U] without one single report to the only authority this organization has and you've been with us for twelve or thirteen years? Is that what you're trying to tell me, [Student G]? When I have, for thirteen years, gone repeatedly out of my way to try to help you? Surely—is that what you're telling me?

Well—

In honesty, is it what you're telling me?

Well, I don't think it's quite like that.

Then tell us all what it—tell us what—why did you just tonight discover this? Is that what you're telling me, you just tonight discovered this? Is that what you're telling me?

... realized my error. [A few words are difficult to transcribe.]

You did—in other words, you didn't realize your error from Thursday night, Friday, Saturday, and Sunday. How did you realize your error? Under what circumstances did this awakening dawn in your consciousness that you had made a mistake?

When [Student B] came up and she said there are really only four standard cassettes.

That's when you realized that you had made an error? All right. We will have to correct that. [Student S], orders are to be taken and you are to check it as secretary of this church.

Uh-huh. [Student S responds.]

Now we have to correct these errors. If the only way you became aware of it is when [Student B] said to you there are only four and not five standard cassettes, then we've got—you've got to have some help monitoring in that area of consciousness. Now you know very well that I have asked the directors to help you, to check up on you until you are able to get through that. Now you know that, [Student G].

Well, it was at that point—

Because it not only causes a lot of grief for the organization, but those realms of consciousness of mental substance overriding spiritual truth, just like with [Student O], are not only detrimental but they guarantee the loss of the student as far as this Light's concerned.

Go ahead, [Student G].

Well, it was at that point that, that the whole subject of running the, the fifth cassette, which would, should not have—

When did you sell [Student U] a cassette?

[Student U] bought a cassette—

Specifically, that class Thursday night. At what time?

During the regular order taking.

All right. Today [Student U] ordered one of the standard cassettes from last Thursday, is that correct?

That's correct.

Did you in honesty, honesty within your consciousness, report to the Council, number one: that [Student B], through [Student B] you had become aware of a mistake you had made, you have, however, an opportunity to sell [Student U] that tape and could you have permission to do so? Did you bring that in honesty to the authority of the church? *[The teacher addresses Student G.]*

No, I did not.

Well, don't you think that would have been a better way for you, [Student G]? We wouldn't have to have this meeting tonight. Not—because not that you're the only one that caused this meeting. I have [Student O] and a few others to take care of.

I don't want it . . . [It is difficult to transcribe a few words.]

I know you don't like it. And I'm trying to find ways to help correct it, [Student G]. So, you won't have to serve that realm. Because it not only is extremely costly for you, it's costly for all of us, because we're all a part of the whole. Don't you see?

Yes.

So, you said that you had become aware that you should have checked. But you overrode that awareness. Didn't you report that to me on another occasion here recently? That you had become aware of what you should have done and did what you knew you shouldn't do?

I have done this many times in my life.

And would you call that temptation?

I certainly would.

And what is it tempting to? Did it—has it brought any good, [Student G]?

None at all.

Well, you see, when it is a person's personal life, that, unless they make that personal life a part of the school, then the light is not exposed over them, you see. But you have to understand—I know you do understand—that the selling of cassettes or taking cassette orders or the philosophy, the tapes, everything involved in this organization becomes the responsibility of the organization. Therefore, I would be greatly encouraged that you are being monitored with that weakness known as temptation, [Student G].

Uh-huh.

For you know very well it's brought you no good.

No.

All right. Thank you. Now I will know, when the Spirit informs me, when your order can be filled. *[The teacher addresses Student U.]* Because you wouldn't even want that cassette under the vibration of which it is being delivered, if it was allowed to be delivered. Because, you see, like a cookie, it carries with it the vibration and the motivation of those people who have anything to do with it. And in all fairness to [Student U], he would not really appreciate receiving the cassette under those vibrations of more temptation. I know damn well I wouldn't. And won't grant to another what I wouldn't grant to myself.

Now, I have been working diligently on the attendance affirmation and I want to see the hands of those who are working daily on it because it's the money out of your pocket—if that's the only thing you people can relate to. I think you can relate to something besides that. *[Please see the appendix for the affirmation.]*

Now, why is it necessary for us to have to flood our consciousness with an attendance affirmation of supply? Why? Because our consciousness is flooded with the direct opposite. That's why. Mental substance has become the priority and that is not the purpose of the church. Therefore, to correct that—to permit—you see, God works through man. God doesn't work to man. God works through man. And as your clouds of mental substance and constant judgments get thicker and thicker, then you have to take corrective measures through affirmations to lighten the clouds in your consciousness so the Light and the Spirit can get through.

Now, we'll get to you, [Student O]. Although I took out the time and spoke to you about your sacrificing your spiritual opportunity, if you remember, today.

Yes, sir.

What—yes, [Student P], you may take care of the washer. What do you have to say about that, [Student O]? We have taken corrective measures. We have lyceum teachers there. And that's just the way that it is. But, you see, you sacrifice so quickly your spiritual opportunity without checking with the Spirit, from whence the spiritual opportunity flows, you see?

I see.

So, what do you think about that, [Student O]? We have taken corrective measures for you. [Student E]—it's interesting—and there are no accidents in the universe—why that little boy picks whenever you have a spiritual opportunity to pull his number on you. Don't you think? Or were you able to perceive that, [Student O]?

Well, I was able to perceive it, but I . . .

Yes, go ahead.

When I try not—I try not to dwell on that too much.

No, one shouldn't dwell on anything. One should take corrective measures. Because, you see, without corrective measures, one just goes into the pit, the pit of temptation. Yes, [Student O].

OK. I had disciplined him twice this morning.

He was doing his number, yes.

All right. So, but that's, that's—what, what really—possibly, also, there was another avenue that I could have taken.

Yes, what was that avenue you could have taken?

If I had known properly what was the schedule for today.

The schedule is always the same. And you mean to tell me you didn't inform [Student O] that he would be taking up the offertory? *[The teacher addresses Student R.]*

No, that's not— [Student O remarks.]

I told him that [Student U] would be bringing it up. [Student R remarks.]

Yes, but I mean, he is one of the ushers who helps take up the offertory. [Student O] does.

Collect it, you mean? [Student R continues.]

Yes.

Yes. [Student R confirms.]

Not that schedule, Mr. Goodwin. [Student O clarifies.]

Oh, which schedule are you referring to?

In, in other words, in reference to the student forum and if I had known that [Student R] had to—was going to speak after [Student S]—[39]

Yes.

—well now, I would, I would have taken that opportunity go out with [Student E] because he was acting up again.

I see. All right. Did you look at the church program?

I didn't look at it.

Ah! What is the sense of us going to all this expense if my own students don't—aren't aware of the schedule?

Right.

See, that's the reason that we spend all that money, effort, and energy, [Student O]. Now you students, especially here at Sunday night group, you have a responsibility to know who the speakers are; you have a responsibility to know who the healers are; you have a responsibility to know who the ushers are; you have a responsibility to know who's speaking or not speaking and which mediums are serving. That's your responsibility. That's your responsibility. Or are you someplace else while you're in church? You see, that's your responsibility.

Now, [Student O], that includes you. Doesn't leave you out. You have that same responsibility as all of the rest of us. You have that responsibility.

I would not think of going to my church not knowing the schedule and every participant. I never have gone to my church not knowing, consciously, who was working and what is going on. Because to do so is a total waste of my life. It's a waste of my energy not to know what's going on. That would be like me just sitting in there continuing the recording for my own students and trying to get that work done and not even bother and come out here to expose [Student G] and her temptation con game and [Student O] and his temptation con game today.

What kind of a school would you have left, [Student B]? How long do think it takes if you let these things go by? It takes no time at all. Because it is a weakness that must be strengthened.

As I explained earlier, you have a very unique school: you have an authority that knows how to handle things. They have already spent years demonstrating that. Years! I would like to see one of you do as well as the angels have done in this organization, [Student B]—or anybody else. I would like to see one of your egos do half as well in your life as God's angels have done and continue to do with this! I haven't found anyone yet, have you, [Student O]?

No, sir.

No. So, now we have taken care of [Student E] and his trips—by the lyceum teachers. Both [Student B] and [Student P] are there. And when it's your duty, a spiritual duty to go up and take that offering, you take him over immediately and set him right beside them. You understand?

Yes, sir.

That's the way this organization runs. And that's the authority of the Council. Now I already spoke to [Student B] and told [Student B] to inform, I mean, [I] spoke to [Student P] and told [Student P] to inform [Student B] today while I was at church.

You must put the brakes on the weaknesses. The weaknesses, temptations, they're doing you in royally. Royally. That's what's doing you in, is that weakness called temptation. Because you become infatuated with your weaknesses. See? You become infatuated with your own weaknesses. It's—you see, we never seem to become infatuated with our own strengths. It's only our weaknesses that we seem to become infatuated with.

There was a demonstrable effect today of the sincerity of the students in bringing about and being instruments through which God could work and bring the goodness into the church and a little more supply. If the only thing your egos can relate to [is] if you don't make the effort, you pay more money, you see? Now the ego can relate to that. Because I am not the Lloyd's of London. Your ego can relate to that. And therefore, perhaps, bring about some incentive to make that effort and continue to make that effort, you see. Because that's right down here in this old material world very clear: two and two makes four; it'll never make five. So, if that is the only thing that can motivate some of you, there is divinity in disaster. There is divinity in disaster.

Now your egos today should have noted at least there was some increase in the flow. Isn't that true, [Student B]?

There was.

Well, it's up to you. The same law applies to the baked goods or anything else in this church, you know.[40] The same law applies. The same law. [If] you don't make the effort, then you dig deeper into your purses. You make the effort, and the burden will not be heavy. But I can't tell you seven days a week constantly right around the clock to make the effort. But you can see that only forces of darkness, [Student O] and [Student G], would take you from your spiritual Light. You can see that, can't you, [Student O]?

True.

Only forces of darkness. So, you have to go beyond infatuation. You have to go beyond attachment. And you have to look if this person or that person is being used as an instrument of the realms of darkness. You have to go beyond the blindness of emotion. You understand that, don't you, [Student B]?

Yes, it's true.

Yes, [Student P].

It's raining.

Isn't that nice. *[Some students laugh.]* Why do you think the Council ordered that these things be covered up?[41]

I really— [Student P begins.]

There is a cushion out here from your lounge. [Student R remarks.]

Thank you.

It's against the wall. [Student R continues.]

Oh, that's fine.

Be all right? [Student R asks.]

That should be fine, be it in Divine order. *[After a short pause, the teacher continues.]* Why do you think the Council ordered—in fact, why do you think they told me this morning to put on a raincoat? *[A few students laugh.]*

I thought it was the dryer. I didn't know what that noise was. And then I realized it was . . . [The last few words of Student P's comment are difficult to transcribe.]

Can't you hear the drip, drip, drip from the drain?

I could . . . I understood what was happening. [Again, it is difficult to transcribe some of Student P's words.]

Oh, I see. *[A few students laugh.]* Maybe someday you'll accept there's a Spirit, [Student P], and they do know what they're talking about.

Thank you.

How many years will it take? *[After a short pause, the teacher continues.]* See, when it comes up against blind desire and infatuation, it comes up against a stone wall, doesn't it, [Student O]? Are you able to see how even a person's son can be used by the realms of darkness to take a person from the Light of freedom? Are you able to see that, [Student O]?

Plainly see it. I was able to—

The Bible teaches it, you know, very clearly.

Yes.

Very clearly the Bible teaches that wonderful truth. So, a person on a spiritual path cannot afford the luxury, the luxury of blind desire, attachment, infatuation. They cannot afford it because they must give up the Light. You'll never have both. There's no way you can. Because, you see, your blind attachments, your emotional needs and infatuations, they will tempt you only at the time you are in service to the Light within you. Can you see that, [Student B]?

[There is no audible response from the student.]

They know when to strike. They always know the moment, the very moment to attack. And they'll always feed your self-pity: how you should have more rest; how you should have more time to yourself; how you should go out to dinner; you should go to the movies; you should go here; you should go here and go there. They will always tempt not your light of reason, but your senses. So that you can get even weaker than you are.

A few people make it on the spiritual path. And you certainly can see why, can't you, [Student G]?

I certainly can.

All of your weaknesses in service to the realms below shall be exposed in order that you may grow and God may become the higher priority. It's that way for everyone.

I really am grateful.

You see, [Student G], it's not just you. It's that way for everyone. Look at here recently the mountains of effort that's been made on [Student M's] infatuation. You know that, [Student O].

Yes.

Untold amounts of energy I have had to pour into trying to help her. To cast a little bit of light over the bondage of that infatuation. The absolute, suffering bondage. See? [Student M] knows that.

Yes. Thank you. [Student M responds.]

Because the bondage has been taking [a] toll upon her, you see. It even shows in her face. The infatuation does that to— shows on women; shows on men, too, but especially women. It's quite noticeable, you see. It's the drawing of the bondage of infatuation. It makes a person look old, tired, and weary, you see. You see, it's been happening to you very recently: here in this past seventy-two hours. You look in the mirror. It'll go away. But, have you noticed it, [Student O]? Can you see it in her face? How her face is—

Yes.

—being drawn, and it does that to everyone. It's the bondage of infatuation. Uh-huh. Don't worry, [Student M], if you remain in the Light, that's in God's hands and his ministering angels.

Thank you.

And your value for something greater than infatuation. That gaunt, exhausted look will disappear. *[After a short pause, the teacher continues.]* It is only the cry and the wail as it talks to the mind, losing its great love. That's all it is, you see?

Uh-huh.

Let the tears flow if they want to flow. I'm well aware of the entity.

Uh-huh.

The sadness, you see? You see the sadness in your face these past seventy-two hours?

Yes.

Exhaustion. You see, the Light, that beautiful Light that just causes a person to look like an angel has dimmed and almost gone out. Look at [Student M]. That's not her. That's the thing, as it cries and clutches to hold on. It's called attachment, [Student B]. That's what it is. It shows, [Student M].

[It is difficult to transcribe Student M's response.]

I had a girl here—sixteen years a student of mine. I used to have her get a mirror to look at [herself]. Same situation. It was her infatuation: her great love affair with her boy. She was totally in love with him to the sacrifice of God, you know. [Student A], you remember, don't you? She was completely in love with her boy. Until I would have her get a mirror to see what [it] was doing to her looks.

You see, you see, the thing feels threatened and is telling your mind, your emotions, it's about to lose. As long as you believe you are the thing that tells you how dearly you love this infatuation, you will suffer. Because that's not God. You see?

Yes, I do see. [Student M responds.]

But it's that thing that's talking to your emotions. It's not you. There is a difference.

Uh-huh.

You know, it'll tell you, oh, [it's] your greatest love of your life. There was never a love like the love you've experienced with your boy. It'll give you all of those wonderful con games as it slowly, but surely—you see, as it's clutching to hold on. That's the only reason you look exhausted, tired, as though you'd been brought through the wringer and look about sixty, instead of the young age that you are.

Uh-huh.

Yes. It's just that darkness of that entity. That's all it is, [Student M]. What have you lost? Creation to gain God? Well, when you—when that thing finally leaves your face, then you will see the difference.

Can't wait.

All you've lost is mental judgments and [mental] substance. You've lost nothing. You'll gain everything. Because God *is* everything good. You're being wrenched by your own Light of your own soul from the clutches of that dependence, you see. You know, if it wasn't that little fellow, it'd be someone else.

Uh-huh.

If—you [have] got to remember when it was big [Student O]. Then it got transferred to little [Student O]. Except they don't call him little [Student O]. I only call him little [Student O] in reference to: it used to be big [Student O]. Do you understand that?[42]

I do understand. [Student M responds.]

See? Remember this phenomenal infatuation you had with big [Student O].

Oh, yes.

Then, after you conceived, you see, it started—the thing, that entity, this great love affair entity transferred to that little, bitty fellow.

Uh-huh.

You see? Yet when you asked the Spirit for a name, they absolutely, blatantly refused to name him little [Student O]. *[Some students laugh.]* Be grateful for your sake.

Nothing personal, [Student O]. There's nothing wrong with the name [Student O], *[More students laugh.]* except what she created with that name. See? See, when the mind creates—no matter what name you give it—a form that is greater than God in your consciousness, you [have] got real problems.

Yes. [Student M acknowledges.]

Real problems.

Uh-huh.

Because the good—good feelings and good experiences and the joy of life and all the happiness and everything, that all goes out, and all becomes subject to what some mental entity and their games—because they're all fickle, those mental forms—decides to do with you at any moment. And because the manipulation has first taken place by the person, they attract like kind. You understand how that works?

Yes. [Student M replies.]

What good is there in that great infatuation love affair, [Student M]?

No good.

You see? You see, that thing doesn't want to let go.

I know.

He's screaming and he's putting that age upon your face. But you must remember, that will disappear. He will go because your soul doesn't want that bondage the rest of your life.

No.

And you have to understand, on a positive side, you were able to transfer this great love affair from big [Student O]—

Uh-huh.

—to little [Student O]. So, it is smaller than it was, in that respect. [Student E's] only a little bitty fellow.

Oh.

And [Student O] is a great big fellow. *[After a pause, the teacher continues to address Student M.]* You'll make it. You'll make it because you are so strong. You're that strong. Your soul is that strong. And God is greater than love affairs.

Uh-huh.

And you're not the first to get in it. And you won't be the first to get out of it. You can be rest assured of that. Anyone around God's angels will get through it. They won't escape it. They will grow through it. They won't turn their back and it's over, because that's not how you grow through anything. See, you have to remember in these love affairs that you're experiencing, [Student M]: it had a beginning. Therefore, it cannot be God!

Right.

Because that which has a beginning has an ending. So, because it had a beginning, it is guaranteed to have an ending. And because it has a beginning and an ending, it cannot possibly be God, for God doesn't have a beginning and God doesn't have an ending. Therefore, in truth it cannot be good.

Right.

Something that lifts you up only to drop you into hell. Would one—would you call that good, [Student B]?

No, I wouldn't.

That's what happens when we sell out God in our consciousness. That's what happens. We become that little puppet at which the strings are pulled at any moment they decide to be pulled. But we should be encouraged. For when the strings are pulled, we know our own weaknesses. And we know beyond a shadow of any doubt where [and] in what areas of our consciousness we've sold out God. See? So in that respect, that's very encouraging, [Student M]!

Yes.

Hmm?

Yes, it is.

You see?

Yes.

You see, there's a part of you that's very dependable. That's the soul. And that which is dependable is secure. So, your emotional security, you don't need to transfer to little [Student O]. You don't need to transfer your emotional security, that need for emotional security, to anything outside of you, for the greatest security of all exists within you. You see?

Right.

Yes, you had quite a night, [Student M]. You had quite a night. You know, I usually don't reveal this to my students: I worked with you practically all night long, 'til the wee, wee hours of this morning.[43] There were *thousands* of screaming demons that wasn't [weren't] about to let you go from that love affair. I know. I know exactly how you felt. And I know the exhaustion you experienced because they're not getting their way as long as you're in the Light. You see, because they come to attack me. They blame me for the Light that shined over that dark area of your consciousness. They blame me for the loss of this great love affair. I know. That's my work. I ought to know, I've been through it. God only knows how many times I've been through that. I went through it with [Student Z]. I went through it with [Student V]. I went through it with [Student Q]. I went through it with [Student E2]. I've been through it with so many people, you cannot imagine how many love affairs I've had to go through.

I don't need to be married or have girlfriends or things. Why should I, [Student B]? I go through them for years of my life. One love affair right after another one. You can't imagine. I know them inside out, upside down, sideways, backwards, and you name it. Because I've spent my life working with people to try to help them through those great love affairs of infatuation bondage.

Uh-huh.

And those entities, they know where the Light's shining. So, they always come to attack me. Oh, I know you didn't sit down there last night and say, "That son of a bitch, Richard Goodwin"—God forbid, it's on tape—or—whatever, it's private. *[Some students laugh.]* And I know you didn't sit there and do that. You were just tearing your brains out with those entities.

Uh-huh.

Are they any good, to put you through such torture all night long? Are those things worth it?

No!

What have they brought you to keep you up all night long, tearing apart at your emotions? That can't possibly be good, let alone God. If I wanted to climb the wall, I'd find something besides some infatuation bullshit to climb it over.

No, I am aware, [Student M]. I am aware that a part of you made a decision in the Light. And I'm also aware you must pay the price to be freed from that bondage of that infatuation. I'm also aware that you're capable of freeing yourself from that bondage. But those entities try to tell you you're not, you know.

Uh-huh.

They work on your weaknesses.

Uh-huh.

But, at least, you know, everybody has weaknesses and you have a few. When you cast the light of reason over that infatuation, you stop and say, "Now just a minute. He's physically still there. I still do my best to guide him. It's just that I'm able to breathe without him present for a few moments. I'm able not to pant like a, a dog in heat waiting for him to arrive." That's freedom!

Uh-huh.

I mean, when a woman can go about her work in the day and not pant like a dog waiting for her love affair to arrive in her consciousness, don't you think that's freedom, [Student B]?

It's true.

That is freedom! Think of that! That you're going to be able to breathe! So, what those insane entities, doing their number on you all night, [what they are] trying to tell you doesn't even hold water. What does it hold?

Nothing. [Student M responds.]

Better for you to be free from that bondage—why, he's just a little bitty fellow—than to go twenty years from this day.

Uh-huh.

You're not being freed for me or for Serenity Church. You're being freed for your own soul—that which you are, not what you think you are. You see? Many another mother before you has had to wait fifteen, twenty years plus. Isn't that true, [Student G]?

That's true.

They, not having this Light that you have received, at that timing—

Uh-huh. [Student M acknowledges.]

See?

Uh-huh. I know it.

Why, they've had to go through those years of suffering and still are torn to pieces by those entities! Isn't that true, [Student B]? At certain times?

[It is difficult to transcribe the response from Student B.]

They, they—you see, the instant you believe the thought of your mind is you, they got you. That's all you have to do, is believe. The instant that entity rises up and tells you about your great love, all you have to do is believe that you're that entity. The instant you do that, they got you. That's all you have to do, [Student M].

OK.

That's all you have to do, is believe that entity when he says, "My great love of my life." You know that, because that's what he tells you.

Yes.

The greatest love you've ever known. Well, if that little fellow that you are infatuated with is the greatest love you've ever known, what happens when he decides to do his number?

Uh-huh. Uh-huh.

Ha! What happens to [Student M], an individualized soul? What happens to you? Is it going to be a repetition of a sixteen-year student of mine, who's torn to smithereens with the greatest love she's ever known? He's now fifteen or sixteen. That's the alternative. That's the choice. And when he doesn't get what he wants—and you never know when he wants it—she's torn to smithereens in the depths of hell. Totally.

More than one of my students has left the Light for their love affair.

What do you think took this exodus [of students]? What do you think rose up that this [these] ex-students of mine, here, [left the church] in this past couple of years? It was these great loves. Aren't you people aware of that? They got involved in the greatest loves of their life. Well, what do they have to say about it now? Without naming their names—what do they have to say about the greatest love they've ever known today, two years later? Go see them and you'll find out. I guarantee you, [Student B], you *will* find out about the greatest love they've ever known and what they've ended up from. Uh-huh. Without—I haven't even discussed it, but I'm very well aware of it. I'm aware of the unbearable regrets, the anger, the resentment, and go on down the list, as they sold out the thing they worked for, for the greatest love of their life. Yes, [Student M].

So, this suffering and this screaming of these demons about your great love affair, they will pass. But not overnight, [Student M], because you did not create the need to find a god of form overnight.

Uh-huh.

You see?

I do see.

So, if you understand that this need to find a god that you could squeeze, touch, and manipulate was not created overnight—it wasn't created the moment that you met big [Student O]. And it certainly wasn't created the moment that you transferred from big [Student O] to little [Student O], [Student O]-[Student E]. You understand that?

I do understand that.

No, no, no, no. You see, that sellout was done long ago.

Yes.

Long ago. This is why we make it so difficult to find the God of Truth, to find the God that doesn't have clay feet. That's why we make it difficult. All of your religions teach you that man has to have something that he can control for a god. So, he has images and he has statues and he has something that he can touch and he has something that he can move. That's the gods of creation, you see? The golden calf, it's a living demonstration in the Christian Bible. Religions before them have revealed constantly how man must have a god that he can squeeze and move and touch. Because that represents control.

The God of freedom, like the air, when man is locked in self and self-identification, that just seems meaningless. He moves his hand through that God. See? He can't grasp it and control it. You understand that?

I do.

Well, that's where you are in evolution, [Student M]. Be grateful for that suffering. Be grateful today because going through it today, you won't have to pay the unbearable prices of those emotional entities of the dark deep twenty years, thirty years from today. If you don't accept it from me, talk to some of the mothers that are students of mine. I know they can help shed that light on that. Isn't that true, [Student G] and [Student B]?

[It is difficult to transcribe the responses of Student G and Student B.]

Because, you see, the law returns impartially. What divine justice. If we just look at these things without emotion—I'd like some coffee, please, [Student P]. Anyone else can have it if they want. Take a look of how just and beautiful the law is. The experience reveals to us our true motivation—not what we try to tell our self, but what our true motivation is. Don't you understand that?

And we must look at it with a joyous spirit and say, "Now just a minute"—Excuse me—"like attracts like and becomes the Law of Attachment. My God, look at this mirror. Look at my suffering. Help me, God, to see *clearly* my true motivation when I set that law into motion that I'm having these experiences as a return. Help me to encourage myself that I'm not totally a bad person. It's just that through my ignorance I stepped off into realms that lacked the light of reason." Wouldn't you agree on that, [Student B] and [Student G]? That's all. You see, you [have] got to talk to yourself: "So, I've made a mistake. Now, hopefully I will learn from that mistake. I will pay my price graciously. I will not cry in self-pity and discouragement because I must pay for what I have set into motion." And then the time will come when you'll be able to breathe fresh air. Now how can you beat that?

You look at it a positive way: to let a god of clay go to find the God of freedom. My God, who could hesitate with that opportunity, [Student B]? Who could hesitate to let a god of form and bondage go from the consciousness to gain the God of fresh air and freedom? Who would want to lock themselves in a closet when they can be out in the meadow of life? I can't imagine. Certainly, no one who is pausing to think would make such a choice to be locked in the closet of hell when the opportunity to walk in the meadows of God was available to them. Yes.

Thank you.

There's another part of you, [Student M]; it's the good part. Those are the parts I try to keep my consciousness on to see the good, because that's where God is; that's where you truly are, though temporarily and at times you have these tendencies to believe you are the thoughts of your mind, which are creation! You must understand—look, thought is form and is limit. Therefore, it is created. You are not creation. You are that which moves creation. So, there's no way possible you can be the thought. You are the mover of the thought. To believe you are the thought is the bondage of living hell. That's how they get you, is the instant you believe that you are this great love affair. When you believe that, you are bound. When you talk to yourself and say, "Hey, just a minute. Just a minute. I'm not the thought. I am not its effect, the feeling. I am not this emotion. Because I am not it, I can control it." Understand that, [Student B]?

Yes.

Because you are not it! That's where the freedom is. Because that's where the truth is!

Certainly, [Student M] suffered all night. I am very well aware of that. I worked like a little demon myself on those entities, knowing they're only creation, you see? And knowing that those kinds of forms blame anyone that shines an ounce of light of reason over them, you know. God is greater than that. I got to work. I did my job today.[44] And I'm here tonight working for the Light again.

Oh, no. No. No, when you've gone through as many love affairs as I've gone through, [Student M], you don't end up cynical or bitter, but you don't serve those false gods with clay feet. I guarantee you that. Not when you've gone through enough love affairs. And each one is the greatest you'll ever know. It's always been that way, hasn't it?

Oh, it's true. [Student M responds.]

You do remember the others?

Yes.

Without me being specific. And each one was the greatest love you ever experienced. Or have you forgotten? Don't take it personal, [Student O]. After all, you had your own. *[Many students laugh loudly and then the teacher laughs.]* If that doesn't help us, [Student O], to turn to God, I don't know what will. *[Everyone laughs.]*

You didn't, really, for a moment delude yourself that [Student M] was a virgin?

No, I try— [Student O responds.]

You try not to hear that. All right. We're all adults; so, let's act accordingly. God is greater than all that. If you have some value for creation, tell me what it is. God's angels will help you watch it fall apart. *[Everyone laughs.]* Uh-huh. Uh-huh.

Yes, well, you know, it's like today, you know, I know you've all witnessed the difficulty with some people coming to church because of their attachment to their babies. Can that be Light? To deprive a person—anything that deprives a person of the Light is not the Light and is not in service to the Light no matter what your mind has to tell you. Therefore, when I witness [Student O] sacrificing the Light of his own soul and freedom, I asked God and his angels for guidance to help him. And they immediately took corrective measures. Because little [Student E] was in no way serving the Light of God and goodness to be an instrument—no matter how small or how big he is—to be an instrument through which his own father and mother, [who] care for him and bringing the Light to his little soul, there is no way he could be serving the Light that his father would have to sacrifice *his* service to the Light. We all know that.

Now, [Student O], you are taking corrective measures, so there's no one complaining about your guidance of your child.[45]

Yes.

Yes.

Very cautious.

Yes, well, that's important, especially in this day and age. Especially in this day and age when everyone seems to know the best way to raise a baby. Everybody and his brother's got their theory. In fact, I don't know anyone who doesn't have some kind of a thought about the matter. Let them do their own thing seems to be the choice that's the most popular way.

[They're] supporting penitentiaries, too. [Student O continues.]

They certainly are. They're becoming so costly to the taxpayers. They're so jammed packed. They're overcrowded—three to a bunk, I hear, there in San Mateo. It's terrible at that county jail down there—was on the news. They're screaming their heads off. And there's no place to put them; so, they're dumping them back out on the streets. That's right. They need to build larger penitentiaries, is what they say on the news.

It isn't larger penitentiaries they need. Spare the rod and spoil the child. Stop sparing the rod when reason reveals it is needed. And you won't have these unbearable costs of mountains of institutions in which to lock people up.

It is the worst system ever devised by the human mind. They should be put out on farms where they can be working from 4:00 am until 4:00 pm with one lunch break and producing for society. Now when society wakes up, they'll stop this number of building concrete buildings with television sets and radios and 4 by 4 cell blocks and phenomenal costs of psychiatrists and psychologists and down the list. And they'll put them on work farms. And they'll put them out and they'll produce for society and pay their way. Isn't that an intelligent way, [Student B] and everyone?

Yes. [Many students respond.]

They should be producing. Then, you see, the cost to the taxpayer would become nil. The salaries of the guards and everything else would be paid by their production. No work—no food. Very simple. You have to work with the senses, you see. Not one of them will lie down and starve to death. I guarantee you. *[Some of the students laugh.]* Yes, certainly. *[Perhaps a student asked to be excused.]* Not one of them. They may cry and wail and scream that they have to work so hard—but if they keep the goody two-shoes out of the system, then the taxpayers won't be so burdened that they can no longer build the institutions, [Student B].

It's the worst, cruelest system they have going. The very worst. Not only for the burden of the taxpayer and society, but it does nothing to transform them into human beings. It does absolutely zero. They go in there and learn how to do it better the next time. That's what the record has proven. I don't know how many years it's going to take for them to wake up that that's not the way. You know, as—I know it wasn't the best thing, but the idea was good. Unfortunately, the mind got ahold of it. They used to have penal colonies, you know. But unfortunately, they were not treated with the light of reason. The original idea was good: to place them out where they could work and produce for society. But unfortunately, it turned into a real devil's island. But the idea itself is the wise thing under the light of reason. Put them where they can work and produce. Then the energy will go to something productive in life.

Well, I'm glad you're feeling better, [Student M], yes.

Thank you, Mr. Goodwin.

Yes, the, the self-pity entity, the love-affair, self-pity entity, it will leave you as you continue on with your effort.

OK.

It will. And [Student O], you should be encouraged. Encouraged during [Student M's] crisis of trying to free herself from that bondage, you know.

Uh-huh.

Aren't you encouraged?

I am.

Good. The Friends are encouraged. She stands at the crossroads of gaining everything good. So, what is the payment but a judgment of the human mind? Huh?! I gladly give up any judgment that stood in the way of my experiencing the goodness of life. Gladly give it up.

Thank you. [Student M acknowledges.]

Uh-huh. You see, [Student M], I do realize if you hadn't been—remember, your soul merited that.

Yes.

If you hadn't been, as a little girl, so dependent emotionally upon your father—

Uh-huh.

—you would not have this struggle at this time in your life. Now you can't blame your father for, through his own ego needs and his own ignorance, he supported that.

Uh-huh.

But you must take a look at the cause. And when you look at the cause, you have more clearly before you the cure. You see? You know very well you've never felt emotional dependence to any woman—sister, mother, girlfriend, or anything else.

No.

Your emotional dependence is totally with the father image. What the hell, [Student O] doesn't even resemble your father.

Neither does little [Student E]. There's nothing close at all. [Student E] looks nothing like his grandfather on your side of the house. Absolutely nothing. He looks like you and he looks like [Student O]—a combination. But he certainly doesn't look *anything* like his grandfather. And you know it, [Student O]—or don't you?

No, he doesn't.

So, you see, when you look at it with a little light of reason, [Student M]—I mean, really! *[Student M and the teacher laugh.]* But it is—the love affair is an early emotional attachment to your daddy, you see?

Yes.

You know he gave you whatever you wanted.

Yes.

He never once bothered to correct you. Because he had his own—and still does—his own ego needs. Now that doesn't make him a good or a bad person, but if you understand why, you have this phenomenal attachment—because early in your life, as a little girl—you have the cure in your hand.

Yes. Thank you.

And when you use the light of reason and you talk to yourself and say, "What the hell, [Student E], you don't look anything at all like your grandfather. This is stupid in my brain. This is real stupid." See?

Yes.

Now that you're feeling so much better, in fact, your face has even changed a little bit with that bondage of that love affair, what do you think, when do you think, and how do you think that clicked, that light clicked on in your consciousness? Because you sure paid last night for it. When did it happen? I—you—are you aware when it went click? "I can't go on like this." When did it go click? When did that, that light go on?

Yesterday.

Yes. What time yesterday?

Ah . . .

Do you remember? Do you remember what happened in your mind? Because, boy, it did infuriate those entities.

I know.

I mean, it really—they went crazy.

No, I . . . [A few words are difficult to transcribe.]

Was it early in the day, late in the day? Did—

I think it was around one—

[The recording ends.]

SEPTEMBER 30, 1984

Class August 17, 1986

[This class was given in the temple garden to a larger group of students.]

Good morning, class.

This morning has revealed that my class here has made themself in need of the opportunity to experience the wisdom of patience. And so, though some of you may think that I have difficulty in waiting— *[Reddy, the church's dog, knocks over a plastic glass of water. The lid comes off and almost all of the water spills into the garden. The teacher drinks water at the close of a class to aid in the return of Mr. Goodwin to his physical form.]* I can assure you had that cover been on properly that never would have happened—however, I can assure you that patience has not been, for a very long, long time, a difficulty for me. And so today we will discuss your need for the opportunity to experience the wisdom of patience.

The purity facade reveals itself to those who are awakened when anyone permits themself, from lack of the spiritual guidance and exercises that have been given, to blatantly refuse to do them in keeping with the necessity of awakening and simply suppresses that which they have created and believe that they are. So, in order to help you, this class here on Earth, you will be required to be on time at class; you, however, will not be aware, in your mental world, of what time class shall begin. Otherwise, you cannot be granted the opportunity to experience what you know in your world as waiting, that you may grow in the wisdom of patience. That opportunity will in turn grant you a slow, but sure, freedom from this facade of spiritual purity and bring about a readjustment in your priorities while you are permitted in class and in the temple that we have founded.

And so this morning you may raise your hands in question of where you think—and that includes our cameraman and especially our directors—where you think your problem is that you have not demonstrated, especially of recent time, an adjustment in your priorities of what you have earned as a spiritual opportunity. *[After a short pause, the teacher continues.]* And I expect the first hands to be from those who have been granted, by the Law of Evolution, the opportunity to be in a position in our school as demonstrators of the Light, especially, and as directors of our little organization. Yes, [Student R].

In answer to your question, I find that sometimes I get caught up with situations and holding in consciousness to those situations and not putting them down and moving on. And losing the moment of now.

You do realize the cause of that problem?

Yes.

And what is your understanding of the cause?

Self-identification.

The lack of daily spiritual exercises that have been given enforce, the lack of those exercises enforce the ever-increasing attachment to the fruits of action for the glory of self. Contrary to the purpose of being permitted in these classes. *[After a short pause, the teacher addresses another director.]*

Yes?

I find that when, when I've discovered that I've been part of a problem or a problem situation that I've contributed to, I over-magnify it in my consciousness so that I allow it to block out any consideration of the whole, of the organization and my other duties to the organization. And that's a big problem. That, that—

Well, it doesn't have to be a problem, for I have come to you over many years now in your world and have revealed to you the necessity of daily spiritual exercises. If those exercises were being done daily, you would not have the problem, which, of course, only reveals to those who have those problems that no matter what they say, known as the purity facade, no matter what they say, the exercises are not being done. And it is only a deception of the mental substance.

Yes? *[The teacher addresses a different director.]*

I feel the problem that I demonstrate is, as you've stated, not making the daily effort to keep my house in order and not being honest within and allow weak areas, like the self-concern, to interfere with my work for the Light.

Thank you, everyone.

Now, there is no way possible in your world that these classes can continue. There is no way possible that these classes of these higher teachings for you students can continue. You have gone as far as what you believe that you are will allow you to go. Unfortunately for you, as students, it is a blatant lack of using the guidance you have received for so many years. There is no way possible, for you allow, for you, no way possible.

The only alternative that is possible is that the lay students of this school demonstrate a care for that which they are receiving and start demonstrating by making effort with the three people who blatantly refuse to follow the spiritual exercises and guidance that has been given for so many years.

As I have just stated, without that care for what you are receiving there is no possible way for these classes to continue. And they shall not continue. If you, as a student body, which is the majority vibration, care, through the living demonstration— it isn't a matter of saying that you care. It is a matter of demonstrating that you care.

You, as a lay body of students, my channel and his responsibility, and I as your teacher have earned in our evolution this experience. You have the opportunity to make the difference, for the lay body of students is the majority over the three directors that you have merited.

Class is not over, [Student R]. Do not be concerned. When my classes become subject to your presumption, I will first let you know.

Yes, [Student Y].

How would, how should we best work with—I know beginning with ourselves . . .

Yes?

And so how would—what would be the best way to work with those that you mentioned?

Yes, with those—because I have mentioned those who bear the greater responsibility and who have been granted the greater opportunity of the Light. On your time, not time set aside for your spiritual classes—should they ever continue—on *your* time, you make arrangements with the three directors to counsel with them. And, of course, it would be in your best interest if there are other students in this class who care sufficiently for its continuity to be with you in your efforts as channels of the Light to help the three who have received so much over so many years and who are demonstrating a blatant lack of use of the spiritual teachings that they have received. It's known as the facade of purity. The demonstration of putting self-interest and self-priorities over spiritual responsibilities that one has earned is known as the facade of purity.

If one did not permit their selfish ego to attach to their fruits of action, they would not be so concerned whenever they were corrected in servicing the light below instead of the Light above, for the darkness is only lesser light. Yes.

Yes, [Student Y].

May we, may we work with them here?

Arrangements can be made. I will speak to my channel. Yes. Yes, [Student D].

Can a student also call at a specific time to check up on how things are going?

Well, who would you be checking with?

I, I could check with [Student S]. Or whoever the—

What assurance would you have, over a gadget called the telephone, when you cannot see into their eyes and be granted the opportunity to view past the mist?

You're right.

Let alone to hear. Hmm?

Yes.

When we permit our minds and our mouths to be used to lie and deceive, then we have less opportunity over a telephone.

Yes, [Student M].

May we have, like, will the Friends recommend, like, a consistent program of which we may be directed to work with these students on, like, while we're, you know, the nights we're here or on a daily basis during this—

Well, a consistency, a continuity and a consistency would absolutely be necessary for my channel has worked from an average of ten to fifteen years with the three directors. And it isn't though they haven't made effort; some effort has been made. But only effort that the forms they have created will permit.

You see, by suppressing a desire, all you do is strengthen it. And receiving these higher teachings, you're receiving and becoming available to a much higher rate of frequency, a much purer energy. And therefore, by not using the spiritual exercises you have been given, those suppressed forms, which, under the facade of purity, you have permitted yourself to deceive yourself, become stronger than ever before. Absolutely contrary to the guidance that you have received for so many years here in this school. This is why it is not possible to continue on with these higher teachings or these classes while the ever-increasing frequency of energy that you are receiving here in these classes is continually being directed to the forms that you have suppressed.

Thank you.

Yes. Yes, [Student B].

Why will the directors be any more inclined to listen to students when they don't listen to their teacher?

Well, they will not listen to me because they can't grab my throat physically. And they won't listen to my channel because they want something out of my channel, you see. And you will find that the three directors are not interested, as a priority, of getting something out of you; therefore, your work with them, as a student body, directly working with that which is their problem (the uneducated ego suppressing the desires, going contrary to the teachings received), you have a possibility of, with a united effort of the student body, to have an impact upon that uneducated ego that is causing the problems.

You see, first of all, one takes pride in the things they create. And when you are working with the uneducated ego, you are working with what is known as the function of pride. Now the function of pride is a function that makes constant effort to polish the image it believes that it is, you see. It's like brass: it's in constant need of polishing. Otherwise, it doesn't shine, you see. And that which does not shine to a world of creation is that which is not attractive to those lower forms, you see. As the moths go to the light, so the forms of mental substance go to the light that is created by the function of pride. And then man experiences, in his mental substance, the thrill of what he understands as glory. Does that help you, [Student B]? Yes. It's known as the lesser light. The lesser light is the light of glory. And the greater Light is the Light of acceptance. Yes.

Yes, [Student J].

I have no comment, sir. My only reaction to any so-called assistance I can give would be in the area of force, which, I'm sure, is not the way to go.

Well, it is not the—the passive resistance is the path of power. However, you are in a world of creation. And in that world of creation, especially where there are these higher teachings and this ever-increasing frequency of Light, changes must be brought about in order for the continuity. The alternative is, is to separate the boys from the girls. To have a class one week just for the boys. To have a class on a different week just for the girls. We have already discussed that with our Council, and it has not been recommended. For it will, instead of solving a problem, it will increase a problem in your world of creation. For we have already found that the majority of the lady students will be offended, not knowing for sure what the men students are receiving. You understand. And, of course, we do understand that type of thinking because anyone, male or female, that totally believes that they're only half there, of course, would be concerned with what's happening in principle to the other half. I'm sure you understand that. And, of course, it certain—it is not recommended.

Not only that, it goes contrary to our efforts to establish for the first time in a world of creation on your planet, for the very first time, to establish a school of spiritual Light of this frequency where both sexes are in attendance. This has never been done successfully in your world of creation. It has never been done. And surely over this, this past year in your world, perhaps, you're gaining a little insight of why it has never ever been successful, you see. For the evolution of the human form on the planet Earth, it is very rare that, very rare, that they are willing—not that they're not able, no—but willing to make the separation, [Student J]. That's the reason it has never before, ever, existed in the midst of your world of creation. Yes. I hope that's helped with your question.

Thank you, sir.

Yes. Yes, [Student D].

Are you telling us that we're still having a problem with the boy-girl thing?

Oh, yes, yes. I would have to say I'm a bit surprised if you're not aware that you have that severe problem in principle right here in your, in your spiritual classes. The priority of creation has risen above the priority of spiritual awakening, you see. And you should have recognized it in so many ways. When you hear the mind say, well, how much they're doing and how hard they're trying, you are speaking to creation and not to God or the Light. You see? You're speaking to creation.

In fact, some time ago our channel was instructed that he would have to learn to whine and complain and tell some of his students how much *he* is doing, which is totally contrary to his upbringing, has caused him a great deal of emotional upset to have to do that because it is contrary to his own upbringing of his own mental substance. It's not only embarrassing but, for him, it's humiliating. However, he has, at our request, done that now for some time in order to, as you would say, to relate to you when you're in those realms of consciousness. Yes.

I have spoken to the three who have received the most and bear the greater responsibility by the positions that they have earned.

Some of you, I know, are not aware that my channel worked after our seminar Thursday night until 3:00 a.m. Friday morning.[46] He went into his meditation at his regular time and got back up to work at 6:00 a.m.[47] He continued to work. Now that was Friday. Friday in your world. He worked all day long. And then the very next morning from about your, prior to noon on, he worked for hours again.

And we cannot continue with these classes as the ever-increasing energy that you are receiving is being used for the forms you have suppressed and requires so much energy out of our channel, for he will not be fit or able for us to come and give you those classes. You understand? So, we would only be defeating the very purpose for which we have founded them. Yes.

Yes, [Student Y].

Is this, this group here of people, are they abnormal in their expression?

Abnormal?

. . . or is it— [A helicopter flies overhead, which makes transcription of a few of the student's words difficult.]

Abnormal? If you mean by normalicy [normalcy], if you mean by normalicy [normalcy], the natural law of what you are, then they are abnormal. If you mean, "Are they average?"—and that means like the rest of the masses on your planet—then they're very average. Yes.

[It is again difficult to transcribe her remark.]

Yes, yes. Yes, [Student J].

If—

But we haven't come, [Student J], here to be average. We've come here to move above average, at least while we're here, haven't we?

Yes.

Yes, go ahead.

If, assuming 51 percent is making some attempt—

Yes.

—or meets the approval of you and—

It's not me. It meets the approval of the requirements for the Light to continue.

The requirements.

Yes. Otherwise, we destroy our self.

Why not give the violating minority a vacation?

Well, that's what should be discussed with them: if a vacation would, would solve the problem. You see, we have made several recommendations. And our—my recommendation to our own Council, of which Isa is our chairper—chairman—she don't like to be called chairperson. I don't blame her a bit. But anyway, *[The teacher laughs.]* these fancy words nowadays.[48] Personally, in my work here, I would like to see an increase financially in the cost of the class by, say, at least 100 percent increase in the class fee in order to pay for professional workers to come in and do the work. Then, you see, my channel would be freed from being so drained that he soon will no longer be able, you understand, for me to enter. For the energy utilized, you see, it's extremely detrimental. The doctor has already spoken to our Council on that.

And so, I know that your minds tell you, well, that's impossible. Well, it's just as impossible as, of course, you make it. But I find that to be the more intelligent solution in your world, should you, by not demonstrating the law, be successful in your efforts to counsel the three students who are in a critical position in reference to this class and our school. Yes. Did that help you, [Student J]?

No.

Well, you'd rather pay the money, yes. *[The teacher laughs.]* But I don't think you'd want to face having to pay several other people's money. No, I don't think so, [Student J]. Yes. I can understand that. Yes, [Student B].

Since this seems to be a fire center problem, are we being asked to meet fire with fire or—

Yes, that's the only thing that's ever successful, you see, is to meet fire with fire. It's the only way to fight fire is with fire. And when the fires of illumination meet the fires of lust, then the fires of illumination must increase. You see? Yes.

Now, [Student R], I want you to look over here and pay attention, for this involves you. And [Student H]. And [Student S]. The position that you are in. Do you understand that? And for you to permit yourself to feel sorry for yourself is just the opposite if you have any value for the teachings that you receive. Pardon? *[After a short pause, the teacher continues.]* You see? You see, when we make a judgment of how well we're doing, we always experience what we're really doing, don't we? So, we don't make judgments of how well or how badly we're doing on anything. We just do.

You see, it's like a person says, "I'm trying." Well, I instruct you: stop trying and start doing. I've heard try—you see, the word *trying*, did you ever stop to consider the difference between the word *crying* and *trying*? *[A few students laugh.]* What is the difference?

A letter.

Pardon?

One letter.

One letter.

Yes, sir.

Just one. That's the problem. You see? So "I'm trying" is telling me "I'm crying." So, let's stop trying so we can stop crying. Oh, yes, yes. It's one of the defenses, you see, and you know that truth requires no defense; so, what is being defended is falsehood and deception. Yes, [Student Y].

So, would the first step in working with these, these three directors, would be to, we really must, the rest of us, face that very level?

Yes, well, I would rather say that, you see, if you want guidance in working spiritually, then it requires the very thing that most minds are not willing to give: a constant monitoring, you see? You see, that's why you have so many orphaned babies in your world. They require monitoring. So you find your world over populated with untold millions of orphans. Oh, legally, your world says they have a mother and a father, but the demonstration reveals clearly there's no parent at all, for there's no one constantly monitoring them, you see. So your world is over populated with untold millions of orphans. Yes. Requires monitoring.

Repetition is the law through which change is made possible. These are the basic laws to use. Exposure frees the soul. You have come with the motive of freeing your soul from the prison in which you have allowed it to be placed. And so, if you do not use the laws which will bring that about, then it shall not be brought about. Repetition is the law through which change is made possible. Exposure frees the soul. You see?

You see, it's like if a person has a problem with the fire center, you discuss it constantly and repeatedly, the detail of it. Certainly, you are consciously directing energy to it. Well, the one that has the problem is unconsciously directing energy to it. So which is the best way to work? You see? Bring it right up to the fore, as our channel was instructed yesterday, that he may have to stay at the door and monitor with two statements to each student, especially the offenders. He was disgusted. He was upset at the very thought of it. And I will tell you clearly—even though we are recording, these are private tapes here, you see— he was instructed to prepare himself to check with the offenders "Did you get your screwing last night?" "Did you bring the money that you owe?" For these are the two problems that are in the way and an obstruction to what you come here for. Now he didn't appreciate that. I have no problem with the word. It's what you think about the word. They say in your world the bees do it, the bugs do it, the rabbits do it, why not do it? Well, why not cut off your hands and glue feet on them so you could walk on all fours? You see? So, I have no problem with those things.

Oh, if I want to go back into recall and I want to think of the few moments of what I considered, at that time, peace, by getting away from her for a short time—it wasn't very long. Minutes usually.[49] And—but I could go through all of that in review. But, you see, it's what you pay for what you get, you understand?

And so, Isa and our assistants worked with my channel yesterday untold hours of, of [on] this problem created by some of the students. He said, "I'm disgusted at the thought that I would have to stand there and not be allowed to say hello; I'd have to ask that." You know, it's funny where it belongs: with the bunnies, the rabbits out there in creation. Here, in a class, you see what it's doing: it's closing it down. You see? But I do not want those realms to take pride that they have accomplished that. No. For the classes will be replaced with other students. Yes. Different classes.

Untold thousands of hours and energy unlimited has been directed to help you as a student body. There is no way possible God or anything outside can bring about changes in your consciousness. There is no way possible that God and the rest of us in any world can take you physically and set you down to do your meditation, your spiritual exercises, you see? You see, we may accomplish it once or twice through various phenomena, but of what benefit would that be?

We find that there are two types of people in your world and on your planet: the awakened and the dependent. And this class is here for the awakening ones. Not the dependent ones. And people who believe they're half there are people who are dependent. Class is not for those people. People who believe that they are in need and their need can be fulfilled by something outside, beyond their divine right and sphere of action, are people who [are] dependent. These classes, these higher teachings are not for them. They are not ready for these kind[s] of teachings. They're not ready for these classes. No. They have reached the point at which their belief forms, that they believe they are, will permit them to go. And you cannot mix water with oil. You see, it doesn't mix. You can stir it, but you cannot mix it. Yes.

So, the choice has to be made. And it's not being made. It's being spoken, but it is not being made or we would not have this lovely class we're having here today. Yes, [Student M].

As we work on, you know, the forms, our suppressed, our own suppressed desires, hopefully to shed some light of reason on them, as we do our breathing and our exercises, this will bring them to the light so we may look at them.

Well, I think if you would please listen to the classes you've already seen, it was—you've already seen and heard, that it was fully described in that. But, you see, you'll have to do your homework.

OK.

Now, if I hadn't already given that, [Student B] and everyone here, then I would discuss it with you. But I've already given that. So, of what benefit is it to pay so much money for a class and pay no attention to it? It has already been given. Speak to your husband and I'm sure he'll be able to help you.[50] It has already very clearly been given and described. You do understand that, don't you, [Student O]?

I certainly do.

And it certainly was given. Yes.

Thank you. [Student O responds.]

Thank you. [Student M responds.]

You're welcome. There are no shortcuts. Yes, [Student Y].

Is it, is it so that it will take constant monitoring first of ourselves to be successful in the—

[The teacher laughs.] Yes. That's what you're here—you're here in school to awaken. Not depend.

You see, it's so easy to take a look and say, "Well, that's a director, and therefore I presume they'll do this and that." And they do it. Well, you do that from your own laziness. That's all you do that from. It's from your own laziness. That's like a director saying, "Oh, well, Richard or his friends will take care of it." Well, that's their laziness. That's what you know as the great deception, you see. That's the great deception.

So, there's no problem. I mean, if the student body is united and they want to make that effort, we're willing to go along for a time—and I'll not tell you how short or how long—with your efforts working with the directors in order to help them and to inspire that which they are and not that which they believe that they are.

If you're not willing to do that, I will say good day and goodbye to all of you. I will, of course, visit my channel in keeping with the laws of the evolution he has started. And so, you make that decision yourself, and while you're not feeling any peer pressure. So, I will say good day. I expect a decision to be made before you ever leave this temple; otherwise, I not only say good day, I say good-bye. And thank you so very much.

Oh, and one thing. You have permission to seat everyone for refreshments in the temple dining room, and reach your decision. And then make your effort, if that is what you choose.

AUGUST 17, 1986

Membership Meetings

Membership Meeting April 8, 1972

—Annual membership meeting of our church.

O Infinite and Supreme Power, we ask at this time that angel loved ones serving the Light may gather close beside us to inspire and to guide us to carry on the duties, the responsibilities, and work of this Serenity Spiritualist Association. We know that when we are at peace, O God, that Thy power moves through us in a harmonious and serene way. And in so doing, this old world is indeed blessed. We recognize, O God, our responsibility, having received a bit of Thy Light, to share it with those who are seeking. We know in truth that we are greater than this piece of clay that we are moving at this time. And we ask your guidance through all the deliberations of this meeting. Amen.

Amen. [Several members speak.]

Please be seated. *[The teacher strikes a table with a gavel.]* This meeting is officially come to order. All deliberations of this association not covered in its constitution and bylaws is [are] governed by the *Robert's Rules of Order*. The secretary will now rise to read the minutes of our last membership meeting. *[After a short pause, he continues.]* I beg your pardon. The secretary will call the roll of officers and members. Thank you.

[The call of the roll is taken and fifty-six names are called, but only twenty are present, including Mr. Goodwin.]

Thank you, Madame Secretary.

A quorum of the board of directors of this church and a quorum of the laymen being present, this meeting is official. *[The teacher strikes the gavel.]* The secretary will now read the minutes of our last meeting, please.

March 6, 1971. Serenity Spiritualist Church Membership Meeting. The invocation was given by President Richard Goodwin. The nomination of officers by a standing vote was President, Richard Goodwin, Vice President, [Student K2],

Treasurer, [Student J], Secretary-Treasurer, [Student S2], Secretary, [Student P2]: eleven votes each, plus four proxies.

The healers of our church are required to have five documented letters for the state board before each healer may become certified by same.

A pianist is needed for our church services.

It is a forty-year law that the charter sit for thirty days before approval by the State Spiritualist Association in Los Angeles, California.

The Serenity Spiritualist Church will open May 2, 1971, at 10 a.m. sharp. One hundred chairs are to be set up each Sunday.

[Student R2] will be in charge of the receiving committee with two cochairmen. [Student F2] is in charge of the social committee with two cochairmen, being [Student A] and [Student P2]. [Student P2] will be in charge of the ladies' guild; the cochairmen will be [Student A] and [Student F2]. [Student J] will be in charge of the podium; cochairman, [Student K2]. [Student T2] will be permitted to sit in the healing chapel for unfolding healing power. [Student R2], chairman of literature committee and [Student F2] to assist.

The Serenity Sentinel *must be promoted.*

[Student F2] to guide the members and friends to the healing chapel. Hands are to be washed by each healer after each healing. The flower girls are [Student A2], [Student B2], and [Student F2] will be in charge. The flowers are to be purchased from the Flower Gallery at $15 per service. A basket will be placed in the healing chapel. The proceeds are for the building fund.

In divine time, in divine order, we should have our own church.

Donations were taken for hymnals. The lending library will be $10 per year. All board of directors are requested to study the National Manual and follow the dictates of conscience. Type of uniformity and dignity. Without reverence, there is *no Spiritualism. The men are to wear suits on the podium. Dr. Waltham has requested that healers wear white coats. White is the symbol of purity, dignity, and respect. [Student J2] has offered to make a small chapel for the building fund proceeds.*

The church program will be $72 every two months. The ad will be placed in the [Marin] Independent Journal.

There will be classes for spiritual unfoldment. A student forum will be held the last service of each and every month. Workers are requested to be at church at 9 a.m. The church is to be cleaned after each service.

[Student R2] made a motion for the meeting to adjourn until the next designated meeting. [Student W2] seconded.

You've heard the reading of the minutes of the last meeting of this church, what is your pleasure? According to *Robert's Rules of Order*, you may accept it as read—or does anyone have a question? *[After a short pause, the teacher continues.]* The chair will entertain the motion to accept the minutes as read. Does someone care to make that motion?

I will make the motion.

[Student M2] has made a motion that the meetings [minutes] of the last meeting be accepted as read. Do I hear a second?

Second.

Seconded by [Student R2]. All those in favor?

Aye. [Many people respond.]

Contrary minded? *[After a short silence, he continues.]* So ordered and approved. *[The teacher strikes the gavel.]*

The next order of business is the reading of bills and references, which we do not have at this moment. The reading of communications. There is no communication present that has not been answered. And, number eight, the reports of officers, pastors, and assistants.

So, if you'll bear with me, I will read my report, as the president of your church—I did not have time to put it into writing, to be perfectly honest with you, but I will briefly tell you what has taken place in the past twelve months from the first Sunday of May.

As you know, this church was organized in February and conducted an organization meeting, at such time your present board of directors were elected by unanimous vote of our membership for the terms of office so specified in your constitution and bylaws. This church has shown a continuous, harmonious, and stable growth. It has become, in less than twelve short months, the second largest Spiritualist church in the State of California. Now that may or may not seem like much to some, but to me, it is a great deal. I have been in Spiritualism for a number of years. And I feel that I'm a bit aware of the great difficulties in growing from level to level as we strive to unfold our soul qualities.

This church has a regular, dignified ad in the local paper each Sunday. You all know that it has one of the largest, if not the largest, book sales department in *any* church in the State of California. It is having, come this coming May, the first spiritual awareness classes for twelve weeks.[51] It will be the first time that a Spiritualist church has given, publicly—to the public—actual techniques on the unfoldment of mediumship and becoming aware of these dimensions that we're in here and now.

Financially, this church has ever managed to pay the bills that it has incurred. It is not without funds to run a church. A church is like an employer. When we go to work to our employer, we recognize and realize that we're being paid in this material world a material salary. Our employer expects, for that expenditure, certain duties to be fulfilled. A church is an employer. And it expects from its membership certain spiritual responsibilities. For a church gives to them—it pays them not in dollars and cents, not with money or things in this dimension, but it pays them in a way of showing them how to help themself spiritually.

An employer recognizes that when a person is disturbed, they ofttimes blame the company for which they work. This is a very common and understandable practice. A wise employer, if he has a good worker, says to himself, "They'll get through that. They do a very good job when they're not disturbed." So, I ask and pray for tolerance. But we know that we don't get tolerance unless we have some understanding. And so it is with a church.

This church was ordained by another dimension. I never asked for it and I never wanted it. But as long as I am the president of it, I will do to the very best of my ability to serve the world of spirit that they may help to continue to illumine mankind, these spirits yet in the flesh.

And I am very grateful, for I know, and God knows, the work and the dedication that the friends, the members, and the directors of this church put in to keep our doors open. I want to thank all of you for supporting your church, for it is your church. It is, in a way, not a possession, for to possess is to destroy. The very thing we possess starts to destroy us. But it is your church in the sense that you have the golden opportunity to serve God and the angel world and, in so serving, your soul and my soul awakens. Thank you.

The secretary will please read her report. *[The teacher whispers something that is difficult to transcribe to an individual near him.]*

I don't feel at this time that I have anything to say, except that I serve as much as I can, as many hours a day as I can. I am grateful for each and every one that does help us in serving, as service is the only path to illumination for all of us. I don't have anything else to say.

Thank you, Madame Secretary. The treasurer will please read his report and the financial statement of the church.

Before reading the financial reports of this church, the chair will entertain—thank you, [Student J]—the chair will entertain a motion whether you wish your financial report collective or *seriatim*. Let me explain what that really means. A collective financial report is a report of the financial income of your church month by month with its expenditures, giving a final total, cash on hand balance. A *seriatim* report is a listing for the past— from May through March—of every penny that was spent and where it came from. That means, that each postage stamp that was purchased would be read off. I do want you—it is only fair to the membership to inform you that a *seriatim* report would take approximately eleven hours. A collective report would take approximately eleven minutes or much less. Financial reports of this association are available—*seriatim* reports—and a look at our books, which are kept in San Geronimo at our office, to any member in good standing upon a written request to the office stating your request.

The chair, now, will entertain the motion of whether or not you wish this report read collective or *seriatim*. [Student R2] is recognized by the chair. *[He strikes the gavel.]*

I move that we accept the collective report of the financial statement for the Serenity Spiritualist Association.

[Student M2] has made a motion that this association accept a collective financial report of the finances of the association. Do I hear a second?

I second it.

Seconded by [Student G2]. Are you ready for the question? Anyone having a question may speak forth at this time. Question: all those in favor?

Aye. [Many individuals speak.]

Contrary minded? *[After a short pause in which no one speaks, the teacher continues.]* So ordered and approved. *[He strikes the gavel.]* The treasurer [will] please read the report.

I'm going to give the date, the income, and the date of the expenditures for each month running from May 1971 through March of 1972. OK, here we go. May 1971, the income was $1,292.05 and the expenditures were $366.49. June of '71, the income was

$973.84 and the expenditure was $1,154.80. July of 1971, the income was $1,362.23 and the expenditures were $1,321.12. In August 1971, income $1,701.69, expenditures $1,729.53. September 1971, income $1,701.67. [The expenditures for September were not read.] *October 1971, income was $1,535.67 and expenditures $1,639.73. November income, $2,051.52; expenditures $2,280.60. December 1971, income $2,464.96; expenditures $1,935.73. January 1972, income $1,503.55; expenditures $1,918.95. February 1972, income $2,148.22; expenditures $2,262.20. In March 1972, income $2,037.66 and expenditures are $1,643.82.*

Our total income to date was $19,242.80. Our total expenditures to date, good friends, are $18,246.45. Our cash on hand to date is $996.35. And I thank you very much.

Thank you, [Student J]. What is your pleasure? You may accept the report as read, if someone cares to make that motion or state your question. The chair will entertain a motion. Yes, [Student G2].

I make a motion that we accept the statement as read.

[Student G2] has made a statement to accept the financial report as read. Do I hear a second?

Second.

Seconded by [Student M2]. Are you ready for the question? *[After a short pause, he continues.]* Question: All those in favor?

Aye. [Many individuals speak.]

Contrary minded? *[After a short pause during which no one speaks, the teacher continues.]* So ordered and approved. *[He strikes his gavel.]* The financial report of the association is accepted as read.

I would like to take a moment and state for the benefit and perhaps clarification with our membership where all this money comes from. As you saw from the report, that it costs a great deal of money to run this association.

And I would like to clarify that we are the Serenity Spiritualist Association with two separate ecclesiastical charters. We have a charter for Camp Serenity in the mountains of Mendocino and we have an ecclesiastical charter for the Serenity Spiritualist Church. Now, it is, unfortunately, illegal for us to combine church and camp membership due to the national requirement that a camp charter is a separate ecclesiastical charter from a church charter. For the enlightenment of all of us, I wish to state that a member of a Spiritualist camp does not have to be a Spiritualist in order to be a member. However, a member of a Spiritualist church *must* accept the principles of Spiritualism to be a member of a church. Therefore, we cannot combine the church and camp membership.

However, I do want to invite those who are here this evening to consider joining our camp. It supports the one association.

Camp expenditures are $120 per month. That is what the mortgage costs. That is what we're spending on your camp. The income, monthly, from the Serenity Spiritualist Camp, from the board of directors alone, is $125 per month. That does not include the membership fees of $10 a month, the membership fees of $30 a year.

When this [these] church doors opened, the Serenity Spiritualist Church borrowed over $1,000 from the Serenity Spiritualist Camp in order to open its doors. However, both of these separate entities are under the one heading of the Serenity Spiritualist Association. At the advice and counsel of our certified public accountant and our attorney, the camp and church were put under a single banking account way back last year in the month of July. And I did want to clarify the financial standing of the camp and the church.

Now, we will go on because we don't want to drag this meeting out any longer than we have to, and there is coming a time here when the membership will speak up for the good of their church.

Now we have the report of mediums. And I would like to have, if you feel free, the report of the student mediums and the certified mediums of this church. [Student M2], would you like to give us a report under the report of medium?

I thank you, Mr. President, fellow members. This is rather a bolt out of the blue for me. I, I didn't expect this. But myself, working in the church, I have found a great deal of happiness in it, that we give out so we can, in turn, receive. To me, I have been most, most happy to see all the new people, taking courage in your hands and letting spirit be your backbone and standing up and, and just letting it out. I wished only I had done so many years earlier myself. I think the decorum of all the student mediums on the platform, the present members, has been of a most high order. I feel very, very proud to be associated with all . . . [It is difficult to transcribe a few words.]

I would like to see more come up. There is one thing, if I might, during the meeting, to report, Mr. Goodwin, [that is,] put out for the benefit of the discussions of further—at a later date, maybe: I have observed, too, that so many people come from a great distance. Mr. Goodwin, your mediumship is a very high order. And naturally everybody would like to have their billets read. I do feel that to enable you to reach as many of the new people as possible and to enable our new mediums that are coming up to be more accepted in their own work that maybe we could ask, in a very nice way, that those who have received messages or would prefer to wait for one, that—then, in turn, there is not a repeat of work. So that then, in turn, you, in your, your more speedy work, would be able to reach the newer people coming in. Thank you very much.

Thank you, [Student M2]. Thank you. [Student H2], would you care to give us a little report, as a student medium of the church?

No, I would not. Thank you very much.

Thank you. [Student P2], would you care to give a report as a student medium of this church?

Yes. I find a tremendous joy to serve the world of spirit.

Thank you, [Student P2].

Our next order of business is committee reports, standing and special. Now our committees, as most of you are aware, the [chairmen of] committees of this church are nominated at its annual membership meeting and all committee chairmen are nominated for one year. Beginning with advertising committee, [Student R2], do you have a report from your committee, please?

I wish to thank all those who have participated in the advertising committee and urge those who are not members in the advertising committee to join. [A few people laugh.] *It's only—it's less than fifteen cents a day—less than a package of cigarettes. Some people don't smoke. But anyway, it's a package of chewing gum. And it, and it does the fine work of bringing the, the ad to many people. To 43,000 readers. The* Independent Journal *has a circulation of 43,000 readers. And each one has an opportunity to see where they can come for spiritual illumination and help. Thanks very much.*[52]

Thanks very much, [Student P2], for that wonderful report. Our auditing committee, we don't have a chairman for that yet. Birthdays committee, [Student S2] is not here. Book club committee, voted last year, was [Student I2], who is not present.

So, we will get into our nominations. Let's see who else is present here. The—

Educational. [The secretary remarks.]

Educational committee is [Student L2]. And do you have any report you would like to make on education? *[After a short pause, the teacher continues.]* Not yet. Classes haven't started. All right. Entertainment—[Student A] is not present. Flower committee has been changed. Food—food committee! Well, the food committee's here. I know that. [Student F2], would you like to give us a report, please, on the food committee?

Seeing as how everyone here donates to our socials and everyone enjoys them, I just want to say that no one—I haven't found anyone in our church membership or people who attend regularly that refuses to, to help. They're gladly helping. And I think because they know they're going to enjoy it later. And we've had a huge success, as you well know, and we expect it to continue on and on and on and on. Thank you.

Thank you very much, [Student F2]. I see your committee is coming right along. Gift committee—[Student W2], do you have any report that you would like to give at this time?

I don't think so.

You just started on that, didn't you? All right. *[The teacher says a few words that are difficult to transcribe.]* Ladies' guild committee for last year, [Student P2], do you have any report to give on the chairmanship of the ladies' guild?

Well, our biggest project last year was—well, this year from when we started in May until now, were the dolls, of course. It is true, what Crystal said, that the dolls would sell as fast as we made them. And they have. I don't have anything else to say about that.[53]

Thank you, [Student P2]. Lyceum conductor . . . *[Again, the teacher says a few words quietly, almost to himself, that are difficult to transcribe.]* Men's club! [Student R2], you have a report to give us on the men's club, please.

Yes. I wish to thank those who have helped make the doll class. And I have seen a tribute to the dolls appear in very unusual places. We have a framing project, which is—will be going very, very well this coming year. We'll be meeting more often. And I would thank those who have come to the meetings very much for their help. Thank you.

Thank you, [Student R2]. The receiving committee, [Student F2], would you care to give us a report on your activities, please?

Well, I don't know if I have any report prepared.

Thank you. The receiving committee has done very well. We've had many reports from people who called at the office, [regarding] the love that they feel in this church. And I know that the receiving committee is very important in emanating that vibration.

The *Serenity Sentinel* subscription committee—[Student G2], do you have a report?

Well, I'd like to just say thank you, one and all, for your help and support. And it's, it's coming right along. Thank you very much.

Thank you very much. Now we will get on to unfinished business. Is there any unfinished business of the church? If anyone is aware of it, would they please—the chair will recognize them for their motion. Yes, [Student R2].

Some time ago I put in a suggestion to the Spirit Council that we host Rosemary Brown for the national convention. It was relayed back to me by the Spirit Council that we should bring this to the convention of the nat—of the state board and ask the state board to host Rosemary Brown for the national convention when it was held here in California. And I would like to, at this time, announce those plans and receive any enthusiasm that may be evolved therefrom.

Thank you very much, [Student R2]. The chair recognizes your suggestion that was sent to this board of directors—and, as all suggestions are handled by your board, that you have voted in, and there is no suggestion that is not given consideration. As [Student R2] has stated, he received the decision of the board that an expenditure of over $6,000 to bring Rosemary Brown from London, England, is a wonderful thing. But your board of directors felt, considering that we go along nip and tuck and we keep our bills paid, that an additional raising of $6,000 would not be in the best interest of the church or membership at this particular time. However, your board of directors did suggest that the suggestion be brought up by [Student R2] at the convention floor this year, in June 20th, 21st, and 23rd. Thank you, [Student R2].

Is there anything else under unfinished business? *[After a short pause, the teacher continues.]*

Well, I have a few things here we would like to read. And no names are read on any suggestions. But this is one suggestion here is stated, is, "To enlighten is to clarify. Perhaps an explanation of our current expenses could make the membership more aware of their obligation. I, for one, wonder which is camp expense and which is church expense particularly since I'm not a member of the camp group. A package meeting—a package membership might be a good sales point. It would certainly add strength or unity to our cause. The less of vagueness the better." I think you will find that that was handled here at the membership meeting when we explained the reasons why we do not have a joint membership between the camp and the church—because of the illegality of it. And the financial reports, of course, are always available right here at the church.

Now, this one here would like, let's see, "like to form a committee to call on members and friends of our church who are confined—ill and confined to home. Possibly send a card; a committee could drop in to see them. Much spiritual good could come about from such an endeavor." The individual member that made that suggestion is not present and was not aware, at the time of making the suggestion, that we do have a healing council committee and always have had one. That [Student N2] is the chairman of that committee and that she—it is up to the membership of the church, if we are aware of anyone who is not well or ill at home, to inform the chairlady of the healing council committee that we may send them a little get-well card. And perhaps some of our members would drop in and see them.

This suggestion here concerns—this [is a] very good suggestion here. This person was a bit disturbed concerning the request for money from a newcomer. And they state here, "This is the reason I left the Catholic church. It seems to me that there must be someplace where one can escape the mundane aspects of this world and not have to be asked for funds. However, I recognize the great need of having our own church building and you can be assured of $52 a year from each Sunday collection."

I think that that rather speaks for itself, unless someone has something to add to it. I don't know if a person recognizes their spiritual responsibilities. The church belongs to God, and we are the servants of it, to raise the funds necessary to pay for the lights and the rent. We have to pay for an ad in the paper. We, your church, sends workers to Fort Bragg to give seminars. It sends workers to Vacaville to give seminars. Your church supplies, without cost, literature to open up new centers in this world. We presently have over a hundred and some dollars in books tied up in Vacaville. Certainly, we will be paid for them as the Vacaville center sells them. And there are many, many expenditures. We have sent out to our membership a little statement that they may choose from one of several items, if they would prefer to tithe 10 percent of their net earnings as their contribution to their church or whether or not they would prefer to sell tickets to our monthly socials and to attend our monthly brunch or whether or not they would care to give $100 or more to our annual building fund.

And by the way, while we're speaking of that, I would like to say at this time that Wednesday morning, under the guidance of Spirit, I called many business houses on a building fund drive to keep supporting this church. And I am very happy to say that the businessmen of this community have been very, very kind in our telephone solicitation for the support of the Serenity Spiritualist Church.

The J.C. Penny Company donated $5. Agavo Litho Printers donated $15. F. W. Woolworth donated a $10 lamp and so on and so on and so on. At the present time, beginning the first of the week, [Student G2] is chairman of that committee, of the building fund committee here. And [Student F2], the cochairman, will continue on with the solicitation. And I—for those who feel that it might not be quite up to their dignit—

[Side A of the audio cassette tape recording this membership meeting ends. At some point later in the meeting, the tape is turned and recording begins again on side B.]

—and in regards to student mediums and the opening of the doors of this church, most of you are aware that this church has an open-door policy to any qualified person trying to serve God and the angel world. We have repeatedly—your church has—opened the doors for mediums, potential mediums from other Spiritualist churches. For one, [Student O2] is presently serving at the Golden Gate Church, of which she has been a member for fourteen years. And it is indeed a wonderful thing to witness how beautiful[ly] her mediumship is unfolding. She studied; she's sat; she's waited for fourteen years. And it was the Serenity Spiritualist Church that opened the door, and she does remind them of it. [Student Q2], who is not a member of this church or this camp, this church opened the door for her to serve as a student medium and she has studied now this [these] past twelve years.

The one exception to the opening [of] the doors for spiritual workers is the requirements of this church in regards to healing. Unfolding healers are required, by policy of your church, that's been established, to be in the healing chapel every Sunday morning for fifty-two consecutive weeks in order to be qualified to go for their certification papers with the state association. This is a requirement of your church.

Now mediums from other churches, students that come up and [are] unfolding mediumship, no matter how long they work at this church, the state and national law prohibits them from being certified if they have not served a full year in their own church. However, your church makes that point very clear. We have a multitude of requests. We have over forty-two requests from students from various Spiritualist, national churches requesting an opportunity to serve on the podium of this church to unfold their varying spiritual gifts. However, this is only one church. It must take care of its own students. And it does its best to take as many qualified students from the other churches to give them the opportunity.

Now, our next order of business—we're still in the good of the church. Is there anything else before we get to our nominations? Anyone else care to speak for the good of their church? *[After a short pause, the teacher continues.]* I do understand and I recognize the sensitivity of new people coming into the church. And we do make all endeavors possible not to hound them for funds or things of that nature. We, we recognize, I'm sure, everyone present—certainly, I know that the dollar seems so very small when we go to the grocery store, and it ofttimes appears to be gigantic when we come to church.

And speaking of dollars, it's time for us to serve in a selfless way and take up our collection before we get into the nomination of many [delegates].

[Student U2], *[He strikes the gavel.]* do you wish to be recognized by the chair?

I would like to be excused from the meeting.

[He again strikes the gavel.] You are, [Student U2]. I understand that you do have to go. And thank you so much for coming to this point.

Will you please come forward for our offering. *[After a short pause, the teacher continues.]* You know, friends, this is one collection that's only once a year. So don't feel bad. *[A few people laugh. There is a pause, during which a collection is gathered. The offertory is then presented to the teacher.]*

Infinite Spirit, we thank Thee for the vibration in which these funds have been released to Thee and we sincerely ask that we may be wisely guided in their use that they may multiply in a limitless way to serve Thy purpose in bringing the light and truth of Spiritualism to this world. Amen.

Amen. [A few people speak.]

It is time now for the nomination of our delegates to our state convention. Now I would like to explain a bit about that—on June 20th, 21st—no, June 21st, 22nd, and 23rd. Those who are interested in going to the banquet may go on the evening of the 20th. This church is entitled to thirteen representatives at the state convention. It is very important that this association be represented by the delegates, the numbers that it is entitled to. Remember, when you are a part of an organization, there is a responsibility that goes with it. And I would like to—those who are not here, present at this time, cannot be official delegates to the convention, for that is contrary to the constitution, not only of Serenity, but of the state and national association. So, we can only elect the thirteen delegates that are present here this evening.

And I would like to ask those who wish to go to please raise their hands. Now we're going to need thirteen. Will the secretary please write down [Student H2], [Student L2], [Student G2], [Student V2], [Student T2], [Student M2]—they need workers down there.

[Student R2].

Yes, sir.

Do you wish to go to the convention?

Yes, sir.

He's nominated. [Student R2]. I think I'd better go. Richard Goodwin.

I better put myself down, too. [The secretary volunteers.]

Thank you. [Student J]. [Student P2]. How many do you have?

Eleven. Was [Student X2] going, too? Or just [Student T2]? [The secretary asks.]

Well, I can't . . . [Student X2 replies. A few words are difficult to transcribe.]

Just [Student T2].

Eleven? I'm sure there's two others here, surely, that are willing to go to the convention. Now what your church is trying to do is to pay the plane fare of those who need it. Now we will give as much as we possibly can from the funds that are taken in from the socials. And most churches do pay the round-trip plane fare to Los Angeles. The hotel is the Hollywood Roosevelt. Now we need two more?

I'm sorry, Mr. Goodwin. It was four more. [The secretary reports.]

Four more. You have nine delegates?

Nine.

Read them off—

How many days do you have to stay?

You don't have to stay the three days. We need you there to register for voting and to do the voting. That's Thursday and Friday.

I—do you have to be there on a Thursday?

Yes, the vote's in the afternoon—the registration, yes. [Student R2] was there last year. Registration's Thursday afternoon?

It was one evening where we had to attend the banquet. That was optional, I believe.

No, no, no. I'm talking about registration to be an official delegate.

The next day. There's two days there.

Then it was a Thursday.

It was Wednesday, Thursday, and Friday down there. Now the Wednesday is optional.

So, it's Thursday and Friday [that] is a must—is required.

Yeah, but what time is registration?

Morning.

Morning.

Nine o'clock.

Nine o'clock.

I have a, I have an appointment on the Thursday and I can't make it.

We need four more delegates. [Student Y2], where are you?

Here.

Do you feel that you could possibly give a couple of days?

I really don't think so because I'd have to close my business because I—

Oh, you don't have—that's right. Tom's going. So, you couldn't have that. [Student A3]?

Got room for kids?

They'd have to stay in a hotel.

Excuse me, [Student G2], you're going? Is [Student B3] going? [The secretary asks.]

Yes. [Student G2 responds.]

[Student B3] is going. [The secretary confirms.]

Read off the number that you have, [Student P2].

Three, four, five, six, seven, eight, nine, ten! We need two more.

We need three more. Now, you see, your charter—your constitution, rather, requires that you be a member of the association, of the church for a minimum of three months. And we cannot nominate someone who is not here. It's illegal. Yes, [Student M2].

Mr. Goodwin, I have understood before that it is a practice when you don't have your members at your meeting that you can put names down as alternate.

Yes, the alternates, we can. But we can't do the official.

No, we . . . [The member says a few words that are difficult to transcribe.]

You see. And we're entitled to thirteen. Thank you, [Student M2]. We're entitled to thirteen. Yes, [Student R2].

Would it be possible for somebody here in Marin County to take care of [Student C3's]—

Children, so she could go?

Right.

Well, I think that'd be a wonderful thing for you to check into. That's a wonderful suggestion, [Student R2]. Your—oh, I—don't you—

Who do I know here?

But [Student M2] is her cousin. And [Student D3] is your aunt, isn't she?

They wouldn't take care of children.

Oh.

I'm down in Los Angeles.

What about [Student E3]?

[Student E3]. Would it be possible for you to go, [Student E3]?

He's probably got to have my niece and nephew if I go.

[Student F2], would it be possible for you to go if somebody drove instead of flew?

Richard, you make it sound so terrible.

Well, I don't want to drive . . . [Student W2] does have a business. *[It is difficult to transcribe a few of his words.]*

I got a good . . .

Yes, [Student G2].

Well, I, I'm of the understanding that by necessarily being the, the primary individual that's going down there, we do not necessarily have to go. That's why we have alternates. Am I correct?

You—no. The alternate is the backup, in the case someone gets sick because those who are registered must appear at the convention. They get very upset if you have an official delegate and they don't show up. So that's why they have alternates, you see. Because there's a great deal of setting up to a convention.

Couldn't we get our full cast on promises? Couldn't we get our full, elect cast on—

Yes, we—yes, we could.

—on members here and substitute them with alternates.

Yes, we could. That's a wonderful idea [Student G2] has suggested. Now [Student F2], would you like to be a delegate and in the event you can't go, send an alternate? *[After a short pause, the teacher continues.]* Several people are going to drive.

How many do you have?

Ten. Two, four, six, eight, ten. [The secretary counts the delegates.]

Pardon?

Ten.

She said yes. [Another student announces.]

Put down [Student F2]. *[Many people applaud.]* That makes eleven.

Eleven. [The secretary confirms.]

Eleven. Now we have one each for our charters. [Student F3]—oh, you're not a member. I'm sorry. Excuse me. Not yet. [Student L2] is going. [Student J] is going. [Student E3] can't go. And [Student G3], it's not possible.

. . . can't get off of work that morning without a doctor's certificate. [A few words are difficult to transcribe.]

A doctor's certificate? Well, I have some doctors as clients, but I'd hate to go to those extremes.

Couldn't you—[Student G3], could you make it for a couple of days? [The secretary asks.]

Well, I think Tom is going down for all three days.

[Student G3], would you be willing to be a delegate and have us send a backup alternate?

What's that?

Well, that means, in the event you're not able to go, we send somebody else in your place.

What if nobody else goes and then—

Well, *[The teacher laughs.]* we will work on that.

All right. If you think—

All right. Put down [Student G3]. How many is that?

Twelve. We need one more. [The secretary observes.]

That's twelve. We just need one more to represent your church in its fullness. One more. [Student H3], would you like to go and have us work on getting an alternate?

Yeah, because I definitely couldn't make it.

[Student H3]! I can't believe it. We got thirteen. Are you sure?

Thirteen. I'm recounting. [Again, many people applaud.] *Thirteen.* [The secretary confirms the count.]

Mr. Goodwin.

Yes.

Why didn't you nominate yourself to go?

He did. [Many individuals reply.]

I got nominated. Thank you. Yes. Thank you. Now, the next order of business is remarks by visitors. I'm happy to see that we have a visitor with us—a couple of visitors—that is, nonmembers at present. Would any of the visitors care to make any comments here this evening?

Can you turn the heat up? [A few people laugh.]

Let them have a little heat, will you, please? It's at 75 now, but we'll turn it up to 90. *[He instructs a director to adjust the thermostat.]*

Thank you.

Thank you very much, [Visitor A]. Anyone else? [Visitor B], would you care to make any comments?

No, I have nothing intelligent to add to what you're, what you're discussing here.

Thank you very much. Now, this Chair will entertain a motion to adjourn. Motions do not need to be seconded.

Mr. President, before—

Yes.

—you do that may I please—

Certainly.

—add something here that I think as we've discussed the convention business, we've taken up a little offering towards this. And I think, maybe, if you put this thought out, Mr. Goodwin—a little something happened at our Easter sunrise service at the chapel over the weekend. It's rather disappointing that not more came, but we did have a very beautiful service nevertheless. We had good music and so on and so forth. The seats got slightly damp. It did rain during the night. And we forgot to . . . However, we put towels and things out.

Now, you all met President Ford.[54] *I know you all know what a delightful person he is. And he truly made the day for me. He sat very bravely through the breakfast. We did have a good breakfast . . . cooking. I didn't know he could do it. He let the cat out of the bag. So, during that, after a little while, President Ford, sitting on that seat, all of a sudden, he stood up and gently raised his pants away and he said, "You know, my pampers are leaking. It's rather damp." Do you not think we could—knowing how he enjoyed the joke so much—at least take care of . . .* [At different times as she speaks, there are a few words that are difficult to transcribe.]

Well, now, [Student M2], I think that was a wonderful suggestion. Would you like to take care of that?

I thought I'd get that. [The teacher laughs.] *I also had a little—other little goody he put it over the . . . but why we're bringing this up. I know—our secretary knows about this. We met Friday evening in Willits. And we all went to eat together. It was really quite enjoyable doing this. Reverend Elbertson and Reverend Ford have a little running battle between each other. It's a very fun thing and a very loving thing to see. What one can't think of, the other one does. They met in the . . . grocery store. Reverend Elbertson was pushing his little basket and he didn't know Reverend Ford was there. And while he was looking at the shelves, Reverend Ford stuck a package of pampers in his basket. And there poor Elbertson was knowing nothing, you know, wondering what spirit had dropped that pampers in his basket.* [Several people laugh.] *But, however, so I do think . . . Thank you.*[55]

Thank you, [Student M2]. The Chair will entertain a motion to adjourn. *[He strikes the gavel.]*

I make to motion.

[Student G2] makes a motion that this meeting be adjourned—to be held a year from this date at a time, place, and date to be stated by your board of directors. *[The teacher again strikes the gavel.]* This meeting is officially adjourned. Thank you very much.

APRIL 8, 1972

Membership Meeting May 12, 1974

All right, friends, let us all rise, please, and open this meeting, this annual meeting of our church.

Divine Spirit, we sincerely pray that we may be receptive to the spirit of unity, cooperation, and harmony and that this meeting may be conducted for the best interest of this church for the work that it has to do and for the purpose for which it was founded. May we be so wisely guided that we may conduct this meeting in the best possible order in the shortest possible time for the good of all. Amen.

[The teacher strikes a gavel.] This meeting will officially come to order. It has always been our policy to take up a donation for the good of our church at all meetings of our association. And so, will the ushers, please, take up the collection at this time. *[The collection is made.]*

[Student R], please bring the plates forward. *[The offertory is presented to the teacher.]*

We thank Thee, God, for this manifestation and demonstration of the faith of our membership in the divine infinite supply and the application of the things that they are learning in this association. May we be wisely guided in its use, knowing that in truth that which is given returns unto its source as the great circle. Amen.

[He strikes a gavel.] This meeting will officially come to order. Will the secretary kindly call the roll of officers—board of directors.

[The call of the roll is taken for the board of directors and then for the lay members. Forty-eight names are called, but only twenty were present.]

Thank you very much, Madame Secretary.

Robert's Rules of Order will govern all deliberations of this association not covered by its constitution and bylaws. Now, the step for here [is] read the minutes of the past meeting. And for efficiency purposes, if it is within your pleasure, we can wave that particular reading of the minutes. [Student R].

I move we wave the minutes.

It has been moved that we wave the minutes of our last meeting. Is it seconded? Seconded by [Student R2]. All those in favor?

Aye. [Many members speak.]

Contrary minded? *[After a short, silent pause, the teacher continues.]* So ordered and approved. *[He strikes a gavel.]* The minutes are waved.

The [agenda says] read application for membership and action thereon: there are no applications for membership at this time. Six: read bills and references. There are no outstanding bills or references at this time. Number seven: read communications. All communications are up to date. We have no communications to bring to the membership at this time. Number eight: the reports of officers, pastors, and assistants.

I will try to keep the progress report here as short as possible and give you the highlights of what your association has done in the past twelve months. Now you'll see over the fireplace—I'm sure you've all seen it—is a sketch of our proposed church building.[56] And we also have initiated an active building fund committee of which [Student S] is the chairlady in this [these] past twelve months. Now, several of our members have established pledges for a building block for their own church. We still have many members who have not yet been so inspired.

Now let me see here. *[After a short pause, he continues.]* I can't see too clearly in this dimension.[57] So, perhaps I can do better by memory. *[He turns a few pages of his documents.]* As you all know, the printing is done, for your church and for your association, at our church offices there in Corte Madera. And your monthly *Sentinel* is now completely printed—and your church programs—at the office.

We have also, in this [these] past twelve months, we have established our own recording department. We have spent a great deal of money—thousands of dollars—on getting the Living Light cassettes available to our students and to the public. The funds for purchasing all of this equipment has been borrowed from your building fund department. The cassettes of the Living Light are going out very, very well.

Monthly bake sales continue to be held at the varied shopping centers. We have averaged, over the year, approximately $155 per bake sale. Last Saturday's bake sale was $170. And the one prior to that was $220, which has given us a yearly average of approximately $155.

Now, you can obviously see I'm not very good at reading off reports because I can hardly see them. *[The teacher turns more pages in his reports.]* But let's see what we basically have done outside of that. We had a publicity release on our philosophy and on our church last June, almost a year ago. And from that, many doors have opened. It's brought many new people in to visit the church.[58]

The students of the association are now in the process of taking their exams for the certification of mediumship and for healing.

Now, everyone knows, that has ever been a member, of course, of any church anyplace in the universe, that becoming a member of a church isn't simply a matter of paying a fee of $27 a year. That does not constitute membership in anybody's church and that also includes Serenity's church. Now there are, in any church, few workers. We all will agree on that. Our membership roll, as you heard it called off—now we must remember that many of our members live in Colorado. Some of them live in Southern California. Some of them have moved to Oregon. And so, however, there are some that we don't get to see very often, but they do seem to pay their annual dues.

Well, I would like to spend my time on the report—I think anybody that's been in this association for any length of time at all is well aware of the workload that the few people in it are doing. Now, so if you've been over to the office or if you've been around for any length of time at all, then you know how much work is involved in printing our own magazine, in printing our own church programs, in producing our own tapes, available for the public. We have this cassette club, which, for $6 plus tax you can get a fine cassette of any of the teachings or the discourses of the Living Light.

But I am more interested, friends—because the progress of this church is obvious. It's [so] obvious that anyone can see at all. I am more interested in your soul and in the unity within your own being. We all have come to this church—and I'll try to keep this lecture, this report very short. We've all come to this church with varying motives, but we have all been helped by being here. Now I know that many come through our doors and they stay awhile and they go on, which is, of course, their right.

But let us not forget when we feel that we have gained as much as we can gain from Serenity, let us remember another soul that may be coming through the door. Let us remember what it has done for us. And let us remember that what it's done for us, we should at least consider letting it do for someone else. Now, how are we going to make that possible? Well, it's very simple: we're going to make it possible by [being] united in our thought and in our prayers and in our acts, by remembering who we work for in this church. We don't work for a building, and we don't work for a person. We're working for God, hopefully. And if we will always remember that it's God we're working for, then we're not going to have to worry about being tired and being exhausted. If all of us present—and it doesn't seem to be that many. But, believe me, where there's two or more, that's all that's necessary to move the greatest mountain in the universe. That's why I've never been concerned in thirty-three years of this work, I have never been concerned with quantity. I know what quantity does. Let's have a little quality. Let's keep the quality that we have.

Now there's been many suggestions turned in and I'm going to mention some of them as part of my responsibility. There's been the suggestion that I give a financial report each month to the general membership, and I have it printed up and sent to them. Well, I think that's wonderful. And the member that made the suggestion doesn't even happen to be present for the membership meeting. I think it is a wonderful idea: *if* the person that made the suggestion wants to come to the office and is qualified to do the bookkeeping, make out a report, do the printing, and take care of the expense, I'll be more than happy to endorse it.

Now we've had another suggestion that our children and the lyceum, they go on their lyceum field trips once a month. And when they go on their field trips and new children that have come into church just for that Sunday, they sit in the congregation because we don't have a teacher, an extra teacher to take care of those new people. Now I was in hopes that one of my members would be inspired to join the lyceum—an adult—join the lyceum and take care of those little children that one Sunday a month when the children are on their field trip. Now the reason that we don't take all of the new children on the field trips is because we have one, two, three lyceum teachers. We have [Student K2] and [Student S2], and we have [Student I3]. And we cannot take fifty or sixty children on a field trip and take that responsibility on your church unless we have the teachers. Now this is the reason why we don't have, on the first Sunday of the month, a lyceum for the new children here. And we cannot have one—it is not feasible—until such time as somebody in the membership who is qualified is inspired to join the lyceum and take care of those little children on that day.

Now, I have the committees to nominate. I hope I can see this page. Beginning with the advertising committee, will [Student S] continue on as the chairlady?

Yes, I will.

You're doing such a fine job. You see, that's what happens when you do a good job at anything: you get to keep it. The auditing committee, [Student J3], would you continue on with that, please?

Yes, I will. Thank you.

Thank you very much. The bake sale committee, [Student G], would you take the chairmanship of that, please?

With some reservation.

Well, if you take it with some reservations, then it will be a reservation back to you, [Student G].

Well—

What, what seems to be the problem?

Would it entail the responsibility of physically carrying the table?

No, it would not entail that responsibility because I'm sure, [Student K3], being relieved of the chairmanship of the bake sale committee, would be more than happy to have [Student R] continue to take the things there. Is that not correct, [Student K3]?

That's fine.

What?

That's fine.

You see, we give to gain. You see, a little bit goes there and then a little bit goes over there. Then everybody's happy. Thank you very much. And then, we now have no reservations, right?

I'm really very happy.

Oh, thank you so much, [Student G]. Now the bingo committee—[Student R], where are you?

Yes.

Would you continue on?

[It is difficult to transcribe the student's response.]

Fine. Thank you very much. And you continue on with that. Now the birthday committee, now, [Student L3], will you take the chairmanship of that? That's sending out birthday cards to all the members. You've done such a nice job on that.

Thank you.

The book department—[Student G], will you continue on the chairmanship of that?

Yes.

Thank you kindly. Now the building, the building committee, the building committee, [Student V] was on that. Will you take the chairmanship of that building committee, [Student V]?

[His response is difficult to transcribe.]

Thank you very much. Now the building church *fund* committee, that's [Student S]. Will you continue on with that, please—

Yes.

—as the chairlady? All right. Now we have the cassette club. Now, I want to take a couple of minutes explaining the cassette club. We're still within our thirty-six minutes here. The cassette club is a committee, or club, to take care of the clerical work and the promotion of these Living Light cassettes. Now [Student G] is already doing all the clerical work. She's already doing the synopsis for each cassette. So, you might as well have the title; you [already] got the job. Would you like to do that, [Student G]?

Yes. Thank you.

Thank you so much. The clerical committee. [Student J3], where are you?

Here.

Would you continue on with that, please?

Thank you.

Now the coordinating committee. Now this is a wonderful committee. Nothing ever gets done on it. *[Some students laugh.]*

And I'd like to know who'd like that job. The coordinating committee. I don't want to nominate someone after making that kind of a statement. Let's delete the coordinating committee. It never did anything.

The decorating committee. [Student K3], you were chairlady on that and you did a nice job. Will you continue on that, please?

I will.

Fine. Thank you very much. Now the educational committee. [Student M3], you're doing such a good job on that. Would you continue with that, please?

Well, maybe somebody else would like the opportunity to . . .

Well, let me see, considering the number here—no, I think the opportunity, you have a right to continue with it.

I'll be happy to do it.

Thank you very much, [Student M3], because you're doing a nice job on that. Now the entertainment committee, now maybe we can get some help here. Now, now, who's got entertainment here? We need some entertainment at these socials. Now, who's got some connections? My connections don't work with entertainment. *[Many students laugh.]* But I'm sure somebody *here* has got some.

[There seems to be no audible response.]

You know, I think that's a nice job, [Student N3]. Thank you very much. Would you take care of the entertainment committee, please?

This is for the social?

Yes.

Beginning when?

Ah, today. *[Many students laugh.]*

[It is difficult to transcribe her response.]

We may exempt you if we don't have entertainment for this, this next week, but after that, there's no exemption.

Thank you very much.

Would you like . . .

. . . it's all taken care of. [Another person speaks.]

Oh, is it? There you are. You see, you're all set. Thank you very much. Now [Student N3] [is] entertainment chairlady.

What does that say there? I can't see. *[The teacher asks a director.]*

Flower.

Oh, flowers. Flower committee. Where's [Student A]? She was on it. Where are you, [Student A]?

Right here.

Would you continue on with that, please?

Yes.

Thank you very much. Now the food committee here, for the socials. [Student F2], you've only had it for three years. Would you carry on with that? After all, you've got an assistant now so you don't have to carry all those—all that silverware.

I will be that.

Thank you very much, [Student F2]. Now the healing committee there. [Student R], where are you? Would you carry on with that, please?

Yes, sir.

Thank you. Now the ladies' guild. [Student K3] has been working along with that, doing such a nice job, we ought to keep you there. Would you carry on with that, please?

Thank you.

Fine. Thank you very much. Librarian. I think [Student G] ought to come under that committee. She's already got the book committee.

Yes.

Yes. Thank you very much. Literature. I think you ought to be on that, too, [Student G]. It all falls in the same category, really.

[Her response is difficult to transcribe.]

Magazines, books, and everything else, you know? Thank you very much. Now the lyceum, [Student K2], will you continue on with being lyceum conductor?

My pleasure.

Thank you very much. The men's club. I see you're in the flow. Would you be the chairman of the men's club this year? *[He continues to address Student K2.]*

Most gratefully.

Fine. After all, you're collecting very nicely on that. *[Many students laugh.]* Thank you. Now the membership committee. Now I think we ought to have someone on this membership committee. The membership committee—people applying for membership so they can get to understand what this is all about. And [Student S], you have a nice way with words. Would you like to take the membership committee?

Thank you.

Thank you very much. Now the music committee. [Student J3]. That's coming along nicely. Will you continue on with that?

Yes.

Photography committee. Now, [Student S], you already got about five committees. Let me see. Photography. Photography. [Student O3], are you good with a camera?

I've never been complimented on my work.

Well, we'll find someone else then. *[The teacher laughs.]* That's all right, [Student O3].

[It is difficult to transcribe her response.]

Oh, [Student A]? Where are you, [Student A]? Would you take care of the photography committee?

All right.

All right. Now publicity. [Student G], you've been doing a lot of work on that. Would you take care of the publicity committee?

Yes. Thank you.

Fine. Now public relations. Would you also continue on with the public relations committee? Public relations.

I did not have it. [Student G responds.]

Oh, would you take public relations this year?

Yes.

Thank you. Now let's see, receiving committee—is [Student S]—you're all set at the front door. They like your smile. You carry on with the receiving committee.

Thank you.

All right. Now, what is this? The records committee. Well, you do that job anyway, will you keep that, [Student J3]?

Thank you very much.

Fine. Now the subscription—now this is an important committee: subscription committee, the *[Serenity] Sentinel* subscription committee. We need some action on that committee. [Student P3] is on that committee, aren't you, [Student P3]?

Yes.

I've been checking the records to see how many subscriptions we've been getting. How about you and [Student K2] jointly taking care of that committee?

Thank you.

Yes. Then, you see, if I don't get any subscriptions, I can blame you, and you can blame him. You see what I mean? You'll have some help there. *[Several individuals laugh.]* Because it's been kind of low lately.

All right, now the social committee. [Student L3], will you carry on with that, please, with our social committee? Now the special events committee. Now let's see, [Student T2], we've got to find a job for you with some action in it, you hear me? Special events—we don't have too many special events. Now let's see, well, maybe [Student M3] would like that special events committee.

I'd be happy to. What are special events?

Well, special events is [are] when we have a special event, then you see that everything is coordinated for, like, if we were going to a have a special lecture here some evening or we're going to have some kind of special something, some special event.

Oh, I see.

Or at the camp. Thank you. Now the stamp committee. [Student R2] was doing well on that. Will you carry on with that, please?

Yes, sir.

Thank you very much. Now the suggestion committee. The suggestion committee was nominated. We have now [Student G], [Student S], and [Student J3] is on the suggestion committee.

Now, friends, please do me a favor. You know, you call the office and I try to answer the phone and to talk to you as much as I can. But, you see, if you come to the office, take a look and see what our workload is and then you'll understand why I can't be on the phone all the time.

Now, all suggestions—do your church a favor, send them through the suggestion committee and give them an opportunity to grow. Because, you see, all the suggestions come to me! See, and I've had them for so many years, it's not fair to my students not to see what it's like and what you have to go through. So, we have a suggestion committee. So would you, please, when you have your suggestions—you know, we even have suggestion forms, you see. But if you still haven't grown to the level to make a suggestion form out and you still need to give verbal suggestions on how to run your church, would you kindly give them to [Student S], [Student J3], or [Student G]. And they'll be more than happy to help you. Now if they—you see, what happens, it's a chain reaction. It goes through that committee; it gets sifted around and goes up to the next committee. That gets sifted around and finally gets upstairs where it belongs, and it all works out just fine. So if you will do that, I will greatly appreciate it.

Transportation committee. [Student R2], will you carry on with that?

Yes, sir.

Ushering committee. [Student M3], will you carry on with that?

Yes, sir.

Ways and means committee. Now, that's a very important committee. That's, that's the ways and the means of making some money to keep everything going. Now let me see who's in the flow. *[The teacher laughs.]* Now let's see, let's see here, ways and means. You know, I can't nominate myself. Oh, [Student J3], that's a good committee for you. That will help your Scotch vibration. *[Some students laugh.]* OK, ways and means committee. Thank you very much.

Now, delegate committee. We're not having a delegate committee this year because we're not sending a delegation to the state convention for one simple reason. I believe that charity begins at home and we take care of our own backyard first. And the, the four, five, six hundred dollars it costs to go to the convention, your church can wisely use that to help pay off some of its equipment and get these teachings out to the world. So if there is anyone that wants to go to the convention, I would like to, first, suggest to them that they at least consider that their church needs funds at this time. We're only three years old. You know we have a spiritual retreat in Mendocino—that forty acres at Camp Serenity with its own little chapel building. You have over $25,000 worth of equipment sitting in your office—printing and recording equipment. And so, I think it's come a long ways for such a short time.

Now, in order that we may finish up this meeting and we may go have lunch—I'm sure everybody's hungry. However, the floor is open, of course, for anyone that has anything to say. I want to say this: I want to thank all committees, all committees, the standing committees for one year. I want to thank all the committees for your efforts, sincerely. And everybody knows what we've been doing. See, we don't have to get up and tell them what we've done. Really, everybody knows, you know, because everybody's here. And so, I do want to thank all committees for their efforts. And all of the committees are nominated for the year.

And if the visitors to the church would like to make any remarks, we'll be happy to listen to them. If any of the members have anything to say—now, remember, friends, the spoken word is life-giving energy. And that's what we're talking about. We need life-giving energy to get the work done. So, I'm finished talking. Does anyone else have anything to say? *[After a short pause, he continues.]*

If not—no visitors?—thank you all very much for your full cooperation. *[The teacher strikes a gavel.]* Let's go have lunch. The meeting is complete.

MAY 12, 1974

Membership Meeting May 11, 1975

Let us rise, please. *Robert's Rules of Order*, the seventy-fifth revised edition, shall govern all deliberations of this association not covered by its constitution and bylaws. The fourth annual membership meeting of the Serenity Spiritualist Association will officially come to order.

O divine, eternal, and infinite Spirit, who has brought this church, Thy church, into being, may we be wisely guided in peace and harmony, in total consideration for the operation and the work of this church that it may continue to serve the purpose for which it was originally founded: to bring the light of this Living Light Philosophy of Spiritualism to a world who is seeking it, that its members and friends may consider more than themselves in the work that is to be done, that we may awaken within our consciousness that though we may be few in number, the work and the spiritual responsibility is indeed great. Let us unite in thought and in purpose that this meeting, the fourth, governing this church since its founding four years ago, may go peacefully, efficiently, and harmoniously that Thy work may continue to be done. Amen.

Amen. [Many people speak.]

Be seated, please. Will the ushers, please, take up an offering for the good and the support of this church that it may continue to carry on its work. *[A collection is made. The collection plates are then presented to the teacher.]*

We thank Thee, O God, for the manifestation of this supply that Thy work may continue to be done. Amen.

Amen. [Several individuals speak.]

[The collection plates are removed to a separate room.]

A full complement of the board of directors of this association and a quorum of its lay membership present, this meeting is officially come to order. The secretary will kindly call the meeting to order and call the roll of officers, followed by the roll of membership. Time to call the roll of officers. And when your name is called, kindly answer by "Present" or "Yes."

[The call of the roll is taken and forty-two names are called, but only twenty-one members were present, including the board of directors.]

[Has] anyone else been omitted? If so, please speak up. *[After a pause, during which he turns several pages of a report, the teacher continues.]* You'll have to bear with me because I'm just out of one dimension and I have a little difficulty seeing in this, this dimension.[59]

[Pointing to a report, the teacher asks a question.] What is point four here, [Student J]?

Read the minutes of the past meeting.

Oh, the next on the order of business is the reading of the minutes of the past meeting. A motion may be made from the floor to dispense with those minutes or you can spend the time to listen to them. Do I hear a motion on the floor? The chair will entertain a motion to dispense with the reading of the minutes from last year's meeting, if you wish to make a motion.

I move . . . [A few words are difficult to transcribe.]

A motion is made by [Student Q3] to dispense with the reading of the minutes from our last meeting last year. Do I hear a second?

I second. [Several students respond.]

Seconded by [Student V]. Please take note—oh, it's being recorded. Are you ready for the question?

Question. [A few members speak.]

Question: All those in favor?

Aye. [Several members respond.]

Contrary minded? *[After a short period of silence, the teacher continues.]* So ordered and approved. We will dispense with the reading of the minutes from last year's meeting. Read the bills and references: there are no bills and references to be read. Read . . . *[The teacher shows the agenda to a director sitting beside him.]*

Communications.

Communications. There are no present—the reading of communication will come under the good of the church, which come under suggestion. Point number eight.

Reports of officers.

Reports of officers.

Pastors.

Pastors and assistants. Well, my good members, I did not prepare a report this year. It is the first year in the history of this association that I did not prepare a report, for I considered the time that it would take me to prepare the report would be more wisely used in making planters and different projects to pay the bills of this church; so, you wouldn't have to be forced into a 25 percent compulsory tithing. So, I took that time to apply to the workload at the office. And so, I will give you a brief report, from my own consciousness, of what's taken place in the past year. Now this association—those of you who visit your church office and who are participating in this church are well aware that your church has taken its funds and it has paid off equipment, printing equipment, recording equipment, and all other kinds of equipment necessary to bring the Living Light Philosophy to the world. And so this is where the monies we're able to take in has [have] gone.

You will have a treasurer's report here in a few minutes of the actual financial status of your association. And considering the few workers that your church has at present, though more are on their way, it has done extremely well. And those of you who are active in your church are well aware that whatever funds come into the church, go right back out in order to bring this Light to the world and to those souls who are seeking.

This past year, I was forced, from a matter of necessity, to refrain from giving any more private counseling to the public, whereas the workload is such at your church office that it is no longer possible for me to give private counseling to the general public, as I have over these past thirty-five years. I have had to restrict that counseling to members of the church and to students who are registered in class.

Last November, this church had the most successful bazaar in its history. And that, of course, was the effect of a few people in this association, united in purpose, united in effort who made it the most successful bazaar in our history.

As those of you—all of you have been to the church office that are present that are members here, and as you all know and know deep in your own heart that this little church is most successful considering the amount of time that is donated to it by its own membership.

And so it is that is my basic report to the lay members. And all of you know that whenever you have a suggestion about how to run this church, you set a law into motion. And you become personally responsible for the suggestion that you have made. And that responsibility is for you, as an individualized soul, to demonstrate what it is you suggest by first doing it yourself: setting the example. Because this philosophy, in Serenity, is a living, working philosophy of personal demonstration, not one of suggestions for somebody else to do the work to fulfill our own desires. And so it is that is my basic report.

I want to thank the membership of this church and the membership of this association for their efforts in making it as successful as it is. We're looking forward into our fifth year. And it is only through your personal efforts of self-control and discipline and moving into the divine will of total consideration that this church will continue to serve the purpose for which it has been founded. I thank all of you for your cooperation in helping me to make this church the success that it is and serve the purpose that it was founded for. Thank you.

Now we have the report. Do any of the officers of the church, our secretary, our secretary-treasurer, or anyone else have—of the officers—have a report to make? *[After a short pause, the teacher continues.]* If there are no reports, we'll get to the treasurer's report here in a few minutes. And I think, [Student J], I still can't see too well. *[The teacher asks for assistance reading the agenda.]*

The report of the mediums.

The report of the mediums. Where's the report of the treasury here?

The next one after mediums is committee reports.

Report of the mediums. Do any of the mediums of this church have any reports to make? If you do, please stand up and make your reports, but remember the law that you set into motion. I hope I'll remember it myself.

Now the committee reports, the standing and special. I want to personally thank all the committees of this association—there are well over thirty-six committees—who work so diligently to keep these church doors open. Do any committee chairmen have anything to say? I know that you're all very busy working for your church and so—but if you have anything to say, any of you committee members, you speak up. *[After a short pause, the teacher continues.]*

If not, we'll move into unfinished business. Well, the unfinished business here at our special membership meeting a few months ago, in accordance with our constitutional bylaws, the lay membership nominated, as an interim officer, [Student R], to fill the vacancy, as a director on the board, that was made by [Student J3], who sent us a letter months ago stating that she felt that your church deserved a full, working board of directors and that due to personal matters at home she would not be able to be a full, working director for your church, and she resigned from the board. And your board did place [Student R] as the interim director.

Now, I don't know of anyone in the membership of this church, if work has anything to do with being a director, who is more qualified than [Student R]. For he works at your church office seven days a week to help keep your church doors open on a multitude of projects. He does all of the printing. So now I would like to hear a nomination for the director of this board for [Student R]. Does anyone care to nominate [Student R]? [Student N3] nominates [Student R] for director. Are there any other nominations? If—

I nominate [Student R].

Yes. It only requires one nomination. Now all those in favor—I don't think we need to take a closed, secret ballot—all those in favor [of] [Student R] being a director of your board of directors of this association, please signify by saying aye.

Aye. [Many students speak.]

Would you raise your hands that we may have a unanimous vote? *[After a short pause, the teacher continues.]* Then the vote is unanimous. The secretary will kindly record such. [Student R] is nominated and officially a director of this association to fulfill the terms according to our own constitution and bylaws.

Now we come to—the business of what? *[He asks a director.]*

The treasurer's report.

Oh, the treasurer's report. Now we have the treasurer's report. Now you have a choice in your treasury report: you may have your treasurer's report read collectively and we can finish this meeting [and] get on with all these committee nominations or you can have it read *seriatim*. Now if you vote to read your treasurer's report *seriatim*, that means every postage stamp is listed and everything will have to be read. It will take approximately eight to ten hours. *[Some members laugh.]* So, you have your choice. Either sit here eight to ten hours and pay the [American] Legion a little more money or have a collective report read. I do want to make it, however, very clear, whichever way you decide to vote, that the official financial records of this association are always open to any member in good standing, in good standing—that means, all dues paid—who writes a letter to the board of directors requesting that they review the financial records of this association, stating the reason for their request; and then an arrangement will be made for the person making the request to come to the office and so study the financial records of the association. For your association has nothing to hide. We have to fill out government reports twice a week on our finances.

Now will the treasurer kindly read the financial report.

The—

I beg your pardon. How does the membership want the report? Do they want it collective or *seriatim*?

Collective. [A number of members speak.]

Is there a motion on the floor? *[After a short pause, the teacher continues.]* There's a motion by [Student R3] for the treasurer's report to be read collective. Do I hear a second?

I second it.

Who seconded it? Seconded by [Student N3]. The secretary take note. All those in favor?

Aye. [Many members speak.]

Contrary minded? *[After a very short pause, he continues.]* So ordered and approved. Will the treasurer kindly read the collective report of the treasury?

The collective—the comparative analysis of income and expense for Serenity Spiritualist Church for 1974-1975. Total income 1974: $35,610.10; 1975: $57,736.21. Comparison is $22,126.11. The total expenses for 1974 is $34,157.26. The total expenses for 1975, $43,367.85. The comparison is $9,210.59. The retained income for 1974 is $1,452.84. And the retained income for 1975 is $14,368.36. Thank you.

You have heard the treasurer's report. What is your pleasure? You may accept it as read or whatever your pleasure is. I'll need a motion on the floor. Yes, [Student E2].

I accept it as read.

A motion is on the floor by [Student E2] to accept the treasurer's report as read. Do I hear a second?

Second.

Seconded by [Student Q3]. Are you ready for the question? *[After a short pause, the teacher continues.]* Question: all those in favor signify by saying aye.

Aye. [Many members speak.]

Contrary minded? *[After a very short pause, he continues.]* So ordered and approved.

Now, the next order of business is the good of the church. Now this here is the opportunity for anyone to speak up or send in their suggestions in reference to the good of the church.

We have one suggestion here combined in a letter to your church. I'll not read it all in detail. No[r] from whence it came. However, I will state this: that it is in reference to the church not serving Oleo margarine at its dinners. Now, I've only been with this church four years and to my knowledge Oleo margarine has never been served. Maybe I'm a little bit egotistical or something, but I had to eat white Oleo margarine years ago when I was growing up. And I made a decision if it was ever possible for me to have good butter that I would make sure I had it. And so, I worked along the years and it became possible for me to eat good butter. Consequently, I have a regulation and a policy in this church that we will not serve Oleo margarine. Now, if anyone is aware of this church serving Oleo margarine at its dinners, its brunches, or any of our other activities, I do wish that they would specifically give us the details so that the situation could be corrected. I can assure you in the four years I've been with the church, I never ate margarine. Never. All right?

Now, the next point on here is suggestions in reference to the church brunches. Now, your church brunch is $2.50 a brunch. Is that correct—
Right.
—[Student P2]?
Yes.
For adults. And how much for children?
Dollar and a half.
And a dollar and a half for children. Now, because I'm not married and I don't have a wife to cook my breakfast, lunch, and dinner for me, I do quite frequently eat out. Now, a peanut butter sandwich and a glass of, of chocolate malt, the other day, cost me three dollars and thirty-some cents. Now, that was a peanut butter sandwich. I admit, it did have jelly on it. And I do admit that I had a chocolate malt. But that was over three dollars and thirty-some cents at Denny's restaurant. That's not known to be the most expensive restaurant in the county. So, I think that $2.50 for a brunch, where they have all they want to eat—if we have it any cheaper, what's going to happen [is] we're going to be known as the charity kitchen for Marin County and it would surely be most unfair to the membership who's spending their hard-earned wages to donate the food to this church. I think $2.50 is very fair.[60]

This church has a policy whereby, if we have any indigent members—that means, that they're not financially able to, to take care of some of their responsibilities, like going to class and etc., this church goes out of its way to try to make arrangements to help the students and the members so they will not be deprived of any spiritual food. But we are not in a financial position to take care of the physical needs of our membership to the extent that we can feed their daily needs, their physical needs, that is, to, to give them brunches for nothing or etc. We're not financially in that kind of a position yet.

Now, I honestly feel that $2.50 for all that they receive on a Sunday morning brunch on the first of the month and a $1.50 for children is extremely reasonable. Let us remember this, friends, that this donation of food is from our own members. It's out of your own pockets. Now if you wanted to give it away for $0.50 a brunch, that is your decision, if you want to do that. But I don't know how many people will continue to bring food for the brunch.

Now I'm leaving it to you. I'm putting it on the floor. If anyone has any kind of a motion that they want to reduce the cost of our brunches or our dinners, please make your motion so it can be taken care of with the membership. [Student R3], would you kindly rise and make your motion, please.

I move that we don't charge for the children and leave the fee for the brunch at $2.50.

Thank you. [Student R3] has made a move that we leave the fee of the brunch at $2.50; that we do not charge for the children. At what specific age, [Student R3], do you wish the charge removed for the children?

It's usually up to, I guess, up to eleven—the end of the eleventh year.

Well, our church records reveal that we do not charge for our, our dinners or for our brunches under the age of thirteen.

I'm always charged. [Student R3 reports.]

You've always been charged? Well, where's [Student S]? You're here at all of our dinners. Have you been charging the children under the age of thirteen?

Not at the dinners, but the brunches. [Student R3 clarifies.]

Not at the dinners. [Student S explains.]

Not at the dinners. All right, a motion is on the floor that we, we not charge children under what—under the age of eleven, did you say, is that your—

Under the age of twelve. [Student R3 speaks.]

That we not charge children under the age of twelve for our brunches. Do I hear a second to the motion?

I don't want to—

It's time for a second. At the question, we can speak up. Thank you, [Student N3]. Do I hear a second to the motion?

Yes, I do.

Who seconds the motion? [Student S3] has seconded the motion. Are you ready for the question? Now is the time to speak up to a motion—it is on your floor—not to charge children under the age of twelve for our brunches every Sunday. [Student N3] would like to speak. Would you rise, please?

I, I don't want to say this because I don't have any children under that age, however I do have my grandchildren once in a while that do come that would cover them. But I do feel that when you go to a restaurant and you take your children, they don't serve them free regardless of what, what they order. So, I don't know—that's my opinion there.

Thank you very much. Now is there anyone else that wishes to speak? Yes, the lady—[Student T3], please. Would you rise, please?

That's very true. I can see [Student N3's] point of view. But we are family-like here. And couldn't we meet kind of a compromise and put, like, fifty cents for children that are under the age of twelve? Or maybe even a donation. But this way it would be fair to our family church and it would be fair to the children. And if somebody couldn't make it, why, we could always—it would be a lesson in humility to come up and say, "I just can't afford it. I've got three children; and can I give this much? But at least I can give a little bit." And that would be—we would be governed by conscience, too.

Well—anyone else wish to speak up? [Student J], please.

As the treasurer, I would like to ask, unless the members support their church, how are we going to pay the bills?

Thank you very much. Yes, you have a motion; so, I'll come back to you after the others, [Student R3]. [Student U3], please.

I would like to know, Does this include the public or just the members? If it's just the members—

My understanding of the motion is it includes everyone. That includes the public. That's my understanding of the motion that's on the floor.

That's feeding an awful lot of people.

That's right. [A different person agrees.]

The lady—Miss [Student U3]—Mrs. [Student U3]. Would you rise, please?

I just want to say I don't think there's that many children that we have to be concerned with that much money. I mean, by saying that the children eat free, we're not concerning ourselves with that much of a loss of money for the church.

Thank you. Now [Student T3] wishes to speak.

I think it should be, if we do give any lenience, it should be strictly for the members of the church and the people that bring the food. Maybe a mother brings the food and has three children and is growing through the levels of, of money and can kind of make a stretching step and say, "OK, you know, I've got two children. And I'm having trouble with a husband at home. And I can afford, maybe, seventy-five cents, I think." But governed by conscience. And it definitely shouldn't be outside [of] members. It should be the members of the church who bring the food.

Thank you. Now [Student R3] would like to speak again to her own motion.

My motion was mainly to keep a spirit of giving because in my own experience it was a lovely experience to come to the church and have my children served, until they were suddenly being charged a dollar and a half. I'm not concerned with the money. That doesn't concern me at all. It was just that the spirit of receiving something, it made me feel very joyful. And that's why I made the motion.

Thank you very much.

What do you think he does when he gives the messages every Sunday? Doesn't he give? [Student J asks.]

No, no, no.

Is that out of order, [Student J]? [A different student asks.]

Yeah, it is. [Student J replies.]

Now, I would like to speak to the motion, if everyone else is finished speaking to the motion. If everyone's finished speaking to the motion, I would like to speak to the motion. Now, I'm trying, and it's my responsibility as your president and pastor, to see both sides of all coins.

Now, we do have at our dinners a policy that we have had since the founding of the association that children under the age of thirteen would not be charged; that children from the age of thirteen through eighteen would pay $2.50, is that correct? *[After a short pause, he continues.]* Now the reason that we had that policy—and we still have that policy—and the reason that that policy does not apply to a Sunday morning church brunch service is very simple. We have found, over the years, that families who make the effort to come to their church dinner socials to support their church are not in the majority. We have also found that on the first of the month at a Sunday church brunch and a church service that it is the heaviest attendance of our church.

Now one of our members suggested here several months ago that the reason that the first of the month church service attracted the most people and was the heaviest attendance was because the people got so much food for practically nothing. Well, that may or may not be true. But what is true is this: what applies to one applies to all who demonstrate that particular law. Therefore, to charge one person because they carry a card and they're a member of the church—don't forget, I'm a member, too—and not to charge another person is personality. And that's not what this church was founded on. It was founded on principle. Now if we open the door to no charge to children on a Sunday morning, the first of the [month] Sunday brunch, your church is going to be so filled at the brunch that the workers of this church will not long sustain bringing the food and making it for their church. So, we've got to reach a point of reason.[61]

I honestly feel that this church gives more than most churches that I have ever been aware of. There is never a time that I am not available—if I'm not out working for your church—that I'm not available to take care of your calls when you are in times of need. If I am not at the office, your church has an answering service. And I call you people back to try to help you. So I don't think that this church is short in the giving vibration in any sense of the word. But I do feel that whatever decision is reached, it cannot and will not be reached in personality: to give to one child a free sandwich and a free brunch and to deprive from another of God's children the same offer is strictly partiality and personality.

Now, last year, you all know that I gave my personal inheritance of almost $16,000 to your church. I do not feel that that inheritance will long last if we start giving away free food at a public church brunch because it's going to attract more and more people for free food and free sandwiches. And we are not a soup kitchen. We were not designed to be a soup kitchen. We're here to serve the spiritual purpose for which this church has been founded.

Now, I can see this: that a child of thirteen, from thirteen, age thirteen to eighteen pay $1.50; from a child under the age of thirteen to pay $0.75. But, believe me, I've dealt with many children—and I have a very good appetite—they certainly can outdistance my appetite, any child I've ever had any dealings with. So, if you would—the motion that's on the floor, if the lady who made it and the person who seconded it would like to withdraw it, then I will be more than happy to entertain a motion from the floor that our, that our church brunches remain at $2.50 for an adult, that they remain at a $1.50 for anyone from the age of thirteen through eighteen and that we instigate a $0.75 brunch for children under thirteen. Thank you very much.

Does the lady who made the motion wish to carry on or withdraw it?

I'll withdraw it.

The motion is withdrawn by [Student R3]. And the person who seconded it, do they care to withdraw it?

[There is no audible response to the teacher's question.]

The chair will entertain a motion that our church brunches on the first Sunday of the month remain at $2.50 for adults—and what constitutes an adult is the age of eighteen up—and that they will remain at $1.50 for children between the ages of thirteen and eighteen and that we will have a $0.75 fee for children who are thirteen or under. [Student Q3], will you care to make that motion?

I second it.

[Student Q3] makes that motion. It is seconded by [Student O3]. Are you ready for the question?

Question.

Question. Now is the time to speak. *[After a short pause, he continues.]* All those in favor?

Aye. [Many members speak.]

Contrary minded? *[After another short pause, the teacher continues.]* So ordered and approved.

Now, in reference to—there's one other suggestion here in reference to compulsory tithing. I think, perhaps, it's only a matter of a lack of communication in reference to these things. Now when your church was founded, it was founded on the principle, the basic principle that the gift without the giver is worthless. And so it is that every year the association has been in existence I have personally spoke[n] up in protest of any forced, compulsory tithing on the membership of this association. Because I know that when you force an individual to [do] something, their soul is not with it. They're not giving it from the right level of consciousness. This is why this church does not impose upon its membership compulsory attendance, as many churches do. We do not impose these things upon our membership; and therefore, I will admit, the struggle, financially, is a little greater than it is in many churches because we do not have forced, compulsory financial tithing.

Your dues have been kept at a bare minimum of $27 per year. Part of those dues have to go to national headquarters to pay what is called the per capita tax. If you people do not pay your dues, one of the other members has to make up the difference and pay that [those] dues and pay that tax. And so it is that we've kept our dues at a bare minimum. We've kept our philosophy classes at the lowest possible minimum that we could of $50 for a twelve-week semester.

Now if you wish to make a motion, as is a suggestion in our files, to have a tithing of your membership, then let it be a voluntary tithing; let it be as it has always been: to give what you want when you want from your heart. Otherwise, it does no good to this church at all. We don't need it when it's forced out of you.

And so, my good friends, let us think about becoming the living demonstration of a voluntary tithing. Remember, we all don't earn the same amount of money. Now I earn my $50 a month from your church and I manage quite nicely, considering that I've learned to become very practical and very conservative. And so, let us think about those things. Let us think about the people in our membership that are on fixed incomes. They've only got X number of dollars, but maybe they donate some time at the office. Because your church is not in a financial position to be paying salaries to secretaries to come and do typing.

So, if we leave it the way it has always been—not that we're not always open for change—but leave it free, so that one donates a dollar bill, somebody donates an hour's work—because, you see, it's all energy. Money is the effect of energy. And so, if a person is directing energy into your church, they're making a financial deposit. For we use that, that energy, and we transmute that into funds to pay the bills and keep the doors open. Some of you come to the office and you help to make planters and you help to make this and you help to make that to sell. Some of you come and you do the typesetting and do the clerical work. And some I don't see at all. But I never call a member and say I haven't seen you at your church office, because I know that many of those members who don't come to the office, they're home working on an afghan or they're working on something else.[62]

And so, your church wasn't founded to dictate that you must do so many hours at your church office. We hope and pray that you will come and do what you can. But at least do something at home. So it's up to you, as a membership, whether or not you want this church to instigate forced, compulsory tithing financially.

The chair will entertain any motion. *[After a pause, the teacher continues.]* If there is no motion to force the membership into compulsory tithing and if there is anyone that wishes to speak for the good of the church—it's twenty minutes to one. I'm sure you're all as hungry as I am. I haven't yet had breakfast, but I will be happy to be patient to listen to any suggestions that are for the good of your church and that you are willing to become the living demonstration by doing it first. Does anyone have any suggestions? [Student T3] has a suggestion. Would you rise, please.

I just wanted to say, Richard, that if there's some way it can be worked out and, you know, and it's in God order, I'll let go of the house.

Well, thank you—

If you still want it.

Thank you very much, [Student T3]. And I ask the lay membership and the directors of this church that [Student T3] has made a statement that if it's in God's divine order that she will let go of the house which we are renting from her. Your church doesn't have much, but it does have a little money invested. And I am sure that [Student T3] is thinking, if it is in order for her that she would sell the house to her church. Is that right, [Student T3]?

That's right. It's—whatever's right.

Thank you very much. So let the membership as a whole pray in their meditation for divine right action that your church may have its own little home to operate the business of its church.

Now if there are no other suggestions, I thank you from the sincerity of my heart for your efforts in keeping these doors open and serving God's true purpose. Thank you. Let's go have refreshment. Is there anything else?

Committees.

Oh—stay. Oops, sorry. I'm just reminded here, by a director, of the committees. This will only take a few moments. You see what happens when you get in desire. I thought about that delicious cup of coffee and I forgot about everything else. *[Some students laugh.]*

Now let me see, I don't have my bug glasses with me. Advertis—now all committees are standing committees for one year. They're nominated each year. Advertising committee: [Student S], would you continue with that?

Yes. Thank you.

Thank you very much. Auditing committee—that's keep[ing] your eyes on the finance: [Student J], will you take care of that?

Yes, sir.

Thank you. Bake sale: [Student G], you're doing such a nice job on that. Will you continue with that?

Yes. Thank you.

Thank you. The bazaar committee. Now [Student S], you had that last year. Would you take care of that?

Yes. Thank you.

All right. Now what's that committee? *[The teacher may be pointing to one line of the list of committees.]*

Bingo.

Oh, the bingo committee. [Student R]—that's for the socials.

Yes, sir.

Would you carry on with that?

[The response from the student is difficult to transcribe.]

Birthdays.

Birthday committee. Now, [Student S], would you take care of the birthday committee?

Yes. Thank you.

Now I want to pause for a moment. Now all committee heads nominated for one year—it is their responsibility to get at least two committee members on their committee. So I'm sure these committee chairmen will be talking to you.

Brunch.

What's that?

Sunday night . . .

Oh, the Sunday group. The brunch committee has been handled very nicely by the members of Sunday night group. And will the Sunday night group carry on with that, [Student R]?

Yes.

Fine. Now what is—that's the book.

Books.

Book department. Now [Student G], would you carry on with that committee?

Yes. Thank you.

Thank you very much. Now the building committee. [Student V], would you take care of the building committee?

Yes, sir.

Yes. Now the . . .

Building church fund.

Ah, the building church fund committee. Now [Student S] has been working on that and doing a nice job, but she's got so many committees. Would [Student E2] like to take that committee this year?

Yes.

Uh-huh. Now, [Student E2], you know the responsibility of that committee. The month of February is designated for our building fund drive. And so, I do want to bring that to your attention, as I did to [Student S]. And remember, friends, let us be grateful: it is through the support of the public and your efforts that this is going so nicely.

Cassette club.

Oh, the cassette club. [Student G], will you take care of that?

Yes. Thank you.

Funny, I can't read—clerical?

Clerical.

Clerical. You're at the office every Monday for eight or ten hours. Would you continue on with the clerical?

Yes.

And what is this committee?

Decorating.

Decorating committee. Oh, [Student Q], would you take the decorating committee this year?

Sure.

Thank you very much.

Education committee.

Education committee. [Student M3], how's the transcriptions coming?

Improving.

Improving? If they're improving, would you continue on with that committee, please?

I'll keep it.

Thank you so very much. Entertainment, there, entertainment. [Student P2], would you continue with that committee?

Certainly.

Flowers. [A director informs the teacher.]

And the flower committee. [Student V3], would you take over the flower committee this year?

Thank you. I will.

And—

The healing.

Oh, [Student R], would you continue on the healing committee?

Yes, sir.

The ladies' guild. Now, [Student A], you've had that, haven't you? Where are you, [Student A]?

Right here.

Are you here?

I've had it.

I know you've had it, [Student P2]. [Student A], you've had the ladies' guild. Would you like to have a break from that this year?

[It is difficult to transcribe her response.]

And now let's see, who comes regular on Tuesday night? I will nominate her in absence: [Student X3]. I'll talk to her Tuesday night. Thank you very much. She wasn't able to attend today, but I'm sure she'll be most grateful for the chairmanship of the ladies' guild committee.

Librarian.

Librarian. Now that's a nice, easy committee. Who wants that? *[The teacher laughs.]* No, I think [Student Y3] should have that. And I didn't mean that facetiously, but you're already a librarian, aren't you?

Yes.

[Student Y3], would you like to take that?

Thank you.

Thank you so much. All right. Now I only got a few more here. There's only about forty [committees].

Literature.

Now, the literature committee, they have to work on the literature table. Where's [Student P]? Would you take that literature committee this year?

Yes, I will.

Oh, that's fine. And help give [Student G] a break there. Literature?

Lyceum.

The lyceum. Yes, now [Student T2] and [Student X2] are not here today and they both have that. So I will check with them as soon as I get back to the office. The men's club. [Student V], how are you doing getting that men's club organized? How many members do you have now?

Members? I think there's only about three of us right now.

There's three. How long have you had that committee?

I guess, probably, probably about eight months or so.

Eight months. So, we have three members. Would you like to have an assistant on that committee, on that club, the men's club? *[After a short pause, he continues.]* OK, [Student V] will continue on with the chairmanship of the men's club. And [Student M3], you're in the radio business; would you mind being the assistant for the men's club?

Yes, sir.

Yes, they're in need of members. All right? Ah—

Music.

Music. [Student P2], would you continue on with the music committee?

Certainly.

Fine. What's this here?

Photography.

The photography committee. Now somebody has a knack for photographing here that's always at the dinner social. Where's [Student Q]? Would you take the photography committee, please?

You skipped the membership. [A director informs the teacher.]

Yeah, I guess so. [Student Q agrees.]

Of photography. Now the membership committee, let's see, we have—how'd I get to the photography?

You skipped membership. [A different director replies.]

Oh, the membership. [Student E2], would you take the membership committee?

Surely.

All right. That's getting new members. Because you've been doing a nice job with that. Now, music committee—[Student P2]. Photography—[Student Q]. Publicity. Now several of the members have been interested in the publicity committee. Now [Student G], would you carry on with the chairmanship of the publicity committee?

Yes.

And would you ask some of the other people present to help you on that?

Yes.

Now public relations. I hear from upstairs that [Student V3] is very good at that. Would you like to take care of the public relations committee this year?

Certainly.

All right. And see what we get accomplished there now. What's this?

Receiving.

Oh, the receiving committee. [Student S], you've been doing a nice job there. Would you like to carry on with that?

[It is difficult to transcribe her response.]

And what is this?

Records.

Oh, the records committee. The records committee. Well, [Student G], you're at the office every Monday, you might as well have that. All right?

Thank you.

Now what does this here—

Recording. [Two directors respond.]

The recording committee? Well, you do the recording, [Student R]. Will you take the recording committee?

Yes, sir.

The subscription committee. Now there's a committee we've got to really get activated. This is your [*Serenity*] *Sentinel* subscription committee. Now, [Student T3], would you take that?

I knew you were going to say that. May I think about it? In—

Well, then I have to get an assistant for you in case you think down instead of up. Don't you see? See, this is the nomination of the committees. Now did you feel that it might be too heavy a cross? I can tell you what it is—

I fear I may not be here, Richard. And then I can't—

Oh, but that—we send *Sentinels* all over the world. It would be all right. That, that's perfectly all right if you're not present on the sub—

Maybe [Student J] would like that. He'd be a lovely assistant.

[The teacher clears his throat.] Well, let us, let us—

. . . I'll be glad to take it. [A few of her words are difficult to transcribe.]

All right. Thank you. So, [Student T3]. And, and would [Student P] work with [Student T3] on that?

Sure. [Student P responds.]

Thank you very much. And in case [Student T3] is out of state, then we can—you can take care of the out of state, new subscriptions, you see. And—

Social.

Social. Will the Sunday night group continue on with the social committees?

Yes, sir.

And special—does that say special events?

Special events.

Special events. Now that's an important committee here to get everything lined up on special events. Would [Student N3] take that? Special events. That's whenever your church has a special event, like an anniversary or things of that nature. There aren't that many.

But what, what is [are] the duties?

Well, the duties are to get it coordinated and organized.

I will certainly try.

Would you? Special events committee.

If I had somebody to guide me. So I know what to do.

Sure. Sure.

Thank you.

Because that's like your anniversary dinner or some big special event for the church.

I hardly know anything.

Right. Now the—

We will all help you. [A director remarks.]

—the stamp committee. Now [Student S3], would you take the stamp committee this year?

What is the stamp committee?

The stamp committee is a committee that accepts offerings to pay for postage stamps. Because we have to have stamps. It costs your church a fortune because we answer all these letters from all over the world about Spiritualism. Would you take the stamp committee?

Sure.

All right. Thank you very much. Now [Student S3] is on the stamp committee. Oh, here's a lovely committee here. This is the suggestion committee. It's a very active committee. [Student G], would you continue on with that committee?

Yes. Thank you.

Transcription committee. Now [Student M3] is on the education committee. Now, [Student O3], would you take the transcription committee?

Yes.

You're personally responsible for those subscriptions [transcriptions]—getting them out—under the education committee. All right?

Uh-huh.

All right. So [Student M3] will see that that's taken care of there. And [Student G]. Does that say ushering?

Ushering.

The ushering committee. [Student R], would you take care of that?

Yes, sir.

You left transportation out. Excuse me.

Transportation committee. [Student V], would you take care of the transportation committee?

All right.

And that's to see that these souls get transported on time. *[A few students laugh.]* Ways and means committee. The ways and means committee. Well, [Student J], will you take that?

Yes, sir.

That's to see that we have enough money to pay our bills. Thank you all very much. Let's go eat. Thank you kindly.

MAY 11, 1975

Membership Meeting May 9, 1976

Is everyone here now? Good. *[The teacher strikes a gavel.]* This meeting officially comes to order. Let us all rise, please.

O infinite divine and eternal Spirit, we ask Thy guidance on this the seventh annual membership meeting of the Serenity Association. May we be wisely guided in the deliberations of our association for the peace and the harmony, the unity and the strength for the true purpose that we have been granted here in this association to bring the Living Light Philosophy to a world in need. Amen.

Be seated, please.

May I check the tape just once before I . . . [Student R asks.]

Yes, please do. Now, we have, in keeping our Article 5 in our rules and regulations on our constitution, a certain order of business. The Friends feel that, after the many years of operating this association and a quorum is present, that we may—the chair will entertain a motion to delete all of these different things of the meetings and get right down to the actual business at hand. And if someone would like to make a motion in that respect, the chair would be happy to entertain that type of a motion.

[The student is far from the microphone; so, it is difficult to transcribe his motion.]

There's a motion made by [Student V] that we delete all of this reading of the minutes and all of these things. Do I hear a second? *[After a short pause, the teacher continues.]* Seconded by [Student P]. All in favor?

Aye. [Several students respond.]

All contrary minded? *[After a very short pause, he continues.]* So ordered and approved. So, let's get right down to business. The first order of business is [Student S] is the secretary-treasurer of your association. We neglected to officially vote her in at our last meeting. And so the—would someone like to nominate her as the secretary-treasurer of your association officially? She's been doing the work for years.

[It is difficult to transcribe the student's motion.]

Motion—you wish to nominate [Student S]? All right. [Student S] is nominated by [Student Q]. Are there any other nominations? *[After a short pause, the teacher continues.]* No other nominations. All those in favor of [Student S] for secretary-treasurer of your association signify by saying aye.

Aye. [Many members speak.]

Fine. Now the longest order of business here—let us have the secretary-treasurer read the financial report. Now the financial report of this association is usually given collectively. If you wish it *seriatim*, then you can make up your minds you're going to be here for at least ten hours because we've got to read off every postage stamp. The financial books of the association are open to any member in good standing upon a written request to the board of directors stating your reason for viewing the books and making an appointment with the office to do so. Do you wish to have the financial report read off collectively or *seriatim*? *[After a short pause, he continues.]* The chair will entertain a motion for it to be read off collectively.

I [so move.]

[Student A4] makes a motion to have the financial report read off collectively. Do I hear a second?

[It is difficult to transcribe the second.]

All those in favor, please raise their hands. Fine. [Student S], would you kindly read the financial report of the association.

Yes. The balance sheet for twelve months ended April 30, 1976.

Assets: cash in savings accounts: $2,024.91; Land, chapel building, and equipment: $37,500. Total assets: $39,524.91.

Liabilities: first mortgage: $1,353.88; second mortgage: $4,443.57; equipment contracts: $16,317.39; accounts payable, general: $15,385.16. That is a total of $37,500. Retained income: $2,024.91. Total liabilities and retained income: $39,524.91.

Statement of income and expense and retained income. Income: dues, $1,086; donations, $25,979.72; seminars, $6,094.22. Interest—

That should be called classes. Excuse me. Thank you.

Thank you. Interest on earned—interest earned on savings, $6,094.22; net from fundraising activities $86—I'm sorry. Interest earned on savings was $86.50.

Next item: Net from fundraising activities: socials, $1,652.83; books and tapes, $8,961.34; bake sales, etc., $5,836.16; cards, $1,363.87. Total $17,814.20. Total income: $51,060.64.

Expenses: equipment payments and purchases, $3,940.09; magazines and books, $636.86; printing and tape expense, $8,524.30; office expense, $2,784.13; President's expense, $1,180; rent, $5,796; utilities, $1,831.59; real estate payments, $1,365; church expense, $1,207.95; automobile expense, $2,691.93; advertising, $1,422.90; dues, $144; fundraising activities expense, $16,943.88; fundraising activities expense—sorry, I did read that—$16,943.88; postage, $732.80; sales and property taxes, $806.30; legal service, $28. Total expense, $50,035.73.

For the deficit or retained income over expense: $1,024.91.

Now, are there any questions in reference to the report? *[After a short pause, the teacher continues.]*

I would like to say a couple of things here. It is very clear where your association is getting its funds from. And I think if you study this report, it can be easily seen. It is from the sale of the cassette tapes, your classes, and it is from your bake sales [which are] bringing in the most money for your association. And so, we should, in wise, common business sense, concentrate our efforts on the sale of the cassette tapes, for which your organization was truly founded—to bring the light of the philosophy to the world—and on your bake sales. Now the card games [have] just started to get underway, and it's done quite well considering.[63]

Now, do I hear a motion on the floor? The chair will entertain a motion to accept the report as read. Is there a motion on the floor?

[It is difficult to transcribe the motion of the student.]

[Student L] makes a motion to accept the report as read. Do I hear a second?

[Again, it is difficult to transcribe the second.]

Seconded by [Student Q]. Are you ready for the question? Now is the time if you have any questions concerning it or you wish to make any appointments with your church office to view the books, you're more than welcomed to. If you're ready for any questions, please state. *[After a very short pause, the teacher continues.]* No questions? All those in favor?

Aye. [Many students speak.]

Contrary minded? *[After a very short pause, he continues.]* So ordered and approved.

Now, we have here—it's my responsibility as president here to get a few of these reports out here. One of the members, who I notice is not present, would like to have the history of the Old Man, who brought our philosophy [to Earth], all put on to one cassette tape. And they would like to have all of the Sunday morning lectures, since the organization was founded, put into a booklet form. Both ideas, your board of directors feels is very wise. However, there is one seeming snag, and that is the workers to do the job. So, we go by a priority system in the association. And the priority is to keep the doors open and keep [giving] the philosophy to the world. And therefore, that is under consideration when we have more workers to do the job.

Also, we have a suggestion in reference to the upgrading of the *Serenity Sentinel* magazine. I, too, would like the members to know that we have been working on that for the past two years. [Student H] was informed months ago that we would like to have some new art work. [Student G] was informed two years ago that we wanted the format upgraded. And that is in process and will come about in reference 'til we get more typesetters and more workers at the office. [Student H] also has a bake sale sign, which is a priority that comes before it.[64] He also has the little model of the church to sit at the billet table which is before that. And so, we will get to that as we get in more workers.

Now, each year we have a standing committee here. That means—standing committees means they are committee heads for one year and then they are disbanded at each annual membership meeting in order that other people may also have an opportunity. So I think we should go right on here and get right to the committees. And I can't see this too well. So, [Student R], start reading off.

First committee is advertising.

The advertising committee. All right. We'll stop here. Now [Student S], you've been doing such a wonderful job on that. Would you like to carry on with that committee?

Yes. Thank you.

That's fine. Thank you. Next?

Auditing.

Auditing committee. Well, [Student Q] is doing the balancing on the monthly books here and the bank accounts. And whereas she's doing that work—would you take the chairmanship this year of the auditing committee, [Student Q]?

Sure.

All right. Fine. And [Student G] also works in doing the typing of these financial reports to the national, etc. Would you take the cochairmanship on that, [Student G]?

[It is difficult to transcribe her response.]

All right. Next committee, please.

Next is audio.

The audio committee. Now, [Student R], you have that responsibility with all of that equipment on that. Would you take that, please—and the classes?

Yes.

All right. Next.

Next is bake sale.

Bake sale committee. Now [Student G] has done such a nice job and is supporting this church through her efforts—and the [efforts of the] members [and] the friends [of the church]. And would you continue on with that, [Student G], please?

[Again, it is difficult to transcribe her response.]

All right.

Next is bazaar.

Now the bazaar committee. Now this is a very important committee. It takes several committee heads. We've got to get the dolls made, which we're always sold out each year. We've got a lot of things that should be in process in the here and now and not waiting 'til November. [Student P2], you've always been on that committee. Will you take a chairmanship of that, please?

Certainly.

[Student S].

Yes.

[Student Q].

Yes.

[Student G].

Yes.

[Student E2].

Yes.

[Student B4].

Yes.

[Student P].

Yes.

[Student V3].
Yes.
[Student L].
Yes.
[Student A4].
Yes.
And [Student T3].
Yes.

All right. Now we've got all the women present, I think, on the bazaar committee. Now that doesn't mean the men aren't going to be doing anything, because it's up to the women that are on the committee to see that the men *do* do something. We should have a wonderful bazaar this November because every woman that thinks anything of her church is present, unless they're out of town. And therefore, that should work out fine. Next committee, please.

Birthday committee.

The birthday committee. Now, [Student S], you've always sent out those nice birthday cards. Would you take that this year?

Yes. Thank you.

All right. Now remember, on these committees, it's up to the committee head to select two helpers or more and submit their names to the office. Now the reason that you submit their names to the office when you select two people to work on your committee is so that the Friends may look in and see if you're going to have any kind of ego-personality problems or it will work harmoniously. So that's the purpose to that. Next committee is brunch?

Brunch.

Brunch committee. The brunch committee is handled by the Sunday [night] group meeting.

OK.

I don't think there's any dissent in that, is there? The group meeting [members are] present. No. All right. Next committee.

Books.

The book department. [Student B4], you have that committee. Fine. Will you carry on with that?

Yes.

Next.

Building committee.

Now the building committee. This is not the building fund committee, is it? This is the *building* committee. This is the committee that's supposed to be painting the office, washing the windows, and keeping that place clean. [Student V], will you take care of that?

Yes.

All right. You take charge of that. And [Student M3], would you [be] cochairman?

Yes.

Considering you're supposed to keep the windows clean, they're awfully dirty up there.

Building fund committee.

Yes.

Now let's see, now let's see, who's in the flow here? We're all supposed to be in the flow. But let me see, the building fund committee. All right, [Student H], considering you're making the little church back there, would you take over the chairmanship of the building fund committee?

Yes.

We'll expect to see a lot of funds in this year. *[Several students laugh.]* Thank you very much. I'm glad to hear you're a Capricorn. Next committee.

Cassette club.

The cassette club. The cassette club. Now who was on that last year? [Student G]?

Yes.

[Student G], she's got enough committees. Now the cassette club has to be somebody—[Student B4], would you take over the cassette club?

Certainly.

Your mother can show you how it's all done, all right?[65] Next committee.

Children's philosophy class.

The children's philosophy class. Now that's an important committee. [Student P] is on the lyceum. Would you—and let's see, where is [Student A]? She's not here today?

She was. She had lyceum this morning. [A director reports.]

All right. That's my fault. We'll have to have a roll call right after this. All right, the children's philosophy class. [Student P], will you take care of that?

Uh-huh.

Next committee.

Clerical committee.

Oh, the clerical committee, that's all the clerical work. Yes, indeed. [Student G], will you take care of that? You're at the office five days a week.

Yes. Thank you.

All right. Next committee.

Decorating committee.

Decorating committee. Who had that last year?

I did.

[Student Q]. [A director whispers.]

Oh, you did? [You] did a nice job. Would you take—carry on with that, [Student Q]?

Sure.

Next committee.

Monthly dinner parties.

The monthly dinner parties are handled by the Sunday [night] group. Will the Sunday [night] group continue on with that?

Yes.

All right.

Education committee.

The education committee. [Student M3], what are you doing with that education committee? You have the education committee, don't you?

[It is difficult to transcribe his response.]

OK. Would you get us a report next month on the education committee? Would you continue on with the chairmanship of that?

Yes, sir.

All right. Good. Next committee.

Entertainment committee.

The entertainment committee, that was cochairmaned [cochaired] this last year by [Student Q] and [Student M3]. And would they kindly continue the cochairmenship of that?

Yes.

Fine. Next.

Flower committee.

The flower committee. [Student V3] has that, don't you, [Student V3]?

Yes.

That's a, that's a beautiful committee. We have to work on proportional balance, however. It seems to me that those flowers are three feet higher than those. So, would you continue on with that committee?[66]

Yes.

And do you need someone for proportional balance?

Do I need someone?

Yes. You know, I mean to kind of . . .

Oh, as cochairman?

Yes.

Well, certainly.

[Student H], considering you're an artist, would you take over the cochairmanship of the flower committee?

Yes.

And would you kindly see that we have proportional balance?

OK.

On our podium. Thank you. In other words, if somebody donates some flowers and they're going to be X high, see that the ones that we make up, you know, [are that high]. OK. Now the next committee.

Healing committee.

Healing committee. [Student P2] has that. Would you carry on with that, [Student P2]?

Certainly.

Next.

Ladies' guild.

Yes, how's production coming on that? [Student P2], you have the ladies' guild. Are the dolls coming [along and] underway?[67]

Yes. Moving right along.

OK. We need a lot of tea towels and things. OK, will you continue on with that committee? Next committee.

Librarian.

Librarian. Hmm. Well, [Student G], you got so many committees, let's see. [Student E2], would you take over that committee and get the information from [Student G] about that?

Yes.

The librarian. Next. Liter—

Literature committee.

And would you also take the literature committee, [Student E2]?

[It is difficult to transcribe her response.]

Thank you. Men's club?

Men's club is next.

Well, there doesn't seem to be many members to the men's club, but there are a few and they do get a few funds in to help the church to keep going. And [Student V], would you carry on with the men's club?

[His response is difficult to transcribe.]

Great.

Membership committee.

The membership committee. Now let's see, the membership committee, now we change that each year. The membership committee. Well, I never was interested in numbers, only quality. Now let's see . . . membership committee—[Student Q], would you take that this year?

Certainly.

You know what that involves? You talk to [Student E2]. That means, talking to people who are interested in members[hip] so they don't think we're a closed club. OK? Next committee?

Motion picture committee.

The motion picture committee. Oh, you and [Student S] are on that, aren't you, [Student R]?

Yes.

All right. Would you carry with cochairmen on that?

Yes.

Next committee.

Music committee.

Music committee? Is that the choir? No. We have an entertainment committee and then we have the music committee. The music committee has to be the choir. [Student P2], would you carry on with that, please?

Certainly.

Yeah. Next committee.

Photography.

The photography committee. Oh, [Student Q], you were chairlady of that last year. Is the film paying for itself yet?[68]

Hmm...

Not quite. Better give you another year's opportunity. Would you take care of that, please?

All right.

Thank you very much. Next committee.

Publicity committee.

The publicity committee. Yes, now let's see. Publicity and public relations we will consolidate this year. [Student G], will you take care of that?

I'll be glad to.

And next committee.

Receiving committee.

The receiving committee. Now [Student T3], she's usually on the front door out there. Would you take the chairlady of that, please?

When I'm in town.

All right. Good. Then, when you're not, you'll see that we have someone, right?

Yes.

Recommended. Thank you. Next committee.

Records committee.

The records committee, let's see. Records committee. That's keeping the records. Who's good at keeping records. Well, better give that job to [Student G]. She's there all the time. And that will help you with organization, [Student G]. Would you take care of that?

Yes.

All right. Good. Now the [Serenity] Sentinel subscription committee. Now this is a committee we've got to get some energy poured on to. [Student V3], would you take over the Sentinel subscription this year?

Yes.

Yes. Now, we'd like to project that we at least get *[After a short pause, the teacher continues.]* twenty-seven subscriptions a month. Starting today. And we need some people that are active. Now [Student M3] has been on the committee. [Student T3] has been on the committee. Different people have been on the committee. And I'd like to give you a cochairman there that's got some energy and enthusiasm—[Student E2], would you take the cochairmanship of the *Sentinel* subscription committee? And there's no reason in the world why we can't get twenty-seven minimum. Minimum. Minimum. Minimum [of] twenty-seven subscriptions a year. *[The teacher may have intended to say "a month" or perhaps this is a clarification of his earlier statement.]* No reason whatsoever. So, would you get that activated? It's a matter of directing the energy. And if you have problems, you let me know. Yes, if you—because, you see, it's a matter of just accepting everybody wants that beautiful magazine. Thirty-five cents. My God, you couldn't even get a magazine with that much spiritual truth in it [for] thirty-five cents.

Now special events committee. Special events. Hmm. [Student C4], where are you?

I'm here.

Yes, I haven't seen you around for a while.

No, I haven't—

Yes, would you like to take on the special events committee?

Well, you see, the problem—my priorities got me out at—down in Southern California pretty near all the time this summer.

I see. Well—oh, that's what you're projecting for this summer. I see. Well, that's a special event. Would you like to take on that committee? Because perhaps you could coordinate with the *Sentinel* subscription committee and get some subscriptions when you're travelling so much now, don't you see? All right. [Student C4] will be the special events committee and he will be a coordinator with the *Serenity Sentinel* subscription committee and turn in subscriptions to [Student V3]. All right? Or [Student E2]. Would you take care of that, [Student C4]? Because, you see, we don't want you to be left out just because your priorities are taking you to Southern California because there's so many people in Southern California [who] would like to have the *Sentinel* magazine. Would you take care of that?

I'll do that.

All right. Good. Would you check with him—fine. Next committee.

Stamp committee.

The stamp committee. Now stamps, by the way, I hope everybody realizes, have increased in cost. They're not six cents anymore. And considering that I'm at the office every day, I've been very short on stamp funds. Now would [Student M3] and [Student B4] cochairmen the stamp committee?

Certainly.

All right. Now that means getting the funds in for the postage stamps. We read off the report how much the postage is costing us. Next committee.

Suggestion committee.

Beautiful committee. Beautiful committee. Now this year, would [Student G], [Student L], and [Student S] take over the suggestion committee?

Yes.

Now that means that the suggestions don't come to me. Because if they do, I know you're not doing your job. All right? Good. Not until after you've approved them and, and gone through it and then sent a recommendation to your board of directors. Next committee.

Transportation committee.

Transportation. That's a wonderful committee. It helps to coordinate to see people have transportation. And [Student H], would you take that committee chairmanship, please? Transportation, yes.

[His response is difficult to transcribe.]

Next committee.

Ushering committee.

Ushering committee?

Uh-huh.

All right. Well, let's see, who do we have on that? There's [Student J] and there's [Student H]. [Student H], would you take the chairmanship of that ushering committee?

Yes.

Yeah, that's good. Next committee.

Ways and means committee.

The ways and means committee. The ways and means committee. Well, who's the best fundraiser we have? Ways and means committee. That means finding ways and means to support your organization. Hmm? Well, well, [Student Q], I've never heard you cry limitation. So, would you kindly chairlady the ways and means committee, please?

I'll see what I can do. Sure.

Does that mean yes?

Oh, yes.

All right. Fine. Now we got through that. Let's get on—kindly read off the roll of members. Because, at least, we have to read the roll call. [Student P2], please, you're secretary. Do you have the membership list?

[The call of the roll is made and thirty-six names are called, but only eighteen members are present.]

All right. Now we're just about come to a close, here, with our meeting. We have our offering to take up for the good of the church. And I would appreciate that we make a little effort in that area because, as you all know, we have gone to great expense to upgrade the quality of your classes as far as the audio department is concerned. And [Student R], what's the matter with this thing? Look at that. It looks like a rocking chair. *[The teacher refers to the microphone and its stand.]*

Yeah, the cable's a little heavier than the previous one. It's been happening a lot lately. [Student R responds, referring to the microphone cable.]

Oh, well, will you take care of that next time, please?

So, we'll get to that in just a moment. We deleted all these necessary requirements—all these reports of the mediums, the reports of the healers, reports of this one, reports of that. But I would like to take just a few moments to share with you—and it's very important that you know a little how your church runs and how your organization runs and where our energies are being directed.

Now you all know that the organization was founded by the Spirit Council in order to bring this philosophy to the world to help the world, as it has already helped us. We have the Serenity Game out. We have an entirely upgraded audio department this year. And we just completed, yesterday, painting the office, that is, most of it. Haven't finished yet. We'll be asking for some volunteers for a couple of more rooms that have to be done to be completed. We've got a new door put on and everything there.

Now the thing is, it doesn't take a lot of people to keep the Serenity Association, the Serenity Church together. It never did take a lot of people. We have a lot of people who are members who aren't present, but as the lecturer said today, of course, these things, all these factors deal with our priority values. Our support has always come from our efforts to include the public, the nonmembers as well as the members, in our association. So, it is through your efforts of peace and harmony and accepting the divine right of different people to express in different ways and still keep your eye on the Light and your work in life.

Now we have several students that are coming up in their mediumship and in the healing and in different areas. And that's the way that it should be. It shouldn't be built around one or two individuals.[69]

Now if we will all try to do what we can, to have an offering here, which is a once a year offering for the good of our church and let us kindly have the ushers, please, take up an offering.

[Speaking in a whisper, almost to himself, the teacher continues.] Give what I can here. *[Speaking more loudly, he continues.]* Here, [Student J].[70]

[A student says a few words that are difficult to transcribe.]

That's fine. *[After a pause during which the offering is completed, the teacher continues.]*

I think this has been the most harmonious, peaceful, and successful meeting the Serenity Association ever had. I'm a firm believer in just get in [and] get the job done. We could whirl in our mind for six hours and not accomplish one-tenth as much. Jobs to be done. We just get in and do it, and that's just the way that it is. *[After a short pause, he continues.]*

Now, are there any questions? Does anyone have any questions? Or if there's any suggestions for the good of the organization, you know, if there are, now is the time to speak up before we go on about our business. If there's anything you want to say—yes, would you kindly rise, [Student C4], please.

I'm not too clear in my head what I'm supposed to do about, you know, the special events.

Oh, you're on special events. Well, the special events committee chairmanship has been specially modified to suit your particular situation at this time and still benefit your church. So, because of your priorities, as you stated that you would be going down south to the Los Angeles area most of the time now, you'd be away from your church, in order that you may continue to help your church, you understand, and be actively participating, the Friends have given you the opportunity, by taking the special events committee, to make it a special event and get subscriptions, you see. Would you like to set yourself a quota? Like, say five a week, perhaps? Or would you rather have three?

I don't want to be negative about it. I'm just not sure I'm going to have these opportunities.

Oh, you have all kinds of opportunities because we're always meeting people. Yes.

I'll sure do the best I can. But anyhow, do I have to have a membership . . .

Oh, no. All you got to do is take some *Sentinels* and show them to people and—

[The student says a few words that are difficult to transcribe.]

—and subscription envelops. Certainly. No problem at all. I think you're going to do just wonderful. In fact, let me know what your address is. If you don't meet the standard quota, I'll give you a call, collect, [Student C4]. OK? Great!

Yes, [Student M3].

If it please the chair, there was a committee announced, the music committee, that I believe dealt with the music for the dinners and—

That's the entertainment committee.

Entertainment. [A different student speaks.]

That's you and [Student Q].

The recorded music. That's a different committee, as I recall. [Student M3 continues.]

Oh, that. That is—no, that is your committee. You're responsible for all the recording. The recording—no—you mean the recording for the choir?

No.

You mean the recording that is done for the church dinners?

It was my understanding this last year there was a committee called the music committee which was in charge of bringing recorded music to dinners.

Oh, yes. I'm doing the recording myself now. So, I have that committee.

OK.

Yes.

Good.

Not that I asked for it, but I got—thank you very much for clarification. The choir committee, however, was [Student P2]. Yes, [Student T3].

May I please have a clarification on the receiving committee?

Yes, the receiving committee is the committee who is responsible for being at the front door under the guidance of the Council that runs the church. Now the Council makes the decision on who is to alternate on the front door. But whereas you have the receiving committee—because you're on the front door quite frequently—when you're not going to be at church, then it is the responsibility of the chairlady to recommend to the church a replacement.

Thank you.

Yes. Will that be all right? Now is there anything else? Anything for the good of the church? Yes, [Student G].

Perhaps this is not the correct time—

We'll soon find out.

The delegates to the National—

Oh, thank you very much. It is the correct time. Now the National Spiritualist Association board of directors is extremely impressed—they have sent us a letter—with the new Serenity Game. And they have requested that we set up a booth at the national convention—is that Phoenix, Arizona?

Yes, it is.

In Phoenix, Arizona, this October, in order to display the game and to make sales of our Serenity Game and of our book, our literature, and etc. And I would like to recommend to the membership that our delegates—you know, we're entitled to send a minimum of two delegates because we have two charters. We have a charter for the Serenity Church and we have a charter for Camp Serenity, which is a camp charter for our retreat in the mountains. And so, we're entitled to send a minimum of two delegates to the national convention. It is in the best interest of the association and the work it has to do to send these two delegates to this convention in October. And therefore, I would like to recommend that [Student G], our public relations chairlady, and her daughter, [Student B4], be sent to the convention as official delegates from the association, which means they will be voting delegates for the convention in Phoenix in October. And I would also like to recommend to the membership that we try to have at least $100 to help defray what expense we can, because they're going at their expense to that convention.

Would somebody like to nominate [Student G] and [Student B4]? [There is] a nomination by [Student Q]. And so, all those in, in favor? Aye.

Aye. [Many students speak.]

All right. Then that's so ordered and approved. And [Student G] you will leave for the convention with [Student B4]. And we will try to at least have $100, because you'll need that just from their collections there.

Is there anything else? Or should we go have coffee and have our lunch? *[After a short pause, the teacher continues.]* Good. Fine. The meeting is adjourned *[He strikes a gavel.]* until next year. Great.

MAY 9, 1976

Membership Meeting May 13, 1979

First order of business is the ushers will kindly take up an offering for our annual membership meeting. *[The ushers take up an offering from the attendees and present that offering to the teacher.]*

We thank Thee, O God, for this manifestation of Thy divine flow. May the sincere motive in the giving multiply out over the world and reap the harvest of its efforts. Amen.

This meeting will please come to order, as the secretary of our church reads the membership roll.

[The call of the roll is made and twenty-seven names are called, but only seventeen members are present.]

Thank you very much. Now at these membership meetings you have the choice—and we'll put it before the membership and the board of directors—to have a formal meeting or to have an informal meeting. And I will explain the difference to you. A formal meeting, which we have had in the past and we've also had informal meetings, will require *Robert's Rules of Order* governing all deliberations of this association. And the financial report can be read either collectively or *seriatim*. Now if you read it collectively, you will find the income that came into the church and the cash outlay. If you read it *seriatim*, then every single expenditure, including postage stamps, must be read. So, if you wish an informal meeting, please raise your hands, those who do—members of the church. *[After a short pause, he continues.]* And those members of the church who wish to have a formal meeting.

All right, then we will have an informal meeting. And the first thing to be read here is the financial report. If you will kindly—secretary-treasurer, [Student S], read off the financial report to the membership and friends of the church, please.

Shall I rise or stay seated?

Rise, please.

Under income, dues $873—

Date. Date, please.

Pardon me.

As of.

As of twelve months ended April 30, 1979. Income: dues $873; donations $54,023.87; seminars $9,051.96; socials $2,151; books, tapes, and Sentinel *$4,537.43; bake sale and fundraising $6,657.66; interest on note (Tingle) $2,172.26. Total cash receipts $79,467.18.*

Expenses: equipment payments $2,178.44; magazine and books $177.16; office expenses, printing, and tapes $6,248.60; president's expense $2,534.99; rent (log cabin) $4,200; attorney fee $1,265.03; utilities $2,214.04; real estate tax $2,098.06; church expenses $3,934.72; church supplies $2,017—pardon me—$2,717.49; automobile expenses $5,875.08; insurance $939.82; interest to Citizens Savings and Loan $10,164.95; dues $120.75; fundraising activities $1,245.98; sales tax $389.53; repairs $479.27. Totaling $46,783.91.

Furniture and fixtures $8,010.52. Investments, residence $17,619.51. Gardening $3,978.06. Total expenses $76,392.

Retained income over expenses: $3,075.18. The balance for all that is $79,467.18.

You've heard the reading of our financial report. What is your pleasure? To accept it as read or do any of you have a question? Now in reference to some of these expenses—to those who may not be aware—we have been paying real estate tax on the property, the church property at . . .[71] We are going to trial tomorrow and it will be up to a higher power and to the court to decide whether or not we have a right, a just right, to a tax exemption on the church property, as other churches do.[72]

Now, the cost of our *Sentinel* magazine has been costing the church approximately $120 a month in the red in order for us to print and to publish it. And so, we've found it necessary to increase the price of the magazine from $0.50 to $1 per issue.

We have a bare minimum subscription of the *Sentinel* magazine. [Student E2] is the chairlady of that committee. And we'd like to have [Student Z] and [Student B] be cochairladies on that. Will you, please? The two of you. *[After a short pause, the teacher continues.]* And let's get a spirit of energy generated so that we can get a lot more subscriptions, because the purpose of founding the church is to bring this philosophy, this religion and understanding to the world. And that is one of the many ways that it takes place.

Now it has, also, in reference to our brunches and in reference to our church dinners, they're presently $4.75 for the brunch, for adults, and they're $6 for the dinners for the adults. Now, as you all know, everyone that's here, that our dinners and our church brunches, that that food is purchased by our own members and by friends of the church. And it is not fair not to adjust the cost of these brunches and these dinners in keeping with the increased cost of purchasing the food by the friends and members of the church when they go to the store to buy that food. And so, it has been recommended that we adjust our brunches $0.25 from $4.75 on Sunday to $5. And to adjust our dinners, which have been a giveaway at $6, to $7 for a dinner. Now any of you that eat out at any time, I am very well aware and I know you are aware, that you can't possibly get a brunch like that for $5 anyplace, let alone can you get a dinner for $6 or even $7.

So, I'm going to leave it to someone that is interested to make a motion to increase our brunches from $4.75 to $5 and to increase our dinners, our monthly dinners, from $6 to $7. Does someone care to make a motion?

I make a motion.

[Student P2] makes a motion. [Student L], you want to second that motion? Are there any questions in reference to that increase? *[After a short pause, he continues.]* All right, if there are no questions, all those in favor say aye.

Aye. [Many members speak.]

Contrary minded? *[After a short pause, the teacher continues.]* So ordered and approved.

Now, the next thing on our agenda here, we do have a few applications pending for membership in the church. They have not been acted on as of this date. I expect that they will be in the very near future. Now I do want to speak to any applicants, people applying for membership in the church, to research the church thoroughly to see what it's really all about, the way that it gets its bills paid, the responsibility that each and all of us have.

You know, you can't bring about, in the short time that this church is organized, $488,000 in net worth—that's after all bills are paid—if you don't have the system that we have. We have no contributors to this church in the numbers of thousands of dollars; it all comes in from the nickels, the dimes, and the pennies.

Now we've often spoken at meetings in reference to compulsory tithing. It certainly would be a much easier path for me in the sense I wouldn't have to spend so much of my time in trying to get all these committees organized and all these nickels, dimes, and pennies. But it would not be in your best spiritual interest or growth in the sense that if you have to face the giving in a small way frequently, you have a much better chance of growing into a level of flow than if you face it once a year through a compulsory tithing that you begrudgingly feel that you're forced to make your check out once a year.

Now, in keeping with the increased costs that we are all experiencing in our world today—and let us not forget in this increased cost of food and all the supplies, let us not forget that we're also experiencing increased wages. And so let us not put our attention totally on the negative without taking a look at the positive side, too.

It has also been recommended—our dues have been kept for some time at $36 a year, which I feel is very reasonable and it has been recommended that we adjust our dues to $45 a year effective as of this meeting. Now I don't think that that, honestly, is going to put a burden on any of the members or the potential members of this church—$45 a year. And if someone would care to make a motion in respect to that increase— [Student L] makes the motion. You don't have to— *[Perhaps the member stood to make her motion, as was the practice at some of the formal meetings.]* We're having an informal meeting. Thank you, [Student L].

I see.

[Student P2] seconds it: that we adjust and increase our dues from $36 per year for membership to $45 a year.

Now, it's only once a year that I get to talk to you at a membership meeting, because long ago I realized that many churches have membership meetings once a month. But when it's so much energy spent at membership meetings and everyone deciding how the churches should be run, they don't seem to be too successful in many respects. Some of them are, and many of them aren't. The thing is that everything is vibration. The success of your church and the growth of your church and the people in it is vibration. The church is a body of people. It reflects the growth of 51 percent of its membership and friends of the church at any given time. So, if the church is successful in growing, then 51 percent of its people, its own people involved within the church, whether they're card-carrying members or they are friends of the church, that is a reflection of what *they* are doing in their own growth.

Now, tomorrow, we go to court and one of the most important things that seems to interest the County of Marin—the county council—is that everything in this church is for Richard Goodwin. Now, they're entitled, of course, to their thinking. But we must ask our self the question, What is it that we have done or are doing that we have merited this type of thinking from the public? What are we doing? Now we can't just say that that's their error of ignorance. We must be honest with our self. And we must ask our self, Do we or have we, at any time, thought in that way?

In fact, one of my members has mentioned to me, on a few occasions, that some people think that I don't work, that I don't have a regular job. Well, I don't know what kind of thinking it is that thinks that a minister's job is not a job, a regular job. I admit that it's different. Instead of a regular eight hours a day, five days a week, it's twenty-four hours a day, seven days a week. So in that respect, there is a difference in what we consider a regular job of working five days a week, eight hours a day and receiving a salary from some company or working twenty-four hours, on-call, seven days a week and receiving an allowance of $50 a week.

Now, I didn't receive $50 a week until approximately two-and-a-half years ago. I made sure, though many times the board had insisted that I increase my allowance, I always took $50 a month. Now, that's more than enough for me, because I don't spend—I just—I make it on my $50. I don't have any extra to be saving, but my needs are not so great that I need more than that much money a week. But what are we doing with our thinking as we are involved in our church—it's our church—what are we doing? Are we looking at our church as a success and comparing it to our self and to our life? Or are we looking at our church as a part of our self? Because that, in truth, is what it is.

You see, you really get to feel a part of your church when you're faced with paying the bills. I highly recommend that all of the members—and I do hope the day will come when they will have the experience of what it is like to raise $4,000 and more every month, like a little clock, to pay the operating expenses of their church. Now if you think $4,000 a month is a lot of money for a church, then you should look at the budget of the churches right here in this county alone. It's a pittance. But for us, it sometimes seems to be a great deal because we're not that large a membership.

I check the membership rolls and I see that we have twenty-seven members. And out of those twenty-seven members, well, you see how many are present. All right? And so, this is what the Council and the Spirit of your church is weighing out with any new applicants to the membership. Is their priority and their interest in the church and in their spiritual growth? For the demonstration, of course, is the revelation.

Now one of the things that helps anyone interested in this church is to be put on to various committees. Because being placed on various committees where they've got to get food donations for the dinners, they've got to get food donations for the brunches, they've got to raise a few dollars for this committee or that committee to take care of the many expenses of the church, [in that way] they receive all kinds of justifications of why this one can't do this and that one can't do that. Now that's the educational opportunity for all of us. Because when we experience all of these justifications, we have to pause in our own thinking and ask our self, Do we ever use this device of justification or are we honest with our self and with our feelings and with our efforts in life?

Now I assure you that this church will survive, and it will survive very nicely, whether or not the court, tomorrow, decides that we are entitled to an exemption for church property or we are not. We pray for God's divine guidance and don't dictate to God how that's going to be. If we get our exemption, that will be nice. If we don't, that will be nice, too, because we will just get stronger.

You see, there's one thing about necessity: it truly is the mother of invention. This church has weathered many storms. And so have all of the people that are in it. And I can assure you it will weather many, many more.

And so, I do want to take the opportunity to thank each and every one of you for your support and to become more aware, more aware—all of us—of our thoughts, of what *we* are thinking, of what *we* are feeling, and of what we are doing. Because all our experience, all of life is an effect of this thinking process. It's nothing outside. It's not circumstances and conditions beyond our control. It doesn't exist there. That is the false god and the delusion that this church is founded to pierce through. It is never ever outside. So, all of us should be very grateful that in the short few years of this church that it not only has been but is, and will continue to be, successful.

I am very well aware of new people coming into the church who cannot understand that the church has to have eighty-one plus different committees. Well, of what benefit is it to a person to go to a church to sit in a seat for a couple of hours and to leave? Not to be involved in the church is not to grow with the church. You cannot grow with anything that you don't involve yourself in. So, if you come just to sit and to visit and to have what experience you choose to have and then you walk out the door and you don't involve yourself in the many, many opportunities that are given to you, then, although you may be a member of the church, you cannot experience growing with the church for you have chosen not to involve yourself.

Now, involvement in this church is not restricted to carrying a card. There are many, many, many friends of this church who are very involved, in their way, in its support and do what they can.

The main consideration that the county council seems to have, outside of "it's all for me" (for Richard Goodwin), is money. They're very interested in what they consider to be all the money that the church has. Well, I wish they could find it for me when it comes time each week to pay the bill. *[Several students laugh.]* Now, if they consider the assets, the land, the house, and the furnishings and everything that's in it as cash money, that's fine. But I can't take off one of the verandas or one of the balconies and pay the PG&E. It doesn't work that way. Or tear off one of the two-by-fours to pay the monthly mortgage, because it doesn't work that way.

Now, our monthly mortgage is $1,350 a month. And if you go to buy a house today, [you will] find out what your mortgage will be, because, I assure you, it [Serenity's mortgage] is very reasonable, considering the property and its location.

But this interest they seem to have in money—my attorney spoke to me just the other day (the church's attorney) and he was very interested in how much money that I made, directly and indirectly, for your church. Now why do you think our church attorney was so interested and has requested the figures of how much money flows into this church from my own personal efforts? *[After a short pause, the teacher continues.]* Because that will be his counteract to what the county is claiming. That all of this money and everything, that I, as the founder of the church and as the minister and the president—everyone else is taking care of me. Well, this morning in my meditation I asked the Spirit Council if it was in order to reveal to me approximately how much money was brought in from my own personal efforts through my counseling and related areas. And a very conservative figure, according to the bookkeepers in the spirit world, was a minimum, a minimum of $1,500 a month that, either through counseling or direct or indirect, related activities, I generated for the Serenity Spiritualist Church.

Now I was really surprised myself. I had never considered the checks that come in periodically from people who had been given private counseling. Certainly, they've left $25 for the counseling. And then the months go by and sometimes years, and they'll send a hundred or two. And sometimes some of my clients will periodically send in a thousand or two thousand dollars into this church.

And so, when I heard that this morning I said, "Well, that seems to be a lot of money. Why we don't make it conservative and say that I bring in $500 a month? Perhaps they'll be more ready to accept that."

But I'm telling you this because of the thinking that has gone out. Not from outside into our church, but from within our church going outside, like a radio station, like a broadcast, don't you see what I mean? And even though every asset of this church, every piece of furniture, every [phonograph] record—of which I happen to have had a very fine collection long before this church was founded that I donated to this church—the automobiles, the flowers, the plants, everything is legally protected for the Serenity Spiritualist Association, is irrevocably dedicated to the national Spiritualist movement. There is no possible way—and the County of Marin has all of those records. They have our church charter. They have our corporate structure. There is no possible way that it can go to Richard Goodwin or any other director of this church or any other lay member. Because if they even try to do such a thing—if you'll ever study corporate structure—they just go right to jail and that's all there is to it.

We were one of the very first churches in the 360 national Spiritualist churches in this country—we were the first to get a corporate structure *before* we got a church charter. I tried for several years, working with the national board and the national president, to get a constitutional amendment changed to the national charter that a charter would not be granted to any group of people who did not first protect the potential assets with a legal corporate structure. They did, however, though they didn't pass that amendment, they did, however, pass a recommendation. Because, you see, unfortunately, some people, they sell out for quantity and totally lose the beauty of quality.

Yesterday, in reviewing—in the two-hour deposition given by me to the county council, I noted with great interest what the Spirit had said to one of the questions from the attorney: why we had to have nice things at the home at . . .[73] And they said it's part of our religious conviction. Quality, we believe, to be a soul faculty. And quality is the direct effect of another soul faculty, known as the faculty of care.

This church doesn't need the most expensive things. It doesn't have the most expensive things. But what it does have *is* of quality. Now for us to sacrifice quality, knowing very well the law that like attracts like and becomes the Law of Attachment, is for us to go against the very philosophy that we're spending so much effort to teach.

I was brought up to do a job and do it well or not to do it at all, but to make my choice either way. So, if we do not stand up for the soul faculty of quality, which is an effect of the soul faculty of care, and we demonstrate that attitude, whatever you do, stop. Don't make any more effort to spiritually unfold. Because who wants those flaky spirits coming in to advise and guide them? And if you don't make the effort to open up those faculties, that's the kind of people you'll attract from the so-called spiritual realm because like attracts like and becomes the Law of Attachment. If you do not care about your life and to be prompt, to be definite, to be positive, then you attract those other kind of entities into your life. And this is not what this church is all about.

And so it is, in reference to, Do I have a regular job or don't I? Personally, I think I have a triple regular job. That's my personal feeling. I have to—if you want to know what I really do do—it is my job to counsel the members and friends of this association. It is my job to come here every Sunday morning and help conduct the service.[74] It is my job to do every single billet, as much as humanly possible, every Sunday. It is my job to give the classes of this church. It is my job to supervise each and every committee of this church and there's over eighty-one. It is my job to supervise the choir. Every, every bit of the music that you hear in this church is personally selected. I'm responsible for having to do that because I'm the guy that has to ask the Spirit because they run the church in the first place because they founded it. Now I think that's a pretty damn regular job myself. Personally.

Now if anyone doesn't think so, please speak up. *[After a short, very silent pause, the teacher continues.]*

Now, there is no reason, in any way, shape, or form, that our beautiful monthly magazine cannot have full subscription at all time[s]. Now we have added both [Student Z] and we have added [Student B] to help give a thrust of energy and a spirit of enthusiasm to our *Sentinel* subscription [efforts]. Now I look forward to this year ahead from this date until the next meeting, which is always, as you all know, on the second Sunday of the month of May—and beautifully chosen because we all know it's Mother's Day.

All right. Now, you see, there's no reason why we should have to carve into our other general funds and take from another department. The *Serenity Sentinel* magazine should at least be paying its own way, you see? We never did expect it to make money for the church, but we would like to see that, at least, it pays its own way. And I know that there are many people that would be interested in a subscription. I am well aware that it has been adjusted so your subscriptions now, for one year, are $11, two years $20, and three years $27. There's a dollar savings for each year. But I think we'll all agree that it's well worth that dollar an issue. And if you ever come up to see the work that it takes to typeset it, to edit it, to proofread it, and to do the entire thing from scratch and you come up and look over the bills and see what it costs for one ream of paper—and it takes many reams each month—and what it costs for the ink and all of the photographic supplies, then you would have more value for that little magazine. And get that little ship of the *Serenity Sentinel* magazine afloat and get it moving. Because, you know, the *Sentinel* magazine is over nine years old. It came before the church. It was [first printed] with our camp days, you see. And it's gone through a lot of growth.

Now I thank you for all of the efforts that you have made over the years, for the efforts that you continue to make to keep this church together.

And if you have any questions about what I do, if you don't see me doing anything, perhaps it's because I'm not doing what you're doing. But is there any law that says I'm supposed to be? I don't feel badly if I look and I see you, perhaps singing in the choir or doing the bookkeeping or doing any of the other jobs of this church. I never feel badly because I'm not doing what you're doing. And I just hope that none of my people feel badly because they're not doing what they think I'm doing. But, you see, the trouble is usually what they think I'm doing is not what I'm doing at all, you see. *[Several members laugh.]* See, there's the difference. I can physically see what you're doing and other ways, too. But you physically look at me and then you make a judgment of what I'm doing, and it's usually not what I'm doing at all. So, I think we ought to try to adjust our thinking on that.

It's getting nice and warm here. And we're just about ready to finish this up. But it's very, very important that you pray for God's divine guidance over our situation tomorrow. I'm going to be all day with the attorney and in court at 1:30 in the afternoon.

Now, some of our members have asked if they felt it would be beneficial if they were present. And I have been assured that it wouldn't be in our best interest, because it'll only upset the judge. It'll just put him totally on the defensive. We're not going to a jury trial, you know. We're going before a judge. And the Friends say very definitely and positively that I have to go because the attorney says I'm the prime witness and I have to be there. But the Friends assure me that the judge will not appreciate it and he will react accordingly if he sees a mass of people coming in. So, we can do our part spiritually. We don't have to have our clay bodies there. They're demanding mine;

so, it will be there, but so will my spirit. But we can work on it spiritually. Because it represents to all of us over $2,000 a year. If it goes this way or that way, if we don't get that exemption, then there's no problem: we will just have to raise [funds for] the taxes twice a year.

But it would be nice if we, as a group, merit the exemption or merit a good portion of the exemption because the house is used for the church activities. I mean, that's where all your printing is done. That's where all your dinners are prepared. That's where all of your bake sales are prepared.

And so, it isn't as though we built it just for Richard Goodwin to have a place to waltz around—7,000 square feet. Because I can assure you right now, if it was just me and not this church, I would not live there. Because I don't know any single person—any one person in their right mind that would live there. They would spend twenty hours a day just cleaning it. And if you come up there and take a good look, you'll see that's what you'd be doing if that's the house you want to live in all by yourself. You wouldn't be doing anything else, you know. I can hardly keep up with the gardening along with all of my other work. You know, that garden is like the Golden Gate Bridge: you keep watering and you never get to the end.[75] You just keep on and on and on. And the hotter the weather gets, the more watering you [have] got to do. And the more you water, the more the weeds grow. And the more the weeds grow, the more you [have] got to pull them out. So, stop and think. It just goes on.

And it's very nice. It's a wonderful demonstration of what a very small church can accomplish.

Now I said during the construction of that house that this house will do more to bring people to the light of Spiritualism than any project this church has ever been involved in. Of course, when the Spirit told me that, they didn't tell me how they would get to the Light—through their negative brains.[76] But that's all right. At least, they're getting there. They're hearing about

Spiritualism. And that's important. Now their motives are quite varied, and I'm sure you will all agree with that.

So let us give some consideration to what you think I really do around here and not feel so badly that you can't do the same. Because if you take a real look, you don't want it. I know that. Because I watch when you make an effort to help some other soul and I watch that intolerance rise up and "That's enough of my time! They got enough of my energy!" *[Some students laugh.]* So, you see, I'm not saying that you don't have a right to self-preservation, but I am saying that I'm sure you'll all agree you could expand a little bit on tolerance.

Because, you see, nobody really wants to be bothered. Do you see what I mean? They don't want to have to listen to all of those crying, negative problems of people. You know why people don't want to listen to that? I can tell you why they don't want to listen to that. They're not yet strong enough to control those levels within themselves. And so, if somebody comes to them with that crying self-pity, the first thing that starts to happen—they relate to self and so that misery, that garbage rises up within them and they get furious. And then they say, "That person—I can't stand it!" And they just move the other way. That's what creates the intolerance, because the work, yet, needs to be done on our self. So, when you stop to think about it, I know very well that deep in your heart not one of you want my job. Not in any sense of the word.

I don't know how I slipped along the divine ladder of eternity, but whatever I did, I'm crawling back up and things sure as—sure are getting a lot better. And they are going to continue to be better.

And let's not forget about tomorrow. Let us know that God, the only power of truth there is in the universes, is at the helm. And whichever way it goes, it's going to be the right way for the best interest of this church and all the people involved in it. I've tried to assure our attorney of that. He said to me the other day—yesterday—that he's just a nervous wreck. And I said, "Well, why?" "Well," he said, "I, I—there's just so much to this case. And I want this. I want to win." I said to him, "It's not always the best thing to win all the time. Because it's from the failures and the losses that we gain the greatest lessons of life that we may grow." He says, "Hell, I don't want to grow. I just want to win!" He says, "I got to be right." *[Many students laugh.]* I said, "Well, that's where the problem is." I said, "Now stop and think." I said, "Now here, you're the attorney, I assure you, I guarantee that you're going to be paid. Whichever way the case goes, *you* are going to be paid. It may not be as quickly, perhaps, as I would like to have you paid"—because we've always paid him very promptly. But I said, "I assure you, you'll be paid. So why should you have any problem?" He said, "Well, I just have to be perfect!" I said, "Well, you'll grow through that someday." *[Some members laugh.]* We can't all be God.

Thank you very, very much. Thank you.

Did you want to create committees? [A director asks.]

No, we don't need to go through—

MAY 13, 1979

Membership Meeting May 11, 1980

Now, let's all rise, please.

We thank Thee, God, for this opportunity of service, at this meeting, to the Spirit, to the angel loved ones who are with us, and for the purpose of this church. May we have the divine spirit of unity continue in this organization that all who serve it may recognize and realize that their purpose is an eternal purpose and is not limited to these daily activities. Amen.

This meeting will come to order, the ninth annual membership of the Serenity Association. All deliberations of this association not covered by its constitution and bylaws will be governed by the *Robert's Rules of Order*. Be seated, please.

Now, the first thing on the agenda: the chair will entertain a motion from the floor to conduct an informal meeting. Anyone who cares to make that type of a motion may do so. [Student L], will you rise, please.

I make a motion we have an informal meeting.

Thank you. Do I hear a second? [Student Q], will you rise, please? You second the motion?

Yes, I do.

All right, are you ready for the question? *[After a short pause, the teacher continues.]* Question. Now this is the time that you can ask your question, What's the difference between a formal meeting or an informal meeting, if you have any question. *[After another short pause, he continues.]* All those in favor say aye.

Aye. [Many members speak.]

Contrary minded? *[After a short pause, he continues.]* So ordered and approved. *[The teacher strikes a gavel.]* We'll have an informal meeting which means we won't have to go through all this formal ritual that takes, usually, at least a couple of hours. All right, now the secretary should, however, read the roll. Read the roll of memberships, please.

[The call of the roll is made and twenty-four names are called, but only eighteen are present, including the directors.]

OK. Thank you. We're having an informal meeting. So, we'll go—what is the total membership count here?

Twenty-four. [A director responds.]

Twenty-four? Well, I think twenty-four people plus the friends of the church have done extremely well.

Now, on the order of business, as most of you are aware, we have three vacancies on the board of directors: [Student P2] and [Student J] and myself. And so, we can handle that very quickly when it comes time to make the nominations. Now I would like to say this. I want to thank both [Student P2] and [Student J]. They have served this church longer than nine years because they were with us during the camp days of the Serenity Camp, before this church was ever founded. And I do hope that their loyalty will be a demonstration to all of us, although sometimes, you know, we think that perhaps they're not as active or haven't been as active recently, but I remember how active they were in the years when they were able to be active. So, if we're active today, let us not make judgments about how long we're going to stay active.

I'm very happy to see that in the nine years of this church that so few people, so few members and friends of the church have done so very, very well in the work that has to be done.

Now for two of the placements on the board, the Friends have recommended that [Student Q] and [Student H], who are able to donate the time and the work, would be—could be very helpful on the board as directors. Of course, that's up to you people to make the nominations.

As far as my term of office, as I told everyone, I'm *not* seeking reelection. I continue on with my work. But that's up, of course, to the membership. So, why don't we go ahead and go on with the nominations. The chair will entertain any nominations that—anyone have a nomination? [Student S] has a nomination.

Yes. With deep gratitude and respect for his loyal dedication to this work, the church, and the spirit people that founded it, I wish to nominate Richard P. Goodwin.

[Mr. Goodwin sighs.] Well—

Second— [Another director speaks.]

No, that doesn't need a second. Nominations don't have to be seconded. I—well, I suppose—well, until we can find someone that can put in the time every day on an eight-hour shift, I guess I just better accept—I don't know—whatever choice. I'm not elected yet, you understand. We have two more to be nominated. [Student L], would you like to make a nomination?

Yes. I'd like to nominate [Student Q].

[Student L] would like to nominate [Student Q]. [Student V], would you like to make a nomination?

Yes. I'd like to nominate [Student H].

[Student H]. Fine. Is there any other nom—are there any other nominations? *[After a short pause, he continues.]* All right. All those in favor of [Student Q] being nominated to the board of directors, please signify by saying aye.

Aye. [Many members speak.]

Contrary minded? *[After a very short pause, he continues.]* No. Well, that's not the way to do it, really. You should raise your hands. Raise your hands for [Student Q] for nomination. OK. Thank you. Now, [Student Q] is nominated to the board unanimously.

And how about [Student H]? Raise your hands, please. [Student H], don't you want to vote for yourself? *[Many students laugh.]* Let's make it all unanimous. Good. That takes care of—that takes care of those elections. Oh, I suppose we have one more. Those in favor of nominating—or electing— electing Richard Goodwin *[Mr. Goodwin clears his throat, and some students laugh in response to him doing so.]* for a few more years, raise your hands, please. Almost unanimous. *[Some students laugh.]* OK. Almost. I didn't vote.

Now, let's have [Student S], you're secretary-treasurer—now in reference to the finances of your church, it's always been that if anyone has any question, the books are available. All you have to do is make a written request and make arrangements to come and study them, if you have the time to do that. But anyway, it's all there and it's all recorded.

And so, we have this financial report. Now you can have it read *seriatim* or collective. *Seriatim* means every single, little, dinky item, you've got to sit here and wade through and listen to. Or you can read it collective, which shows you the cash flow: what came in and what went out. Which is your preference? Do you want it collective or *seriatim*?

I make a motion that we read it seriatim.

That's every single item, [Student R].

Oh, I mean collective. I'm sorry. [A few students and the teacher laugh.]

All right. Do I hear a second?

I second it. [Another member seconds.]

All those in favor signify by saying aye.

Aye. [Many members speak.]

Contrary minded? *[After a very short pause, he continues.]* Then we'll have it read collective. Now [Student S], would read the finances of the organization, please?

It's twelve-month [period] ended April 30, 1980. Assets: cash in savings account $5,907.70.

Uh-huh.

Note receivable (Colter) $20,376.61; auto (Corvette and General Motors Chevette) $28,778.88; residence [in] San Rafael $920,000; furniture and fixtures $103,437.71. Total assets $1,078,500.90.

Liabilities: Citizens Savings and Loan first deed of trust $107,920.92; Wells Fargo Bank second deed of trust $24,304.64; auto, Bank of Marin $1,584.52; auto, Wells Fargo Bank

$7,778.88. Total liabilities $141,588.96. Net worth $936,911.94. Total liabilities and net worth $1,078,500.90.

Thank you very much. Is there any question on the finances? Anything you want to know? If there is, you speak up now. But as I say, I think you've done extremely well, all of you, for such a short period of time with the assets through the effort—you see, it shows the effort that has been made.

Now, in reference to all these committees and everything, I—the chair will entertain a motion that everyone on their committees remain on their committees. God knows, we need the workers. Anyone care to make that kind of a motion?

I make a motion that we maintain the present committee chairmen.

Do I hear a second?

Second. [Many students speak.]

Seconded by [Student H]. Are you ready for the question?

Question.

[After a short pause to allow for questions, the teacher continues.] All those in favor of us maintaining the committee chairmen and the committees that we have, please signify by saying aye.

Aye. [Many students respond.]

Contrary minded? *[After a very short pause, he continues.]* So ordered and approved. That takes care of all committees.

There is no current correspondence that I am aware of to take care of. In fact, I don't have my list here; so, I don't know what I'm supposed to be reading. So, we don't have to go through that. There are no pending applications for memberships—is that correct? To my knowledge, there are no pending applications. Because everyone that applies for membership has to go through a minimum of one semester of class. So, we have no pending applications to be voted on here today.

And is there anything—now, we mustn't forget to take up the offering—can you imagine? I forgot the offering here—before we conclude this meeting. Is there anything that anyone [would] like to say for the good of the church? *[After a short pause, the teacher continues.]*

Well, if there's nothing that you have to say, I don't have too much to say myself. Because I really believe, from what I've seen over these nine years, that things are going along very, very well. There's a little more cooperation. There's a little more unity. We have people with us that are interested in the philosophy and are trying, in their ways, to apply it. So that makes a much better organization. You can be rest assured of that.

Now if [Student D4] will kindly pass the plate, we'll—and I want to tell you, you ought to feel real good, too, because, you know, we just spent $1,600 for a new [tape] recorder because the other one went totally out on the fritz, and I didn't even ask you for a donation towards it, though I'm willing to accept some kind of a donation. Here, let me give something there. *[The teacher asks the usher to pause for a moment in order that he might contribute to the offering.]* Thank you. Out of the goodness of your heart, if you want to give something [toward the new recorder] at class—otherwise, you wouldn't have no [any] recorded classes, you know. It went totally on the fritz.

Oh, I forgot. [Student D4], come back to me. I'll write out a check. [A student speaks in the background as the teacher speaks.]

And we got a Revox, which is a professional, German-make, [tape recorder]. It's the best you can get. But it's supposed to last us about twenty to twenty-five years, with good care. So [Student D4] and [Student R] are responsible. If it goes on the fritz, they can pay for it out of their pockets. *[A few students laugh.]*

I second that motion.

There, [Student E4] seconds that motion! *[Student R laughs loudly.]* Good for you, [Student E4]. They better take good care of it. That's all I've got to say. But at least it's paid for. That's nice. OK. Are you here, [Student D4]?

Yes.

Well, let us all rise, please. If there's nothing more to talk about, then we can just conclude this meeting. *[Student D4 presents the offering to the teacher.]*

We thank Thee, God, for this opportunity for this meeting and for these funds that have been given for the good of the church. May those who are with us this day ever remember that through the Law of Continuity of Effort, no matter how small that effort may be, if it is continuous, each day and every day, it will reap its abundant harvest. Amen.

This meeting is concluded. Thank you all very much.

MAY 11, 1980

Membership Meeting May 10, 1981

Will the secretary of the church kindly read the roll of members? Members will kindly answer their call "Present."

[The call of the roll is made and twenty-four names are called, but only nineteen are present.]

You've heard the roll of membership. What is your pleasure? To accept it? If so, please make a motion.

I move we accept it.

As read? Do I hear a second?

I second the motion.

Are you ready for the question? *[After a short pause, the teacher continues.]* All those in favor?

Aye. [Many students respond.]

Contrary minded? *[After another short pause, he continues.]* So ordered and approved.

Now I would like to step down from the chairman of the meeting for just a moment to make a motion that we conduct this meeting with the most efficient, speedy action as possible. And that can be done, if you care to vote upon the reading of the financial report either collective or *seriatim*. If you choose to have it collective, we could do it in minutes. If *seriatim*, you're going to have to read off every single little item. That's up to you. And I also, with that motion, would like to make the motion that we dispense with all of these various *Robert's Rules of Order* that'll take us hours and go ahead with an official, but informal meeting. Anyone wish to second the motion that I have made?

I second the motion.

Fine. And all those in favor?

Aye. [Many members speak.]

Contrary minded? *[After a short pause, he continues.]* So ordered and approved. And I'll take the chair again. And let's get right on to the business at hand.

Now, the treasurer of the church will kindly read the financial report of the past twelve months of operation of the Serenity Church Association.

Serenity Spiritualist Camp Association, Incorporated, balance sheet twelve-month ended April 30, 1981. Assets: cash in savings account $1,419.32; note receivable [for Serenity Camp in Mendocino] $19,493.79; auto (Corvette and General Motors Chevette) $28,778.88; residence at San Rafael $920,000; furniture and fixtures $128,437.71. Total assets $1,098,129.70.

Liabilities: Citizens Savings and Loan, first deed of trust $107,109.81; Wells Fargo Bank second deed of trust $23,105.89; auto (General Motors) $5,185.92; IBM typewriter $620.86; Total Liabilities $136,022.48. Net worth $962,107.22. Total liabilities and net worth $1,098,129.70.

Income: dues $730; donations $59,563.30; seminars $3,097.20; socials $4,857.21; books, tapes, and Sentinel $4,129.47; bake sale and fundraising $7,482.15; note receivable $2,130. Total cash receipts $81,989.33.

Expenses: equipment payments $702.15; magazines and books $80.64; office equipment and printing $5,180.66; President's expense $2,600; rent (log cabin) $6,000; bazaar $1,128.75; utilities $2,833.62; real estate tax $1,651.80; church expense $2,225.50; computer expense $5,158.87; automobile expense $4,037.11; insurance $1,777.65; dues $84; fundraising activities $1,128.75; sales tax $380.71; advertisement $12; postage $125; tapes $691.43; mortgage payments (first deed of trust) $11,893; mortgage payments (second deed of trust) $3,467.75; furniture and fixtures $12,793.79; gardening $8,333.39; household supplies and expense $4,349.11; library $3,934.33. Total expenses $80,570.01. Retained income over expenses $1,419.32, which is a total of $81,989.33.

Thank you very much, [Student Q]. Now, you've heard the treasurer's report. Are there any questions? If there are any questions, it's time to speak up. *[After a pause, he continues.]*

Now, in keeping with our regulations here, even though this is informal, you do have a pastor's report. Well, I have spent my twelve months trying to demonstrate the report rather than write it down for you. Now what I mean by that—of course, they say it pays to advertise and I'm happy to see that it only cost us $12 for the year. That figures out to about $1 a month. And we certainly haven't been short of supply in the church, which only goes to prove that all of this, what we call the divine flow and this abundance, is in our consciousness. And when we move the judgments that stand in the way, we won't have any problem with the flow.

I'm very happy to report, with twenty-four members, that your organization is able, not only, to stay afloat but it is able to prosper and to grow, not only materially, but spiritually, [which is] the true purpose of the organization; that there is a more harmonious and unified spiritual flow; that your new *Sentinel* magazine, which is in process, which has already been typeset on your new computer, should be coming out within the next couple of weeks. Is that correct, directors?

Correct. [One director replies.]

Well, let's give them—if I tell—ask them two weeks—let's give them at least three. But very soon. We are combining this issue because we have had quite a change over. The Living Light Philosophy on the class tapes of over 350 tapes is now being printed in the new *Sentinel* magazine. Now that magazine has had, over the years, a lot of struggle. But anytime you work at anything to get the Light to the world, you [have] got to be willing to pay the price of it. We have struggles in our brain; so, we have struggles in getting the message out to the world. And so, we have combined the May-June issue and, be it in Divine order, there will be a greater flow with the *Sentinel* magazine.

Now it's just like your dinners. Your dinners have been growing and improving ever since the first of the year. I spoke to your directors last December in reference to that because it is not only impractical but it is absolute stupidity to work so hard at a dinner and not have the proper remuneration, not that we judge what that should be. We take a look at life and see if you put effort in, then you should receive equal compensation back in keeping with the Law of Effort. And so, it is not practical to work so hard to have a church dinner and not have the reservations that you've worked so hard for.

So, it's a matter of changing our judgments. Our anniversary dinner, which the Spirit of your church has made the request that you work hard to get, hopefully, over 100 reservations, is now, I understand, at 58 confirmed reservations; is that correct, [Student Z]?

[It is difficult to transcribe her response.]

Now I know that in reading of the financial report, it seems like a lot of money. Of course, to my mind it seems like a great deal of money considering that I had such a struggle, years ago, in raising $120 a month just to pay a camp mortgage. That's the land we used to own up north, that we sold and built that house up there off . . .[77]

What is important is this, not that we have taken in $81,000 nor that we have $81,000 in the bank to lose money on. And if you don't believe me, open your eyes, that's where you lose it. The more you stuff in the bank, the more you lose. You don't need money in the bank if you have, in your consciousness, an acceptance that there is no shortage, that the only experience of lack and limitation is a judgment that in an error of ignorance we have made. Now if God is truly at the helm, whether it's your church or your personal life, if God is at the helm, then God *is* the source of the continuous, divine, abundant flow.

This church works very hard to demonstrate that we don't need to rely upon a piece of paper in a bank to survive. The only thing we need to rely upon is moving our judgments out of the way so God can ever be present. Now God is not a doer and does not do it for us. *We* have to get the obstruction out of the way. Then the Divine Intelligence, of which we are an inseparable part, will see, as it sees that the daisies in the field have sufficient nutrients to grow, will see that we have sufficient nutrients to grow.

So let us be grateful for the efforts of all the people—twenty-four members—of all the people that have made the effort, for they in truth, we all know, we're helping our self. That's just what it's all about. If we don't make the effort to help our self, we're never qualified to be the instruments through which someone else is helped. That is not a selfish view of life. That is a practical, reasonable, sensible view of life.

The Bible teaches you, physician, heal yourself. And so, this philosophy teaches, don't preach what you don't make the effort to demonstrate. If you preach God's divine, abundant flow, then let us change whatever judgments are in our consciousness so that we can demonstrate what we preach, whether it's in our health, our wealth, or our happiness. Let's be the living demonstration. None of us, none of us like to be a hypocrite. So, let's not try teaching what we do not make effort to practice. Then we won't have to worry about being hypocrites.

Now, if we feel that we are short, then be rest assured the Power that is the power of the universe will help us to be even shorter; so we can prove how right our mind is. I have the same mind that everyone else has. I can think and think how short I am. After all, several of the directors, over the years, have asked if I couldn't have a raise from my $50-a-week allowance. The Council themselves have said that perhaps I could use a $5-a-week raise. But I do feel that a raise is not necessary for the president of this organization. And so, I have once again asked the Council not to increase my salary, if you can call it a salary. It grows into a great loaf. I have no needs for I have no shortages. If I decide that I have shortages, you may be rest assured I will be so filled with need the frustration alone will drive you out of the church. Because that's what those levels of consciousness have to offer.

You will note in the financial report that over $8,000, in twelve months, was spent for [the] garden. Well, we didn't buy any fancy lawnmowers or anything. We just planted a lot of trees, a lot of flowers, a lot of grass seed, and everything that's necessary to make a beautiful garden. We don't believe in golden temples, but we do believe in the divine, healing power of Nature herself. And we have made great effort up there at the house, at God's house, to put in as beautiful a garden as possible, considering we don't have twenty gardeners to take care of it. And so, we do the best that we can. And we have put a lot into the garden because it does take years for the trees to grow. Now, as the trees grow and bring more shade up there, then we have to water less; then you have to spend less money for the water bill. And so, you see, it all returns unto you.

Now, I would like to live here on Earth to see the day when all of us are demonstrating, in our personal life, the divine, demonstrable truth of God's abundant flow. Believe me, my friends, it is in our thought; it does not exist in our heart. The only place it ever was is in our mind. And what we do, we set our self up.

Now, I'm going to take a couple of minutes out of this meeting, in my pastor's report, if you don't mind, to show you how we set ourselves up. And I will use an example of a member of the church. Some time ago, a person made a decision—a judgment—that they would spend six months in Northern California and six months in Southern California. And for many years that has taken place, in keeping with the judgment established. Time passed. Inflation came about. Things cost more money today than they did ten years ago. Much, much more expensive—plane fares, motels, hotels. Everything's more expensive. Everything was more expensive and changing, except the judgment. And so, what happens to us—all of us—we make a judgment and we set our self up to support the judgment that we have made to prove how right we are. And we pay a terrible, terrible price for that.

I could have, many years ago, made the judgment, "It will always be a terrible struggle to raise $120 a month to pay a camp mortgage." Simply because twice we almost lost the camp from the struggle. Now, I could have established that law and a few years later blown my brains out because that's no way to live. No one wants to live that way. Therefore, stop and think. The experiences that we have—we're being controlled repeatedly by what yesterday had to offer us. We are not living in yesterday, unless we're foolish. So, whenever you make a judgment, believe me, friends, in the moment of judgment, you lose God, because in that moment, you lose the eternal moment where the power really is. And all you're doing, whenever you make a judgment, you're living in the shadows of yesterday and setting yourself up with your tomorrows. Because it's those shadows, cast upon your path before you, are the experiences that bind us.

Now, many things take place in our lives from moment to moment, many different things. If we will pause long enough—and it takes about nine seconds to see it, or less—if we will pause long enough, we will see exactly how a particular level of consciousness, from years past, is working its tail off to set us up in the moment of now.

That's what we came to this church [for]: we came for truth and freedom. And, believe me, friends, that's exactly what this church has to offer you, is truth and freedom. But you have to give up one thing to gain truth and freedom: you have to give up your bondage. And your bondage, like my bondage or anyone's bondage, is called, in this philosophy, judgment. Because the moment you permit your mind to make a judgment, you are pulled into the shadows of yesterday and establish the Law of Repetition of what has already been for you. In order to transform yourself, you must let everything that has been go in consciousness.

Now we all know how strong we are when we have a thought in our mind and we can't get rid of it. Look what happens around December-time, when we start thinking about a cold. Then we get the cold and we work like hell to forget we got a cold. And the cold keeps saying, "What are you doing? I'm still here." Because that's where *we* are. So, you see, we do have the will power: we really do have the power within us to order a thought to be still and to put something that's worthwhile in its place. And we're never left without that power.

Now, as [Student E4] knows here today—she was a little upset: she didn't get her notice. Is that correct, [Student E4]?

It is.

She said she didn't get her notice. I checked with the directors. And according to the directors, it was mailed. I'm going to check on her proper address to see that she gets it. Now, I did say to [Student E4], I said, "[Student E4], well, we always have the membership meeting on Mother's Day." After all, [Student J] thought that was a great idea ten years ago, didn't you, [Student J]?

Yes, sir.

We always have it on Mother's Day. And I said to [Student J] at that time, my mother says, "If it's important to them, they will be there. And if it isn't, they won't. And we really don't want members that it's not important to them. So let them go on their thing." But what was it that upset [Student E4]? She had made a commitment without thorough investigation, is that correct?

Yes.

So, it wasn't really that she didn't get her notice. What it *really* was: she had made a commitment without thorough investigation, you understand, because [Student E4] is a good member of this church and [Student E4] knows, but had forgotten, that always on Mother's Day we have a membership meeting.

I bet I remember now.

I'm sure you will; it's called exposure frees the soul, [Student E4].

[The student responds, but it is difficult to transcribe her response.]

Be grateful for it, because that's what goes on at the house all the time. You see, this is what—I know—and I want to finish here, but this is very important. It's extremely important that a sufficient impact be made in consciousness to balance out any judgment that's got control of us, you see.

Uh-huh.

So, when we have a judgment in control, if we are fortunate, we will merit someone, someplace to not only expose it for us, but give sufficient input into the consciousness so we don't do it again, you see.

Now remember, fear is negative faith or placing one's faith in the great force of the mind, all right?

Uh-huh.

Now the thing we fear the most befalls us. We all know that. So, we establish a judgment and we *fear* it's coming to pass. And it's that very fear that makes it happen for us, do you understand? So now, in exposing these things, what happens to the mind—say, a person is trying to make a change and they're having a great deal of difficulty because they've got a judgment of doing things a certain way. But another part of them wants to be freed from that. All right, it is fear and judgment that's keeping them from making the change. It's called fighting fire with fire: you must give fear to fear. So something with a little reason and intelligence can rise up and be free from all of that.

Now, the Christian faith, for over 2,000 years—well, almost 2,000 years now has used the principle of fear to keep their people bound to what they understand to be God. We use the principle of fear (or faith in the mind) not to bind people to God—because you only bind them mentally to a mental god—but to help them to use it to free themselves. Now if a person says, "Oh, I'm not going to do that again. I'm damn sure they'll expose me," therefore, they make an intelligent decision: they consider *everyone*. Isn't that true, [Student E4]?

Uh-huh.

So, you see, because our mind, the first thing it does is blame some other poor slob. And that some other poor slob is usually your church. That's who that poor slob is that gets all the blame. It's what's called your church, see? And that level—isn't that true, [Student E4]?

Yes.

It rises up. "They didn't send me my notice! I made this commitment to go someplace. And had they sent me my notice, I wouldn't have made that commitment the way that I did and I wouldn't have to go through this frustration and emotion with that other person that I made a commitment with." Isn't that correct, [Student E4]?

Yes, but it didn't seem that difficult.

It didn't seem that difficult. No. So, don't you see, friends, fear binds you. Fear can free you. For that that binds you is that that frees you, if you use it wisely. Man is freed in hell and he's saved in heaven. Now you can't get to heaven to be saved, in consciousness, until you go to hell to get free. Now I know that sounds like a pretty strong statement, but all you [have] got to do is say, "Well, how have my years been around here at Serenity?" Oh, they've been nice and smooth and serene? No hell at all? Well, you're a long ways from getting to heaven. *[Some students laugh.]* Believe me. Because all the hell is what has been, and it doesn't want to let you be! Try to remember that, friends.

You see, it's a lady here at the door this morning.[78] She said, "Oh, my God, you don't know what it was like, what a struggle I had to get here this morning!" I said, "But you got here." [She said,] "Yes, but you don't know what it was like!" I said, "Well, let that go so you can move into the moment." I mean, don't you understand? What good is that that has been, what good is it going to do you to reattach yourself to it?

Now if you think the good old days were so good, then grab ahold of them and bring it up to the present [and] say, "How was I thinking in the good old days?" And let's have the moment of now the good, old days. Don't you see? They weren't so good or we would never have left them. Now if we think they're so good, we keep holding on to them in our head and—you see, my friends, what I'm trying to show you—it's a shadow. It's not the Light. It is a reflection.

All past events are shadows or reflections. In and of themselves, they are hollow. The power of the Divine is not there for you to move forward in your universe. So you must, sooner or later, let them go. Take a parent. Say that the child is to go. Well, look at what they go through. Not because of the child, God forbid. But because of this thing in their head: what they think and judge about the child. It's not the child. It's this up here: what they have in their head concerning the child. That's where it is.

Now, are there any questions about the operation of your church? You should all feel very wealthy. I feel wealthy. If you feel wealthy, then you will attract more. And by "wealth," I mean health, wealth, and happiness. I mean the whole kit and caboodle. I'm not interested in just green paper. I'm interested in what's behind green paper. Because green paper is the effect of energy and I'm interested in the Source itself, not the effect of it. Because [if] you go to the Source, you'll never go without.

Now try to get that through your head. Go to the Source and you'll never go without. And I had to learn that the hard way.

But my head's pretty hard. Just as hard as everybody else's. So go to the Source and you'll never go without. If you feel you're going without any goodness in life, it's because you stopped at a judgment on the way and you haven't got to the Source yet. Go to the Source and you'll never ever go without.

And so, remember, when you're going without anything that you desire, then you haven't got, yet, to the Source: you're standing at one of those judges that you created in days of ignorance. Boot him out of the way and travel right on up the mountain. Believe me, I know, sooner or later, we'll all get there. But once getting there, let us not forget how we climbed up there; because if we do, we'll fall down the other side.

If you have no questions about the operation of your church—I hope—no questions at all? Because I was looking forward to putting someone on a new committee. We only got about a hundred committees now.

Now, everyone is on the committees they were on last year, the year before, the year before. No sense in changing a good thing. You get something working, stick with it. Thank you all very much. The meeting is concluded 'til next year.

Ah, collection. [A director reminds the teacher.]

Election?!

Collection.

Oh, God forbid! How could I talk about abundance and not have the offering! *[Many students laugh.]* Oh, that's terrible! Let us, please, have our offering. My goodness' sakes alive. Thank you. Who reminded me? [Student S]. Good. You're on—I'm glad to see you're in the flow.

Thank you.

We can't have that. Let's be seated until they get all this—oh, sorry—all this offering taken up. It's a beautiful day today, beautiful day. *[After a short pause, he continues.]* Well, I guess I'm not going to get a raise. *[Some students laugh.]*

Well, your pay is running right along with the utilities. [A member observes.]

[The teacher laughs loudly.]
A little below it. [A director replies.]
Below? [The member asks.]

Oh, yes. I'm below the utilities. I am below the utility bill. But I'm above the advertising bill. *[Some students laugh.]*

The utilities might go down. [A member offers.]

I don't think they'll go as low as my salary though. *[The teacher laughs.]* We're working at it. Is the offering—all right. Let us all rise, please. [Student D4], would you bring the flow forward, please. I like to have it in front of all the members. Thank you.

We thank Thee, O God, for the blessings of this abundance that Thou has inspired our people to be the instrument through which it may flow. Let it go out in the universe to carry this Light out to the world, not only in this physical world, but in all these other dimensions that it may serve the purpose of the Light: to lift a soul from the errors of darkness that they may become a worker in the vineyard, that all of this, O God, we know, is ever in keeping (its goodness) with our motive. May our motive be pure and free from all restriction. And in so doing it shall grow and prosper and fulfill the purpose of Thee: to bring the peace that passeth all understanding and the goodness to all life. Amen.

Meeting is concluded 'til next year. Same time. Same place. Be it in divine order. Thank you.

MAY 10, 1981

Membership Meeting May 5, 1983

OK. Got enough chairs for everyone? Isn't that nice, I think I've counted eighteen. How many have you counted?

Eighteen.

Out of how many that are—

Twenty-two.

Good! There's only four missing. Let us all rise, please. The twelfth annual membership meeting of the Serenity Spiritualist Church will now come to order. Let us pray.

O Infinite Divine Spirit, we are grateful to serve Thee in this most important occasion, the annual membership meeting of the Serenity Spiritualist Association. For all that has been, we are grateful from the lessons that are granted to us to perceive. Let us perceive them joyously that we may move from this moment onward in our service to the Light that flows through our being. For only in the service to the Light are we freed from the disturbance, the discord, the disaster, and the despair that is offered in a duality of mental substance. So, in that service, we are not only uplifted to realms of consciousness that are peaceful and are harmonious but we are awakened within, the Light within us, that all of life is ever at our disposal. It is a matter of moment-by-moment, conscious choice that we may pause long enough—only a short moment—and declare the truth within our being, that "My mind is an instrument through which I, the true eternal being is flowing moment by moment. Because it is my mind, it is subject to the light of reason, that which I am." Let us never forget that and we shall truly enjoy the service to the Light that we are. The abundant good, in keeping with the law that like attracts like, shall return unto us on the divine circle of just return. This meeting officially comes to order. Amen.

Be seated, please. Will the ushers kindly take up an offering for the support of our church? *[The ushers take up an offering.]*

[Student O]. *[The teacher addresses an usher, perhaps in order to donate.]* Thank you.

[The offering is brought to the front of the membership and presented to the teacher.]

We thank Thee, Divine Spirit, for the demonstration of this abundant flow. May those through whom it has flowed awaken in consciousness that it may return multiplied and ever increase in the goodness for which it has been sent unto us. And in keeping with that divine law, may we use it wisely, that the Light may shine ever onward and ever upward, bringing the good that is the Law of Service to Thee. Amen.

The secretary will please take the roll of members. And everyone will kindly answer, please, "Present." Thank you.

[The call of the roll is made and twenty-two names are called, but only eighteen members are present.]

A quorum being present of the board of directors and the lay membership, we can now take a vote whether you would like to have a formal or an informal meeting. If you wish a formal meeting, we'll go religiously by the *Robert's Rules of Order* and take the time to accommodate that. Or we can have an informal meeting and we can have a financial report collective, if you wish it, or *seriatim*, which dictates the expense of every postage stamp. Which do you prefer? And do I hear a—

I move for an informal meeting.

I second.

It has been moved by [Student R], seconded by [Student Q], for an informal meeting including a financial report collective—does your motion include that?

Yes.

All right. Do I hear—All those in favor?

Aye. [Many students speak.]

Contrary minded? *[After a short pause, he continues.]* So ordered and approved. So, we'll have an informal meeting and start off with the effects of your efforts over these years, which—I think this time I'll let the secretary read and save my energy *[The teacher laughs.]* for, hopefully, earning more to pay the bills. Go ahead, secretary, please read the report.

OK. Twelve months ended April 30, 1983. Cash in savings account $2,972.78; note receivable [from sale of Camp Serenity] $17,907.65; auto (Corvette and Chevrolet truck SR-10) $39,800; residence San Rafael $990,000; furniture and fixtures $190,275. Total assets $1,240,955.43.

Liabilities: Citizens Savings and Loan first deed of trust $106,571.79; Wells Fargo Bank second deed of trust $22,872.62; auto GMAC $10,724.96; Sherman Clay $5,506.34; Leonard's Player Piano $3,408.75. Total liabilities $149,084.46. Net worth $1,091,870.97. Total liabilities and net worth $1,240,955.43.

Well now, you've heard the reading of the report here, of our financial report. Are there any questions? Any questions? Now is the time to speak up. *[After a short pause, the teacher continues.]* Do I hear a move, then, to accept the report as read?

I move to accept.

[Student R] moves to accept. [Student L] seconds the motion. Any question? *[After a short pause, he continues.]* All those in favor say aye.

Aye. [Many students speak.]

Contrary minded? *[After another short pause, he continues.]* So ordered and approved.

Now, just viewing, of course—in viewing anything, one wisely views more than one dimension. One certainly views the dimension with which we're all the most familiar; that's the dimension of a material world. Because of our identification with a material world, of course, we are more familiar with a material world. We're certainly more familiar with a physical body than we are with a mental body, let alone a spiritual body. And so, we work with that which we are familiar with.

The purpose of the Serenity Association has never been to gather and to garner, to hold and to abuse. Its purpose, in keeping with the law, is to serve the Light. And the Light shines through a mental world, as well as through a physical world. So it is, of course, most encouraging that through the efforts—and you note there are eighteen members present out of—what did the secretary say?—out of twenty-two. You note that through the efforts of eighteen people plus the supporters, the friends of the membership, that the Serenity Church and its purpose to serve the Light and bring this beautiful philosophy to the world—because it works when we apply it—is indeed revealing its own success.

Now you can't bring about a philosophy that teaches living demonstration and not live the demonstration. So, this is the day, of course, that we should reflect in the light of reason and see that effort has indeed been made: that in spite of all of our various levels of consciousness—and we all know at least more than one level—some of us have moved to forty, fifty, and hopefully to eighty-one—that the work is truly being done.

Now, the work is being done within the Serenity Church and Association. That is composed of people. And those people, making that effort, under the guidance of the light of reason, are establishing the law—have already demonstrated the potential to demonstrate in their personal lives the same law. The only difference is quite simple: that within the association there is firm discipline and guidance in consideration of all of our people and the purpose for which we belong to our own church.

Now, in time, of course, that very same law, that very same effort will increase and grow in our own personal lives through a constant monitoring of the vehicle through which we're expressing, known as the human mind. Because you cannot teach and demonstrate a law that says life is ever as you take it and just the way you make it, you cannot teach that without the living demonstration. Because you are all a part of the Serenity Church and the Serenity Church is revealing, demonstrably, that each year it grows, that it prospers, then, because you're a part of that, you are making the effort in spite of what your mind says or doesn't say. Otherwise, it could not be.

I want to just have you see that it's quite clear. That it does require rigid discipline, and rigid discipline is not something that is distasteful. When you understand the benefits of self-control and you understand the benefits of what you call discipline and you reap the harvest thereof without attachment thereto, then you have the joy of life that's your own birthright. And I know you cannot help but agree with that.

I vividly recall the days in Corte Madera, before we moved to [the temple], when I spoke to a small group of our members, that if you want a house, more space in which to work, then you'll have to be willing to have a brunch every single Sunday in order that it can all be brought about. You'll have to be willing to make these various changes.

I'm very happy, especially this day, that one of my own students in a temporary slip into the darkness of the human mind, of the self, felt that she was under an attack and being abused, in the Law of Abuse, I'm very grateful that she managed—and [she] was not going to stay for this membership meeting—and that I had a few moments [with her] and mentioned to her she was demonstrating the Law of Abuse, the very law she cried that somebody else, she was the victim of.[79] Now that's growth. That's [moving] out of the childish realm of pity and rejection and the attachment to the self, the limit. And that's an expansion and that's the purpose of the church: to help us broaden our horizons, to expand our consciousness by freeing us from self-thought.

Now, we all have these wonderful experiences. Every day we have the opportunity. Self-thought is self-destructive. Now anyone interested in destroying themselves, I'll be more than happy to share with you the very law—it's so simple. Think of yourself and destroy yourself. Destroy the goodness within you by self-thought. Because the law is demonstrable and very, very clear: God helps those who help themselves by helping others. That's how God helps us. God doesn't help us by our thinking of our self. Because it is the process of our thinking of our self that builds up a substance that prevents us from seeing clearly. The mist that is in front of our path is the mist of self-thought. Now the Light cannot penetrate that mist. But when you redirect your attention and you help another soul, then, you see, that mist just disappears. And in your service to the Light, you help them because it's right to do so and it's right to do right, [in so doing], that mist will disappear and God will get through in your consciousness. *You* will benefit by not trying to benefit yourself.

It's when you tempt to benefit yourself that you build this great mist and this cloud. Through that self-thought, the mist gets more dense, until you're so far down you can't see any Light, let alone any harmony, any peace, or any good.

Now that's the purpose of a church. The people within it, here, eighteen people and many friends of the church, we are very grateful for, in keeping with the law. No longer—as I spoke with the directors today who mentioned that we are so happy that we don't have the public coming into our church in bare feet, in this and that, you know, and [with] no respect for the church's efforts. Those days are long gone. Well, those days are gone because our own people—the men in their nice suits and everything, the ladies in their long dresses and etc.—we established a law and we attracted something different, you see. Now we could say we never came to church in bare feet. But did we spend our energy in looking just as good as we possibly could, with what was available for us, or did we just throw on any old thread and go with what kind of an attitude to the church? So, *we* made that change, and in keeping with the law, we attracted something better from without, you see.

So, when we go to look without and we see problems out there, try to remember, what we're looking into: we're looking in a mirror that is reflecting back to us where the problem really is.

That's why I'm so pleased for one of my own students, who this very day, it was brought to my attention that she was the victim of the Law of Abuse. I very patiently waited for the law on the divine circle of just return, the principle of the law, to reveal back to me and my own directors that this victimization of the Law of Abuse was what she had established. And so, it returned to me as she wanted to abuse her own church under the justification she had to go to work. And I explained to her: you are demonstrating the Law of Abuse; the one you cried about being the victim thereof. For if you have an employer who will not grant you an hour for a membership meeting to serve your God and your religion once a year, then you [have] got to take a good look and get rid of that employer by getting rid of him inside of yourself because he's a selfish, greedy thing and cannot take you anyplace but right down to the bottom.

Fortunately, she was able to see that demonstrable truth and rise up and declare her right to breathe fresh air in the light of reason. Because remember, my friends, it's inside of our self. And because it is inside of our self, we can change *everything*. The instant we permit our mind to think it is beyond our control—that it's outside of our self—that instant we suffer and pay a terrible price.

That's not what life is all about.

So, if you have any questions, fine. I am very grateful for the dedication of the board of directors of this church to the Light, the purpose for being here, to all of the members, the friends, and the supporters. I am very pleased about the wonderful music department that we have, that some of you are aware of and many are not. But we have this wonderful singing and harmony time up at the house.[80] And we are doing very well and are very grateful for that.

Anyone who wishes to make a little effort to put a little time in that beautiful garden, which is in *dire* need, dire need of being weeded, I expect them to make proper arrangements and put a little bit of time in so that the weeds don't take over the untold thousands of dollars that we poured into that beautiful garden for the flowers. Now anyone who doesn't know how to weed, I'll be happy to personally show them how to do so. So that at least at this critical time of year—the springtime—that we can get it in some kind of shape.

Now remember, we have, moment by moment, that wonderful opportunity to look down there, where self is, or look up there, where freedom is. And we know the only difference between freedom and license is that license has the delusion that it can get something for nothing. That's why it's not freedom. So, let's continue to work for the freedom inside of our self, knowing—and be joyous that we're paying in consciousness every step of the way.

Now I've said what I have to say. I give my directors an opportunity to say anything they would like to say and then we can conclude, close up, and have a nice afternoon and, hopefully, a nice evening. First, do the directors have anything to say? If you do, now is your time to speak up. Believe me, I won't jump down your throat. Not on such a lovely day. I've got a temper, but hopefully I've learned to use it a bit wisely. Some of my older members know what my temper is like. *[After a pause, the teacher continues.]*

Anyone else have anything to say? *[After another short pause, he continues.]*

Let us all rise, please, conclude the meeting, and have a wonderful day. Thank you very much.

MAY 5, 1983

Membership Meeting May 13, 1984

[The previous membership meetings were held at the American Legion log cabin. This membership meeting was held at the Serenity temple.]

Infinite divine Spirit of Light and Truth, we're gathered here to conduct the business of the Serenity Association. We ask for Thy guidance of reason that we may act accordingly, that we may gain control over our judgments, for in so gaining control are we free from the bondage and the suffering of creation. This meeting officially comes to order. Amen.

Please pass the offering, [Student H]. Be seated, please.

[After the offering is made, it is presented to the teacher.]

We thank Thee, God, for this demonstration of Thy abundant good. May we be guided to use it wisely in the best interest of the Light that we work to serve. Amen.

Thank you, [Student H].

You're supposed to stand and hold it. [A director instructs the usher.]

The secretary please read the list of members in good standing.

[The call of the roll is made and eleven names are called, but only nine are present.]

Thank you. Now, we may vote to have an informal meeting or a formal meeting. So, I'll present it to you for a vote. All those in favor of an informal meeting, raise your hand. Thank you. Contrary minded. *[After a short pause, he continues.]* So ordered and approved. We'll have an informal meeting. Thank God. Perhaps it won't take so long. *[Some students laugh.]*

Number one—and it's very important—the philosophy, this philosophy teaches the demonstrable Law of Evolution, which is change. So, we're constantly faced, in all of our activities, with changes. Therefore, we evolve graciously or we evolve with great struggle. I could easily state that after working this week, based upon my judgments *[Student E, who is a young child, begins to vocalize.]*—you may excuse [Student E]—based upon my judgments, this meeting is not convenient for me. But duty has a higher priority to me because I know the law: that you get out of a thing what you put into a thing and not one iota more. So, I am here in keeping with my value of duty. And so, I look about me and I see that there are a number of people who also are here in keeping with their value of duty.

Now this meeting is the most important meeting this association has conducted in the thirteen years of its existence. For you are not aware, most of you—and those of you who have some awareness—do not understand what mental force is like. Oh, you may have read about it in a book dealing with that subject. But that's questionable that you've read about it. Or perhaps you have heard about it. But you have all had the experience of it.

Now this association, over this past year, in keeping with its own evolution and its own merit system, for it's composed of people, has had over one year of a vicious, vindictive attack upon the character, upon the responsibility to the Light that it has to conduct this school.

It is sad, yet it is understandable, when you pause to think and apply this philosophy, that when the Light is cast upon anything that is hidden, it is the natural process of survival for it, whatever it may be, to defend itself. Now as the church, the school especially, has evolved, in keeping with its basic principle—that exposure frees the soul—more exposure has been cast [and] continues to be cast upon that which is hidden. Therefore, that which is hidden, having light cast upon it, known in this philosophy as exposure, has risen repeatedly to defend itself.

Now if that is still a little difficult for you to comprehend, I will make it a bit clearer. We all enter different schools for various motives. Our motives change in keeping with our own effort to free our self from the judgments that we have served or continue to serve. So, as we continue in our efforts, we find a shifting or a changing of the motives that we came to anything with. Now in keeping with those changes, which is known as growth, we find, in time, that what we valued, that is, our judgments of the past, no longer has [have] as much value to us. And so, our motive in evolution gradually, slowly but surely, becomes purified. And so it is with my students past, present, or yet to be: they all come with various motives to a school of Light.

I have witnessed the slow, but sure and gradual changes with those motives of my own students. Through the efforts of exposure, those motives have begun to purify themselves. How does that take place? You see, that which we serve—that meaning any judgment that we judge and decide to serve it—in keeping with exposure, the mind begins to make intelligent choices. It chooses according to how much threat its particular judgment is receiving, whether or not it wants to put itself through another process of exposure. And so gradually, slowly but surely, like little children, we begin to grow up.

Now without discipline, there is no way possible for the light of reason, through exposure, to benefit us. We find our self out in the world of creation where there's no one interested in telling us the truth, for they are so prejudiced. They tell us what they first judge that we want to hear in order that they may get from us what *they* want to get. And so we find that we are, slowly but surely, in this school, freeing our self from prejudice or prejudgment, for we're filled with prejudice. Everything we see, we have prejudged. Everything we hear, we have prejudged. Everything we feel, we have prejudged. And therefore, that is the extent of our own prejudices.

Unfortunately, we have restricted our thinking to being prejudiced in reference to race, color, and religion. But that's a very limited, narrow view. We go to speak to someone and we are already in the control of prejudgment of how they're going to react based upon how they reacted in experiences of similar kind in past events. Now that's not freedom in any sense of the word.

So, over this past year, the motives, gradually, slowly but surely, through the light of reason, through exposure cast upon them, became revealed. And as that took place with some of my students, now long gone, fear rose. And when fear rises, the survival, the self-survival instinct rises with it to defend and to protect that which a person may believe that they are at any given moment.

The purpose of the founding of this school will not change. We have gone through the worst year this organization has [had] and it has survived or I would not be here today to speak to you. Therefore, it is important for you, as members and students of this school and association, that you understand beyond a shadow of any doubt that the light of reason, which you call and understand to be exposure, shall continue to shine.

Now our teaching reveals that if the Light is too bright, it is best that we see it not now. You should be encouraged that the Light is brighter than it has ever been in this organization, for it reveals that some students have made adjustments in their motives for being here and, therefore, have sufficient value, in keeping with the Light that exposes those motives, sufficient value to remain and to grow with the organization.

Now this organization has received applications for new membership. It is being considered by the Council and the authority of the organization. For there are very few who will be allowed in this school, as this school grows in its own purpose to serve the Light. For this organization is not dependent upon numbers for its survival. It never has been dependent upon numbers for its survival. It *is* dependent upon truth for its survival. And so, truth shall not be sacrificed for any, *any* thought of creation. Because they're two entirely separate things.

The greatest struggle and difficulty over this past year has been the bombardment of thought force upon the organization. I have worked on myself daily not to be saddened, let alone discouraged, knowing the law, that so-called ex-students of mine would so deny the Law of Personal Responsibility that they would serve such a realm of degradation and deprivation and vindictiveness and vengeance to be so foolhardy to be tempted to destroy the Light that is indestructible. And by that I am not referring to myself or to any form, but that which sustains a thing is greater than the thing. My temptation to sadness or heartache is not for me personally. It is for what I know: the law is like a circle and it returns unto the sender. That is a weakness of my emotions to feel sad for anyone who would be so vindictive [as] to viciously, daily call every single one of the financial supporters of this association by having first taken their names and their phone numbers and their addresses as an ex-bookkeeper of this association that they may call and state such poisonous untruth and lies.

Fortunately, truth crushed to earth shall rise again. And the only financial supporters, who have been clients of mine for over twenty years standing that were even tempted to discontinue the financial support which keeps this organization together, are only those of recent time who are tempted by their own personalities and has nothing to do with truth.

Now, for your information, there is no way possible that this school and this church could have continued its existence without the financial aid and support of various clients over the many years of my service to God and the ministering angels. For there is no way that such a small group of people can put in, for this year alone, over $100,000, which—over $100,000 has been spent for your school and your church to continue.

Now I know, I know the records. This is the first year that we do not have the financial report completed because [Student R] has been given that bookkeeping job and has to clean up a titanic disaster that was left for us. *We* earned that. *We* have merited that experience. And we are coming through it.

But many of you, as students of mine, know one thing: that whoever chooses to leave the Light that I serve, I am pleasant to, but I am not so foolhardy to ever associate with. Because, you see, it's like anything. You go to school and someone flunks out before the graduation. Only a foolish student, only a foolish student would continue to associate with those who have chosen something different. It's like a person studying to be a singer or a musician and they have a friend that is studying with them. The friend decides that they no longer want to make the effort to learn to sing or be a musician. Well, if you associate with them, knowing the law that like attracts like and becomes the Law of Attachment, then you soon find you don't graduate yourself. You don't become a singer or you don't become a musician. Does anyone not understand that simple law that like attracts like and becomes the Law of Attachment?

Well, I have refrained from speaking to you members and students directly in respect to this vindictive, vengeance campaign until the law was fulfilled. The law has been fulfilled. A year has passed. Fortunately. Fortunately, I have survived. I was never concerned about the Light's survival. I have to admit: at times I was a bit concerned about my own. But to, to be a victim of that vengeance and vindictiveness, you must realize that you, yourself, must let your guard down. There's [It's] one thing to be aware of a campaign against yourself, against what you spent forty-some years of your life working for, and it's something else to permit yourself to overidentify with it and, therefore, to be controlled by it.

Because we are all human and anyone who is under a constant, daily bombardment is bound to weaken at times, especially when the very thing that they are working for and the people associated with it are weakening themselves.

Now, I am encouraged that greater effort is being made. And I want to reveal to you clearly, as members and students of this school and church, where the weaknesses are. First of all, let us clearly understand that we have accepted, when we enter this school and church, one authority and one authority only. Now, this offers to us the daily effort, while involved with this school and this association, to gain control of our own judgments and selfish desires.

Now, for example—and what is so very important—we come here with the thought and with the belief that we are serving something greater than our mental substance and that in that service, which we understand to be selfless service, in that service we are instruments directing intelligent energy to something that is greater than what our mind is capable of conceiving. Now we come here with that belief, with that understanding, in various words or phrases; that's our motive for being here: to free our self from what our mind has already offered to us in life. All right.

Time and again, that is not the demonstration. The demonstration is the direct opposite. Now what does that mean to us as students? What does it mean to us? It means that we, at times, are deceiving ourselves. We believe that we are serving something greater than our mind, and then we awaken and find that we've been serving our mind all the time. That's a terrible waste of energy. It is a terrible waste of effort.

Because we spend twenty-four hours day and night serving our mind, we already know what the experience and the effect is of serving our mind. And we also—some of us—have had some experience of the effect that we have when we serve—whatever you may call it—something beyond our mind. And that which is beyond our mind is beyond our mind's control.

Now, when we, in service to the Light (something greater than what our mind has offered us), when we are tempted to go against the very thing we come to the Light for—to serve something greater than our mind—we are a house divided and are destined to fall.

Now how does that take place? You have a unique school and a very unique association. It was established on an agreement that—I am grateful to say I have never shirked my duty in that agreement—that a Spirit Council, which asked for a school and a church to be opened, would make all decisions governing the church and the school: to the purchase of a toothpick, to the payment of a mortgage, you name it, they agreed to make the final decision.

When you go against the very purpose and foundation of this school and association, you are serving what you're used to serving: mental substance. You are bypassing and going against the very authority that has founded it, for the purpose that it has been founded: to free you from the bondage of creation. That's where the problems are. How do they manifest? I give you many examples.

As recent as Friday, [Student Y], a student allowed here in the school, went against her spiritual purpose for being in this school. She went against her spiritual purpose. Now, how did she do that? It's quite simple. She judged that streusel cake, baked for our bake sale, in service to the Light, was not in our quality standards; it was burned.[81] Is that correct?

Yes.

All right. This is how you go against your purpose of being here. This is how you are a house divided and you defeat the benefit that is waiting for you. If you wanted to bake a streusel cake for yourself, you would do so. But to believe you are baking it for a spiritual realm of Light and freedom, to believe you are doing that and demonstrate the direct opposite is self-destructive. Now, of course, it's not all [Student Y's] fault.

This is the Light I'm speaking of. The Light shall continue to shine. It doesn't matter whether it's [Student Y], it's [Student S], it's [Student G], or [Student B] or anyone else.

You have come here for the purpose of freeing your soul. You have not come here for truth at your convenience, for truth at your convenience is total falsehood, and I will not serve that realm of consciousness for anyone.

Now, [Student G], who, this very day, shall be voted in by the membership of this organization as director—I'm a little positive about that. Perhaps because I know and I accept who the authority really is here. All right. Now [Student G] took a look at the streusel cake she baked—am I correct, [Student G]?

[It is difficult to transcribe her response.]

I was not physically present, but I was well aware of what was going on. It happened here in the kitchen. Now you may think it's a minor thing. It's not a minor thing to you! It is a major thing when we deceive our self! That's a major thing. And so, she didn't like the looks of them because, to her view, they're too dark. But then [Student G's] mind and [Student G's] prejudice [are] not the quality standard of your organization. For [Student G] is prejudiced about the coloring of the top of a streusel cake. She prefers them light. Do you understand? Fine.

She did not—and this is an error; this is an error, an omission—she did not check with the only authority the organization has. That was her error. But she's human and she makes errors. And that's why you're here: to be freed from that, to see how serious these errors really are *for you*. I will survive. So will your school. Will *you* survive? That's the question. That's the question you must ask yourself.

And so, based upon her prejudice, for she prejudged that it was not quality, based upon her personal likes and dislikes. Do you understand, everyone? And so, in order to support her prejudice, she spoke to [Student Y]. Is that correct?

Yes.

And [Student Y]—like attracts like and becomes the Law of Attachment—[Student Y] has similar prejudice. She doesn't like them dark. She likes them light. I came down here late that evening and I personally—and, worse than that, the prejudice even went so far as for [Student G] to spend all her money to purchase them and put them in a bag—all four. Is that correct?

[Again, it is difficult to transcribe her response.]

Which deprived [Student G] of the spiritual benefit of baking them for something greater than her mind in the first place. Does everyone understand? It not only cost her money out of her pocket, it cost her the spiritual essence that goes into the divine bank of spiritual grace. That's what's at stake. Not just the four streusel cakes. All right.

I was told to take one out immediately and to pick the darkest piece of the streusel cake that I may demonstrate and prove beyond a shadow of any doubt to my own students that it absolutely and positively was not burned. Is that correct, [Student Y]?

Yes.

And so, I took the darkest piece I could find, on the side, in front of everyone and I ate it. And I had everyone present also take a taste, because I was told—and I told [Student G], "There is absolutely nothing wrong with this streusel cake, absolutely and positively not. And it meets the quality standards of this association." Everyone tasted it and everyone agreed.

Now I said nothing to [Student G] in reference to why they were dark—did I?—the next day.

Think of what's at stake. In baking salmon loaves over the years, the Council of your church has always chose[n] the more expensive red salmon over the pink salmon. You know that, you people who have been around for many years. Because that is what they have chosen. They could [have] chose[n] the cheaper pink salmon, but they have always chosen the more expensive red salmon. And so it is with the streusel cake. [Student G] had always chosen the darker brown sugar instead of the cheaper light brown sugar. The Council had, years ago, approved it or it could never have been done.

Now think, the light of reason was nonexistent. Had the light of reason been existent, [Student G] would have said, "Well, I don't like it so dark-looking. However, dark brown sugar is what's approved. Dark brown sugar is what I have used for many years. What's the matter with me?" You must try to understand at this meeting—it is so important—what is happening to your mind, your spirit, and your soul. You are here to be free from that realm of consciousness that is ever present and that is being served almost constantly. Here, you have the opportunity—not the guarantee—here you have the opportunity to free yourself from that realm. You have no guarantee for no one can step inside your ego and make the changes that are necessary.

Now the only time—[Student O], are you with us?

Yes, sir.

Then—my eyes are open. So, open yours. Because I don't fool around after spending a life in this work. I don't fool around with anyone. Whatever the trip may be, it has nothing to do with the very purpose *[The teacher hits his fist on the table for emphasis.]* of being [under] this roof! Do you understand?

Yes, sir.

Don't forget it! Now this organization will continue! I am not interested in anyone's mental forces! I'm not interested in their judgments! I'm not interested in their egos. I am interested in their soul. And that's the only reason they're allowed within two feet of me. Do you understand that, [Student O]?

Yes, sir.

Then don't forget it! Do you have a problem with your eyes?

No, sir.

Then you open them up. I'm not here to listen to myself talk, young man! My work shall continue on. You students have the benefit of being exposed to it! But you students also have zero guarantee! Zero guarantee! So, open your eyes. And if you think you've been awake too long and you're tired, you just remember, young man, that I got up at 3:00 am this morning and my eyes haven't closed since!

Now, we'll continue on with this. You people that want the benefit of what this school has to offer, you clean up your act and you follow the one and only authority that runs the organization. And if you feel that you don't want to follow that authority, you join those who have gone, for my work will continue on. Do you *all* understand? Is there anyone who does not understand that?! If there is, speak now or *forever* hold your peace. *[After a short, silent pause, the teacher continues.]*

Now I will continue on with *my* work.

Now, you've come a long ways. All of you. If you want to go any farther, then remember there's one authority in this organization. And if you don't want to follow that authority, then please leave graciously. May that be in my divine merit system.

Now, are there any questions in reference to this meeting before we vote on the acting secretary-treasurer to become secretary-treasurer? *[After a short pause, he continues.]*

Now I have spent my life teaching that honesty will lead us through. Now, [Student O], do you feel that, in all honesty, you may have something to say in reference to your vibration there of being tired or whatever caused your eyes to close? *[After another short pause, he continues.]* And while you're thinking about it, I'll speak to anyone else who chooses to close their eyes while I'm working. Because I have more value for God and his angels. I don't have such a temptation that I close them out any time my ego decides or I would not be here right this moment. I'd be someplace else at *my* choosing. Be rest assured of that!

Now I've told you people before, you students who have been permitted close to me, that I'm not fooling. [If] you want the benefit of what this school offers, [then] clean up your act when you're around me! I have never been short of people and I have no intention of being short of anything. Because I've worked to know the law and—more important—I work to apply it!

You have anything to say, [Student O]?

No, except I was conscious that, that, I was, trying to go to sleep because my eyes had closed a couple of times before. But, I mean, evidently—

The Spirit was well aware. They gave you two chances and the third time, [Student O], they act, whether it's streusel cake or anything else. I have already instructed my student down there—I've already instructed [Student Y] that she is not to permit her ego to run this organization by making judgments of what quality control is when she has never earned that authority. I made that clear to you, didn't I? I am not interested in whether it's a song or a streusel cake. I am interested in *who* has the final authority in this school. And be rest assured, those who do not have value for this philosophy or this school, they will go their way. But as long as I'm on Earth, their egos will not even begin to run it. Did I not explain that to you? I don't want to see it again. *[Student E, a young child, is in another room and begins to vocalize.]* Yes, go ahead, [Student O].

Well—

[Student M], you're excused to take care of your son. Because, after all, this is the first time, as you well know, that any small baby was allowed in a school that I'm operating.

Yes. Thank you.

So, it's a privilege that you have earned, but [it is] not guaranteed. Yes, [Student O].

Yes. So I just when I—I accept the exposure because, it, evidently, was something I needed.

Thank you, [Student O], you have no alternative. Your presence here is the Law of Solicitation.

Right.

So it isn't a matter of whether you choose to accept or not. The matter is to grow or go. That's what's at stake. Because here, the Law of Presence is the Law of Solicitation. And you are present. Therefore, you have solicited what this school has to offer, including its discipline and including the light of exposure. And so has anyone else who enters a door that this school has the divine right of controlling! Do you understand, [Student O]?

Yes, sir.

Now I realize you are a relatively new student, but you should know, after the months that you've been around me, that I am not here to play with those realms. Because if that would be my interest, I shall go into the commercial business and I shall not be earning $3,000 a year, as the vice president informed me yesterday that was my earnings for the past year. I shall put my talents into other areas in which the remuneration of this world shall really blow your mind.

Do you understand?

[The student responds, but it is difficult to transcribe.]

Fine. Then don't sit there and go to sleep in school. I hope, for your sake, you don't!

Now, that's the purpose of being here. That's your purpose for being in this school, is to grow up! No matter who you are, you come here to grow up. Because you already know what your growing's been like out there.

Now this school will continue on, as you witnessed yourself. You at the bake sale were fortunate enough to have a visitation from one of my ex-students and all of you were present in church today to have a visitation from another one of my ex-students. And so, that which has been always returns to the wise man who has patience and knows the law and applies it.

And what I spoke to you earlier about, "Vengeance is mine, saith the Lord," [which] means that vengeance belongs to the law and how foolhardy is the one who is tempted to take into their hands vengeance and vindictiveness, for it shall only return unto them. That's heartbreaking and saddening, but then again, one must not interfere with the right of someone else's law. And look at life the way life really is: if someone is going through a varying struggle, then that is what is necessary;

they have made it necessary for them. If they solicit your help, then they have also established that law. *You*, then, have established the law to help them in keeping with the light of reason that you are receptive to at any given moment. For how long shall you be an instrument through which they may benefit? That is ever in keeping with the law that you alone have established in evolution.

So here, you come to grow, or you come to visit and to go. That's what the organization was founded on thirteen years ago, and it continues to serve the very same purpose. I know what this school has to offer! I know! I know its benefits. I cannot know for you. If you do not know what this wonderful philosophy can do in your life through your little bit of effort to apply it, if you do not know that, I cannot know it for you. But I assure you, to me, it has sufficient value to keep my eyes open when it's being revealed! Do you understand? And if it doesn't have enough value *for you,* to keep *your* eyes, [Student S], open—you understand?! If I flashed a certain desire of yours in front of you, your eyes would open very quickly!

[If] you want this class to continue on, then you keep daring to close your eyes and to insult the Spirit that I serve. You just go ahead. You're excused to get a glass of water, [Student S]. It seems interesting to me that you should be so tired. How dare you insult my life's work! How dare you insult the Spirit that you claim to be benefiting from! How dare you!

[Student J], you've known me for over thirteen years. Don't you think it's time that a few people woke up?

Yes, sir.

[There is a pause in the class as the student gets a glass of water.]

Well, some of you who aren't around every day, working here in this school, perhaps you'll get your eyes open. This is what it's been like: selfish desire entering the school of Light. Selfish desire. The demands of the human, uneducated egos to force this school to serve creation. There's no way it's going to. There's no possible way it's going to.

I receive[d] from the students that have left the ultimatum, which is nothing more than a threat, to either operate this school the way their egos dictated or they would leave. They left! Didn't they, [Student B]?

Yes.

And we're still here! I not only received that ultimatum or threat here, under my own roof, right in our own library, but right in front of physical witnesses. And then, when I would not bow to their ego's dictate and demand, they not only sent a written letter of *irrevocable* resignation but they were the very instrument that started the vindictive, vicious campaign to destroy my character and the forty-some years of my service to God. They haven't got to first base! But I have had to live and witness what they're doing to themselves.

I assure you who are left, and those who are yet to be, I assure you this school will not bow to any threat, to any ultimatum in changing its principles and its policies to reveal the truth through this philosophy that has been dearly paid for and continues to be dearly paid for. There is nothing inside of me that can tempt me to sell out to creation when I know what creation really is. And I know what it really has to offer.

So, I want the full cooperation of the board of directors in no uncertain terms to stop serving creation while they're in this school, to stop interfering with the divine right of the Spirit Council to establish quality control, to be the only authority—because that's why this organization is the way that it is—and not to be so tempted with their weaknesses to interfere with just who is the final authority! I want the full cooperation of my board of directors. Is there any problem with that full cooperation?

[There is no audible response.]

Now, you'll all be very harmonious here—and especially you directors—if you stop going against the authority of this school. Then, everything will be peaceful, harmonious, and the abundant good would flow as it never has before. But you're going to have to work on your weaknesses, your temptations while you're here. And [Student S], as a secretary and a student of mine for over ten long years, you of all people with your titanic will power—how dare you be weakened to start to try to sleep in that chair in front of me.

I apologize.

You should apologize! When I see when you're chasing a desire that you can stay awake right around the clock twenty-four hours day and night, you should apologize! You most certainly should! And so should [Student G] when she dared to be tempted by that titanic ego of hers to go against the authority of this school for *her* to be the authority on the quality, which they alone established. You should be, [Student G]! I know it's errors of ignorance, but let's get rid of the errors and let's move on to goodness and prosperity around here.

Do you understand? Because you have applied for membership, [Student O].

Yes, sir.

You know me well enough. I don't play those kind of games. Those who do are long gone! And if I can survive the thought force of living hell for over a year, I sure as hell—God forbid—I sure as *hell* am strong enough to survive anybody's ego trip, no matter who is weakened into it, whether it's sleeping or anything else or money, sex, or anything else. I'm strong enough for God never failed me, no matter how far down they kick me.

You want to know something, now that the great wave of a whole year of unbearable thought force is over? You want to know something? I used the last ounce of my will power to put on the best image when I expose myself to any of you. And you want to know why? Because when those realms sense you're weak, like the dogs after a wounded animal, they rip them to pieces! And if you don't believe me, ask [Student R]. They're always waiting to attack. Not the people, no, not their soul, but those *things* that we, in our weaknesses, called temptations, that we serve! That's why I made such phenomenal effort to show my restoration, no matter what it took out of me!

Now perhaps you understand. When you go to try to force the Light to serve your desires of creation, you be rest assured if it in any way involves that which I am responsible for, you will have to meet me first! And I guarantee *you*, you'll meet your match and eighty-one others right behind me. Because I've never considered myself a pantywaist for anyone to mow over.

Now, I would like a vote on the recommendation of the Spirit Council that [Student G], who has been a member and a student of ours for over ten years, who was voted in last year as acting secretary-treasurer of this church to replace the vacancy created by one who has left, be voted into the board of directors. Now, understand your constitution and bylaws: that the membership votes to fill the vacancy of director; they do not vote the position. So, all of those in favor of [Student G] being voted to fill the vacancy as a director of the Serenity Association, please raise your hands. *[After a short pause, the teacher continues.]*

Anyone contrary minded? *[After another short pause, he continues.]* So ordered and approved. [Student G] you are officially, as of this day, filling the vacancy as director of your church, Serenity Church.

Now, is there anything that any of us have to say? And perhaps, [Student O] and [Student S], you won't close your eyes again and open up that Pandora Box when God's angels are working. Look—understand, sonny, I have other desires, too, than to sit here and use my energy to straighten out your little ego. I do have other desires. There are other things that I would like to do. Why, I may even want to sit down, relax, and watch the television or something—the boob tube. There's all kinds of things. I would like to go out there and do some watering there of some of those plants that are wilted. So, I do have other priorities, you understand.

All right. Now for those of you who would like to have a cup of coffee and conclude this meeting—are there any questions? Remember, I'm the one that had to adjust that the bookkeeping isn't balanced yet. We're still—he's still working on finding a few errors—a few thousand, you know. It's not bad. He started with thirty-some thousand. Now it's down to only a few thousand, about seven or eight thousand. I already found two thousand. But, you know, I can go down there and do it. I mean, after all, he didn't come here in any sense of being a bookkeeper. The truth of the matter is we're very fortunate; he has spent his life—[Student R]—in not being able to balance his checkbook. *[Many students laugh.]* So, we get the most qualified ones to work on our books.

At least it's honest; there's nothing being pilfered off. That I know. But the errors have got to be corrected, because the report has to go into the federal and the state, you see. So he brought me the report and I said, "It balances?" "No, it's $8,000 off." But he says, "It's getting better." I said, "Yes, a couple of days ago it was $37,000 off! Now it's only $8,000." And I said, "Worst of all, it's on the short side." *[The teacher laughs.]* That I don't appreciate. But anyway, to say the least, it's getting there. But I will not give forth a[n] official report until it's balanced. But it's errors and it's additions because, as I say, he's already spent his life never being able to balance his checkbook. And to think we've merited him balancing our books. Oh, God forbid. Well, anyway, something good will happen out of it.

You see, it's just like the disaster the other day. The divinity of disaster. There's always something good you can take out of any experience if you want to make the effort. So, we had an experience in cutting down on the amount of food that could be baked by some of our people. So, the Spirit turned around and adjusted the prices. I'm a little bit, perhaps, disappointed—and I don't want to be because it's based upon experience. But we should make greater effort to make some changes in our levels of consciousness over our bake sale. You see, for your information, our dinners bring in the highest revenue to keep this organization together next to the donations from our members, our students, from my clients, and from people who have received benefit from this organization and from counseling over these many years. The dinners bring in the next largest amount of revenue consistently. And the bake sales would bring in more revenue if we, the people responsible for the bake sales, will change our attitude—you may be excused to take care of your son, [Student M]—we will change—if he's willing to take control of his ego, he can come in. But if he's not, I don't want him in here.

OK. Thank you.

He's lucky to be out there. If he'd gain control of that ego of his—he needs more discipline.

[If we will] change our attitude in reference to the judgments we have over our bake sale, [they will bring in more revenue]. It's our attitude. You see, I teach get God in it or forget it. But, you see, putting God in anything depends on how willing we are to make the effort to get judgments out. You've got to get the judgments out, and then God will get in and you'll have success. It's just like the dinners. We have success—I have been working diligently, haven't I, [Student B] and [Student S]? Pardon?

[It is difficult to transcribe their responses.]

[I have been working] diligently on these dinners to try to get it through your egos that it is in your own best interest to get your judgments out, to let God in, and you'll have no problem with attendance. But you must *give* to gain. So, on the bake sales, you must give up your judgments to gain the abundant flow of God. And it's that simple.

Now if you're not willing to give up your judgments over any project you're involved in, then you be rest assured God, the goodness, is not going to flow. Because, you see, it's your judgments that are proving to you how right you are, see? The energy that flows through us goes to the judgments; and then we can say, "Yeah, I was right all the time. It was a lousy bake sale." [It] was this or that, you see. We've got to make the changes deep in our subconscious. Because that's where it is. The prejudice is way back here.

You see, what happens with our mind—and try to understand. When we judge something to be a certain way and seeming circumstances or conditions or authority does not allow that, our subconscious retaliates because our conscious judgment is based upon our subconscious addictions. And if you will understand that simple principle, you'll know what you're dealing with, for that's the key to the truth that was given to you years ago—that "Man is a law unto himself. What are you doing with the law that you are?"

You've got to understand your mind and how it works if want to get yourself free from the bondage of mental laws and judgments.

Thank you very much. Let's have a cup of coffee. Thank you.

MAY 13, 1984

Membership Meeting September 21, 1988
The Last Wishes of Mr. Richard Goodwin

[This meeting was held at the Serenity temple. An earlier recording of Mr. Goodwin's last wishes was dated January 19, 1983, and published in Volume 19.*]*

Good evening, everyone.

Good evening. [Many students speak.]

Thank you. We'll make this as brief as possible. *[The teacher coughs.]* Excuse me. I'm covering all bases in my responsibility to the Light and the church of which you are a part. Does everybody understand that?

Yes. [Many students speak.]

Fine. Now, this is a legal corporation, protected legally by the corporate laws of the State of California.

You are now going to receive the Council and Isa Goodwin's direction of intent. When I'm gone physically, I'm gone. This is the request, direct from me, of the angels, Isa Goodwin, the chairlady of the Council that founded this organization and runs it these many years to this moment through myself, this piece of flesh, Richard Goodwin.

This is for your benefit. So no one, no matter who it is, will be tempted to try to destroy, when everything is set for this Light to go to the world of several books. I may, however, just be here for many years. But I will do my responsibility and I will get to it quickly, for your sake.

Now, first, in the event of my transition, it is my request, speaking for the true and only authority of the Serenity Church and this association, that you remaining shall be considerate of the following direction: one: in keeping with proper corporate structure and at our request, the board of directors shall harmoniously move Vice President [Student R] to president, in the event of my actual transition, which may or may not be any day. You understand that? *[After a short, silent pause, the teacher continues.]* I don't hear anyone understand that.

Yes. [Many students speak loudly.]

Very well. The secretary is secretary of this church and has, like anyone else, the opportunity to remain in that position. [Student H] is secretary-treasurer [and] has the opportunity to remain in that position in the event of my physical transition.

I wish it very clear that no one remain in their positions after I [have] gone who do not wish to be. The Living Light is the only purpose this organization is founded. The Living Light is not a person. It is not a place and it is not a thing.

Now there is one vacancy on the board. I have personally investigated for three years who would be willing to donate that much time, temper and all, and be loyal to the Light. It is my request that [Student O] be placed on the board of directors. In the event that I am here Sunday morning, I will call for a legal request of the legal membership that he be so placed. In the event that I am gone physically, it is my request that you fulfill that.

Now, in the event that I am physically gone, it is my wish that this property be harmoniously sold within a year, within a year. I foresee, harmoniously, approximately six months to a year. It is my request, harmoniously, that the last broker used not be used. I do not want this property to go in a disaster sale when it is absolutely not necessary.

We are almost finished with the computer equipment. Within two months—for those of you who don't know, we're waiting on the RAM chip and there's a world-wide shortage. Now perhaps [I'll] explain that to you later, but we have already made our payment, partially. I was in hopes to stay to see the first page. I may or may not. I never have been a medium that dictates to the angels. I've never been a medium that has tried to use them. So, let's make that all clear. I cannot guarantee you the hour of my transition because they won't give it to me and not because I haven't asked for at least three years. Period.

Now, let's get down to all of these details. The property sold harmoniously, for those who are still on the ship. No one is to stand in the way of anyone who wishes to leave the Light, no matter who it is. I want that clearly understood. However, for those who choose to remain, harmoniously, for the purpose of serving the Living Light, to which I dedicate my life and have for many years, it is my desire and it is our wish—because we're not going to stay down here in your physical world. Should I pass, I'm passing. I'm going to my world to stay.

Now I want it very clear that this property be sold within a year so there's not a disaster loss. And I want it clear that in the event of my flight that a humble, clean, dry house in the country, out of this county, preferably close to the ocean—the office be placed there. You have [Student R], the president. You have [Student S], the secretary. You have [Student H], the secretary-treasurer. And I'll do everything I can, if I am here Sunday, to get a legal vote for [Student O] to be on that board of directors.

Now, the place should consist of one bedroom. It should consist of sufficient space, which would require another large bedroom or two bedrooms just to take care of the master Living Light tapes, of which not even the directors of this church—some of them—have ever heard. Now some of the directors—a couple—have heard very advanced teachings. None have heard the advanced, advanced teachings. Nothing selfish; you weren't quite ready. You hear me? And you never will be ready if you choose to leave the Light after I'm gone because I'm staying in the Light, God willing.

Now, let's get right down to business. A shelter to be purchased for an office by this association, preferably—and there's no reason why not—out of this county. Not Del Norte County.

I know—you don't have to be on the ocean. It'll be there. So that the computer equipment can be placed there: untold thousands of dollars already invested and paid for and many thousands will be cleared up—and I'm not asking you for money and don't worry about it—if I'm still here, but I will not leave you stranded.

This is a legal corporation. There's no money for anyone. I don't want any [battles] and I'm not going to stay in the astral realm to see it torn apart by dissension by attorneys, you hear? And I want that very clear in my breath, my—whether it's my last or my first.

Now, to the details on this shelter. I want that purchased. Nothing fancy. Clean and dry. I want it maintained by the funds from the sale of this property. You understand? I want it—that's the utilities and the maintenance. That's the church office for the Living Light.

Meetings? Once a month. If you don't want to make the journey, you won't long remain in the Light. I know that. You hear? Once a month. Once a month to see how the book is coming. Telephone calls? The telephone is to be in the name of the Serenity Association. Nothing else. I'm not ashamed of being a Spiritualist. You get out into the country near some small town: "Those are kooky Spiritualists." I don't want any of that bullshit! I want that equipment in that shelter purring seven days a week.

Now if the president, [Student R], is not willing to keep it purring seven days a week—I know he will. I won't stay in the astral realms to watch him, but I know damn well he will. You call the office when you care to call the office. If he answers, he answers. He may well be on the computer. So don't make judgments too quickly. You understand?

Now the purpose of that office will contain all computer equipment to do our own printing with the latest technology of the Apple laser writer/laser printer. You hear?

I'm almost at the last step of that equipment. Telephone—now, I'm not finished yet. Telephone, of course, is paid by the association. Utilities are paid by the association. That's the church's office. Maintenance of the property is paid for by the association.

Now, [Student O], are you willing a minimum of twice a month to—after all, you'll be on the board if I have a breath here on Sunday—on Saturday. Let's see, [are] all the directors here on Saturday?

Sunday. [Student R responds.]

Sunday. Sunday. Everybody's here Sunday that cares about the Light. [Are] you willing to make that journey by yourself, yourself twice a month—it might be a hundred miles—just to clean that property?

Yes, sir. [Student O responds.]

Are you willing to do that?

Yes, I am. [Student O confirms.]

Pardon. Because there's no housekeepers up there. You understand?

Yes, sir.

And far enough—well, several miles, ten miles maybe, approximately, from a town. All right?

Yes, sir.

Or possibly even twenty. All right. So that the work can be done every day. Now you can't put a human being, no matter who they are, in that kind of a situation without some kind of [video]tapes, because they probably will have no satellite dish. And you're not dragging that one out of here. It cost too much money; it would be a waste of money. So, the laser [disc] library, complete, is to go to the church office.[82] So, it can't be so damn small so that it won't fit those things. And I want that house dry. Absolutely dry! There are master tapes that cannot be destroyed, unless you just wasted all your effort in life. You got the message?

I want that laser library to go. I want my 8-mm [videotapes to go], which is the church office's; those are 8-mm movies. I want those to go to the church office. I want the EDV-T1, my little, dinky TV-combo VCR, by my bed, that *has* to go. That's a monitor in the final tail end of the video-laser system downstairs. I presently got it by my bed. All right? Now you know why I really bought it. All right? Six months or so—I don't know how long, [Student S]—

I think that long, yes.

—before the laser computer even came. Now let's get all this stuff clear because I won't be discussing it again. You hear me? If I'm back here, you understand, [on] Sunday.

Now, the XB—oh, God, what number is it?—XBR in the sitting room, that's a TV so you can put an 8-mm [tape] in. You live in the country by yourself and see how long your sanity lasts. I mean, I can do it. But the new, the new president, when I'm gone, what do you expect? You wouldn't do it yourselves. I know that. I know that very well. That TV, I want to go to that office for his use. You hear me?

Yes. [Many students respond.]

And when he's not using that EVD-T1, that little, dinky one by my bed, at present, which is the tail end monitor when the video work—which is all ready—the equipment. Most of it's down there in the software. I've worked every day and night with it, when I can. So? If you see it by his bed, that simply is quite clear: we're not producing, at that time, the laser discs. Got the message?

The book's in process.

Now, what else do I have to take care of? I think I got that all—No, I didn't! He presently gets, for his work here, to survive, you know, that—he's been considerate. Is it $600 a month?

Yes. [Student R responds.]

A month! Let's get it clear. A month, everyone. Don't relate to me. I get $60 a week. All right? I'm not complaining. But then I'm not him, and he's certainly not me. All right? It is my request, from this Council of this church, that he get $1,000 a month. You understand?

Yes. [Many students speak.]

The property will be sold. One thousand dollars a month. Now if you, anyone, got the wrong idea, that they're not going to pay their monthly dues or they're not going to pay for the utilities, don't get too far out. You get something for nothing, you'll go balmy in creation. You pay your just share, every one of you. And I won't be hanging out in the astral realm for a hundred years waiting for everybody. So, get the message straight.

Now, is there anything—any other details? [Student S], [Student H], [Student R], you're directors. Tell me. Spend some of your energy for a minute. Anything that you think I've left out? Speak up.

I don't feel that you've left anything out. [Student R offers.]

I want all bases covered in the event. Because I could be here until I'm 89, but I'm no fool. Now, you got to remember this is my request from the Council of your church. This is not a will. I will not put this church—besides, it's a corporation. Do you understand that everybody?

Yes. [Many students respond.]

You want to waste this money, your hard-earned money, on personality, battling and fighting? And you think there's only one book? It is a series of at least twenty-seven. [Student B] or [Student S] or [Student R], do you want to share how many millions, billions of words there are?

There's a lot. [Student R remarks.]

[Student B]?

I couldn't begin to count them. I don't know how many there are.

To be transcribed.

Years of work.

Now, the transcriptions can be mailed in, of course. The board of directors, wherever they live, on their own, can check them. I want—you fight and you will destroy yourselves.

Now if I'm still on Earth, if there's the slightest forces in the atmosphere, just say goodbye to me. I don't kick out anyone. You're just making another step. You're not here at night. I'm not crying or complaining. I don't know the day, the hour, nor do I know the year. Do not be deceived that God's angels give me enough energy to make it very clear—their intention. Does anybody not understand that? If so, please raise your hands right now.

There will be no women living in the Serenity Church office. You don't have to worry. Isa Goodwin's got very good eyes and somebody will appear someday. You hear me?

I do. [Student R responds.]

Now, he has agreed. So, you don't want—now, if he wants to shack up in some town, that's his business and that's really none of your business. All right? With some broad, that's—

May I say something? [Student R asks.]

Yes.

I made a commitment to your mother—

Yes?

—[this] morning that that would not be the case.

All right, I'm making it very clear to these students, your right of choice. Now you don't have to be president when I'm gone, but you want to complete that work on those computers and the Living Light.

That's the only purpose of my being here.

Thank you. There is untold years of work, you understand? The Living Light will come out in a series. Do you understand that? Paperback after paperback. It will be printed in the little house in the country, if I'm gone. Otherwise, it'll be printed wherever God puts me. Presently, the angels have me here. You understand?

Yes. [Many students respond.]

I've already cut down the work schedule so that I can last longer for *your* sake. I'm ready to go any minute. I would like to—the RAM chip. There's no way that I can make the RAM chip appear suddenly. Tell them about the RAM chip. I've paid for half of that laser printer.

Yes. [Student R affirms.]

Black and white.

Yes. [Student R continues.]

Now, oh, I've got to clear that first. Next year, the word is out that a $60,000 pure color printer can be obtained.

Uh-huh. [Student R confirms.]

Now we've got to make a reversal change. Out in the country, now, it would be in our best interests, with all of these diagrams—many you have never seen—you hear me?

Yes. [Many students respond.]

For the church, with the funds that are left, to invest and get the color printer if I'm not here. I can't get it now because, do you understand, it's an executive secret. *[Many students laugh.]* I don't control Macintosh, Apple Computer. You understand?

Yes. [A few students respond.]

Pardon?

Yes. [Many more students speak.]

I have special software that I have personally talked to Europe, to the Continent, to the north, to the south, all over, to get this underway, hopefully, not knowing the hour that I go. I would like to—that's my request, as long as there's peace and happiness here and joy—I would like to, at least—I've made my request—see the first completed page. That, I would like. But that's my own personal—I'm not afraid to go. I [could] go any second. But they won't tell me the hour or day. And I get a little upset that my mother's been able—and she's still able—[to] tell everybody else when their aunts and uncles will go, [when] [Student P4] is to go, when everybody else is to go, but not me.

And not you students! *[Many students laugh.]* She's not telling you; so, don't bother me. She won't tell me for me, don't you even—oh, that's another thing. No personal, personal notes and questions and bullshit. Just your health. No romance. No affairs of the hearts. No money. No nothing. If I'm still here Sunday. Do you understand that everyone?

Yes. [Many students speak.]

Huh? All right. Fine. Now let me think, is there anything else before . . . Oh, God . . . all right. *[The teacher pauses for a few moments.]* That's what it is. I'll take a vote right now—and any of you dare, if I'm gone later to, to try to tear this humble, little Living Light apart, well, you pay your own way. I want a nomination from the floor for [Student O] to be placed on the board of directors.

I nominate [Student O] for board of directors. [A director makes a nomination.]

I'd like someone off of the board, off of the board.

I nominate [Student O] for board. [A different student remarks.]

Fine. The nomination—who seconds that nomination?

I second it. [Many students second it.]

I want someone off the board. [Student B], did you second it?

I second it. [Student B says.]

[Student B] seconds that. So—but it's on the tape. Is that tape still working?

It's on the tape. [Student R confirms.]

Fine. All those in favor of [Student O] being placed on the board of directors—and no bullshit [or] I'll kick them in the butt myself—please say aye.

Aye. [Many students speak.]

Those not in favor. *[After a short pause, the teacher continues.]* One hundred percent in favor. Is that right, [Student J]—

Yes, sir.

And everyone?

Yes. [A student confirms.]

All right. So, I got all that taken care of. I don't have to bother [with] that Sunday. Isn't that nice? All right. All right. Then you get to work a little more, but not too much more because I got to last as long as I, I can, [Student O]. And I can't have people around too much. Nothing personal, kid, nothing personal.

Yes, sir. [Student O responds.]

All right. It's going to be done, God. The laser printer. What else?

My personal—my will? Well, that's really my business. What do I own? I own some clothes in my closet. What else? I own a ring. I want the new president of the church to have it. That was donated to me by my students years ago. Or did they want to reclaim it? You remember, my amethyst ring.

Yes. [Student R and Student S reply.]

And I have a nice, thin watch. It's in—it's up there. It's not locked up. *[Some students laugh.]* I want the president to have it. The greatest wealth you'll ever get from me is the eyeball of Isa Goodwin around the clock, *[Many students laugh.]* getting the Light to the world. All right? But then, that's my business. I have my last will and testament. Don't worry, I'm not reading it to you. It's none of your business. *[A few students laugh.]* I have my last will and testament. I [have] already been through that bullshit. I'm prepared. And if there's anything I left out, I got the basic essence on paper. God help you if you dare to drag the Living Light through that public bullshit! The documents of my request are not filed with the county of Marin, just my personal will.

That's all I have to give materially is what—well, some of you seen sitting right in my room: my clothes. My own personal clothes. And I got quite a few that I haven't worn. You used to see them when the church—they happen to fit him. That's all. That's practical. My ring? You want to tear my good ring apart?

You rarely see me wear it, right? It happens to be my birthstone, not his. Well, if he don't [doesn't] want it, say so now. I don't give a damn.

I do. [Student R replies.]

Fine. What else do I have? My clothes. My ring. And I want the EVD-T1 by my bed to go to the church office. And I don't want no [any] fighting over it. Because, God help you, that's really the monitor at the tail end. So, there's another monitor! It's a bigger one. It's in the A/V room. Tough shit. *[Some students laugh.]* Everything else, God forbid, you sell. And I want the money here and I want it all accounted for if I'm gone. Every single penny.

Secretary—[Student S].

Yes?

There's no way—now look, let us all be honest. If you want to leave after I'm gone, please feel free. But remember this, I won't physically be here to stand in your way, do you understand?

Yes, sir. [Student O replies.]

If you don't care enough to see this organization—and I'm not talking about meeting and fighting with people—through one, short year of physical transition, then you really don't give a shit about me. Because I'm down here whatever time it is, not fighting with any of you, for the Light. And if you're not willing, that's your right. You understand? But I hope, for the sake of your beautiful souls, you will at least bow your titanic egos—and I got a big one myself and I try to keep it under the reins. There's something greater. Because your flesh and bones, you never know the minute they're going to go. You better have something in reserve. And that's the Living Light. For me.

Now, if you want to go, I understand. I won't stand in your way. But for God's sake, think clearly for your sake. I'm doing everything—the last breath. There'll be no fighting. Period. There's no money to get. Forget glory. Forget—God—all the bullshit. Forget that. Demonstrate! And I won't stay in that astral realm to keep hollering at you. Demonstrate that you really care for the Light in your soul more than your pride. I'm here. I care more than my pride. I don't expect you—any of you—to be me. I expect you, as students, to enjoy life! You don't have to be here every day. What the hell. Can't you care enough in your heart for your soul? The organization is moving to the country to a humble shelter. What the hell is six months or a year? What's the personality bullshit—do you understand me, everybody?—

Yes. [Many students speak.]

—when the Light is at stake? And I mean it, because I love every one of you. But don't you forget, the Light is first. And no fighting bullshit! Now if you can't survive, you directors—or the rest of you—on one one-hour meeting, legally, a month, after I'm gone—one—then you have no business being on the board of directors and you have no business wasting your time even if I do stay. Do you all understand that?

Yes. [Some students speak.]

All of you!

Yes. [More students speak.]

[Student H]? [Student S]? [Student R]?

Yes, sir. [Student R replies.]

Sorry, I can't hear [Student H] and [Student S].

Yes. Yes. [Student H and Student S reply.]

Thank you. I'm not fighting; I just want it damn clear. You got that recorder on?

It is. [Student R confirms.]

Is it run—it better not run out of tape.

No, we got fifteen minutes. [Student R replies.]

Oh, that's fine. I'll take a breath. *[The teacher pauses for a few moments.]* All right. Don't waste your lives fighting. Don't do that. I've kept it open for the Light. Not for my ego and certainly not for yours—any of you. [Student J] has known me over twenty years. Doesn't matter whether there's things or not. I used to—you remember. I had a shirt and the collar was yellow. My poor pride just—and a gray suit, you remember?

Uh-huh. [Student J replies.]

That's all I had. You know that.

Uh-huh.

I was in Forest Knolls. So? What the hell's the big deal? I'm not into these things. They'll have them converted. Don't fight over any shit. Doesn't matter to me. I've lived with them and without them, haven't I, [Student J]?

Yes, you have.

Without them when I met you [and] most all of my life. This is not mine. This belongs to the angels. But it's in a material world. Now convert it. Don't give it away. What's a fair price? Look, I can't do everything. You got six months to a year. All right? Don't go by the letter of the law. You know I wouldn't let them have it for 695 [$695,000] that certainly—and I wouldn't even let them have it for 795 [$795,000].[83]

That's right. [Student R confirms.]

And that's a pretty good—I think you got the message. Huh?

Yes. [A few students speak.]

You understand?

Yes. [A few more students speak.]

Now, I don't expect you to meet here like you have been. I expect once a month. I expect [Student O] to get up here and spend a day cleaning.

Yes, sir. [Student O replies.]

Would you like to donate that one day?

Yes. [Student O replies.]

Fine. I expect once a month [you] come here. You know, I won't be here on that day. He [can] come up here and clean. Right?

Yes, sir. [Student O again replies.]

[Student H] [can] get up here and clean.

Yes. [Student H replies.]

What the hell is once a month? Oh, twice a month to clean. I'm sorry. Twice a month to clean. Once a month for a meeting. And [Student S], you certainly, certainly, I think you care enough—I know in your heart you do—to see once a month meeting, twice a month cleaning. What's the big deal? Tell me. If you don't—that's all right. I'll understand. But I have no secrets. You understand? [Student P] or anyone? None of this bullshit fighting. What's the big deal? Until it's sold.

I'd like to— [Student S begins.]

Yes, [Student S].

I'd like to—

Thank you. Am I asking too much?

No. [Many students speak.]

When I'm gone, that you don't give this away? That within six months to a year, that it's sold. You think he [Student R] wants to live here in this huge house by himself? *[The teacher laughs.]* I have no problem with it. But he *will* do it. And it's up to you directors. He's down there working on the computer for the Living Light. That's where his time is donated before I go. If I'm gone Sunday or Saturday or tonight, then I expect his butt to be down there doing that. Not sixteen hours a day, but I expect a full shift without interruption.

You know, many people don't have the pattern of not sleeping for a day or night. I'm getting old because I can't make it three days and nights without sleeping like I used to. I collapse, all right?

Yes. [A very few students speak.]

Fine. So, I don't expect anybody—president, vice president, whatever—now remember, on the board of directors—when I'm gone, it is the board of directors—your corporate structure's down there [in the office]—who place the positions legally. My request, from the Council of this church, that it be [Student R], [Student S], [Student H], [Student O].

When I'm gone, I'm gone. And I'm not coming back here to fight with nobody. Have I missed anything? *[After a short pause, he continues.]* For God's sake, [Student S], [Student R], [Student H] speak up. Yes.

I don't think so. [Student R replies.]

Yes, [Student S], yes. Thank you.

Could you clarify the positions then?

I've already clarified it. There's your president. There's your secretary. There's your secretary-treasurer. And—what's the next one that's on the line of the directors? We've been with four—short for so long.[84]

Vice president. [Student R speaks softly.]

Huh?

Vice president. [Student R speaks louder.]

Oh, well then, that's where [Student O] would be. Thank you, [Student S].

Thank you very much. [Student S replies.]

I'm not perfect. You'll find out when I'm gone. If you ever [were] deluded—and no, no ego bullshit. You'll destroy yourself, you gentlemen. OK? And [Student H], you stay right where— well, you're the ones that [are] voting. I mean, that will be after I'm gone. I'm, I'm giving you my request, ladies and gentlemen.

Thank you. [Student S replies.]

And [Student E]. All right? Because I happen to know that [Student H] cannot be expected to get up here and do all the work after I'm gone, with a family and making a living. Now [Student O], he's willing to do that. But he can't be having his family up here, you know, all the time. I expect your child and your wife to come up a couple times to clean. Do you hear me?

Yes. [A few students reply.]

Everybody?

Yes. [More students respond.]

When I'm gone, you know, I know you—just keep it out of the courts, OK?

Yes. [A few students speak.]

Keep it out of the courts. And I guarantee you—from my brain now—I guarantee you because there's no warranties or guarantees in spirit. But my ma has given me a chance to speak. And I guarantee you, myself, Richard P. Goodwin, if you do any fighting of any kind and any ego bullshit, you will throw away hundreds of thousands of dollars that you can't see. And you will pay your own way. I'm not going to tell you how. Period.[85]

Right now, I'm great. But you won't be here the rest of the night, so that's it. All right. I'll say good night to you because I know you've got to take care of things. OK, [Student J]?

Thank you, Richard.

OK. Thank you.

Thank you.

And I'll say—you, you people start cleaning up. You wait around here. *[The teacher addresses a specific student.]* Could everybody else—any questions from you people? My God, [they] made it short, did—Yes, [Student S], certainly.

The new office in the country— [Student S begins.]

I won't be here, you know, when that day comes, yes.

I know. I'd like to clarify, Is [Student O] the only one to clean that with no women present? Is that—

Yes, that's correct.

Thank you.

Twice a month.

Thank you very much.

Yes. Twice a month. That is absolutely correct. Because the main interest—and he's a very good cleaner.

Uh-huh.

The main interest is the Living Light. You understand, children?

Yes. [Many students speak.]

That's the main interest. Don't expect to see the book in six months. I know how much I've been working. But you will see—when you do get up there once a month, you will see some progress. And unless you make the effort to understand electronics, like I have been making effort just only in these past weeks since getting that—because my mother herself has kept me away from computers. She says, "You have no time, Richard, for that. Stay away." She wouldn't even let me touch them. And now, when you, [the] skeleton crew[86], arrive, I was working my butt off and I'm getting it through my brain, finally, she lets me—only because I happen to know I've got to help on the, "Shall this software be? What's your recommendation?" And I got to check. Well, you know that. "No, we're not spending money for that. We'll buy no pig in a poke." Got the message?

Yes.

Yes, [Student S], go ahead, please.

Thank you.

Yes. So, when the office is in that place in the country, you meet once a month. What's the big deal? Isn't the Living Light worth that to you?

Yes. [Many students respond loudly.]

Isn't the Living Light worth a short transition of six months to a year to get rid of all of this?

Yes. [Many students respond.]

Pardon?

Yes, sir. [Many students respond.]

Well then, by God, you say "Yes" and show me that after I'm gone. God help you if you don't. I'm not trying to scare the shit out of you. *[A few students laugh.]* I'm telling you that if I have to hang around this earth realm to straighten out any bullshit, you will wish—ghost or not—that there was no ghost called Richard. You'll think Casper is a real joy. *[More students laugh.]* All right. Good night.

Good night. Thank you. [Many students speak.]

If I'm here Saturday, I'll see you again. Now, you wait. *[He addresses a specific student.]* Good night. Good night, everyone. Thank you very much for coming.

Thank you. [Several students speak.]

Thank you. And I, I will see you if I'm physically here. And if I'm not, then I will look down for a short time—oh, my body. Damn it, this piece of clay. I want to be cremated. No problem. Don't you dare have me burned prior to seventy-two hours.[87] Surely, you can afford that. And the ashes? Well, what the hell. Get them away from that and throw them out, well, you throw them out in that ocean out there. Just let the breeze take them. Period. And, damn it, stay there [as the remains are cremated]; they won't let you do it. They won't want to [let you stay]. You directors, one or two of you, stay there because they want to give any ash.

Uh-huh. [Student R replies.]

Or don't you know that? Why should you be throwing out some other asshole's ash?

That's right. [Student R replies.]

I don't give a shit about the ash. But you, you people might not like that. I know the shenanigans. When you pay that money and you get stuck with somebody else's ashes?

Uh-huh.

It's only a little bit, you see.

Yes.

Just—phsst! Don't throw them out on the freeway! God damn it. *[Many students laugh.]* At least throw them out—well, well, of course you could throw them out in the back yard. But don't tell anybody where. I don't want no, no—you know, just [throw them out] on a nice windy day. You know, none of this horseshit. All right. Now, no funerals. God forbid you dare, you dare be so mean to me. No mourning. Ah, shit, I've covered everything. Have I forgotten anything?

Not that I can think of. [Student R replies.]

[Student R]? [Student S]? Directors?

No. [Student H replies.]

Thank you. Good night. Good night.

Good night. Thank you. [Many students speak.]

Let the men take away—get the chairs later.

Thank you.

Go out in the kitchen and have something and close up. Just close up. All right?

Yes. Thank you. [Many students speak.]

And close those doors. Thank you, everyone. All right. Thank you very much. And [Student O]—

Yes, sir.

And [Student U], take care of things in the garage, would you, please?

Yes.

We'll take care of this. I'll have [Student R] call you in a few minutes. OK?

Yes, sir. [Student O replies.]

All right. [Student U answers.]

Yes, sir. [Student O again replies.]

Close those doors, please. And [Student E], go with your daddy and [Student M], please.

Thank you. [Student M replies.]

OK. Thank you.

Shall I stop [the recording]? [Student R asks.]

Yes.

SEPTEMBER 21, 1988

Membership Meeting November 28, 1988

Now in reference to the law of the National Spiritualist Association of Churches, of which this church is a legal auxiliary, there shall be no disrespect of one member to another. The authority of the organization alone shall decide what is disrespect and what is not disrespect. In this church that authority has always been, in this organization for twenty-four years, God's ministering angels. When our secretary reported to me personally, in front of a board member, that [Student B] was being disrespectful to her in the kitchen of this church home, that she was standing in the kitchen smoking a cigarette and having a cup of coffee, and when she asked [Student B] to get to work, [Student B] was disrespectful to her.

No member or director of this church has ever decided what is respectful or disrespectful. I, Richard P. Goodwin, took this matter directly to the Spirit Council. And with full consideration of all factors involved, no reprimand was given to [Student B].

Therefore, no member of this church, as long as I am its leader, its pastor, its minister, its medium, and its founder, shall decide for God's ministering angels and this church who is disrespectful and who is not. The report is to be given directly through the chain of commands, respectfully, to a board member. That report comes to me. If there is question of no action, you have the privilege to speak to me directly.

No right or privilege has ever, ever been implied or granted to any member or director of this church to reprimand another member of this church, let alone to tempt physical violence or threat or implication thereof. Should that ever happen again, the full, legal law of this organization, the Serenity Spiritualist Church and the national Spiritualist organization shall exempt that member from membership through the legal process of the grievance committee. The accuser may face the accused in front of God's ministering angels and all legal processes. Does anyone not understand that?

If you do not understand *that*, then raise your hands, if you wish not to speak, just raise your hands. *[After a short pause, the teacher continues.]*

Now great effort has been made by God's angels to look into each individual case.

Mental substance has risen, through m and s, that function of which we are so well familiar; that has risen higher than God's angels. Because if it had not risen higher—over 51 percent in this church—then there would be respect for God's angels. And respect for God's angels has been deteriorating at a rapid rate for over seven long years. That will no longer be tolerated. That will no longer ever again be tolerated. It shall never again rise its ugly head in this church.

Now, if you don't understand those corporate bylaws of this corporation and the National Spiritualist Association of Churches, then it's your responsibility to ask for and to receive, from this church, the constitution and bylaws. That's *your* responsibility. As it is *your* responsibility to show respect for God's spirits, the founders and the authority of this church.

This is a Spiritualist church. This is not a mental church. It never has been. It is not now. It is not going to be.

I shall now read the financial report of this church, the balance sheet, twelve-months, that ended April 30, 1988, of which you are now well familiar as a director and treasurer. Did you have any questions over the expenditures or the income?

Nope. [A director responds.]

Fine. Because if you did, you never reported it to me.

Current assets: cash zero; cash on deposit $11,097. Cash is zero because we bank all cash every week to pay the bills. Does anybody not understand that? Savings $542; accounts receivable $17,504. Total current assets $29,143. Fixed assets: residence San Rafael $1,020,210; furniture and fixtures $318,606;

machinery and equipment $274,065. If you can't find it, then you'll have to take another look. Total fixed assets $1,612,881. Too much gold in the temple of God, that's my mistake. Other assets: auto $23,727; total other assets $35,205. Total assets $1,677,229.

Liabilities. Current liabilities: accounts payable $5,059; sales tax collected $690. Total current liabilities $5,749. Long-term liabilities: notes payable $23,923; first deed of trust as of April 30, '88—you know we just refinanced for $213,000. So, let's understand this. Long-term liabilities: notes payable $23,923—I read that before. First deed of trust $104,697; second deed of trust $18,716. That's the old Wells Fargo second mortgage. The first was the First Nationwide first mortgage. We just refinanced. Total long-term liabilities $147,336. Total liabilities $153,085. Net worth $1,524,144. Total liabilities and net worth $1,677,229.

I have an accounting of every penny for twenty-four years. At least I've been that interested in *my* church.

Serenity Spiritualist Camp Associated, Incorporated, NSAC statement of income and expenses, twelve months ended April 30, 1988.

Income. Dues $270; donations $73,452; seminars $12,390; classes $39,610; books and tapes $8,830; accounts receivable $4,564; miscellaneous income $6,676. Less cost of sales $4,210. Total income for the year $141,582.

Expenses. Office supplies $1,312; utilities $3,795; auto $624; contract labor—electrical, if you will recall—$525; insurance expenses $7,031; dues and fees $231; tax on the property $4,001. That's because our own attorney betrayed me. Repair and maintenance $2,279; household expenses $2,027; library—go take a look at it—$4,691; church expense $22,920. Now, they'll want to know what the church expense is. Did you want to explain to them or don't you even know? *[After a short pause, the teacher continues.]* He doesn't know. Yes?

The healing assistance comes out of that. [Student R explains.]

That's right. Church expense. Is that a church expense or isn't it? And other things come out of that. The president's expense, $3,000; interest paid $17,211; depreciation $17,556; miscellaneous $5,002. Total expenses $92,205. Retained income over expenses $49,377. A total of $141,582.

Now, I think it's time that you have a little bit of awareness. Under miscellaneous income—I've kept my mouth shut year after year. I have taken from this church in the year of 1988 $3,000. I have given under miscellaneous $6,676. I've never considered that anybody's business. *[After a short pause, the teacher continues.]*

Shut this off. *[He refers to the tape recorder.]*

NOVEMBER 28, 1988

[On February 24, 1989, Mr. Goodwin passed from this world to his true home. His ashes were dispersed over the Pacific Ocean off the coast of Marin County, California. The last class that he gave was A/V Seminar 35, on February 16, 1989, which was published in Volume 7.

This concludes the teachings of the Living Light Philosophy that were given through Mr. Goodwin's mediumship and recorded on audio or videotape. More teachings that were not recorded on tape but were written down at the time they were given survive. Be it in Divine order, those teachings will also be published.

If a particular class resonates with you, consider purchasing an audio recording of that class. Much information is available on the recording that was not included in these transcriptions, like the tone of the teacher's voice when he admonished or encouraged his students, the sound of his laughter, which was filled with such joy, or the varied feelings in the tone of the students' voices. That additional information may be helpful in broadening your understanding of these beautiful teachings. In addition, although great effort was made to ensure accuracy, it is possible that errors exist in the transcription. Also, consider that the punctuation may imply a meaning that was not originally intended by the teacher. So, to be free of those constraints and to enjoy the added benefits, consider listening to any of these classes.]

No Doubts or Fears

No doubts or fears
Nor rivers of tears
To sail my ship away
A joyous heart
Before we part
A smile to sail me on
To shores that's known
To God alone
Where Light and Love impart
A brighter dawn
Before I'm gone
The joy of health to sing
From harmony and unity
The bells of freedom ring.

[The teaching above was hand-written by Mr. Goodwin on December 8, 1988.]

APPENDIX

The Divine Healing Prayer

I accept that the Divine Healing Power
Is removing all obstructions
From my mind and body
And is restoring me
To perfect health, wealth, and happiness.
My heart is filled with gratitude
For the Divine Law of Acceptance
That is healing both present and absent ones
Who are in need of help.
Peace, the power that healeth,
Is guiding my thoughts, acts, and deeds
As God and I go hand in hand
Living a life of joyful abundance.

The Total Consideration Affirmation

I am the manifestation of Divine Intelligence. Formless and free. Whole and complete. Peace, Poise, and Power are my birthright.

The Law of Harmony is my thought and guarantees Unity in all my acts and activities, expressing perfect Rhythm and limitless flow throughout my entire being.

Without beginning or ending, eternity is my true awareness and sees the tides of creation, as a captain sees his ship.

As the Light of Truth is sustained by the faculty of Reason, I pause to think and claim my Divine right.

>Right Thought. Right Action. Total Consideration.
>Amen. Amen. Amen.

Divine Abundance

Thank
(Gratitude)

You
(Principle)

God
(Divine Intelligence)

I'm
(Individualizing)

Moving
(Rhythm)

In
(Unity)

Your
(Realization)

Divine
(Total)

Flow
(Consideration)

The Controlled Spiritual Environment Affirmation

You are in a controlled spiritual environment of truth and freedom
Where peace and harmony reign supreme.
Be awake, be aware, be alert.
Your purpose of being is freedom from what has been.
Thoughts of self are foreign to this environment.
Take control of your mind and experience the joy of living.

The Law's Be

Our being is the consciousness, Truth.
Holy be the identity
The joy of Life
The totality of Acceptance
In mind as it is in heart
Grant us the Light
Our daily sustenance
And forgive us our has-beens
As we forgive those has-beens who tempt to steal our joy
Free us from the romance of self-love
Deliver us from the service to the false king of shadows
For Light is the kingdom
And the power and the glory forever
Peace be, the order of Divinity.

The All That Has Been Affirmation
From A/V Class Private 12

All that has been cannot be
That's not Good and I'm not free
Until I give then I be
The joy of life that sets me free.

The All That Has Been Affirmation
From a Recording of Affirmations

All that has been cannot be
That's not God and I'm not free
Until I give then I be
The joy of life that sets me free.

The Beseeching of the Angels

[The version below is as it was spoken on the class recordings. The alternative fourth stanza is from a printed version.]

O ye who once were mortals,
Enrobed like us in clay,
Come down from heaven's bright meadows
And be with us today.

Instruct us, loving angels,
The way your glory came
And wreathe about our foreheads
Truth's glowing ring of flame.

Come down, O blessed angels,
Make earth and heaven one.
And when our paths are shadowed
Be ye our rising sun.

Unfold us in God's wisdom,
His beauty and his love,
And may the earth life fit us
To be like you above.

[An alternative ending to the last four lines is:]

Enfold us in thy wisdom,
Thy beauty and thy love,
And may the earth life fit us
To be like you above.

The Attendance Affirmation

[This affirmation was referred to in Class September 30, 1984.]

Like the blades of grass in the meadow of God, Serenity Church attendance is ever growing, increasing, and multiplying in service to the Light.

[The affirmation below, "The Call of the Soul" is sometimes referred to as "The Eternal Call of the Soul".]

The Call of the Soul

Rhythm, Harmony, Balance, Peace.
Hold release, hold release.
Thank you, God, I am at peace.

Oh, Love Divine

Oh, love divine, a servant be
'Til selfishness imprisons me
And warps the reason of my mind
Into the madness of the blind,
When truth cries out, "Not mine but Thine"
And frees my soul with love divine.

[The following text is from the personal notes of the vice president of Serenity, a man who also served as the recording technician for these classes. This procedure is referred in A/V Class Private 29, which was given on January 5, 1986. The exercise may be the one the teacher refers to in AWF 22, which was given on December 29, 1985.]

Acupressure of Circle of Logic

This procedure, as given by the Friends, is to help students restore balance in their universe, as long as effort is being made by the student who is the recipient of the procedure.

Procedure:

The student who is seeking help should sit, with back perfectly straight, on a stool or low back chair. Hands in lap, body completely relaxed.

Student to be helped, and one who will administer the pressure, should do the cleansing breath, three times. *[Note: A/V Class Private 30 also recommends that the person administering the pressure have clean hands and that their hands be rinsed with water immediately before and after the procedure.]*

The student who is to administer the pressure should stand behind the seated subject. Referring to diagram, place the index finger on top of middle finger. Be sure your finger nails are short enough so they won't dig into the other student's neck. Place the middle finger on the spot, point "A" on diagram, press firmly, and rotate tip of finger in small circle to the right, clockwise, 14 revolutions. Change fingers so that the middle finger is on top of the index finger, see diagram. Press index finger firmly, on same spot and rotate counterclockwise 13 revolutions.

Find spot "B" on diagram, and repeat procedure. Rotate middle fingertip 14 clockwise, then rotate 13 counterclockwise with the index finger. That completes the procedure.

APPENDIX 547

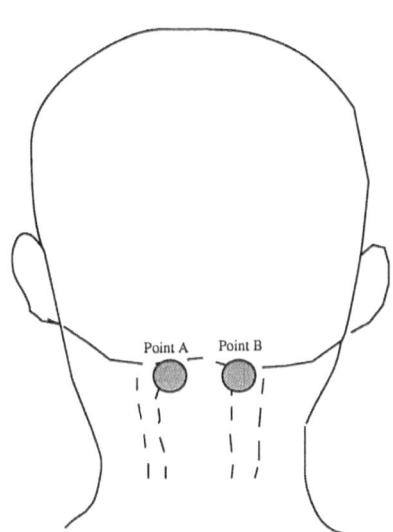

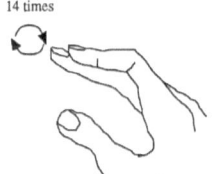
Step one

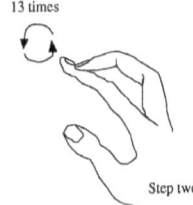
Step two

[In A/V Class Private 71, the teacher refers to a pamphlet that was published by Serenity many years earlier, entitled, "The Celestial Marriage". Here is the text of that pamphlet as it was published. An asterisk indicates a page break.]

THE CELESTIAL MARRIAGE

OR

THE DESCENT OF MAN

A FABLE
FROM
THE BOOK OF LIFE

*

GIVEN IN HUMILITY
TO ALL
HUMANITY

*

One day in great **ASPIRATION GOD** sent forth from itself **WILL**, and the sons of **WILL** became. Now the sons of **WILL** were of **GOD**, yea, they were **GODS** sent into form, but knew not because of form. The sons of **WILL** roamed the universes for eons and eons of time ever seeking other forms. After much searching they met to consider what they must do. For seven days and seven nights they discussed, and at the seventh hour **ILLUMINATION** fell upon them and said, "Behold, sons of **WILL**, within thyself is **COMPASSION**, know it, and unto thee shall be given." Alas, the sons of **WILL** knew **COMPASSION** and that night the daughters of **DESTINY** became.

In the morning when the daughters of **DESTINY** awoke to the sons of **WILL**, the **GODS** and **GODESSESS** of nature danced in jubilee.

Now the sons of **WILL** married the daughters of **DESTINY** and all nature wept with joy.

One day in **TRUTH** a son was born, his name was **INEVITABLE**, and the sons of **WILL** were greatly pleased. Now the daughters of **DESTINY** were quite unhappy for they **HOPED** for a daughter, and so that night in **DESIRE** a girl was born, her name was **LUST**.

Now **INEVITABLE** grew in the warmth and sunshine of the day. Oh how he loved the sun, for to him all **LIFE** was **LIGHT**.

LUST grew up to be a beautiful and lovely woman with a great fondness for the moon and darkness, for had she not been born in the night of **DESIRE**.

Time passed on, and one day **INEVITABLE** felt he would go into the night to find **LUST**, for he had heard so much about her, and had sent her many messages asking her to come into the **LIGHT** so that they may know more of each other. **INEVITABLE** went down, down into the darkness of night, and as he descended a great **FEAR** overcame him, but he found **LUST**, her face glowing so beautiful by the reflection of the sun. From the shadows where the **LIGHT** of the moon shone not, a voice spoke unto **INEVITABLE** and said, "Behold the beauty and the glory thou hast found, is it not worth the descent into our realms?" But from within, a voice spoke to **INEVITABLE** and said, "Take her to the realms of **LIGHT** that you may see more clearly in a day of **REASON**."

The senses won, and that night in **DESPAIR** a child was born, her name was **GRIEF**. The years passed and **GRIEF** could not be comforted, for she had been born of **LUST**, in the night of **DESIRE**, by the promptings of **PASSION**, and knew not of **TRUTH**.

INEVITABLE wandered on and on with the daughter **GRIEF**, hoping to return to the realms of **LIGHT**, but no, the centuries passed and only **SORROW** did they know.

Then one day a bird from the realms of **LIGHT** landed on his shoulder and sang this song, "In **SORROW** doth thou stay for self-pity knows no way."

INEVITABLE thought and thought of the meaning of those words, then he thought of his homeland **TRUTH** where he had been so very, very happy; and in **CONCENTRATION**, he found himself leaving the realms of darkness, passing through the lands of **IGNORANCE** and **EXPERIENCE** to return to his blessed land.

LOVE ALL LIFE
AND KNOW
THE LIGHT

*

OH MAN THINK HUMBLE
YET WELL OF THYSELF
FOR IN THY THINKING
IS CREATED
THE VEHICLE OF
THE SOUL

Cover Image of 1972 Edition of *The Living Light*

[The cover image of the 1972 edition of The Living Light *is displayed on the frontispiece of this volume. Reference to the symbolic image is discussed in excerpts from the following volumes of* The Living Light Dialogue:*]*

[Volume 2, Consciousness Class 44, pages 480-481:]
"And we'll begin with the outside of it, which is the snake, representative of wisdom consuming itself. Now why does the symbol of wisdom consume itself? Does anyone know? Does anyone know why wisdom is self-consuming? Because, my friends, if it's wisdom, then it can gain nothing from outside of itself: it already is wisdom. So all that wisdom is—you understand, you don't gain wisdom and neither do you give wisdom. Wisdom is self-sustaining. When you rise to a level of consciousness where wisdom expresses itself, then you will become it and it is self-sufficient unto itself. So the snake consuming itself is representative of wisdom, in comparison to what one might call knowledge. Now, knowledge is something that you gain. It's something that you put into your brain and you feed back at your discretion—but not wisdom.

"The next step is the interlaced double triangle, which is a very, very ancient symbol. It is the meeting of the spirit with matter. It is the power above that meets the forces below. And at that junction, when those two triangles meet, that's the negative and the positive poles come together in creation and the divine spark, the rays of light, life is so-called born into matter.

"Now you all know that all poles are triune. The negative pole is triune and the positive pole is triune. In fact, my friends, as we've stated before, all things that are manifest are triune and that is why three is the number of manifestation.

"Inside of the interlaced triangles you'll notice on the top of the pyramid in the rays of light is the all-seeing eye. Now the all-seeing eye is that that is not distracted, because it sees everything and so nothing gains its attention. And that is why it is the all-seeing eye. The triangle itself, the pyramid upon which all knowledge, the all-seeing eye, all wisdom, and all life rest, is the pyramid of manifestation. All things in all universes (physical, mental, or spiritual) are triune. There are three parts to all things: that is an absolute fact of physics and it is a truth of the universe."

[Volume 4, Consciousness Class 78, page 172:]
"Then, we'll be happy to share our understanding. The serpent so designed—consuming itself—is the ancient and eternal symbol of everlasting and eternal wisdom. The double triangle, with its apex downward, is the manifestation of the Divine Power and the balance of nature, its own creation. The pyramid with the all-seeing eye on the top is the eternal Light that never closes, that sees all things, that knows all things, and that ever is and ever has been."

Notes

1. The missing text, which was not recorded, is from a student's personal notes that were written as this class was given.
2. The missing text, which was not recorded, is from a student's personal notes that were written as this class was given.
3. If students saw a snail while in the garden, they were encouraged to step on the snail, and say a prayer for the snail as they did so. The sound the teacher makes may refer to that practice.
4. The teacher may again refer to the practice of stepping upon any snails in the temple garden and, in so doing, free them from their physical forms.
5. The microcassette tape recorder had an automatic on and off setting, which stopped the recording after a short period during which no sound was registered or recorded, and it began recording when sound was registered. When the automatic recorder began recording, it had a tendency to clip the first sounds of the first word spoken. In earlier classes recorded on microcassette, the recorder was started and stopped manually.
6. At this point, the recorded teachings may have been played back for the students to take more complete notes.
7. The recorded teachings may have been played back for the students to take more accurate notes. The recordings of informal classes, like many in this volume, were generally not made available to the students.
8. This class was given after that evening's work assignments were completed, which is when many of the informal classes were held. Students were given different work, including cleaning, watering the garden, working on a church project like the monthly magazine, or working in the cabinet

shop. Students working in the cabinet shop were a bit isolated from the rest of the students and may not have been as informed as other students as to what transpired that evening.

9. When the Spirit Council asked Mr. Goodwin to open a church in order that these teachings may reach a wider audience, one of his conditions was that the Council would make all of the decisions regarding the operation of the church. And so, each question, issue, or recommendation was presented to the Council and a decision was reached, all through Mr. Goodwin's mediumship. Thus, the Spirit Council was the true and only authority of Serenity. So, when procedures that were approved by the Council were not followed, directors were responsible to inform Mr. Goodwin, and there usually was some form of exposure. Exposures were a common experience at the temple, but it was very rare that they were recorded.

10. The teacher very rarely swore. So, when he did, it made a significant impact on his students.

11. The teacher may be referring to the first book of teachings, entitled *The Living Light*, the entire text of which is included in Volume 1.

12. The temple was equipped with an intercom that allowed an individual to broadcast an announcement into every room. There were even intercoms on the outside of the building, which facilitated communication with students working in the garden.

13. The east wing of the temple, which was the private apartment of Mr. Goodwin, was located one floor above the main floor.

14. Editor's Note: Although the process of exposure was feared by the forms the students were temporarily overidentified

with and emotion, the defense of the forms, was often expressed, the result of the exposure was always a greater degree of freedom, harmony, and peace. That greater harmony lasted as long as the student made the effort in consciousness to remain free from the forms that had controlled him or her.

15. Student O and Student M were married and the parents of Student E.

16. The significance of the streusel cakes is also discussed in the Membership Meeting of May 13, 1984, which is also in this volume.

17. Each Sunday morning, after Serenity's devotional services at the American Legion log cabin, a brunch was held as a fundraiser. All church attendees were invited to attend. The brunch items as well as the chairman of the brunch were approved by the Spirit Council weeks in advance of the brunch. Then, as the brunch was finishing, the brunch chairmen would offer students the opportunity to select a brunch item to prepare and to bring the following Sunday. Each brunch item had an approved recipe, and if a student did not have the recipe for their item, the brunch chairmen arranged for a copy to be provided. Students were not reimbursed for the cost of the items; it was their donation to the organization and an opportunity for selfless service.

18. Students had recently been given the opportunity to purchase (at the cost of the tape) cassette tapes with music of their choice, and along with the music there were spiritual affirmations spoken by Mr. Goodwin. The affirmations were recorded at a very low level and were not consciously audible; however, in very quiet passages, they sometimes could be heard.

19. The teacher may be referring to Student E's behavior during church service.

20. In the recording entitled Membership Meeting May 13, 1984, which is also in this volume, we learn that the streusel cakes were to have been baked for Serenity's monthly bake sale. As with the items made by the students for the Sunday brunches and monthly dinners, all bake sale items had recipes that had been approved by the Spirit Council.

21. Editor's note: Some individuals who were in a level of consciousness of discord would call Mr. Goodwin and deny personal responsibility for their own experiences. When Serenity merited those types of experiences, it would indicate that the students were directing 51 percent or more of their energy to that realm. By bringing this experience to the attention of the students, Mr. Goodwin was encouraging them to make greater effort to be aware of where they were directing their attention while at the temple or while engaged in a spiritual duty.

22. St. Anthony's is a nonprofit in San Francisco that provides a range of free services, including meals, to the indigent residents of that city.

23. Serenity's monthly dinner had been held the previous evening at the American Legion log cabin. Mr. Goodwin would always attend, but not always speak at those dinners.

24. The affirmation had been playing over the temple intercom when the students arrived.

25. The microcassette recorder may have been set to auto-stop at silences and auto-record when it registers sound. That is, after a matter of seconds, when no audible sound is registered by its microphone, the recorder automatically shuts off. Then, when the recorder registered sound, it began recording, which frequently meant the portions of the first words spoken were not recorded. Additionally, if students spoke so quietly their words did not register with the recorder, it may have shut off.

26. When Mr. Goodwin was asked by the Spirit Council to open a church, he asked that the Council make all the decisions and he agreed to support whatever decision they made, regardless of his personal feelings.

27. Perhaps Student B refers to her youngest child.

28. The teacher may be referring to his experiences as a child. His mother, Isa Goodwin, is a medium through whom the spirits could materialize in physical forms.

29. This language is very unusual for the teacher.

30. Editor's note: At this point, the recording ends. Although this class includes several exposures, which was always a serious matter, the last half of this recording is filled with joy, which may be more fully appreciated by listening to it.

31. This class was given on a Thursday evening.

32. The teacher may be referring to the microcassette tape speed of 2.4 cm/s.

33. Student G painted the flowers that decorated the dinnerware that was used at the temple for holiday and special occasion dinners. Each of the twenty-five settings featured a different flower.

34. Student O and Student M are the parents of Student E.

35. Student S and her friend had had a recent automobile collision.

36. The upper east wing of the temple was Mr. Goodwin's living quarters. On some occasions when students were present at the temple, he would remain in his quarters and not give a class or even interact with the students as they performed their assigned work.

37. After the offertory had been collected from the congregation, an usher presented the donations to Mr. Goodwin, who would then say a prayer.

38. Students could order cassette tapes after a class, after Sunday church services at the log cabin, or any time they visited the temple. It was the responsibility of one student to record the orders and report them so that those tapes could be made. Tapes were paid for at the time they were ordered and were generally available for pickup within a few days.

39. On the last Sunday of the month, it was the practice of Serenity's devotional services to hold a students' forum. Mr. Goodwin gave a lecture or class on the first Sunday, and other directors gave lectures on the second and third Sundays. And on the last Sunday, several students would give short, extemporaneous lectures on various aspects of the teachings.

40. The teacher refers to Serenity's monthly bake sale and other fundraising activities.

41. Many of the chairs on the balconies of the temple had cushions that soaked up water in the rain. To prevent that, the furniture was covered or the cushions were put away before the rain. The teacher may refer to that procedure.

42. Student O and Student M are the parents of Student E.

43. Under spiritual guidance, Mr. Goodwin would work in consciousness to help dissipate the forms of mental substance of the students.

44. The teacher may be referring to his work at the Serenity Church service that morning.

45. The teacher may be referring to the instance when Student E had become disruptive during church services and his father, Student O, took him outside the log cabin and disciplined him. It seems that someone who lived near the log cabin became involved.

46. The teacher refers to A/V Seminar 16.

47. Mr. Goodwin meditated at 4:00 a.m.
48. Isa Goodwin is Mr. Goodwin's mother. She is chairman of the Spirit Council.
49. The teacher may be referring to a time when he was married.
50. Student M was married to Student O.
51. The date of CC 1 is January 11, 1973. So, the classes given in May 1972 were not recorded.
52. Committee chairmen were responsible for a committee that had a specific task and often involved raising funds to support Serenity. For example, contributions to the advertising committee helped to fund the ads in the *Marin Independent Journal*.
53. Crystal was one of the spirit guides who communicated with Mr. Goodwin. One of the tasks of the ladies' guild committee was to make Raggedy Ann and Raggedy Andy dolls.
54. Rev. Ford may have been president of the state or national association.
55. At the time of this meeting, the Serenity Camp Association owned land in Northern California, outside of Willits, and the land was known as Camp Serenity. On that property, a small, wooden chapel, the Chapel of Awareness, was built. Before the Serenity Spiritualist Church was formed and had its first service at the American Legion log cabin on May 2, 1971, Serenity held festivities and services at Camp Serenity several times a year, including a sunrise Easter service. As more energy and attention were directed toward the church in San Anselmo, there was less time for activities at the camp.
56. The American Legion log cabin, where the church services were held and where this meeting was held, had a large fireplace.

57. The teacher may have been trying to read from a printed agenda.
58. The teacher may be referring to the feature article in the *Marin Independent Journal* on Mr. Goodwin and on Serenity that was published on June 2, 1973.
59. This meeting was held directly after church services, during which Mr. Goodwin served as the medium.
60. Through the mediumship of Mr. Goodwin, the menus for the brunches and dinners were approved in advance by the Spirit Council. Members and friends of Serenity volunteered to provide specific menu items. The volunteers purchased the ingredients and prepared the item they had chosen. Volunteers were not reimbursed for the costs of their brunch or dinner items. All the funds raised at the brunches and monthly dinners went to Serenity.
61. At this time, Serenity held brunches only on the first Sunday of the month. Later, after the temple was built, brunches were held every Sunday.
62. Students were given the opportunity to make various things, like planters, Raggedy Ann and Raggedy Andy dolls, afghans, and other household items, that could be sold at the annual bazaar.
63. The teacher refers to the Serenity Game, which is a card game that features the teachings of the Living Light, which was printed in 1975.
64. The model of the Serenity temple that Student H was building had a slit in its "roof" to receive donations. When the model first appeared at a church service, Mr. Goodwin was the first person to donate. Just a few years later, the temple existed.
65. Student G is the mother of Student B4.

66. In addition to raising funds, the flower committee made large flower arrangements that were on both sides of the podium for church services at the log cabin. That committee also made several smaller bouquets that were placed on the tables where people ate brunch. After the service, the larger bouquets were given to members of the congregation to aid in their healing, and the smaller ones were sold to the people attending the brunch. In his comment, the teacher may be guiding the committee to ensure a greater balance between the two larger arrangements.

67. The ladies' guild made hand-sewn Raggedy Ann and Raggedy Andy dolls, as well as other household items, that were sold at the annual bazaar.

68. The photography committee would sell Polaroid photos and portraits to attendees at many of the church's activities.

69. There were a number of student mediums and student healers who were developing their talents as they served during the Sunday devotional services.

70. The teacher contributed funds to various church endeavors from his monthly stipend, which, at that time was $50 per month. In 1976, his stipend was increased to $50 per week.

71. In consideration of its present owners, the address of the temple has been deleted.

72. In late 1976, Serenity purchased an empty lot and, on January 20, 1977, broke ground to build the Serenity temple. Previous to that, Serenity rented a house, which served as the home of Mr. Goodwin, the church office, and the location where the committees met to perform their selfless service. Spiritual awareness classes CC 137-139, which are published in Volume 5, provide a progress report on the building of the temple and share a number of the challenges that were faced in that process. Much of the labor involved

in the construction of the temple was volunteered by the students, but not all the workers were volunteers. The net worth includes the value of the temple at that time. The real estate tax also refers to the temple property.

73. The address of the temple has been deleted.
74. This membership meeting was held at the American Legion log cabin, directly after Sunday devotional service.
75. The Golden Gate Bridge is continually being painted. By the time the paint crew has finished painting the bridge, it is time to repaint where they began. Perhaps he refers to that process.
76. Mr. Goodwin may be referring to an article in the local newspaper, which was printed on February 21, 1978, that featured the temple and was critical of the expenditure and of Serenity.
77. The teacher refers to the Serenity temple and makes reference to the name of a road, which has been deleted.
78. This membership meeting was held in the log cabin after the Sunday morning devotional service.
79. It seems that after declaring she was not going to stay for the meeting, the member decided to stay.
80. The teacher refers to the temple. This membership meeting was held at the American Legion log cabin, following Sunday morning services.
81. For additional teachings related to the streusel-cake opportunity, please see Class May 20, 1984, which is in this volume.
82. Serenity had an extensive collection of movies on laser discs.
83. The teacher refers to the sale price for the Serenity temple.
84. The corporate structure of the Serenity Association calls for

five directors, but it had operated for a number of years with only four.

85. Editor's note: Although plans had been made for a timely sale of the temple, the students merited a different experience. The warning given by Mr. Goodwin manifested and a large portion of the funds from the sale of the property, which were to aid in publishing these teachings, did not materialize. That all the volumes of recorded teachings have now been published is a demonstration of the value the students have for the Living Light Philosophy, as well as their great regard and esteem for Mr. Goodwin. Even with all the efforts of the students in this endeavor, this good work could not have been accomplished without the steadfast guidance and support of the Spirit Council and all the other workers on the other side of life, for it is the Light that doeth the work.

86. The "skeleton crew" is a reference to the significantly reduced time that the students had been permitted at the temple.

87. Cremation should only occur after a period of seventy-two hours has passed from the time of transition.

www.ingramcontent.com/pod-product-compliance
Lightning Source LLC
Chambersburg PA
CBHW030507080526
44586CB00011B/100